THE MEMORY TRACE:
Its Formation and Its Fate

THE MEMORY TRACE:
Its Formation and Its Fate

Erich Goldmeier
*Franklin Delano Roosevelt Veterans
Administration Hospital
Montrose, New York*

LAWRENCE ERLBAUM ASSOCIATES, PUBLISHERS
1982   Hillsdale, New Jersey

Copyright © 1982 by Lawrence Erlbaum Associates, Inc.
All rights reserved. No part of this book may be reproduced in
any form, by photostat, microform, retrieval system, or any other
means, without the prior written permission of the publisher.

Lawrence Erlbaum Associates, Inc., Publishers
365 Broadway
Hillsdale, New Jersey 07642

Library of Congress Cataloging in Publication Data

Goldmeier, Erich.
 The memory trace.

 Bibliography: p.
 1. Memory. I. Title.
 BF371.G64   153.1'2   81-15161
 ISBN 0-89859-172-4   AACR2

Printed in the United States of America

Contents

Preface   ix

PART I: THE FORMATION OF THE TRACE

1. **The Visual Trace**   3
   1. Human coding   2. Grouping   3. Coding by function   4. Coding of features

2. **Singularity**   20
   5. Features and their values   6. Monotonic dependence and dimensionality   7. Phenomenally realized parameters   8. Singularity as sensitivity to change   9. Regularity, Uniqueness and goodness   10. Singularity as self-consistency   11. Singularity as norm   12. The general nature of singularity   13. Encoding of nonsingular features   14. The three regions of singularity

3. **Extensions of the Theory**   67
   15. Extrinsic effects   16. Visual concepts   17. The trace versus the stimulus   18. Verbal Memory   19. Synopsis of encoding

PART II: THE FATE OF THE TRACE

4. **Theory of Memory Change**   105
   20. Memory change   21. Intrinsic stress   22. A model of stress   23. Predicted results   24. Stress versus fading theories   25. Experimental Considerations   26. Recognition versus reproduction

5. **Intrinsic Change in Recognition**   130
   27. Experimental Design   28. Corrollaries of the experimental design   29. Change toward singularity—designs 61c and f   30. Change toward self-consistency—designs 63d and b   31. Symmetry—figure 64g   32. Self-consistency as figural integration—figure 65g   33. Self-consistency continued—figure 66g   34. Slant—figure 67d   35. Memory for gaps—I. design 68e versus 68h   36. Memory for gaps—II. tendency to consistent structure—designs 68d and h   37. Memory for gaps—III. gap strength—figure 70 versus figure 68   38. The evidence for directed change in recognition

6. **Intrinsic Change in Reproduction**   164
   39. Change in several dimensions   40. Fragmentary reproductions and reconstructions   41. Procedure and sources of experiments   42. "Forgetting" in Hanawalts figure 17 (here figure 71a)   43. Prostructural and countrastructural features—designs 72a and b   44. Directed change in figure 64g   45. Symmetry as self-consistency in figure 65g   46. Self-consistency in reproductions of figure 66g   47. Balance and rectangularity—design 67d   48. Parallel lines and self-consistency   49. Designs 63b and d—change of taper   50. Designs 63b and d—change of elements   51. Closure in figures 68 and 70

7. **Change of Nonvisual Traces**   203
   A. The story task   52. The empiristic fallacy—recognition   53. Self-consistency in reproduction   B. The symbol task   54. Structure of the symbol patterns   55. Reproductions of the symbol pattern   56. Changes of the number sequence   57. Generally preserved features   58. Is there law and order?   59. Recognitions of the symbol patterns   60. Relation between visual and nonvisual memory

8. **The Dynamics of Change**	**229**
61. The time course of change 62. Gradual versus sudden change 63. Change of singular traces 64. Trace systems 65. Synopsis of memory change	
References	**243**
Author Index	**251**
Subject Index	**255**

Preface

There is agreement that memory traces are not mere snapshots or tape recordings of the stimulus, that traces are not "first-order isomorphisms" in the words of Shepard and Chipman (1970). But there is hardly any agreement about what *does* characterize the memory trace. The word trace itself seems somewhat disreputable. Its theory is left in the twilight between perception and memory proper. Yet, models and theories of memory cannot help making implicit and often unrecognized assumptions about the memory trace. This book aims to strengthen the meager base on which memory theories now rest. It challenges old assumptions and introduces new concepts, foremost the notion of singularity, as they become necessary to understand traces adequately. Some research data of the past are found in need of reinterpretation. The result is a new theory of the memory trace.

Trace theory, and therefore this book, addresses itself to two aspects of trace structure: the *formation* of the trace, and *its fate,* once the trace is formed. Neither aspect has been systematically investigated. In fact, it is still not universally agreed that the fate of the trace is a topic worthy of investigation.

The treatment of the trace presented here concentrates on a broad framework, leaving of necessity many details open. A number of issues, or pseudoissues, at present under debate are not covered at all because this theory is neutral to them. Examples are the controversy of propositional versus imagery representation, the debate between inborn, individually acquired, or culturally or socially determined cognitive processes. The theory is neutral to the question of short-term versus long-term memory, and also to many assumptions in perception. It does not address the problem of the nature of the trace (Palmer, 1978b) or whether traces exist, a question discussed in a novel way by Kolers (1979). The theory does not make direct contact with the distinction between episodic and semantic memory (Tulving 1972) and with the notion of levels of processing (Craik & Lockhart, 1972). However, the viewpoint presented here is eminently compatible with both Tulving's and Craik's ideas, especially in the form they have taken subsequently (Cermak & Craik, 1979). I have briefly indicated the relationship between the two theories in Section 18. This theory makes it possible to understand the trace as an independent variable, with retrieval the dependent variable supporting the notion of encoding specificity.

Any theory of the trace imposes limits and constraints on memory theories. The present theory seems to fit in better with the notions of Kintsch on memory for gist, the theories of Bransford and his associates, and the ideas of Norman and Bobrow (1976) and (1979) and Norman and Rumelhart (1975) than with the associative memory theory of Anderson and Bower (1973). However, it is difficult to match up theories that were formulated independently of each other. Sometimes differences are more semantic than real; sometimes similarities turn out to hide unbridgeable gaps.

Although my treatment of the topic is unmistakably gestaltist, this is not a treatise on gestalt. I hope it is read for the issues it raises rather than judged by the many misconceptions still current about gestalt theory.

The emphasis in this treatment of trace theory is on visual memory. I have tried throughout to show that the theory can be generalized to all of memory.

According to Jenkins (1979), who has been taking the pulse of memory research for quite some time: "the field is open to new paradigms and new research ideas in a way that it never was before [p. 430]." I hope that the ideas here proposed furnish new paradigms, shed new light on current research problems, and serve to advance the understanding of human memory.

I wish to thank Stephen Palmer and Carol Krumhansl for helpful suggestions and Westchester Community College in Valhalla, N.Y. and Pace College in Pleasantville, N.Y. for generously providing large numbers of subjects.

What remains to be said is that this work owes its existence to the inspiration I received from my teacher, Max Wertheimer, and owes its completion to the encouragement and support I enjoyed in my association with the Veterans Administration since I began this work in 1966.

THE MEMORY TRACE:
Its Formation and Its Fate

THE FORMATION OF THE TRACE

we have every reason to believe that... sensory channels ... (have) a tremendously higher information capacity than... the perceptual machinery at higher levels. A drastic simplification of the input must occur... (It) may take the form of throwing away information or of recoding it more compactly
—Attneave, 1967 [p. 63]

1 The Visual Trace

1. HUMAN CODING

Today's ideas about trace formation have their roots in the coding theories developed for telecommunication (Shannon & Weaver, 1949) and for imparting information to computers. The thrust of these theories is, firstly, to avoid loss of information, secondly, to find "efficient" codes (for elaboration, see Simon, 1972), and, thirdly, to keep down noise or, as psychologists put it, to avoid error and ambiguity. These considerations apply to all information transmission and storage systems, whether they are machines or organisms. In memory research, they have yielded a large if not very impressive body of results, described, for instance, by Kintsch (1977) and Norman (1976). This approach is however becoming less and less productive. It limits research particularly in two areas.

1. Until the 1960s and even today, many investigators have paid little attention to conceptual (gist) and perceptual (visual) memory compared to verbal memory. The representative account of "Human Associative Memory" by Anderson and Bower (1973) treats visual memory with no more than a few pages describing the work of Winston and others (Winston, 1975), work that is of very limited scope and, so far, more a research program than a reality. Theories that handle memory for gist are in their infancy (Kintsch, 1974, 1977), and memory for concepts has been investigated only sporadically, as in the case of chess positions by Chase and Simon (1973). According to Lockhart (1979):

> Memory research was and still is, too dominated by the traditions of verbal learning. The essence of this tradition is to present 'items' to subjects with instructions to

'study' them and then to test the subjects memory for these items. The task of a theory of memory is then seen as that of providing an account of what a subject does when confronted with this peculiar set of circumstances [p. 77].

The focus on verbal memory ignores the fact that the human brain was not designed for the task of remembering disconnected sentences, words or syllables, or nonsense, least of all verbal nonsense. From an evolutionary point of view, nonverbal, especially visual memory, has primacy over syllables, words, and "lists." It seems unwise to base research in a field on one, very extreme and unrepresentative type of material, especially after almost a century of meager success with lists of disconnected "items." Biologically, perceptual memory antedates verbal memory. Visual traces are at least as likely to be paradigmatic for the investigation of the memory trace as words. Any theory that ignores this relationship is implausible from the start.

2. Traditional memory research has paid little attention to the enormous amount of data processing that intervenes between the stimulus or item and the formed trace. Two kinds of processing are involved. The first depends on the specific episode surrounding the encoding (Tulving, 1972) and on the particular orienting task guiding the subject's learning activity (Craik & Lockhart, 1972). This kind of processing is open to experimental manipulation and has given rise to a literature of its own (Cermak & Craik, 1979). We deal with these problems here only incidentally. The second kind of processing has been investigated mainly with regard to visual patterns, originally by Wertheimer (1923) and the gestalt school (updated by Metzger, 1975), and sporadically since Wertheimer's work. This coding problem is treated in some detail by Kolers (1968a) and figures in the thinking of the Pittsburgh group (Reddy & Newell, 1974). There is agreement that perception translates the stimulus pattern into a code suitable to the brain, into brain language as it were. But, unlike the situation in telecommunication, this code: (1) is not a one-to-one mapping, like a snapshot or a tape recording; (2) is not unique; (3) loses information; and (4) changes information in specific ways, for example, by categorizing a percept in an egocentric system of categories, to name one of many mechanisms of change.

Data reduction in the latter sense has been virtually overlooked in memory research or has been considered as merely a problem for those who study perception. It emerges, however, as the key to the understanding of trace formation and consequently trace structure. The trace structure, in turn, constrains all theorizing in memory. The trace structure is related to both the formation of the trace and to the subsequent fate of the trace. The theory developed here covers both these aspects of trace theory and is intended to apply to all kinds of traces, verbal and conceptual as well as perceptual, but the emphasis lies on the visual trace.

2. GROUPING

In visual perception, data reduction takes place in two respects: establishment of true parts and assignment of features and feature values, which are treated in Chapter 2. The assignment of parts has variously been called organizing, parsing, chunking (Miller, 1956), categorizing (Rosch, 1973b), and schematizing (Bartlett, 1932; Neisser, 1976; Norman & Bobrow, 1976). Wertheimer (1923) thought of the assignment of parts as structuring and considered features as gestalt qualities. His studies were extended by his students, notably Gottschaldt (1926, 1929), Ternus (1926), Kopferman (1930), Goldmeier (1936/1972), and Metzger. Some of their results are described by Kolers (1968a) and Rock (1975). The most comprehensive and authoritative account is Metzger's *Gesetze des Sehens* (1975), which unfortunately is to date not available in English.

Wertheimer (1923) writes:

> I stand at the window and see a house, trees and sky. And now, from a theoretical viewpoint, I might count and come up with . . . 327 brightnesses and hues. (Do I perceive "327"? No. I see sky, house, trees. The perception of "327" as such nobody can achieve.
>
> And if, in this abstruse reckoning, the house is 120, trees 90 and sky 117 then I experience, phenomenally, this particular grouping, this particular subdivision, and not, say 127 and 100 and 100, or 150 and 177 [p. 71].

This concept of grouping implies a hierarchy of levels: a background, surrounding figures, which in turn have parts, which have subparts, and so on. The hierarchy is created by the transitive, asymmetric relation "part of." In the usual sense, derived from Aristotelian and Boolean logic, this relation partitions the objects of the visual world exhaustively into nested sets. The array could be diagrammed as a tree with relatively few branchings. This picture is, however, both incomplete and misleading.

What is perceived and therefore what is incorporated into the trace are the units and subunits, figures on a background, which result from perceptual grouping. Instead of "327 picture elements," the percept and hence the trace is composed of but a few parts. The process of organization reduces the stimulus data in two ways: Firstly, it groups a large number of picture *elements* into a small number of seen *objects* and their parts. Secondly, out of an astronomical number of possible groupings, the perceptual process selects one particular one. For example, in Fig. 1 with its 17 dots, we see 3 connected lines, 5 and 9 and 5 dots (the corner dots are shared between adjoining lines); not 4 and 10 and 3, not 1 and 16, as in Fig. 6a. (In both these examples, we have treated the dots as the ultimate elements. Actually, there is no a priori reason why parts of dots could not be grouped with parts of the background, etc., further multiplying the number of possible groupings.)

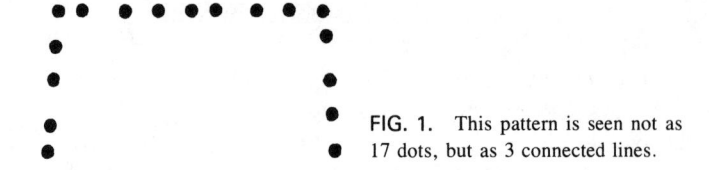

FIG. 1. This pattern is seen not as 17 dots, but as 3 connected lines.

Since Wertheimer identified the problem of grouping, much work has been done on how grouping is accomplished, both on the phenomenal and on the neurophysiological level, with very unimpressive results. But memory theory need not wait for final insights into the mechanism of visual grouping. Memory deals with the *result* of grouping, however arrived at. Perception extracts information from the stimulus array by zeroing in on the one—occasionally more than one—grouping of the final percept out of the gigantic number of possibilities in the stimulus array. The trace, as a consequence, is composed of objects, things, their form, their parts and subparts, rather than of an enormous list of stimulus elements. The trace specifies figure and ground and what might be called the structure of the field. In addition to partitioning, grouping has two results:

1. The subsets (phenomenal parts) are more or less strongly unified into *subwholes*. For example, the dots of Fig. 1 are grouped into three "lines." These lines possess phenomenal reality even though the stimulus array does not contain physical lines. Alternative groupings, say, the first 7 dots, the next 7, and the remaining 3, are difficult to visualize simultaneously and almost impossible to maintain even with much practice. On the other hand, the pattern 7.7 or 9.7 of Fig. 42 can easily be perceived in a variety of partitions. In the first case, the partition is unique and compelling, the pattern is a *strong whole,* and it rates high on "goodness." The other two patterns are open to many different phenomenal groupings, none of which is very compelling; they are loosely organized, rate low on goodness, and represent *weak wholes*.

In a strong whole, the parts depend on each other. In Fig. 1, for instance, removing or even slightly displacing a corner dot affects the appearance of the whole pattern. In pattern 7.7 and 9.7 of Fig. 42, removal or slight displacement of any dot causes negligeable phenomenal changes. The dots in the weak pattern are only weakly interrelated; in the strong whole, they support each other strongly. Strength and weakness, like goodness, are attributes of the whole pattern. They are not due to associative bonds between individual elements. On the contrary, the bonds between the elements are created by the overall configuration, are dependent on it, and will change if changes occur in other, distant parts of the array.

Strong and weak wholes form also among syllables, words, word pairs, and sentences, the traditional objects of memory research. The concentration on *weak* wholes has kept this research both uncontaminated by extraneous effects and, I believe, peripheral in its results.

2. Even though the grouping within a strong pattern is fairly unique, it can change drastically with various additions, within or outside of the pattern (Gottschaldt, 1926; Palmer, 1977). Figure 2*a* shows a pattern usually seen as *one two-dimensional polygon with two concave angles*. Adding two internal lines, in Fig. 2*b* and *c*, regroups the pattern into *two overlapping squares*. Figure 2*b* in the context of *d* is seen as a *square next to an L-shape* (Dinnerstein & Wertheimer, 1957). In Fig. 2*e*, the lower square seems to be *transparent* and *overlapping* an imperfect upper square. In Fig. 2*f*, the two halves balance. One sees *"a" with an interior design*. The balance is also restored in the case of Fig. 2*g*, but in this case the result is not *"a* with an interior line" but *"a pair of abutting convex polygons* in the same plane, no transparency, not one polygon as in 2*a* and 2*f*.

Grouping sometimes decides whether a pattern is seen in two or in three dimensions (Julesz, 1971; Kopfermann, 1930), as in Fig. 3*a* versus *b* from Metzger (1975). Stereokinesis also is a matter of grouping (Metzger, 1935, 1975), in this instance, grouping in four dimensions, the fourth being time.

A difference in grouping accounts for the two ways in which ambiguous figures can be perceived (Rock, 1975) or for the change in the appearance of a figure with rotation (Dinnerstein & Wertheimer, 1957; Goldmeier, 1936/1972; Rock, 1973).

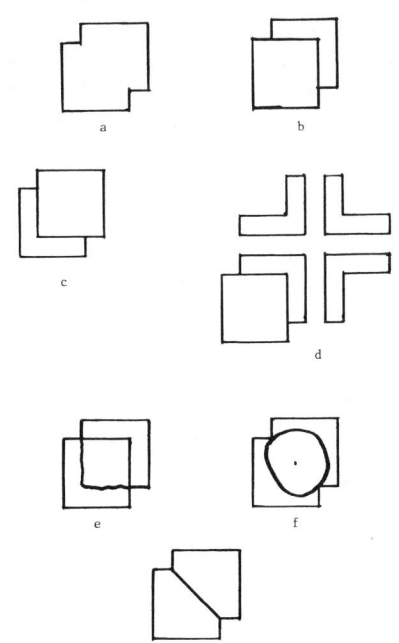

FIG. 2. The grouping of the parts of pattern *a* is changed in various ways as the context of pattern *a* is varied. Pattern 2*d* is from Dinnerstein and Wertheimer, 1957.

8 1. THE VISUAL TRACE

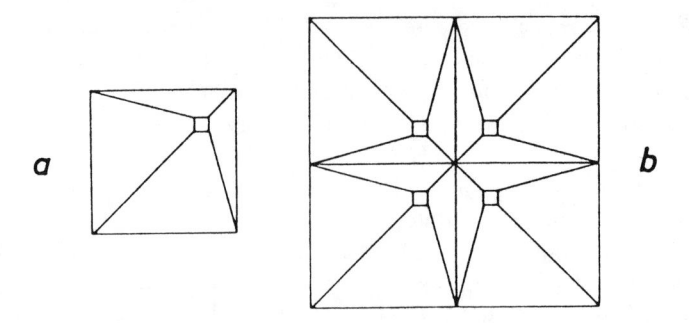

FIG. 3. Design *a* by itself is seen as three-dimensional. In the context of *b* it appears as part of a two-dimensional pattern. (From Metzger, 1975.)

Grouping effects make it difficult or impossible to identify a pattern embedded in another array, if the other array evokes an overridingly different grouping (Gottschaldt, 1926, 1929). Figure 4 shows an illustrative pattern. Pattern *a* is contained in *b* geometrically but does not exist in *b* phenomenally. It is almost impossible to see *a* in *b*. Other grouping effects are due to visual noise that likewise can hide part or all of a pattern. Whether a pattern is submerged depends on the kind of noise. Figure 5 shows a triangle on a background of lines. The oblique sides of the triangle are easy to see, unaffected by the horizontals. But the bottom side of the triangle is lost in the "material" of the background (Galli & Zama, 1931). Instead of a triangle, one sees an inverted V. The third side of the triangle is grouped with the other horizontal lines. One can easily *verify* that there is a third side that completes the triangle, but this grouping is not *seen spontaneously* and is difficult to maintain if found.

The change in grouping of the whole in response to small local changes (Fig. 2) and the change in grouping of an isolated part compared to its appearance in context serve to simplify the trace and increase the efficiency of the coding. The improvement may consist in greater symmetry, fewer parts, or simpler structure of the whole, compared with alternative groupings.

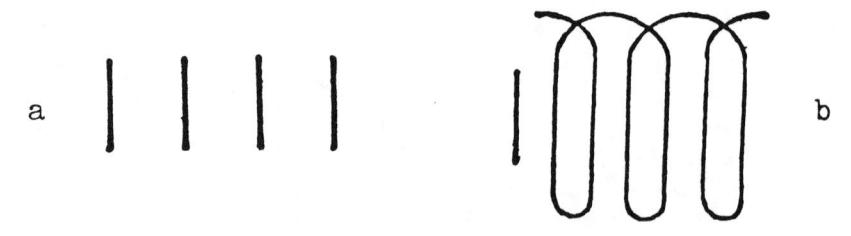

FIG. 4. Pattern *a* is geometrically contained in *b*, but does not exist in *b* phenomenally. (From Köhler, 1947.)

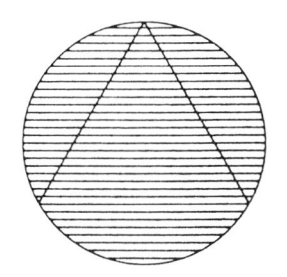

FIG. 5. This design shows a triangle on a background of lines. The horizontal side of the triangle is phenomenally part of the background. (From Galli & Zama, 1931.)

3. CODING BY FUNCTION

If phenomenal parts were no more than independent fixed subsets of elements, coding would entail no more than representing the parts and their relations. This is true only in the extreme of very weak aggregates, for instance, stars in the sky, dot patterns like 7.7 and 9.7 of Fig. 42, or the pictures of "unorganized collections of objects" used by Mandler and Parker (1976). In general, elements or subsets of elements (i.e., phenomenal parts) have a *function* within the whole. According to Mandler and Parker (1976), the function may be derived "through *experience* with the world, which organizes incoming information relative to previous experience [p. 39]" or may originate from figural *attributes* of the pattern, or both. For example, the middle line of Fig. 1 *plays the role of* "centerpiece" to the two "side lines." Phenomenally, the two side lines are related because they have the *same function*. They form *a pair*. The role of the center line is *connecting*. The structure of the design is phenomenally not $1 + 1 + 1$ but $1 + 2$, where the 1 is not one of the side lines and the 2 are not, say, the middle plus the right side line. Similarly, Fig. 71a is phenomenally not $1 + 1 + 1 + 1$ but $3 + 1$, where the straight line is "an appendix" of "the triple curve," which is "arching up." The three curves are on an "equal footing," form the "main part" of the design, a "trinity," a "crescendo," not a $1 + 2$, not the middle curve connecting the other two as in the previous example, but a "rising sequence" made of three similar curves. The three curves form what is called, in Section 2, a *strong* subunit. On the other hand, the relationship between the triple arch and the line is *weak*. The pattern as a whole would be little affected if the line was longer or shorter, turned slightly relative to the main structure, or even omitted.

The title of Wertheimer's 1923 paper was not *Laws of Grouping* but *Laws of Organization in Perceptual Forms*. The term *grouping* is a misnomer. It suggests that the stimulus elements have psychologic reality and that, additionally, they have been assigned membership in some set or subgroup, as associationism assumes. What Wertheimer proposed and what is suggested here is that *psychological reality attaches in general only to the end product of*

1. THE VISUAL TRACE

grouping, the phenomenal parts, and that elements in general have no independent psychologic reality. Consequently, the trace consists of coded phenomenal parts, *including their functions in the whole,* whereas individual elements are not necessarily coded and in general not represented in the trace. Even the parts are not necessarily represented as independent components but merely as *carriers of their function within the whole.*

This idea is supported by a variety of observations. Figure 6*a* is a dotted circle with a center dot. While the center dot is coded or represented as an individualized carrier of the function CENTER, the 16 peripheral dots are coded only collectively as the material of a dotted circle. They lack individual function and therefore individual representation in the trace. Figure 6*b* has a center dot, but the peripheral dots are rearranged and there are only 15 of them. Figure 6*c* has

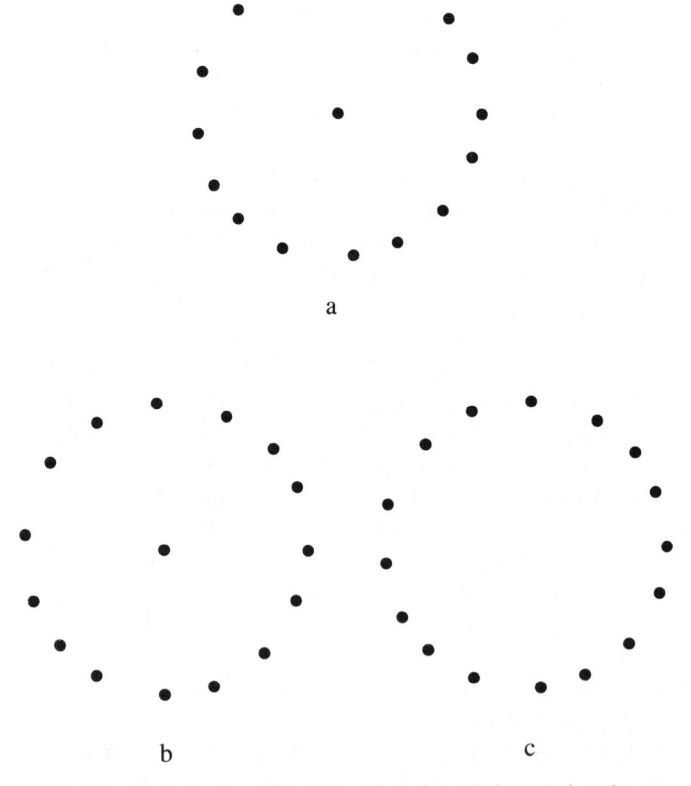

FIG. 6. The standard *a* has 16 peripheral dots, irregularly spaced, and a center dot. Figures *b* and *c* are variations of *a*. In *b* one peripheral dot was removed and the remaining dots rearranged. In *c* the center dot is removed, the peripheral dots are present in the same position and same number as in the standard.

the 16 peripheral dots of 6a in exactly the same positions but has no center dot. Figure 6b is perceived as more similar to *a* than is *c* by 13 of 14 subjects, even though in both *b* and *c*, one dot has been removed, and, moreover, in *b* but not in *c,* the relative positions of the remaining dots have been disturbed. The experiment suggests that the center dot is coded individually as CENTER, whereas the peripheral dots are coded only collectively by their function as MATERIAL of a dotted circle; furthermore, that the position of the center dot is *precisely* coded, whereas the positions of the peripheral dots are only *approximately* coded.

Results like these are often dismissed as due to different "placement of attention." The argument goes that the absence of a dot in 6*b* is "not noticed," whereas in *c* it is "noticed." The difference in noticing is undisputed. But the difference is not due to "attending." The mechanism of grouping and of perception does, in general, *guide* attention rather than being guided by it. It is difficult *not* to attend to the center dot, whereas it is just about impossible to attend to the exact number and distribution of the peripheral dots. In accordance with the laws of grouping, the center dot is perceived and hence coded differently from any of the peripheral dots. As a consequence, there is no perceptual difference between the standard and Fig. 6*b* to attend to.

In the experiment of Fig. 6, subjects could possibly be trained to perceive the differences between irregularly spaced 15 and 16 dot circles, just as laboratory technicians (but as yet not computers) can be trained to recognize each of the 23 specks that are the human chromosomes. Possibly, such well-trained subjects, confronted with experiment Fig. 6, would notice a difference between 6*a* and *b* and would "attend to" the equality between the dot arrangement and dot number of the circles in *a* and *c*. On that basis, they might find *c* the more similar pattern, in spite of the missing but "irrelevant" center dot. Coding and similarity depend on what is seen. Seeing is governed by laws that incorporate both figural characteristics and aspects of experience (see, for instance, Krolik, 1934, on the effect of experience on induced motion; Mandler & Johnson, 1976; Metzger, 1975; Palmer, 1975 a, b). Too often, the effects of past experience have been misinterpreted as arguments in favor of associationism.

Theorists often feel they have made a case for pure empiricism by demonstrating the shortcomings of pure nativism. Both issues are by now discredited as alternatives. We return to the role of past experience in later sections.

In experiment Fig. 6, attention effects are ruled out, because it is impossible to attend to the unnoticed differences between *a* and *b*. But even plainly noticeable and attendable differences do not deflect the laws of perception and coding, as demonstrated by the following experiments.

Figure 7 *a* is a dotted circle, 7*c* is a *proportional* enlargement of *a*. Figure 7*c* has the same number of dots (17) and the same ratio of dot diameter to circle diameter as 7*a*. Figure 7*b* is enlarged by the same factor (two) as 7*c* but has 35 unenlarged dots. The three patterns differ noticeably from each other. In this

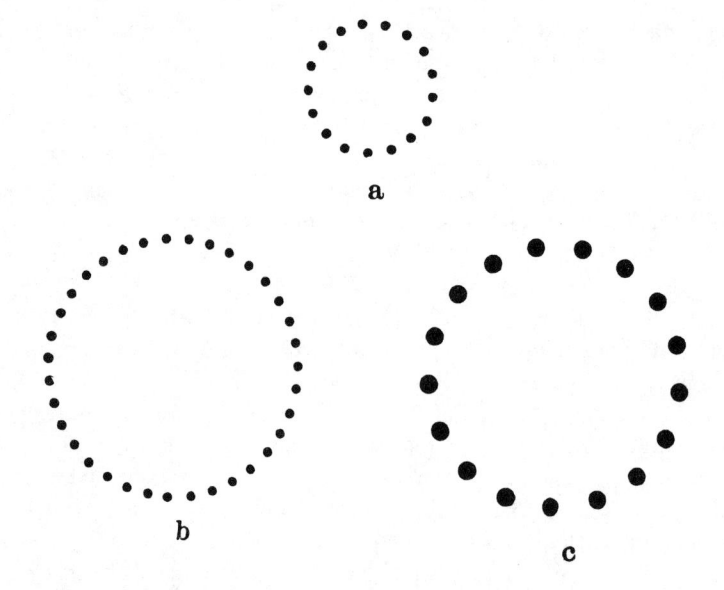

FIG. 7. Figure 7a is a dotted circle. Figure 7c is a strictly proportional enlargement of a, has the same number of dots (17) and the same ratio of dot diameter to circle diameter as a. Figure 7b is enlarged by the same factor (two) as 7c but has 35 unenlarged dots. (From Goldmeier, 1972.)

case, 10 out of 10 subjects find *b* the more similar of the two enlargements (Goldmeier, 1972). As I have argued there, the dots are not coded individually but collectively, as MATERIAL. Therefore, the one-to-one correspondence between the dots in *a* and those in *c* is not phenomenally realized, even though it is a geometric fact. On the other hand, DOT DENSITY along the line (and other, related features) is coded, and, in that respect, *a* and *b* agree closely. The dots are not coded individually, are not phenomenal parts, and therefore do not enter into the similarity judgment. The material function (regular, etc.) of the dots is coded independently of overall form (circle) and overall size (enlarged). The dots are noticed and therefore coded in all three patterns. But, whereas CIRCULARITY is coded at the *form* level of the hierarchy, the dots are coded at the *material* level, collectively, as "dottedness," not individually.

The lack of individual coding is characteristic of *material* elements (Goldmeier, 1972, Chapter 3), and, as Tulving's principle of coding specificity implies, what is not coded is not remembered. The experiments of Fig. 6 and 7 suggest that reproductions of these figures from memory, especially long-term memory, would at the form level preserve the CIRCULARITY and, in Fig. 6, the center dot. At the material level, reproductions would preserve the density and degree of regularity of the dot arrangement, and the shape and density of the dots. But reproduction or recognition would not preserve individual peripheral

3. CODING BY FUNCTION   13

dots. Specifically, the number of peripheral dots, if tested in the paradigm of the memory experiments in Chapters 5, 6, and 7, would vary, whereas there would be no variation in the number of center dots, namely one.

Coding by function in the whole rather than coding part by part or element by element is not restricted to the hierarchical subordination of "material" under "form." To illustrate the generality of coding by function, here are some further experimental findings, one on similarity with rotation (Goldmeier, 1972, Chapter 6), the others on phenomenal identity (Ternus, 1926).

Similarity experiments suggest that in Fig. 8a and c, the two lower, unequal "spokes" are grouped together and perceived as BASE for the upper ARM. In Fig. 8b, the two equal spokes are grouped together as a (spreading) TOP; the short spoke is seen as a (shaky) SUPPORT. Geometrically, Fig. 8b is derived from a by a 50° counterclockwise rotation. Figure 8c is derived from a by a 100° counterclockwise rotation. Even though c is rotated twice as much as b, it is significantly more similar to the standard than 8b ($p < .05$). Figures 8a and c are relatively similar because the transformation, in this case rotation, preserves the grouping and the functions of the standard a, even though the parts have exchanged their roles: In a, the left big spoke is upper ARM, in c, the right big spoke has that function. In a, the BASE is formed by the little spoke plus the right big spoke, in c, by the left big spoke plus the little spoke on the other side.

Although the bases of a and of c differ if considered piecemeal, they have whole qualities in common. These whole qualities are perceived, and they account for the *functional equivalency* of the bases. For instance, the endpoints of both bases fall on an (imaginary) horizontal base line. Both bases have an excentric apex from which a long arm takes its origin. Both bases have three angles, a convex angle on the left and two concave angles on the right. The upper ARMS of a and c, although differing in direction, point (almost) straight UP. Both ARMs arise from the apex of the base, are kinked, concave to the left, and have two about equal subparts.

If these whole qualities and structural homologies are encoded and the individual pieces of the subparts are not encoded, then a and c are perceived and

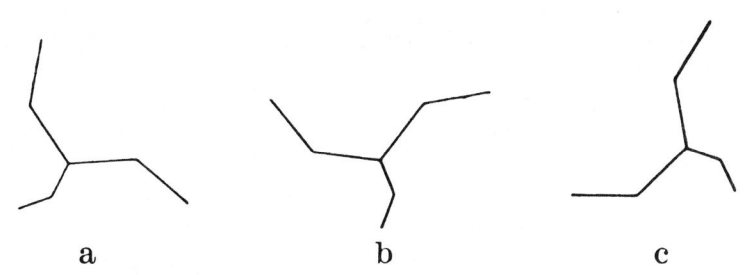

FIG. 8. Figure 8b is derived from a by a 50° counterclockwise rotation. Figure 8c is derived from a by a 100° counterclockwise rotation. (From Goldmeier, 1972.)

coded in almost identical terms and should behave almost identically in long-term memory. The trace of *b* on the other hand should comprise quite different parts, different features, and fare quite differently in long-term memory. And all this in spite of the fact that the individual elements and their relative angles and distances are the same in all three patterns.

Ternus (1926) addresses the preservation of function with exchange of function carrier even more directly. His experimental paradigm is the following: Two patterns are projected in quick succession on a screen, so that stroboscopic motion ensues. Some elements of the two patterns occur in the first exposition. They are marked in Fig. 9 to 13 as dots or solid lines. The elements of the second exposure are marked as open circles or dashed lines. Some elements are part of both exposures. They are marked with a dot within a circle or with both a solid and dashed line. The basic experiment of Ternus is shown in Fig. 9. There are four, equally spaced dots. The first exposure shows the first three dots, the second exposure shows the last three dots. The two middle dots, marked by a dot inside a circle, are shown in both exposures; they are repeated in the same location; they are "identical." With optimal timing, one sees not the two identical dots stationary in the middle and a third dot first to the left and then to the right of the stationary dots. Instead, one sees three dots moving as a unit from left to right. If the dots are numbered from left to right, dot 1 moves to the position of dot 2, dot 2 becomes dot 3, and dot 3 moves phenomenally to the right to location 4. *The dots exchange identities but retain functions.* The three functions preserved in the stroboscopic motion are LEFT, CENTER, RIGHT.

In Fig. 10, the transformation amounts to a rotation plus translation. One sees an arc move as a whole on a circular path. The first dot in the first exposition becomes, in the second exposition, the fourth dot, the second dot becomes the fifth, and so on. Each dot appears to move three places along on the arc. Actually, only the three left dots in the first exposure are replaced by the three right dots in the second exposure. The five center dots are present in the same position both times. Again, all dots exchange identities; that is, are seen as moving, but the functions (left end, interior, right end) and the grouping (one dotted circular segment) are invariant.

Ternus' experiments depend strongly on grouping and on the function of the elements in the particular pattern. The slight modification of Fig. 10, shown in Fig. 11, leaves identities fixed, although, geometrically, it is almost the same as Fig. 10. The pattern is perceived as a horizontal bar plus an oblique "appendage" dangling from one end, a grouping similar to the partitioning of Fig. 71*a*. One sees an immobile horizontal line with the appendage moving independently. No change of functions, hence, no exchange of identity of the points.

In experiments 9, 10, and 11, the transformation consists merely of the rigid motion of one unit. Experiment Fig. 12 amounts to a translation with added distortion. Figure 12*a* diagrams the experiment; 12*b* shows the two presentations separately, the first exposure above, the second one below. The second and

3. CODING BY FUNCTION   15

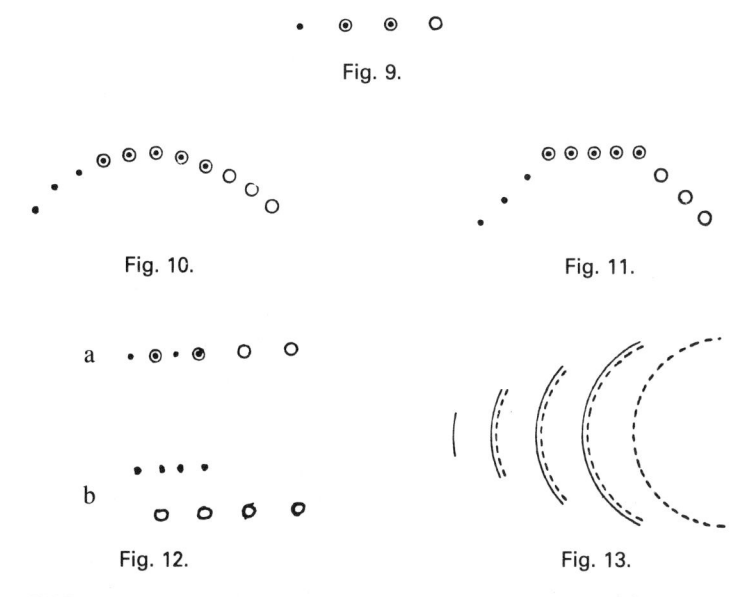

Fig. 9.

Fig. 10.   Fig. 11.

Fig. 12.   Fig. 13.

FIGS. 9 to 13. Two patterns are projected in quick succession on a screen, so that stroboscopic motion ensues. Some elements of the two patterns occur in the first exposition. They are marked in figures 9 to 13 as solid dots or solid lines. The elements of the second exposure are marked as open circles or dashed lines. Some elements are part of both exposures. They are marked by a dot within a circle or with both a solid and a dashed line. Figure 12a shows the two exposures together as just described, 12b shows the two presentations separately, the first exposure above, the second one below. (From Ternus, 1926.)

fourth dot of the first exposure reoccur in the second exposure as the first and second dot. One sees a group of four dots that moves to the right and at the same time expands to twice its previous length. Identities are not conserved: The first dot of exposition one becomes identified with the second dot in exposition two. The second dot phenomenally moves to the position of the fourth dot, the third and fourth dot identify in the second exposure with the two added new dots (shown as empty circles). Distances among the dots also are not conserved; they are doubled. The equality of the distances, however, is preserved. The four functions, left end, left interior, right interior, right end, are conserved, although, in the second exposure, all functions have been taken over by other carriers.

In the experiments mentioned so far, the elements are all equal dots. One might assume that *equality* of elements is necessary for a smooth exchange of function among the elements. Ternus addressed that question with the following two patterns. One experiment is like the basic experiment, Fig. 9, except that exposition I consisted of one white, one light gray, and one medium gray dot;

exposition II omitted the white dot, repeated the two others, and added on the right a dark gray dot. In spite of the inequality of all elements, the identities transferred exactly as in Fig. 9, the three dots move to the right as a unit. *At the same time the whole array darkens.*

A final example is diagrammed in Fig. 13. The first exposure shows arcs 1, 2, 3, 4; the second exposure shows 2, 3, 4, 5. With proper timing, one sees four arcs move to the right as a unit, and at the same time all arcs grow larger. In the last two experiments, identity is transferred between *unequal* elements, and functions are conserved in the face of physical and phenomenal change of each part of the pattern, darkening in one, enlargement in the second.

The end product of grouping, or better, organization is then not a list of parts or a hierarchy of parts and subparts. Rather, the end result is a *structure in which the parts are perceived and coded as carriers of specific functions.* The functions have phenomenal reality and therefore are part of the trace. Often the functions are coded without, or independent of, the carrier or embodiment of the function. As a consequence, traces can be curiously deficient in detail. Palmer (reported in Norman & Rumelhart, 1975) tested students' mental representation of the facade of a building that each student had seen and visited for several years. The building was low and squat, had a windowless ground floor with an entrance in the middle, and two upper floors, each with three groups of 14 identical narrow windows. Both in recall sketches and in recognition choices from four drawings, the students grossly understated the number of windows and the elongation (squatness) of the building. Also, in recall, the entrance was often not in the center. *Functionally,* such a building requires the front to exhibit a ground floor entrance and a variable number of upper stories with a variable number of windows. All this was indeed remembered. However, the parts are not constrained by their function with regard to: (1) the exact number of upper stories; (2) the placement of the entrance, as long as it is located on the ground level; (3) the exact number of windows; and (4) the exact proportion of height to width of the building. If the parts are coded by function as is here proposed, the trace will be *indeterminate* as to the number of stories, the exact placement of the entrance, number of windows in each row, and the elongation ratio. That is not to say that this additional information could not be acquired, but acquisition is *difficult, useless,* tends to be *imprecise* and *impermanent,* as is described in Section 13 dealing with nonsingular features of the trace. The experiment is an excellent illustration of data reduction in coding. The analogy between the number of windows and the number of dots in the periphery of Fig. 6 is striking. The understating of the squatness and number of windows is probably due to a central tendency or a ceiling effect, both common with nonsingular features (see Sections 13 and 14). Nickerson and Adams (1979), on the basis of experiments with familiar objects, came to similar conclusions. They state: "The details of visual stimuli are not retained . . . unless there is some functional reason for them to be [p. 306].

4. CODING OF FEATURES

In general, wholes and parts at all levels of a hierarchy have properties, attributes, or features. Little thought has been given to the number of possible phenomenal attributes. Just as in principle, there are enormously many ways to partition the stimulus elements into visual objects; so is there an enormous number of possible relations among the stimulus elements, each giving rise to potential attributes.

For example, in Fig. 1, the distance between the bottom dot of the left side line and the left corner dot is a phenomenal attribute of the line, being perceived as its *length*. But the distance from the same bottom dot to the third dot up is not phenomenally realized and is not a psychological property or feature of the design. In fact, most of the ½ × 16 × 17 = 136 distances between any two dots are phenomenally not realized and are psychologically not features of the design.

The same is true of relations: In Fig. 1, the left side line is as long as the right side line. That means, numbering the dots consecutively starting bottom left, the distance between dots 1 and 5 equals that between dots 13 and 17, and this equality is psychologically realized and is a phenomenal feature of the design. On the other hand, the distances from dot 1 to 8 and dot 9 to 16 are almost impossible to visualize. These two distances also are about equal, but neither the distances themselves nor their geometrical equality are phenomenally given or even realizable. Each of the 136 distances can be compared with any of the others. So, geometrically, there are ½ × 136 × 135 = 9180 relations of this type, but very few of them are phenomenally real; very few are features of the design and are so coded. There are relations of still higher orders, most of them unrealized. But some high-order relations are realized as phenomenal features; for example, the relations that make dots 1 to 5, 5 to 13, and 13 to 17 collinear, and the relations that make dots 5 and 13 apices of an angle. These relations are phenomenally real and coded in the trace. That is attested to by the fact that the design is seen as having three *straight* lines and two *corners*.

Figure 14a is seen as two curves, the right one with a cusp. We perceive the S-shape of the left curve, the triple curvature with cusp of the right curve, and the separateness of the two curves in spite of: (1) the *local nearness* of some of their dots that tends to group them together; and in spite of (2) the *factor of closure* (Wertheimer, 1923) that, acting unopposed, would separate out a phenomenal part like 14b. This grouping demands of the perceptual machinery a very high-level curvilinear regression that would do a pattern recognition computer program proud. People do it with just one glance. The curves of the left line are perceived as *shallow* and *opposite*, on the right curve as *"deep"*, and *"two larger and one smaller and tighter* curve. The two large ones are seen as *concave to the left,* the smaller one is seen as *concave to the right*. All these features are of high order. Many lower-order features, in this instance, are not perceived. However, some are (e.g., the equality and roundness of all dots).

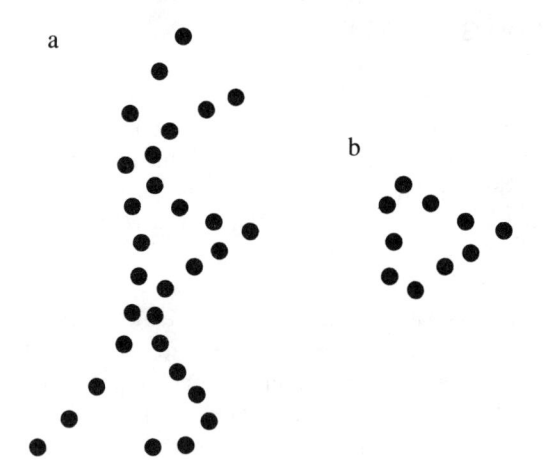

FIG. 14. Figure 14a is usually seen as two dotted curves. The subset of dots in 14b is not seen spontaneously as part of 14a.

As in the case of grouping, we need not know how perception manages to create perceptual attributes like equality of the side lines, or straightness, or curvature, and why it fails to encode the enormous numbers of other geometric relationships not perceived as attributes. Memory theory is only concerned with the role that attributes or features play in the structure of the trace once they are established, and with their encoding.

Attributes have a referent. Figures 8a and c look *broadbased;* 8b appears *unstable*. These attributes refer to the whole figures. They do not apply to the three component lines. The three component lines might be characterized as *angled* or as *made of two equal halves,* which is not true of the whole figure. Our mental representations are so constructed that the referents of attributes tend to be coextensive with *true, psychologically realized parts,* with the phenomenal wholes or subwholes, arrived at by grouping. For instance, in Fig. 2e, the attribute *transparent* attaches to the entire front square and only to it, not, say, only to the piece of the front square that transparently covers a piece of the square behind it. Camouflage and protective coloring are based on this tendency of perceiving the area of each color as coextensive with a true part of the scene. On the other hand, we perceive objects that continue each other as one, even if they are separated by interruptions, as in the case of an object seen through a picket fence, or, even more extreme, in Rock and Halper's (1969) patterns seen through a slit.

A number of factors enter into the establishment of an attribute as a phenomenal feature. One factor consists of the presence of other features (Asch, 1946, 1961). Another factor is the feature structure (Whitman & Garner, 1962); yet another is category membership (Rosch, 1973a). Except for context effects, (see Section 6), this research is still in its infancy. Further exploration of this area is of considerable importance to coding theory. We do not yet understand what ele-

4. CODING OF FEATURES 19

vates some but not other attributes to the status of obvious and promptly encoded features. Asch (1946, 1961) commented on this fact in regard to character traits:

> the impression of a person grows quickly and easily. Yet our minds falter when we face the far simpler task of mastering a series of disconnected numbers or words. We have apparently no need to commit to memory by repeated drill the various characteristics we observe in a person, nor do some of his traits exert an observable retroactive inhibition upon our grasp of others. Indeed they seem to support each other. And it is quite hard to forget our view of a person once it has formed [p. 238].

Similar comments would fit the famous experiment of Shepard (1967), in which 98% of 600 pictures could be recognized when mixed with 600 "new" pictures.

2 Singularity

5. FEATURES AND THEIR VALUES

Many parameters of visual stimuli can assume a continuous range of different values. There is, for example, a continuous range of brightness or redness. One can shift the dots in a dot pattern and shift the corners and change the angles in polygons. Corresponding changes then occur in the phenomenal values of the perceived features. Experiments in the tradition of classical psychophysics, performed in the 1950s and 60s, suggested the hypothesis that continuous variation of a geometric parameter, say, a shift in the position of the dots in Fig. 15 or the peaks in Fig. 21, results in perceived changes that are monotonic functions of the degree of shift. Posner, Goldsmith & Welton (1967) and Peterson, Meagher, Chait & Gillie (1973) actually demonstrated this for dot patterns. Attneave (1950), using parallelograms like those of Fig. 16, showed that in general the phenomenal distances between two of his figures covaries with the change in base angle. For example, the psychological distance from Fig. 16a to c is 1.08 (on his scale, see Attneave, 1950), the distance c to d is 1.07; the two add up to 2.15. The observed distance a to d is almost exactly equal to that sum: 2.12. Similarly, the distances b to c (.83) and c to d (1.07) add up to 1.90, and b to d was observed as 1.93. The results of Peterson et al. (1973) with Posner's dot patterns are just as clear-cut. We refer to this assumption as the Hypothesis of Monotonic Dependence. It is similar to Hypothesis I and II of Goldmeier (1936/1972) and can be regarded as a generalization of the Weber–Fechner law.

The hypothesis implies that: the varied parameters, in this case, dot position and base angle, are (1) phenomenally realized or represented; (2) the representation evokes a corresponding dimension or *feature,* let us call them, respectively,

5. FEATURES AND THEIR VALUES   21

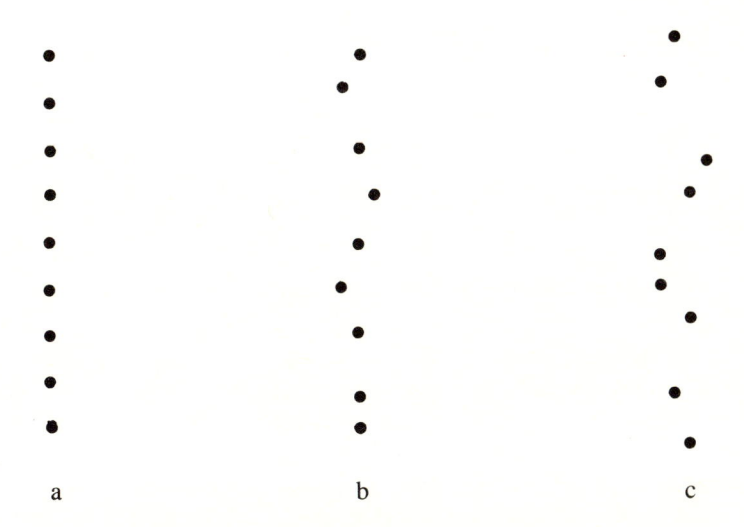

```
  •              •              •
  •              •                •
  •              •                •
  •              •                •
  •              •              •
  •              •              •
  •              •                •
  •              •                •
  •              •                •
  a              b              c
```

FIG. 15. Design 15a is a straight line of 9 dots. The total change from *a* to *b* is 4.4 units, (one unit equals ⅓ of the distance between dots in 15a) and the changes affect only the second, fourth, sixth and eighth dot. The change from *b* to *c* involves only the five previously unchanged dots and totals 7.4 of these units. Consequently the change from *a* to *c*, involving some shift of all nine dots, adds up to 11.8 units.

dot location and *angle;* and (3) this feature is coded as having some specific value. Similarity between two patterns then means that the particular feature is coded at a similar value, whereas phenomenal distance corresponds to a difference in the coded values. If pattern *a* in Fig. 15 is more similar to *b* than to *c*, the Hypothesis of Monotonic Dependence implies that the internal representation of all three patterns has a feature—dot location—and that differences in the *average of the dot locations* are coded as phenomenal distances between the patterns; likewise, that the base angle of the patterns in Fig. 16 is *realized* as a feature in the internal representation and that the angle is coded according to its phenomenal size.

Posner et al. (1967) were even more specific. They postulated that:

> the subjective distance between an original pattern and its distortions is a logarithmic function of the average distance which a dot moves... It apparently matters very little how the distance is distributed across the dots. That is, perceived distance is about the same whether the rule requires every dot to move a little or a few dots to move a great deal, provided only that the average amount of movement is constant [p. 29].

Here the monotonic function is specified as logarithmic, and the dependence is based specifically on the *average shift of all dots*. Attneave also found that, in

2. SINGULARITY

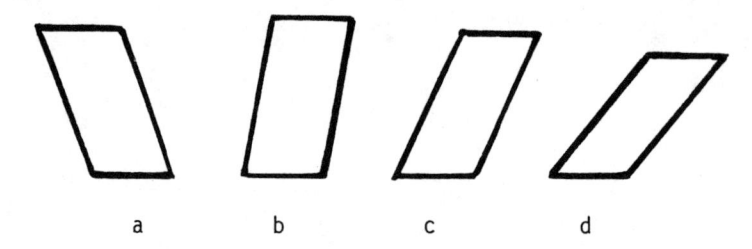

FIG. 16. Parallelograms used in experiments by Attneave (1950).

general, perceived distances are monotonic functions of the base angle. However, unlike Posner and his colleagues, his primary concern was not the monotonic dependence but the problem of dimensionality.

The appeal of this form of Monotonic Dependence lies in the complete predictability of the effect of stimulus changes. Its weakness is the inability to discriminate between realized and unrealized geometric change. The following experiments, mostly from Goldmeier (1936/1972), test the validity of Monotonic Dependence.

In Fig. 19, the four corner points of 19g are shifted inward by a small amount in 19d and by a larger amount in 19a. The average shift in d is less than in a, but, contrary to Monotonic Dependence, the greater geometric change causes the smaller phenomenal change: 14 out of 15 subjects ($p < .001$) consider a more similar to g than d. The same failure of Monotonic Dependence can occur if the changes are random. Experiment Fig. 15 was quoted earlier in support of Posner's findings. With 15a as the standard, b is indeed more similar to a than is c, in conformity with the Hypothesis of Monotonic Dependence. The change from a to b is 4.4 units (one unit equals ⅓ the distance between dots in 15a), and the changes are limited to the second, fourth, sixth, and eighth dot. The change from b to c involves only the five previously unchanged dots and totals 7.4 of these units. Consequently, the change from a to c, involving some shift of all nine dots, adds up to 11.8 units.

In a second experiment with these three patterns, b was used as standard. As we just mentioned, the difference between b and a is 4.4 units; the shift from b to c is 7.4 units. Yet, in this comparison, c is phenomenally closer to b than is a. Monotonic Dependence fails.

Conversely, if the "average amount of change" of two distortions is the same, then they should be equally similar to the standard. In both Fig. 29b and c, the standard a is distorted by shifting some dots. In 29b, the shift involves the dots on the short sides only and results in an increase of the two angles. In 29c, the two angles—two "form" features—are the same as in a, but the dots are shifted *along* the lines, changing the "material" of the lines from regular to irregular. Posner's *"average amount of movement"* is held to the same quantity

5. FEATURES AND THEIR VALUES   23

in both comparison patterns, yet *b* is significantly more similar to *a* than is *c* for 9 of 10 subjects ($p < .02$, Goldmeier, 1936/ 1972).

The use of dot patterns to test the Hypothesis of Monotonic Dependence is a matter of mathematical convenience and historical precedent. Actually, the hypothesis is intended to be applicable to any pattern at all, including drawings like Fig. 31. Both 31*c* and *d* are distortions of *a*, derived from *a* by rotating the five "intermediate" lines. The right lower and the bottom line are turned clockwise; the other three lines are rotated counterclockwise. The amount of rotation in the case of *c* is less than in *d*. The shift of each point on the lines is monotonically related to the degree of rotation. The rotation from *a* to *c* is greater than that from *c* to *d*, and the rotation from *a* to *d* is greater than that from *a* to *c*. With *c* as the standard, *d* is more similar to the standard than is *a*, in agreement with the Hypothesis of Monotonic Dependence (*a* to *c* > *c* to *d*). But using *a* as the standard, *d* is phenomenally closer to *a* than is *c*, even though the intermediate lines are rotated less from *a* to *c* than from *a* to *d*. The hypothesis fails.

The hypothesis also fails in at least one of Attneave's comparisons. The psychologic distance from Fig. 16*a* to *b* is 1.23 (in his units); from *b* to *c*, it is .83. If phenomenal distance changes monotonically as the base angle changes from *a* to *b* to *c*, then the distance from *a* to *c* could not be smaller than one of its components, *a* to *b* (1.23) or *b* to *c* (.83). However, it is 1.08, less than *a* to *b* alone. As Attneave (1950) remarks: "*a* is within 5° the mirror image of *c* ... (This) introduces a new dimension [p. 525]," which accounts for the failure of Monotonic Dependence.

There seem to be obvious explanations for the failures: circularity of Fig. 19*d*, straightness of Fig. 15*a*, different *levels of organization* (Form versus Material, see Goldmeier, 1972) in Fig. 29 *b* and *c, parallel* course of the intermediate lines in Fig. 31*c*, and the *near-symmetry* between Fig. 16*a* and *c*. But an explained failure is still a failure. Cognitive psychology has traditionally relied on confirmatory cases as prototypes, like dot patterns of the Posner type, Attneave's parallelograms, rotations like those investigated by Shepard and Metzler (1971) and Cooper and Shepard (1973), and on enlargements, like those reported by Bundesen and Larsen (1975). They are accepted as typical of one-parameter variations monotonically related to phenomenal change. They are quoted in support of Monotonic Dependence. Actually, the failures of the hypothesis are universal and can be found wherever one looks for them. I would like to suggest two places to look.

The work of Shepard and Metzler (1971) and Cooper and Shepard (1973) suggests, *although the authors do not make the claim,* that a figure becomes increasingly dissimilar to its initial appearance as it is rotated out of its initial orientation. But we have seen that in the case of Fig. 8*a*, the variant *c*, which is rotated by 100°, is more similar to *a* than 8*b*, which is rotated by only 50° against

24   2. SINGULARITY

a. I suspect that chronometric studies like those of Cooper and Shepard would show results different from those they have previously obtained, if patterns like Fig. 8 were systematically investigated (Goldmeier, 1972, Section 51).

In the same vein, chronometric studies by Bundesen and Larsen (1975) on enlargements have shown that comparison times increase monotonically with the degree of enlargement. But studies on similarity (Goldmeier, 1972, Chapter 3) have demonstrated that psychologically there are many different kinds of "enlargement." Figures 17 and 18 show examples of different kinds of enlargements, some much "better" than others. Mathematically, enlargement is uniquely defined as a change of scale. Psychologically, enlargement is not unique. Because of this difference, chronometric studies should show shorter

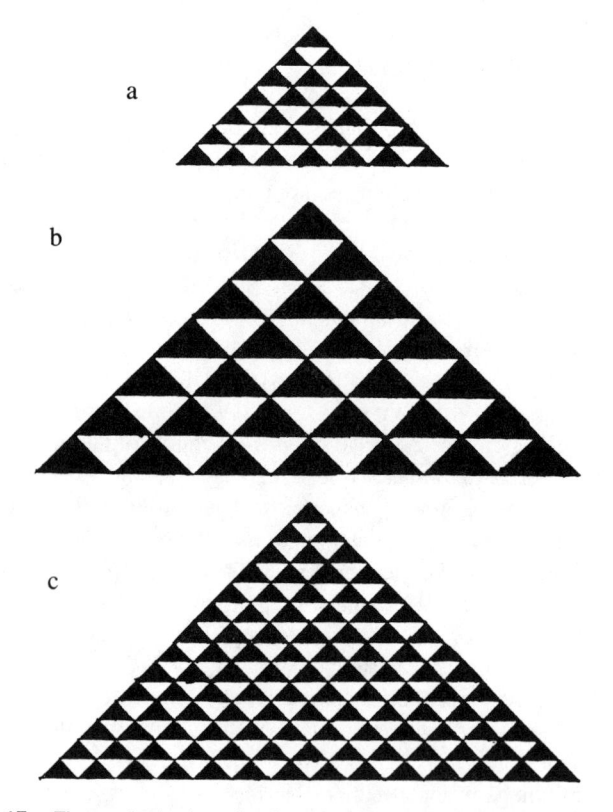

FIG. 17.   The standard *a* is a triangle made of 7 tiers of smaller triangles. Both 17 *b* and *c* are twice as big as *a*. Figure 17*b* is a strictly proportional enlargement of *a*. Each element of *b* is twice as large as the corresponding element in *a*. Figure 17*c* has twice as many elements as *a* and each element is exactly the same size as the elements of *a*. Usually the disproportional enlargement of 17*c* is more similar to the standard *a* than the proportional enlargement 17*b*.

5. FEATURES AND THEIR VALUES   25

●●●●●●●●●●●●●
a

●●●●●●●●●●●●●●●●●●●●●●●●●
b

●   ●   ●   ●   ●   ●   ●   ●   ●   ●   ●   ●   ●
c

●●●●●●●●●●●●●
d.

● ● ● ● ● ● ● ● ● ● ● ● ● ● ● ● ●
e

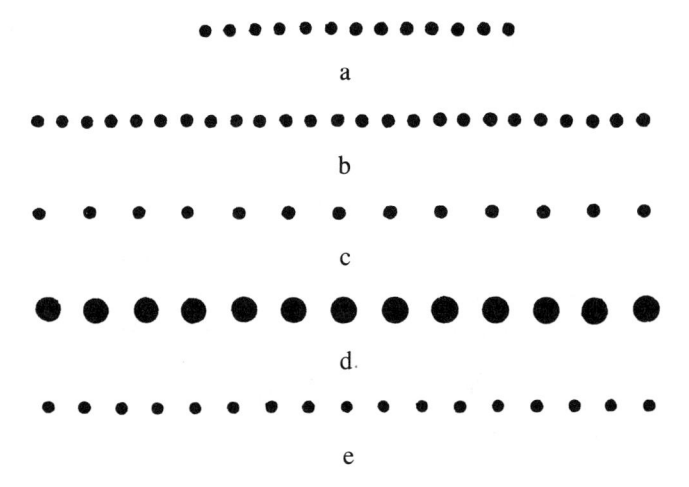

FIG. 18. The standard a is a row of dots. All other rows are twice as long but only in 18d have all measurements been doubled proportionately, including the size of the dots. In 18c the distance between the dots has been doubled; the diameter of the dots is the same as in the standard a. In 18 b and e likewise the dots have not been enlarged. In 18b the distance between dots is the same as in the standard. In 18e the distance between dots is larger than in 18b but smaller than in 18c: the distance was so chosen that the gaps between two dots are the same size as in 18d. In both c and d the number of dots is the same as in the standard (13). Figure e has 17 dots and b has 25. Similarity experiments indicate that b is most similar to the standard a, next is e, and c and the proportional enlargement d are least similar to a. (From Goldmeier, 1972.)

comparison times for psychologically "good" enlargements (17c, 18b) than for some strictly proportional ones (17b, 18d).

The ambiguity of enlargement has parallels in the way we conceptualize size change and in the way nature effects growth. We code an overly tall (or precocious) child differently from an adult of the same size (properly tall) and a normal child differently from an adult dwarf of the same height. An elephant has *more* cells than a mouse, not the *same number of cells* of larger size. A large molecule has more, not bigger, atoms than a small one. We don't build a large house from the same blueprints as a small house by merely using a larger scale (ceilings and stair steps twice as high, etc.), nor a small office building by scaling down a skyscraper. In other words, operationally, conceptually, and also in cognition and visual perception, enlargement is in most cases not a geometric change of scale. In fact, strict change of scale, for all its mathematical simplicity, is a poor model in almost any field: astronomy, physics, biology, economics, art, as well as psychology.

The inconvenient exceptions to Monotonic Dependence discussed here and the many more exceptions likely to exist (e.g., with rotation and enlargement) are more than curiosities. It appears, as Attneave suggested (1950), that Monotonic Dependence applies only *within one psychologic dimension*.

6. MONOTONIC DEPENDENCE AND DIMENSIONALITY

The various failures of Monotonic Dependence seem related to the intrusion of an additional dimension of change, sometimes obvious, sometimes unexpected and subtle. Thus, the question arises, when does a change create or activate or lead to a new dimension, a dimension that was absent or dormant in the original pattern? Indeed, what determines the number of dimensions that are active or realized in a pattern, say, in a circle drawn on a card? Some features of a percept are evoked by the context, as Garner (1974, p. 184) has suggested. A circle shown by itself is phenomenally a circle, say, on a rectangular card, or possibly a black circle on a white card, etc. The same stimulus shown side by side with a card bearing a dashed circle will, by contrast, acquire a new feature: *solid-lined*. Alongside a card bearing a smaller circle, the original becomes *a larger circle*. Alongside a circle drawn as a double line, the original becomes *single-lined*. The context activates the features of solid line, large, single, and it could activate innumerably more features not called forth without the context. In fact, as Palmer (1975a, 1975b, 1977) has emphasized, there are hierarchies of contexts, all active in encoding. The features of a pattern evoked by widening the context are extrinsic to the pattern but are intrinsic to a higher level of the contextual hierarchy. Widening or manipulating the context and creating different types of contexts are *synthetic* strategies used in most of Garner's work (Garner 1974), also Palmer's (1975b).

Investigating the relation of Monotonic Dependence to dimensionality calls for an *analytic* strategy. It requires variation of individual patterns, holding the context unchanged. This is the strategy in the work of Goldmeier (1936, 1972, 1941), Rosch (Rosch, Simpson, & Miller, 1976), Bear (1973, 1974), and Palmer (1975b, 1978a), among others.

Intermediate between the analytic and synthetic strategy is the approach of Shepard (1963, 1964) and Rosch (1972). It is based on Shepard's insight that within any one dimension, psychological proximities allow of a linear ordering, and, conversely, if the proximities of a set of objects cannot be ordered linearly, then the distances between the members of the set must lie along more than one dimension. This is the basic principle of multidimensional scaling. I think it is also a key to understanding the nature of dimensionality.

Multidimensional scaling, for all its mathematical elegance and its power to extract information from seemingly amorphous data, *does not yield up dimensionality*. The number of dimensions is chosen intuitively before the mathematical analysis begins. In deciding on the number of dimensions, one is guided by rules of thumb (Kruskal, 1964). Essentially, by two rules: (1) choose as few dimensions as "possible"; (2) choose "interpretable" dimensions. Even though multidimensional scaling is based on linear ordering *within* dimensions, it does not guarantee recovery of the effective dimensions hidden in the data. I hasten to add that the method was never intended to identify effective dimensions uniquely, and also that in principle, given a sufficiently dense set of data or a continuum of data, the exact dimensional structure would be recovered. But as it stands, neither synthetic nor analytic methods succeed in uniquely defining *psychologically realized* dimensions.

In addition to the failure of Monotonic Dependence, we now find an inability to identify the psychologically active dimensions in a perceived object. In spite of great efforts, no objective rule to determine phenomenally realized features or to define the effective dimensions has been found. It seems that these two failures are linked, that *monotonicity and dimensionality define each other*. Shepard (1963) observed early on that "a trading relation exists . . . between the two basic requirements of (a multi-dimensional mapping); namely the requirement that the space be of minimal dimensionality and the requirement that the relation between the . . . (similarity data and the) interpoint distances be monotonic [p. 36]." What Shepard found true of mappings reflects an underlying tendency of human encoding: *A single dimension is mentally established only if there is an attribute that varies monotonically.*

Figure 19 illustrates this relationship. The top, bottom, right, and left dot of 19*a* are stationary. The other four dots are moved outward monotonically from *a* to *g*. While geometrically this variation proceeds monotonically, the phenomenal variation involves several attributes or dimensions, only one of which, overall size, follows monotonically the outward shift of the moved dots. Others are: roundness, which runs monotonically from *d* to *c* to *e* versus pointedness, which runs from *a* to *g* to *b* to *f*. Concaveness, which includes *a* and *g* versus convexness, which runs from *b* or *f* to *c* to *e* to *d*. Roundedness is perceived if the angles between all adjacent triples of dots well exceed 90°. Roundedness increases *monotonically* as the difference between adjacent angles decreases. Pointedness arises if every other angle between adjacent dots is below about 100°. It increases monotonically with the difference between adjacent angles. Concaveness depends monotonically on how much every other angle excedes 180° and vice versa for convexness. An additional property, *orientation,* runs monotonically from *a* alphabetically to *g,* as does size, but it has three subdivisions: diamond-like, neutral, and square-like (see Fig. 19 and 20).

It should be understood that the patterns in Fig. 19 represent only seven examples out of an infinite number of variants created by the *continuous, monotonic change* of one parameter, the outward shift of the four diagonal dots by equal amounts.

Of the dimensions studied, two clearly depend monotonically on this one parameter. Size probably depends almost linearly on the amount of shift.

28   2. SINGULARITY

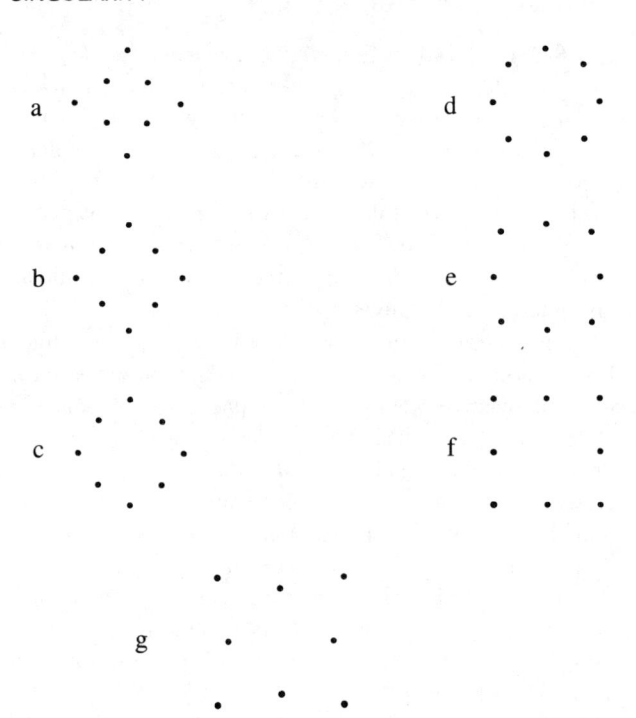

FIG. 19. This design consists of eight dots. Four of these remain stationary, the other four are moved outward by increasing amounts (*a* to *g*). Figure 19*a* is pointed and concave; the qualities decrease in *b* and start to reverse in *c*; *d* has neither points nor concavity—it is completely circular, and at the same time the design has increased in size. Beyond *d* it becomes pointed again and finally, at *g*, concave again. (From Goldmeier, 1972.)

Another dimension, orientation, also follows this parameter monotonically, but with quite a different mapping function (Fig. 20). The functional dependence of orientation, although monotonic, is almost a step function: The orientation is diamond-like from *a* to *c* and beyond, almost to *d*, where it abruptly changes to neutral, and just beyond *d* to square-like, remaining square-like through *e*, *f*, and *g*. There is hardly a difference between *a* and *c* as regards diamond-like orientation and between *e* and *g* as to square-like orientation.

Two other pairs of dimensions, roundness–pointedness and convex–concaveness, both depend on the relative size of the two sets of alternate angles. If the two sets are nearly equal, as in *c*, *d*, or *e*, the pattern is rounded and convex; if alternate angles are markedly different, as in *a* and *g*, they are pointed and concave. The two sets of dimensions differ, however, in the location of the neutral zone. Specifically, *c* and *e* are slightly pointed but not concave. Like size and orientation, the two dimensions rounded–pointed and convex–concave depend monotonically on a geometric parameter: the absolute value of

6. MONOTONIC DEPENDENCE AND DIMENSIONALITY

the difference between the two alternating sets of angles (the angles with vertices on the diagonals minus the others). The *difference* is a monotonic function of the first-mentioned parameter, the outward shift of the diagonal dots. But *the absolute value of the difference* is *not* monotonically related to the amount of outward shift. Relative to the absolute value of the angle difference, the seven patterns are monotonically ordered as *d, c, e, b, f, a, g,* both geometrically and psychologically.

This ordering was obtained by means of similarity rankings. Figure 19 *d* was used as the standard, and the subject was asked to select from all other patterns of Fig. 19 the pattern most similar to *d*. The design chosen was then removed, and the subject had to select the pattern most similar to *d* among those remaining. This procedure was repeated until only one pattern was left. Ten subjects were used. The ordering *d, c, e, b, f, a, g* represents the average of the 10 rankings. Not all rank differences are statistically significant. For instance, *c* and *e* do not differ significantly from each other, but they differ significantly from *b, f, a,* and *g*. (Other details of these experiments, not relevant here, are reported in Goldmeier, 1972, Chapter 7.)

The same kind of ranking was carried out with the patterns Fig. 68 *b* to *j* (excluding *a, k,* and *l*). Using Fig. 68 *f* as the standard, 68 *e, f,* and *g* are significantly more similar to each other than to any of the other designs, which have gaps within the lines ($p < .01$). Conversely, with *d* or *h* as the standard, *f, g,* and, in the case of *h,* also *e* rank lowest, and in both cases are significantly ($p < .01$) less similar to the standard than the designs with the gap on the same side as the standard (*b* and *c* for *d, i* and *j* for *h*). In other words, if a one-step change goes from *h* to *i,* it makes a small difference; if the change goes from *h* to *g,* the difference is significant. A one-step change from *d* to *c* makes little difference, whereas if the same change goes from *d* to *e,* the difference is significant.

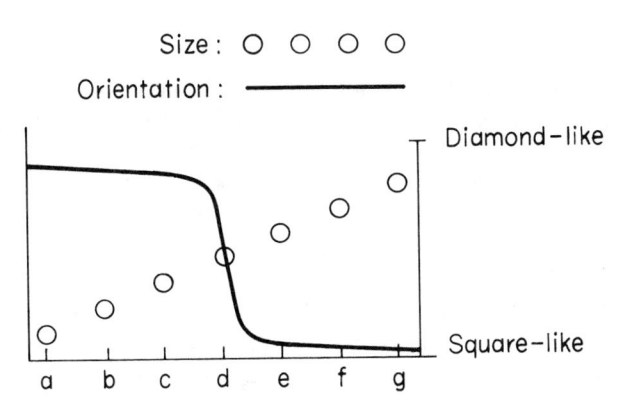

FIG. 20. The abscissa represents the designs of figure 19 *a* to *g*. The ordinate represents increase in size from *a* to *g* (empty circles) and change from diamondlike orientation, *a* to *c*, to squarelike orientation, *e* to *g* (solid line).

2. SINGULARITY

Similarity rankings of this kind were performed for the patterns shown in Fig. 19, 31, 61, 63, 67, 68, and 70. The results were reported and discussed in Goldmeier (1972), Chapter 7, and also here, Section 28, and in connection with the aforementioned designs. In the case of Fig. 68 *b* to *j*, the rankings suggest that the geometrically monotonic shift of the gap from *b* to *j* results psychologically in *two* features: gap-within-curves, as in *b, c, d* and *h, i, j*, versus *gapless*, separate curves, as in Fig. 68 *e,f,g*. The gap-within-curves feature is monotonically dependent on the geometric gap shift, *excluding e, f, g.*

Four points emerge from this discussion:

1. A feature or dimension always depends monotonically on a stimulus parameter. Example: Roundness – Pointedness in Fig. 19 depend monotonically on the absolute value of the difference of neighboring angles.

2. The converse is not necessarily true. Example: Whereas in certain random dot patterns (Peterson et al., 1973; Posner & Keele, 1968), one-dimensional geometric change monotonically leads to phenomenal change, this is not always the case (Fig. 15 *b* to *a* to *c*). In fact, many geometric parameters are not psychologically realized at all (dot relationships in Fig. 30*a*), so that a change in these parameters leaves the psychological representation unchanged (dot relations in Fig. 30*c*, dot changes on the periphery of Fig. 6).

3. Even if a stimulus parameter is psychologically realized, that is, gives rise to a feature or dimension of the representation (such as the position of the gaps in Fig. 68, the angle of the lines in Fig. 31, the dot positions in Fig. 19), then a monotonic variation of this parameter can take the variants through different appearances not monotonically related to the geometric variation. In the preceding examples, Fig. 68*h* is closer to *d* than to *e;* in Fig. 31, variant *a* is closer to *d* than to *c*, even though in *c* there is less rotation than in the other variant. The monotonic dot shift in Fig. 19 takes the pattern through several independent dimensions, so that, for instance, the most changed pattern *g* is closer to the original pattern *a* than to the intermediate pattern *d* (Goldmeier, 1972).

4. More than one dimension or feature may depend on the continuous variation of a single parameter (e.g., size, orientation, roundedness, and concaveness in Fig. 19). The dependence may be: (1) monotonic, in the case of size and orientation; or (2) not monotonic, as for roundedness and concaveness in Fig. 19. *However, if not monotonic, there always exists, according to point 1 earlier, another parameter that varies monotonically with the feature,* in the case of concaveness of Fig. 19, the absolute value of the angle difference. The other parameter is, of course, nonmonotonically related to the original parameter.

Furthermore, if two features depend on the same parameter, whether monotonically or not, the functional dependence on the parameter must be different, as sketched in Fig. 20 for size and orientation of the patterns in Fig. 19, or "parallel course" and "balanced partition" in Fig. 61 and 62 (see Section 29).

The four points converge to this conclusion: Whereas every feature depends monotonically on some stimulus parameter, not every parameter of the stimulus is psychologically realized (i.e., represented in the stored percept). In fact, just as in the case of grouping, an enormous degree of data reduction occurs. Only relatively few stimulus parameters are coded as features.

7. PHENOMENALLY REALIZED PARAMETERS

To determine which parameters of the stimulus are phenomenally realized, we start, much like Posner and Keele (1968), with some standard pattern a and increasingly distort it to a pattern b, and beyond b to c. We then ask our subjects whether b or c is more similar to a. The five examples are from Goldmeier (1936/1972).

Experiment Fig. 21 deals with distortion of angles: 21a consists of a series of spikes or angles. In both variants, the heights are increased and consequently the angles are decreased. In variant b, the heights of the spikes are increased by various amounts (2 to 7 mm, average 5 mm, in the original drawing), whereas in c, all spikes are higher by an equal and larger amount (10 mm each in the original). If heights or angles are realized as phenomenal features, like the angles in Attneave's parallelograms, b should be more similar than c, because the average change in b is only half as much as in c. But of 11 subjects, 6 judge b more similar, 4 choose c, 1 is undecided. There is no significant phenomenal difference between the two variants.

In the following three experiments, distortions affect first one half, then both halves of the original pattern. In Fig. 22b, the lower angle of the standard a is decreased by 15°; in variant c, both angles are decreased by 15°. For 8 of 10

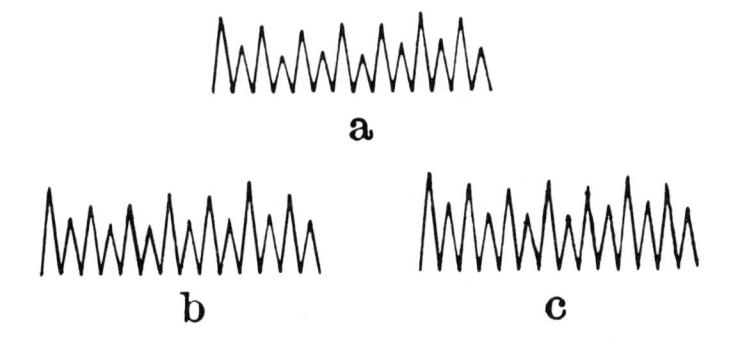

FIG. 21. Design a is an irregular series of spikes or teeth. In 21b these "teeth" were raised by various small amounts (2–7 mm. in the actual drawing); in 21c they were raised by an *equal* and larger amount (10 mm. in the actual drawing). (From Goldmeier, 1972.)

2. SINGULARITY

FIG. 22. Each design has two angles with the following measurements:

	Upper angle	Lower angle
a	120°	60°
b	120°	45°
c	105°	45°

(From Goldmeier, 1972.)

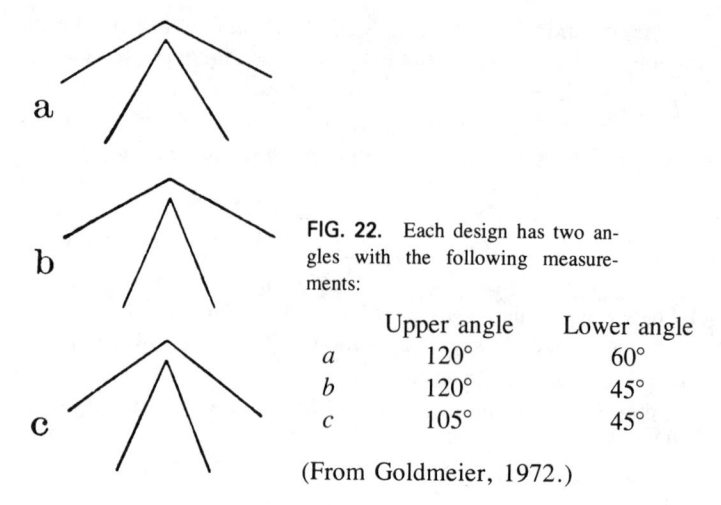

subjects, *b* is more similar to *a*. This result weakly (p < .1) conforms to Monotonic Dependence.

In Fig. 23*b*, the curvature of the upper line only is increased; in *c* the lower line is also more curved, so that in *c* both lines are changed. Of 12 subjects, 8 find *c* more similar to *a*, 4 choose *b*. The variant with less distortion, *b*, should be more similar.

Finally, in Fig. 24*b*, the left half is identical with the left half of the standard *a*. The right half is distorted. Variant *c* has the same distorted right half as *b*, but additionally a distortion of the left, so that both sides of *c* are different from *a*. The additional distortion of the left side of *c* was equalized to the distortion on the right by restoring the relations of homologous points, marked 1–1, etc. in

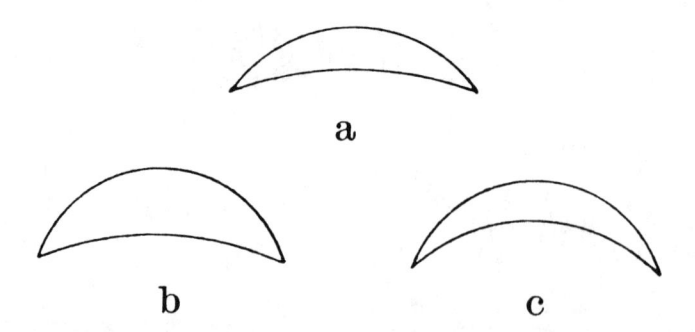

FIG. 23. Design *a* has two curves. In 23*b* the lower curve is the same as in *a*, the upper line is more curved, and the thickness (the difference in the height of the two arcs) is thus increased. In 23*c* the upper curve is the same as that of 23*b* and the lower line is also more curved. Neither line is the same as in *a*; however, *a* and *c* have the same thickness. (From Goldmeier, 1972.)

7. PHENOMENALLY REALIZED PARAMETERS   33

Fig. 24a. Both variants were judged equally similar to the standard, five subjects chose b and five chose c, even though c was changed exactly twice as much as b.

In all four experiments, pattern c was changed twice as much as b; yet, in none of the four was b preferred at the .05 level of confidence. There are two possible explanations. In the absence of a new dimension in the two variants, the degree of distortion, the amount of shift of the changed parameter, could be too small to be psychologically effective. That is unlikely with the clearly noticeable changes used. Furthermore, as we see later, the same amount of change is effective under other circumstances.

Secondly, the Hypothesis of Monotonic Dependence might have been applied to the wrong parameter. This possibility was not envisaged by the proponents of Monotonic Dependence. On the contrary, the appeal of Monotonic Dependence lies in what was thought to be the unambiguous way in which it predicts psychological change. This has now proved to be illusory. In the patterns of Fig. 19, we found two different parameters, both psychologically realized, leading to two different monotonic orderings. The parameter governing concavity-convexity turned out to be the "absolute value of the difference of certain

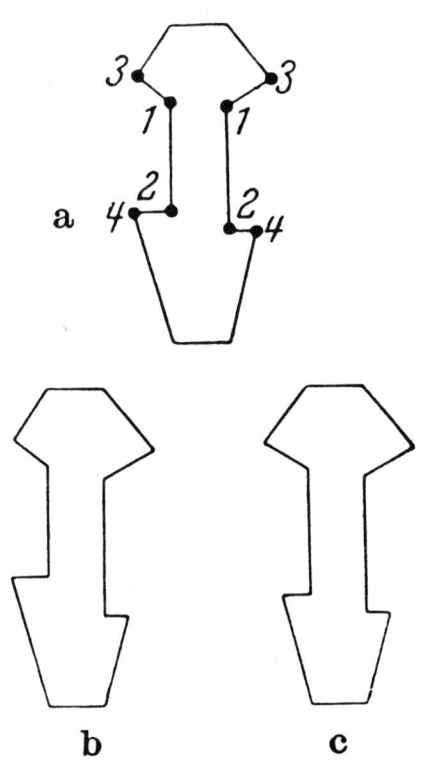

FIG. 24. Figure 24b is identical with the standard a in its left half. On the right side points 1 and 2 are shifted downward, point 3 outward, point 4 closer to the middle. Figure 24c is not identical with 24a on either side. Its right half is identical with the right side of 24b. On the left side points 1 and 2 are shifted downward, point 3 outward, point 4 closer to the middle with respect to the corresponding points of 24b. (From Goldmeier, 1972.)

angles" that was related, but not monotonically so, to the parameter "outward shift of certain dots." In each of the present four experiments, the same situation obtains. In each case, a geometric parameter varies in the opposite sense from the parameter we have used to define the change. In Fig. 21c, the relationship of the peaks, the "skyline," is the same as in the standard, whereas in 21b it is altered. These *height relationships,* suitably defined, describe the distortions just as uniquely as the heights themselves and can serve to predict similarity via Monotonic Dependence. However, they predict the opposite outcome. In Fig. 22c, the *divergence* of the two angles is 60°, the same as in the standard 22a. The divergence in 22b is 75°. Divergence, which is changed only in b, is as valid a parameter as the change of each individual angle. The two parameters predict opposite outcomes. In Fig. 23 a and c, the "thickness," the *vertical distance between the two arcs,* is the same, whereas in 23b, this parameter is increased by two thirds. Based on "thickness," Monotonic Dependence predicts c to be more similar, whereas based on "average amount of change of individual lines," b is less changed. In the fourth experiment, Fig. 24, the left-to-right relations, that is, the relations between points marked with the same number in Fig. 24 a, are identical in a and c but altered in b. Using the *average shift of homologous points* as the parameter, c is less changed than b, whereas based on whether one or both sides are changed, b is less changed.

The ambiguity illustrated by these four examples is not peculiar to these designs but applies widely (see, for instance, the findings of Palmer, 1978).

Because in all four examples the experimental outcome is equivocal, one might assume that both parameters are psychologically active and more or less in balance. In Experiment 21, both the average height and the skyline could be encoded and could give rise to two phenomenal features that are perceived as opposite changes. If in Experiment 22 both divergence and individual angles are coded, their opposite change could lead to equivocal similarity judgments. The same could hold in Experiment 23 for thickness and individual curvature, and in Experiment 24 for left–right relations against individual change of the two sides separately. The results then would be due to different saliency, different weighting of two competing features or dimensions. The similarity of each variant would depend on the relative weight of each feature within the representation. While relative weights cannot be deduced from the Hypothesis of Monotonic Dependence, they could be determined empirically. For instance, in Experiment 21, a change of hight by an average of 5mm plus a change of skyline, as in Fig. 21b, can be compared with change of hight of 10mm and no change of skyline, as in Fig. 21c. Because 6.5 choices went to b and 4.5 choices to c, these could be the relative weights of the particular combination of changes. If we make the same changes, that is, if we increase the hight in one variant by an average of 5mm, as in Fig 21b, producing the same change of the skyline, and compare the variant with another one in which all hights are increased by 10mm leaving the skyline raised but otherwise unchanged, then we should again find similarity

7. PHENOMENALLY REALIZED PARAMETERS 35

/\/\/\/\/\/\/\/\/\/\/\/\

a

/\/\/\/\/\/\/\/\/\/\/\ /\/\/\/\/\/\/\/\/\/\/\/\

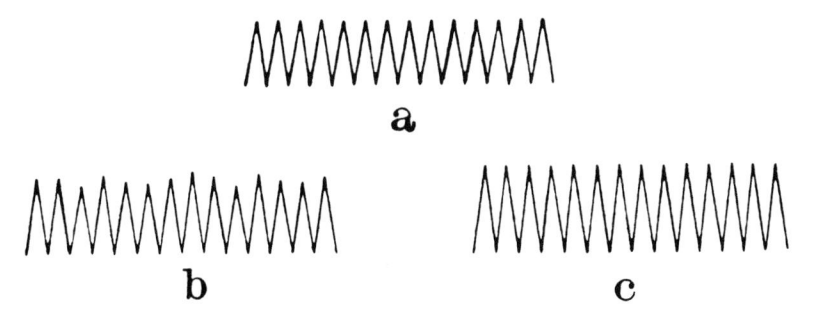

b   c

FIG. 25. Design *a* is the standard. Designs *b* and *c* are variants of *a* derived from the standard by the same amount and kind of change as figure 21*b* and *c* relative to 21*a*. (From Goldmeier, 1972.)

judgments split about 6.5 to 4.5, even if we start with a standard different from Fig. 21*a*. Experiment Fig. 25 is so constructed. Starting from pattern Fig. 25*a*, variants *b* and *c* are changed *by the same amounts* and in the same manner as Fig. 21*b* and *c*. Specifically, the two features, "hight of individual spikes" and "skyline," are changed exactly as in Experiment 21. But now *c* is more similar to the standard than is *b* for 11 of 11 subjects. The experiments compare as follows:

Experiment	Number of subjects choosing	
	b	c
Fig. 21	6.5	4.5
Fig. 25	0	11

The two outcomes are significantly ($p < .005$) different. Negatively, this shows that one cannot, in general, calibrate one change against another. Positively, it suggests that the same amount of geometric change of a feature has widely differing effects on the phenomenal change of the feature, *depending on where in the range of values it is applied*. In this instance, a change of the skyline has relatively little effect if it is applied to Fig. 21*a*, but the same change, if it is applied to Fig. 25*a*, has a large effect.

Figure 26 is a comparison experiment to Fig. 22. In this case, *both* angles of the standard *a* are 120°; their divergence is therefore zero. The two variants are prepared as in Experiment 22. In *b*, the lower angle, in *c*, both angles are reduced by 15°, which increases the divergence in *b* by 15° but restores it to the original amount in *c*. Now *c* is more similar for 10 of 10 subjects tested. The results compare as follows:

Experiment	Number of subjects choosing	
	b	c
Fig. 22	8	2
Fig. 26	0	10

36   2. SINGULARITY

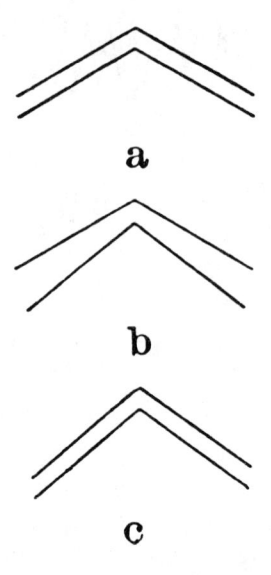

FIG. 26. This is a comparison experiment to figure 22. Both angles of the standard *a* measure 120°. In *b* the lower angle, in *c*, both angles are reduced by 15°. (From Goldmeier, 1972.)

The two experiments have opposite results ($p < .0005$). A change of divergence starting from zero, as in Fig 26*a*, is phenomenally much more effective than the same change added to a starting divergence of 60°, as in Fig. 22*a*.

Figure 27 exactly duplicates Fig. 23 except for the starting values of the two curvatures. In this case, the change of the individual, lower curve is so salient that it outweighs the change of "thickness" in 27*c*. (As in Fig. 23, *a* and *b* share the lower line but differ in thickness, *a* and *c* have the same thickness but differ in both lines.) The experiments compare as follows:

Experiment	Number of subjects choosing	
	b	*c*
Fig. 23	4	8
Fig. 27	11	1

FIG. 27. This a comparison experiment to figure 23. As in figure 23, *a* and *b* have the same lower line but differ in "thickness," *a* and *c* have the same thickness but differ in the curvature of both lines. (From Goldmeier, 1972.)

7. PHENOMENALLY REALIZED PARAMETERS 37

"Thickness" is a more salient feature when both lines are "curved"; curvature is more salient when it has the value of zero. The difference is marked ($p < .005$).

The changes applied to Fig. 28b and c are the same as those for Fig. 24b and c: Only the right half of *a* is changed in *b*, whereas both halves of *a* are changed in *c*. However, the right–left relations of homologous points of *a* are preserved in *c*. Now, all 10 subjects find *c* more similar to *a*. The two experiments compare as follows:

Experiment	Number of subjects choosing	
	b	c
Fig. 24	5	5
Fig. 28	0	10

If the left–right relation is symmetry, as in Fig. 28a, it is more sensitive to a measured amount of change than the nonsymmetric, left–right relations in Fig. 24a ($p < .01$).

There is one previously mentioned example, Experiment Fig. 29, in which the outcome is clear-cut. The "average amount of change" of the dots is the same in Fig. 29b and c, but b is significantly more similar to the standard than is c. The

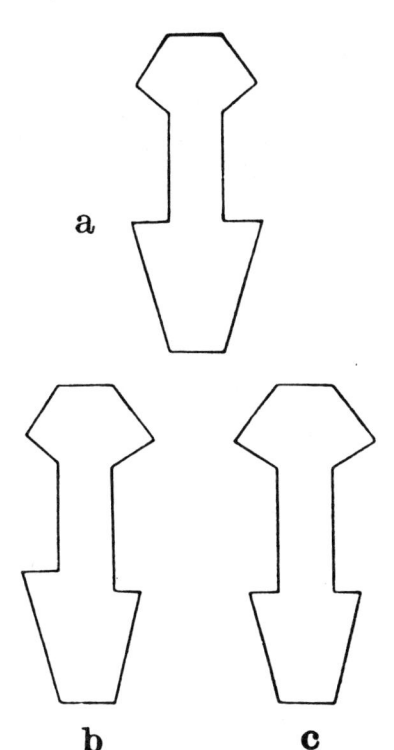

FIG. 28. This is a comparison experiment to figure 24. The changes applied to 28b and c are the same as those of 24b and c: only the right half of *a* is changed in *b*, while both halves of *a* are changed in *c*. However the right–left relations of homologous points of *a* are preserved in c. (From Goldmeier, 1972.)

2. SINGULARITY

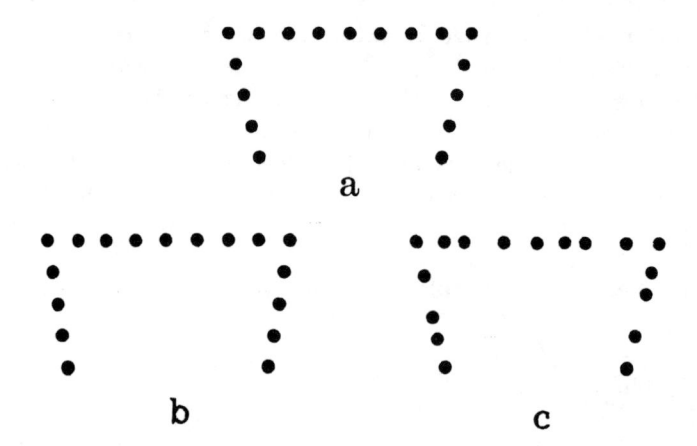

FIG. 29. The standard *a* is changed in *b* by increasing the two angles by 5°. The change in *c* consists of shifting the dots along the lines. The total dot shift in the original amounted to 26 mm in *b* and 28 mm. in *c*. (From Goldmeier, 1972.)

change in *b* is one of *form:* the two angles are increased by 5°. The change in *c* is one of the *material*, the texture of the dot distribution. This exempts the comparison from the rule of Monotonic Dependence, each change being in a different dimension. The total shift of dots in the original was about 26mm in *b* and 28mm in *c*. In this instance, the change in *material* prevailed over the 5° change in *form*. Does this mean that a 5° change of the two angles is phenomenally always "smaller" than a 28mm shift of the dots along the lines? Or does the saliency of both changes depend on the initial angle and initial dot distribution to which they are applied? Figure 30*a* has angles of 90° and an irregular dot distribution to start with. Figures 30*b* and *c* are varied exactly as Fig. 29*b* and *c*, a change by 5° in *b* and a shift of dot distribution within the lines in *c* equal to the dot shift in *b*. In this case, *c* is judged more similar by 18 of 20 subjects. The change of *form* is salient, the change of material (texture) is not. The two experiments compare as follows:

Experiment	Number of subjects choosing	
	b	*c*
Fig. 29	9	1
Fig. 30	2	18

The two results are significantly different ($p < .0005$).

We began by asking which parameters are psychologically realized. We end by discovering that the same parameter, say, the angle in Fig. 30 and 29, is psychologically realized if it takes one value (90°) but not at other values. We call such values *singular* and say the pattern has a singular feature. The next

8. SINGULARITY AS SENSITIVITY TO CHANGE

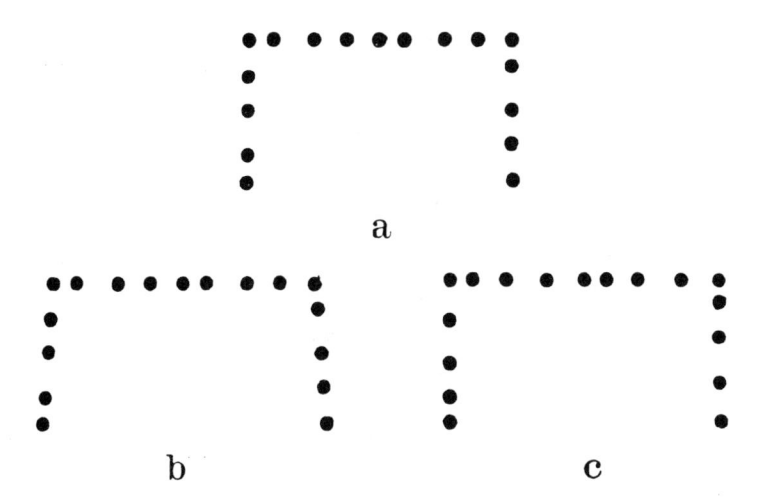

FIG. 30. The same dot shift as in figure 29 is applied to the standard 30a: In 30b the angles are increased by 5°, in 30c the dots are shifted along the lines by about the same amount. (From Goldmeier, 1972.)

sections elaborate the notion of singularity. Singularity emerges at the key to the understanding of trace structure and as the instrument of data reduction in feature space.

8. SINGULARITY AS SENSITIVITY TO CHANGE

The reversal of the similarity relationships in the experiments of the preceding section demonstrates that a one-parameter variation can evoke psychological change in more than one feature (e.g., "hight" and "skyline" in Fig. 21 and 25). But the paired experiments demonstrate another aspect of one-parameter variations. As the parameter moves through the full range of values, the psychological attribute varies only slightly in most regions of its range but very markedly in other, very narrow regions. The skyline in 21a is insensitive to variation, whereas in 25a it is very sensitive to even slight variation: The equal hight of the spikes is sensitive; the unequal hight is perceived as little changed over a wide range of stimulus variations. We call equality a *singular* value of the attribute spike-relations, whereas irregularity, which extends over a broad range of values, represents the *nonsingular* values.

In this terminology, zero is a singular value of divergence in Fig. 26a and c, whereas 15° in Fig. 26b, 60° in Fig. 22a and c, and 75° in Fig. 22b lie in the *nonsingular range*. Zero curvature in Fig. 27a and b is singular, nonzero curvature in Fig. 27c and Fig. 23 is nonsingular. The thickness is relatively nonsingu-

40   2. SINGULARITY

lar in all six of these patterns. Symmetry, in Fig. 28*a* and *c,* is a singular value of the left–right relations of homologous points. The relations in Fig. 28*b* and Fig. 24 are in the nonsingular range.

The phenomenon of singularity pervades all cognitive activities. It has been found in perception, categorization, trace formation, and trace transformation. Under the heading of Prägnanz, Wertheimer described singularities in number concepts (1912a) and in the organization of visual percepts (1923). Rosch identified singular color values as "focal" colors (1972) and singular objects as "basic" (Rosch, Mervis, Gray, Johnson, & Boyes-Braem, 1976a) and singular members of categories as "semantic prototypes" (Rosch, 1975b). Goldmeier

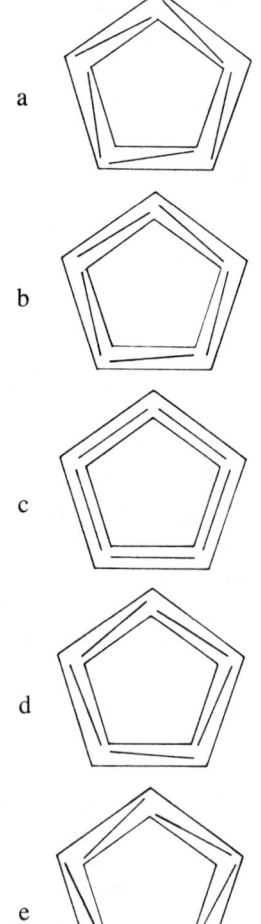

FIG. 31. Starting with pattern *a* the five "intermediate" lines are rotated by steps. The right lower and the bottom line are turned clockwise, the other three lines are rotated counterclockwise. (From Goldmeier, 1972.)

8. SINGULARITY AS SENSITIVITY TO CHANGE 41

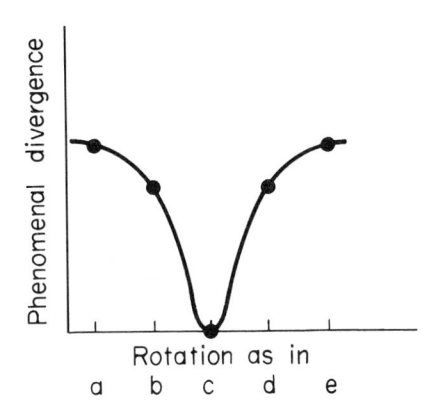

FIG. 32. Plot of phenomenal divergence of the "intermediate" lines versus the rotation of these lines in figure 31 *a* to *e*.

(1936 / 1972) and Rock (1973) found what amounts to singular *orientations* of patterns. The notion of singularity, under whatever label, is not widely accepted and is often not understood. The defining characteristic of singularity (or Prägnanz, as the German literature calls it) is *sensitivity to change*. The following two examples are paradigmatic of the singularity of visual patterns.

As the middle lines of Fig. 31 are rotated in small steps, as described in Section 5, the appearance of the pattern changes. If the degree of phenomenal change is suitably quantified and plotted against degree of rotation, the curve of Fig. 32 results. Small rotations in the region of *a, b,* and *d, e* of the curve, resulting in patterns like Fig. 31 *a, b, d,* and *e,* cause hardly any phenomenal change, whereas the same degree of rotation in the narrow region around *c* influences the appearance profoundly. Obviously, the rotation is most effective in the small range of values that correspond to a *parallel course* of the lines. This value of the parameter is singular, and the broad range of values away from *c* is nonsingular.

In many instances, it is next to impossible to define the singularity in geometric terms, although the existence of the singularity is no less evident. Figure 33*d* is an example. Figure 33*a* shows two groups of dots. The nine-dot group on the left moves to the right, moves through the other group, and appears on its right side in Fig. 33*g*. In Fig. 33*a, b, f,* and *g,* the two groups are perceived as separate. In *c* and *e,* they form one irregular group of dots. But the small shift from *c* to *d* or from *e* to *d* gives rise to the singular wavy line seen in *d*. The steps between *a* and *b, b* and *c, e* and *f,* and *f* and *g* are 4 times as large as the steps from *c* and *e* leading to *d*. The wavy line is perceived only in the very narrow range of lateral shifts around *d*. This *phenomenal linearity* of *d* is sensitive to even small shifts, whereas the phenomenal irregularity in Fig. 33*c* and *e* and the phenomenal separation in 33*a, b, f,* and *g* are very little affected by much larger displacements.

The difference in sensitivity to change must be reflected in the mental representation of the variants. Evidently, the trace of singular patterns, like Fig. 31*c*

42   2. SINGULARITY

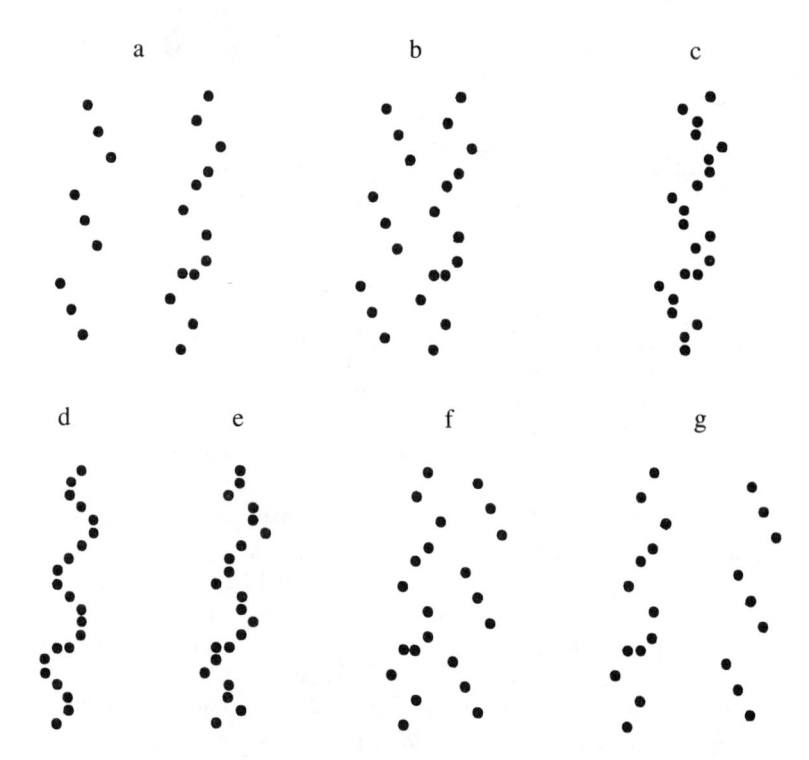

FIG. 33. The nine dot group on the left in 33a moves to the right by steps. The left group moves through the other group and in f and g has emerged on the right of the other group. The steps between a, b and c and between e, f and g are 4 times as large as the steps from c to d to e.

and 33d, *precisely* codes for parallel course and linear unity, respectively. The trace of the corresponding nonsingular patterns codes only *approximately* for divergence, irregularity, and separateness. One may picture the trace as having "click stops" for the singular values of each feature. If the divergence of the lines is zero as in Fig. 31c, it "clicks in" at zero; if the dots line up sufficiently as in Fig. 33d, the two dot groups "lock together" to form a line. If, on the other hand, the feature has a nonsingular value, then this value is represented only approximately, loosely or vaguely, and *the trace represents a larger range of values* of the parameter without precisely defined stops.

There are essentially three sources of singularity. The first is physiologic, "hardwired" in computer terms. "Focal colors" seem to fall in that category (Rosch, 1971). The reason why a certain shade of red is the *reddest* possible red seems to be related to the color sensitivity of the retinal pigments. The singular locus of the best red is independent of cultural upbringing, of color names, of age, and of practice effects (Rosch, 1972).

The second source of singularity is exemplified by *imprinting*. For a limited period of time right after a bird is hatched, the sight and sounds of its mother are indelibly "imprinted" on its memory. That is how a young bird recognizes its mother. To what extent something like imprinting occurs in mammals is not established. Imprinting is a very special kind of learning. Unlike ordinary learning, it is not open to erasure nor to later modification. Once imprinting has taken place, it appears to be permanent and indelible. Some ethnic and cultural preferences may well belong in this category.

The third source of singularity is acquisition by learning. This mechanism enables us to recognize people and things or to identify complicated patterns, say, faded inscriptions on stone or patterns of the Posner type (Sections 5, 13), to diagnose a tissue section as cancerous, or to recognize functional groupings on a chessboard (Chase & Simon, 1973).

Associationism, because of its empiricist leanings, has opted for an exclusive explanation of all singularity effects by learning. Obviously, this is correct for the examples of singularity by learning just given. The ability to recognize a cancer pattern under the microscope can only be acquired through experience. On the other hand, many of the figural singularities like equality, rectilinearity, and singularities depending on nearness, closure, or connectedness (Palmer 1977, 1978a; Wertheimer 1923) are either programmed at birth or arise at an early stage of maturation of the central nervous system. The same probably applies to the singularity of the horizontal and vertical extension in space (Rosch 1975a). The complex processing required for depth perception (Kopfermann, 1930; Metzger, 1975) is also largely preprogrammed (E. Gibson & R. Walk, 1960; Julesz, 1971). In the case of a circle and a square, Rosch (1973a) has shown that the goodness or typicality of these forms is invariant over cultures and therefore probably built into human form processing.

There seem to be many intermediate situations, like imprinting, the homing of some birds, the information on which migration of birds depends, and most importantly, human language. Language may well rest on a preprogrammed, gradually maturing language processing capability that develops under the stimulus of exposure to a particular language.

This sketchy survey shows that we know as yet very little about the genesis of the singularities in our world picture. This gap in our knowledge need not detain us, however. Once singularities are established, whether programmed or newly acquired, they form the matrix, the schema, the framework, the filing system within which new information is assimilated. By and large, feature values are assigned by their relation to the singular values of the features. The value is coded either as singular, d in Fig. 33, c in Fig. 32; nearly singular, at the steep slope near c in Fig. 32, or nonsingular, in the large, almost level region before b and after d. As discussed in Sections 13 and 19, this system combines coding accuracy in the narrow singular range with information reduction in the broad nonsingular range. With respect to coding economy, it matters little whether

2. SINGULARITY

singularities are inborn or acquired yesterday, whether they mature with age or are established by culture and tradition, or possibly are just idiosyncratic or ad hoc. Much fruitful research is under way in this area (see Rosch, 1975b, especially experiment 9). What matters for trace formation is that *features have a small range of high resolution, here called singularity, and a broad range of low resolution, here called the nonsingular range.*

The word *singularity* is my translation of the German word Prägnanz. The two words mean the same thing, except that I have elaborated this concept further, both here in Chapter 2 and in a previous publication (Goldmeier, 1972). The two words are however intended as synonyms. The following sections deal with several aspects of singularity as it affects trace formation and trace structure.

9. REGULARITY, UNIQUENESS, AND GOODNESS

Many of the examples of singularity discussed in the preceding section appear to be *more regular, better,* and *more unique,* "one of a kind," than their nonsingular counterparts. By contrast, the nonsingular patterns are *irregular, poor* patterns, and also are nondescript and resemble each other. The poor patterns, in other words, *lack* regularity, goodness, and uniqueness. The close correlations among regularity, goodness, and uniqueness had long been noted by gestalt theorists, but the three characteristics remained undefined and unconnected.

Garner set out to establish the correlation between goodness and uniqueness and developed a hypothesis to link the two characteristics with a special form of regularity. To test the hypothesis, Garner and his coworkers (Garner & Clement, 1963; Handel & Garner, 1966) used the set of dot patterns obtained by placing one dot into five of the nine cells of a 3×3 square matrix. Figure 34 shows examples of the 126 possible 5-dot patterns of this type. For this well-defined set of patterns, Garner and Clement developed one objective measure of regularity and two subjective measures, one for goodness and one for uniqueness.

According to Garner and Clement (1963), the patterns were objectively characterized by: "the number of equivalents for each of these patterns . . . using an arbitrary rule concerning equivalents [p. 447]." The rule involves reflections and 90° rotations. One simply counts for each pattern how many different patterns are produced by these two transformations. The number of the resulting patterns is the "size of the equivalence set." For example, Fig. 34*a* and *b* both are members of an equivalence set of size 1, because no matter how many 90° rotations or reflections are applied to the patterns, they remain unchanged. Patterns Fig. 34*c, d,* and *e* are each members of a set of 4, the patterns Fig. 34*f, g,* and *h* each belong to a set of 8. Altogether, there are 2 equivalence sets of size 1, 11 sets of size 4, and 10 sets of size 8. Garner and Clement used a subset of 90 of the 126 patterns.

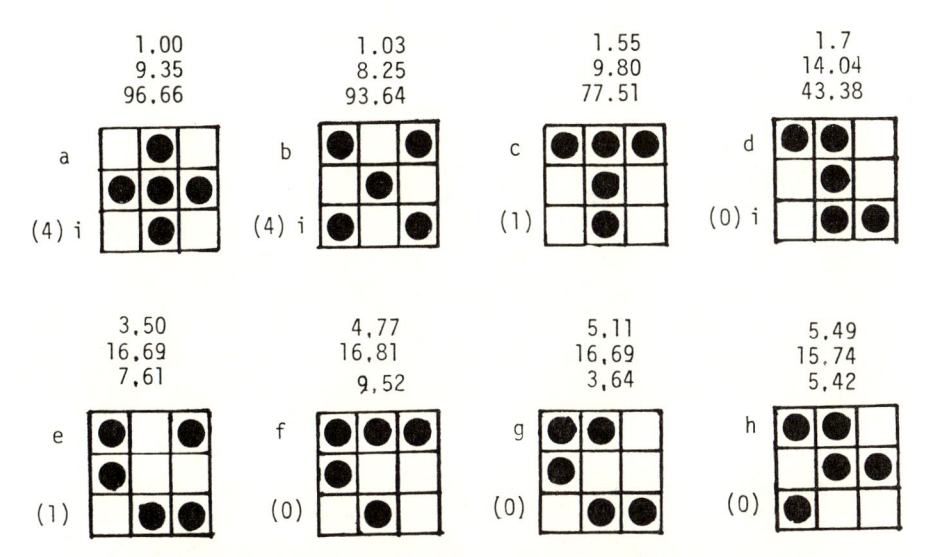

FIG. 34. Examples of Garners five-dot patterns. The top number over each pattern is the mean goodness rating on a scale of 1 = best to 7 = worst. The middle number is the size of the group of similar patterns (inversely related to uniqueness). Both numbers are from Garner and Clement, 1963. The last number is the "mean predictability score" from Bear (1973), a measure of self-consistency. All numbers are averages over the whole "equivalence set" of which the pattern is an example. The number in parenthesis at the left gives the number of symmetry axes and the letter i, where present, indicates that the pattern is invariant to inversion through the center.

Goodness was rated on a scale of 1 to 7. The top number in Fig. 34 is the goodness rating. The smaller the rating, the better the pattern.

Uniqueness, or its inverse, the size of the set of relatively similar patterns, is harder to measure. A panel of 20 subjects was asked to sort the patterns by similarity into about 8 groups. Actually, they used 7, 8 or 9 groups, except for one subject who used 10. The average size of the group of which each pattern was a member (the middle number in Fig. 34) is inversely related to uniqueness.

Garner and Clement found a correlation of .84 to .88 between goodness ratings and uniqueness score. They also found that membership in the different equivalence sets defined by rotations and reflections accounted for most of the variance of goodness ratings. For instance, membership in sets of size 1, 4, or 8 alone accounted for 73% of the total variance. There were other objective factors. For example, 20% of the variance depended on whether a pattern contained 0 or 1 or 2 straight lines. In short, Garner and Clement found strong correlations among: (1) regularity, defined by smallness of equivalence set; (2) uniqueness, defined by the smallness of the set of patterns judged similar; and (3) goodness,

46   2. SINGULARITY

measured by ratings. Garner was led to an explanation for this relationship by information-theoretical considerations. He proposed (Garner & Clement, 1963):

> that each pattern which a person sees is perceived not just as this one pattern, but as one of a set of alternative or equivalent patterns. In this case, we could speak of the relative size of the set of alternative patterns, and the greater the size of this psychologically inferred set of patterns, the greater would be the uncertainty of all patterns in that inferred set.... (Then) pattern goodness (and uniqueness) is inversely related to the size of such psychologically inferred sets [p. 446].

There is little doubt that the sorting task of Garner and Clement measures uniqueness, although the authors do not use that term. However, a good case can be made for considering what Garner calls the "inferred set of patterns" to be a consequence of each pattern's degree of *regularity*. Just as each pattern has its individual, intrinsic goodness, independent of membership in any set, the pattern also seems to have an intrinsic degree of regularity, regardless of the size of an "inferred set of equivalent patterns" perceived along with the actually presented pattern. These regularities in turn determine the size of the equivalence set. Figure 34*a* and the only other pattern with an equivalence set of size 1 (shown as Fig. 34*b*), for instance, are the only two patterns having four axes of symmetry *and* invariance under inversion through the center dot. This is indicated in Fig. 34*a* and *b* the notation (4)i. The 11 equivalence sets of size 4, for example, patterns Fig. 34*c, d,* and *e,* either have only one axis of symmetry, like Fig. 34*c* and *e, or* they are invariant under inversion through the center dot, like Fig. 34*d*. This is indicated by (1) or (0)i, respectively. Finally, the 80 patterns that are members of equivalence sets of size 8, like Fig. 34*f* and *g*, have no axis of symmetry, marked (0) in Fig. 34, and also lack the "i" for invariance under inversion. Regularity is thus defined *intrinsically* as highly regular, with *four* axes of symmetry *and* inversion invariance; regular, with *one* symmetry axis *or* invariance under inversion; and irregular, without either.

What Garner and Clement's experiment proves is, therefore, a close correlation among *intrinsic regularity, uniqueness,* and *goodness,* without the need to invoke a "set of inferred equivalent patterns."

That should not detract from the great value of Garner's notion of an inferred equivalent set. In some contexts, it is exceedingly illuminating and productive, particularly with verbal material. For example, the word "country" evokes a large set of nations of various geographic or population sizes, whereas the word "power" evokes a small set of nations of great political and military might, and "superpower" a still smaller, more unique set.

Whether regularity is measured by the size of the inferred set of equivalent patterns or by the number of intrinsic invariant attributes, Garner and his coworkers succeeded in quantifying regularity and to define uniqueness operationally by the average number of patterns sorted into the same bin. But their

9. REGULARITY, UNIQUENESS, AND GOODNESS 47

measures and definitions are tied to the special case of a restricted and discrete set of patterns. They cannot be applied to continuous "families" of patterns, say, the patterns of Fig. 22 and 26, or 21 and 25. In the continuous case, uniqueness attaches to the narrow range of values around the point of parallel course (Fig. 22 and 26) or equality (Fig. 21 and 25), whereas the nonparallel or unequal values encompass the wide range of nonunique members of the family. Instead of a bar graph of uniqueness where each bar represents the number of items in one bin, the result is the more or less sharply peaked graph of Fig. 32.

Garner used discrete and constrained sets of patterns, because in information theory information is quantified in discrete units (bits). Consequently, discrete, countable, finite sets of alternatives lend themselves best to the calculations of information theory. But as Shannon has already indicated (Shannon & Weaver, 1949): "To a considerable extent the continuous case can be obtained through a limiting process from the discrete case by dividing the continunm . . . into a large but finite number of small regions . . . As the size of the regions is decreased (the various parameters involved) approach as limits the proper values for the continuous case [p. 49]." In the psychological case, Shannon's "small regions" could be for instance the famous just-noticeable differences. They also could be the degree of "sensitivity to change" introduced in Section 8, the saliency in A. Tversky's theory of similarity (1977), or the "density" of Krumhansl's similarity theory (1978).

Here lies the connection between singularity, operationally defined by sensitivity to change of continuous parameters, and uniqueness, defined by the smallness of the set of similar patterns. In the limit of continuous families of patterns, regularity becomes "sensitivity to change." Just as sorting by similarity measures uniqueness in Garner's discrete case, so do similarity comparisons measure singularity in the continuous case investigated in Goldmeier (1936/1972).

There may be stimuli that are inherently singular or nonsingular. But, in general, singularity derives from a setting. In isolation, Fig. 35*a* is singular compared to *b*, but, in the setting of *c* and *d*, the singularity relation is reversed. Singularity does not exist in the abstract and the same is true of goodness, uniqueness, and regularity. We return to the question of the nature of singularity at the end of Section 12.

It has often been said that the notion of singularity, like goodness, is vague and, to quote Garner and Clement (1963), relies on: "*ad hoc* explanations about particular patterns, the type of explanation which has plagued classical Gestalt psychology for so many years [p. 451]." This criticism applies not only to singularity but to any general characterization of whole qualities. For instance, Garner's notion of "inferred set of equivalent patterns" depends on an ad hoc defined set of patterns with ad hoc defined transformations. However, there is agreement that key concepts need to be defined operationally. The following sections are devoted to an effort to make singularity a more precise concept.

48   2. SINGULARITY

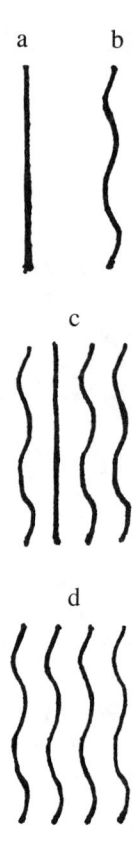

FIG. 35. In isolation the line of 35a is singular compared with 35b. In the setting of 35 c and d, the singularities are reversed.

10. SINGULARITY AS SELF-CONSISTENCY

Singularity attaches to particular values of a feature. The feature may be global, as the singular roundness of Fig. 19d, or it may only involve part of a pattern, as the singular "cadence" or "rhythm" of the ascending part of Fig. 71a. The singularity of the feature has consequences for the part or whole that is endowed with the attribute. One consequence is that its elements require or specify each other. For instance, in the pattern of Fig. 36a, each element conforms to the overall rule of the design, a rule that is intuitively clear even though it is difficult to formulate explicitly. Each element is perceived as *fitting* or *proper*. If one element deviates, as in Fig. 36b, the rule is violated. Because this is true of each individual element vis-a-vis all the other elements, we say the pattern has internal consistency or, borrowing a term used in atomic physics, has *self-consistency*.

Not all kinds of singularity involve self-consistency. For instance, an all-white object is not more self-consistent than an all off-white object, even though white is the more singular color. But self-consistency can be the most obvious

10. SINGULARITY AS SELF-CONSISTENCY 49

and striking evidence of singularity. Fig. 33*d* is a nondescript, irregular curve; yet, psychologically, it predetermines most of its points and constrains their location severely. This is true even though it would be hard to specify the overall rule of the dot sequence in a nontrivial way. (Trivially, a list of coordinates would do). There is much less consistency in the other patterns of Fig. 33, along with less singularity and less constraint.

Self-consistency, more so than singularity, is a matter of degree. Figures 25*a* and *c,* 26*a* and *c,* and 28*a* and *c* are more self-consistent than their nonsingular counterparts.

Self-consistency is *transposable.* Parallel course in Fig. 31*c* or 26*a* and *c* can be achieved whether Fig. 31 is a pentagon or a triangle, whether the angles in Fig. 26 are 120° or 105° or 85°. What matters for singularity and self-consistency in Fig. 26 is *the agreement or disagreement in the direction of figurally related parts* of the patterns. Self-consistency in Fig. 36*b* is achievable by suitably shortening all but the fourth line, lengthening the fourth line, or any combination of these.

In the examples discussed, self-consistency depends on a continuously variable parameter. Self-consistency can also vary within a discontinuous set. A well-researched example of the latter is Garner's set of all possible arrangements of five dots in the nine cells of a 3 × 3 matrix discussed in Section 9. There, it was shown that these patterns range from good, unique, and in a certain way regular, to poor, nondescript, and irregular. If these attributes are expressions of singularity, then the dot pattern should form a "strong" unit in the best configurations and a "weak" unit in the worst ones. In this terminology, "strong" means essentially the same as self-consistent, and "weak" refers to an aggregate that is irregular, randomly assembled, having nonsingular values of its attributes.

Bear (1973) came to equivalent conclusions: *"Each element of a good figure should be strongly suggested or implied by the other elements of the figure, but this close relationship should not obtain among the elements of a poor figure* [p. 32].''

Bear tested this assumption by removing one dot at a time from each of Garner's patterns and presented the resulting 4-dot patterns to his subjects, with the instruction to add one dot in that empty cell which "is implied or suggested by the dots already in" the matrix. Bear found his subjects nearly unanimous in selecting a fifth dot when it resulted in a "good" pattern. For example, as each one of the dots in Fig. 34*a* was omitted, it was restored spontaneously by 98, 93, 97, 97, and 98% of his subjects. (Reading left to right, top to bottom). In the case of the "worst" patterns, some of the dots were never spontaneously chosen as being "suggested" by the remaining four dots. For example, as each of the dots of Fig. 34*g* were omitted in turn, only 10, 10, 0, 2, and 5% of the subjects replaced it to the original position (again, reading from left to right, top to bottom). The average of the five scores results in a "mean predictability score" of the whole pattern.

2. SINGULARITY

The "mean predictability score", taken from Bear (1973), is given in Fig. 34 as the bottom number for each pattern. In effect, it measures the self-consistency of the pattern. The completions tended to make the resulting 5-dot patterns as "good" as the four given dots would allow. Bear found a correlation of about .89 between the rated goodness of a pattern and the mean frequency of choosing its dots. Patterns that rate high for goodness and that are found to be more "unique" by means of similarity grouping are also patterns in which any four dots limit the choice of a "suggested" fifth dot most severely. The narrow limits of acceptable completions in the good and unique patterns connote a high degree of self-consistency. Thus, Bear's findings imply that singular features of the dot patterns result in a high degree of self-consistency. In short, a good and unique pattern is self-consistent and vice versa.

The opposite of self-consistency is random juxtaposition of items, like the pairing of two otherwise unrelated objects in paired associate lists. A visual analog can be found in Mandler and Parker's (1976) paper. They compared pictures of objects in a random arrangement with the same objects arranged in a coherent scene. On a more abstract level, Chase and Simon (1973) compared meaningful Chess positions with randomly arranged chess positions. In both cases, memory for the location of the objects was better in the meaningful arrangement. In both cases, the random version lacks self-consistency; the coherent arrangement is more self-consistent.

Self-consistency may extend to only a part of a pattern. If in pattern Fig. 34d the center dot is missing, then this dot is selected by 91% of Bear's subjects, whereas the other dots suggested themselves to only 38% (middle) and 25% (corners) of the subjects. Presumably, the three midline dots unite into a strong subpart, whereas the corner points are not as strongly determined by the remaining dots. In pattern a of Fig. 71, the three arcs form a self-consistent subunit, whereas the straight line appears to be an arbitrary, inconsistent "appendage." This pattern has been used in memory experiments (Section 42) that support this assessment, but no independent evidence is at hand.

11. SINGULARITY AS NORM

Although singularity does not always lead to internal consistency, singular values of a feature always are *normative;* First some illustrative examples.

It is difficult to specify what is singular, or "good," about the curve formed by the upper ends of the lines of Fig. 36a. Nevertheless, it is easy to specify what is defective, or "wrong," about Fig. 36b: The fourth line is *too short*. Pattern a is *normal;* pattern b deviates from that norm.

Similarly, in the dotted curve of Fig. 37, one dot is *in the wrong place*.

Finally, the color of an egg is *off-white,* but a white object is not perceived or

11. SINGULARITY AS NORM   51

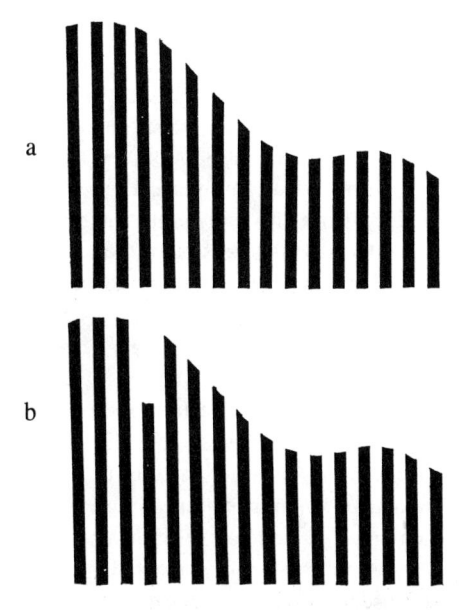

FIG. 36. Design 36a is "good," compared to the "flawed," defective design 36b.

coded or remembered as "off-eggshell." The color white is the norm, as well as singular.

Some forms, colors, or structures are perceived as singularly *right*. In the case of straightness (upper edge of Fig. 25a or c) or parallel course (Fig. 26a and c, Fig. 31c) the singularity is easy to define geometrically. In the case of Fig. 36a, 37, or the color white, a definition on geometrical or physical grounds is elusive. Yet, phenomenally, the singularity is salient and unmistakable. In all these examples, we perceive something as *deviant from a norm,* as flawed, derivative, imperfect, almost but not quite as it *should* be. Preferred values were characterized by Wertheimer (1912) as singular (ausgezeichnet) or (1923) as prägnant; Woodworth (1938) referred to the coding of nearly singular attributes as

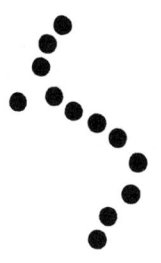

FIG. 37. Curve with an imperfection.

schema-plus-correction; Rosch (1975a) speaks of the singular values as reference points.

Normality judgments are an everyday occurrence in human perception. A person "speaks with an accent" (i.e., the speech deviates from a norm). A fruit, or a face, has a "blemish" (i.e., deviates from an ideal). A work of art "lacks perfection," and so on. Norm, ideal, and perfection all point to a singularity. If an object deviates slightly from this norm, its internal representation, so we argue, *contains implicitly* the singular version of the object and, superimposed, a particular modification. For example, Fig. 36*b* is perceived "essentially" as *36*a, *but as* a *with too short a fourth line*. This trace structure occurs even in an observer *who has never experienced 36*a. However, in other instances of near singularity, prior experience with the unmodified object is required, as in the case of a foreign accent. The role and the limitations of prior experience as an explanatory principle is discussed in Section 51. Here, neither the origin of the singularity nor its definition are at issue, as long as its function as a reference point in the trace of a *nearly* singular pattern is agreed upon.

It would be convenient if a general formula existed for constructing singularities. But, as discussed in Section 12, this goal is far off, possibly unattainable. However, in the absence of a general solution, it is possible to identify singularities empirically and then to show by experiment that singularities are indeed normative. Here are some experiments of this kind.

Rosch, in a series of studies (1971, 1972, 1973a, b), found that in the color continuum, some colors are *representative* of the color name and also are "focal" in the sense that they are better remembered than nonfocal colors. Rosch found this true even for young children and primitive people. In other experiments, Rosch (1971) established that focal colors, singular directions (horizontal and vertical), as well as round numbers serve as "cognitive reference points." There is an asymmetry between singular and almost singular values of a feature. Rosch found that an 80 or a 100° slanted line is phenomenally "closer" to a vertical than a vertical to the slanted line, a nearly focal color is closer to the related focal color than the reverse, and 9 or 11 is "nearer" to 10 than the number 10 is to 9 or 11.

How far the realm of the *almost singular* extends varies from case to case. Surely, 999 or 1002 is "almost" or "essentially" 1000, whereas 110 or 1851 are not. Singular values are in the middle or at the edge of a comparatively narrow range of *almost* or *essentially* singular values, followed by a broad range of nonsingular values. The relationship is illustrated in Fig. 38. Mathematically, singularity approximates a Dirac δ function.

This important question is discussed in detail in Section 23.

In another experiment, Rosch (1973a) compared each of three *good* forms, a square, a circle, and an equilateral triangle, with six more or less severe modifications of each of these three prototypes. Figure 39 shows one of them, the square, with its six variants. Rosch then constructed derivative series by using

11. SINGULARITY AS NORM   53

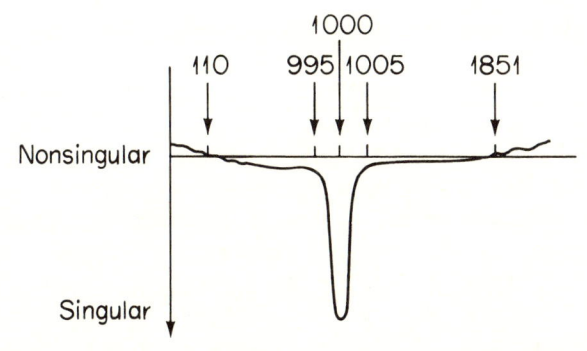

FIG. 38. Singularity, near-singularity, and nonsingular range around the singular number 1000.

each of the six modifications as prototype and applying the same modifications to them also. For example, when the square with gap was used as the prototype, the same modifications as shown in the illustration were performed on the square with the gap, except in case of the original square, which had no gap, so that it, too, was a modification of the square with gap. In other words, the series included the first two patterns of Fig. 39 plus the other five patterns with the gap added, so that all but the square itself had a gap. The derivative series were thus twice modified variants of the good figures and once modified variants of one of the original variants shown in Fig. 39.

The subjects were members of a stone-age people, the Dani of New Guinea, without previous experience with geometric forms or line drawings.

Rosch's experiment called for pairing the members of each set with a word label, one label for each set. There were seven groups of subjects for the seven kinds of prototypes and modifications.

Rosch found that for all those patterns, the set with single modifications was associated with the correct word label after fewer errors than were the doubly modified sets. Quoting only significant ($p < .05$) results, Rosch also found that the unmodified square and circle were learned with fewer errors than any of the modifications, even if the unmodified patterns were learned as members of once or twice modified sets. That means the unmodified square and circle were associated with the set label after fewer errors, even if the label belonged to a set otherwise containing only singly or doubly modified members. Also, the unmodified square and circle were chosen as "most typical" examples of the set label even by subjects who had encountered the unmodified patterns only in the con-

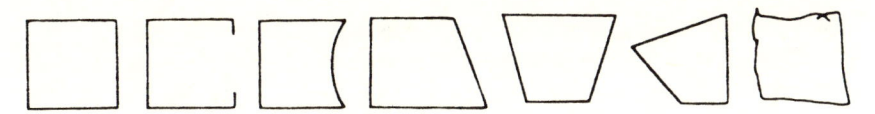

FIG. 39. The square and its six variants used by Rosch (1973a).

text of sets with double modifications. The experiment suggests that even with a doubly modified square or circle as the standard, these subjects perceive the unmodified square or circle as most representative of the label for the standard.

There is a limit to the degree of distortion that is still referred to the original starting pattern. This limit is quite apparent with the dotted triangle of Fig. 42. As Peterson et al. showed (see Section 13), slight distortions are seen as "imperfections" of the original triangle, but when the global attribute "triangularity" is lost, it is not recoverable no matter how much training is provided on the higher level of distortion.

In Rosch's experiment with the square, circle, and triangle, the triangle was the least singular pattern. Equilateral, isoceles, and scalene triangles were learned with about equal ease by these aboriginal subjects. Only two of the modifications, the variant with one line replaced by a curve and the triangle drawn in freehand, were learned with more errors. Apparently, any three-sided figure with straight lines represents triangularity equally well and is coded in nearly equivalent traces by these subjects. Only the line-to-curve and the freehand versions are coded as triangle-with-modification. These two versions also were ranked lowest on typicality for their set.

Another pertinent observation is due to Bear (1974). He used the accumulated findings of Garner and his associates (Garner 1974), especially Handel and Garner (1966) and Bear (1973), on the 5-dot patterns mentioned in Sections 9 and 10. These patterns had been ranked for goodness (singularity), encodability, number of "implicit alternatives" (inversely related to regularity), and number of associations between each other (inversely related to uniqueness). Bear (1973) determined for each dot how "predictable" it is from the other four dots in the pattern and from that calculated the "mean predictability" score for the whole pattern, what we call self-consistency. There are high correlations among goodness, encodability, regularity, uniqueness, and self-consistency of the patterns. Handel and Garner asked their subjects to draw for each presented 5-dot pattern another one "suggested by it." Rotations and reflections were frequently produced in response to this request. However, Bear (1974) found that a considerable number of Handel and Garner's responses were not rotations or reflections but modifications of the stimulus that differ from the original stimulus by the position of *just one single dot*. In most of the latter instances, the shift of one dot changed the stimulus from a less "preferred" to a more "preferred" position (i.e., toward a more self-consistent pattern). Bear argues that the chosen pattern is perceived and coded as the norm or "schema," whereas the stimulus pattern is perceived as a variant of this norm, in which a single dot is in a less preferred or "wrong" position. For example, the frequent choice of Fig. 40*a* as "associate" for 40*b* or *c* suggests that 40*b* and *c* tend to be perceived and coded as "40*a*-with-one-dot-displaced." Not only was the shifted dot in a more preferred position, but the associated pattern as a whole was "better," judging by: (1) goodness rating; (2) *greater average preference of all five dots in the context of the*

11. SINGULARITY AS NORM

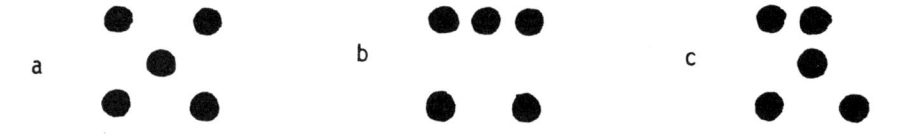

FIG. 40. Design *a* is frequently chosen as "associate" for *b* or *c*. (Bear, 1974.)

new pattern (i.e., self-consistency); (3) regularity (singularity) as measured by having fewer "implicit alternatives" (i.e., more 90 or 180° rotations or reflections that leave the pattern unchanged); and (4) *greater ease of encoding*.

There were a few cases of change in the opposite direction. The countertrend was apparently a ceiling effect, due to constraints inherent in Handel and Garner's procedure. The subjects were not permitted to add or subtract a dot. In many patterns, these seem to be the most natural "suggestions." Figure 41*a*, for example, might suggest 41*b* or *c* rather than any pattern with exactly five dots. Because the square in Fig. 41 is a stable subpattern, it really "has no use for" a fifth dot. If a change of Fig. 41*a* is forced, the square tends to remain intact so that the fifth dot must move instead. However, the fifth dot is already in the best available position relative to the square. Given the square and asked to add one more dot, about 80% of the subjects put the fifth dot where it is in Fig. 41*a*, whereas only 8% put it in either of the two open corners and 2% in each of the remaining cells (see Fig. 41*d*). Because of the limited choice of "associates" allowed in Handel and Garner's procedure, Fig. 41*a*, which ranks sixth in self-consistency, ends up being "associated" with Fig. 41*e*, which ranks only twelfth in a set of 23.

Bear (1974) concludes that: "the trend toward a stronger competitor in which the noncommon dot is more predictable from the remaining elements is also a trend toward a pattern whose other elements are more predictable, one from the others, and a trend toward a pattern which has fewer implicit alternatives and is more easily encoded [p. 364]." In other words, the trend is to *normalize* the "poor placement" of one dot.

The normative aspect of singularities is reflected in the language. There is a word for zero curvature, *straight,* but not for other specific degrees of curvature. There is transparent and opaque, but nothing precise in between. Something is either correct or incorrect to various degrees. Friendly and hostile describe two ends of a continuum, with a word for the midpoint, indifferent. Not every scale has singular points or words for specific values. Warm and cold are relative terms, but there is the freezing and the boiling *point* and *absolute zero*. There is *level ground* and then various degrees of incline. There are saints and sinners.

Rosch (1975a) has called attention to the use of "linguistic hedges" (Lakoff, 1972) to indicate a feature value that is near but *not quite at* a singular value. For instance, 85° is *almost,* or *essentially,* or *practically* vertical, and 998 is *essentially* 1000. The normative character of singular values is revealed by the asym-

56   2. SINGULARITY

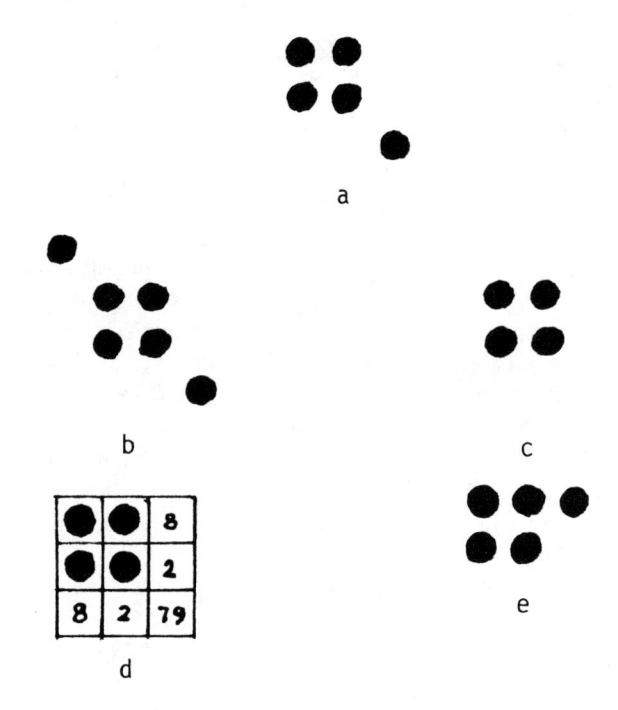

FIG. 41. Possible improvements of figure *a* if addition or removal of one dot were permitted: figures *b* and *c*. The numbers in 41*d* give the percentage of choices when subjects were asked to add one dot to the four dots given. Figure 41*e* tended to be "associated" with 41*a*. (Bear, 1974.)

metry of these statements (Wertheimer, 1912). A level road is not thought of as "lacking incline," a vertical is not "nearly 85°," and 1000 is not "essentially" 988. Tversky (1977) has shown the same kind of asymmetry between members of the same category. For example, North Korea tends to be perceived as more similar to China than China to North Korea. This asymmetry is part of a very pervasive aspect of cognition, namely, to choose a normative, sometimes egocentric system of reference: It is the *dog* that wags the tail and the *sun* that rises and sets as it *circles* the earth (see Metzger, 1975, Chapter XVIII, on reference systems).

The fact that the "good" patterns, the basic square and basic circle, are easier to learn and are rated most typical of a set of modifications supports the contention that: (1) these patterns are coded in a simpler, more direct way than the modifications; and (2) that the modifications are coded *with reference to* the basic pattern, specifically, as a perturbed form of the singular pattern. The fact that sets with single modifications are learned better than sets containing modified modifications suggests that second-order perturbations are coded as the singular pattern with (two dimensions of) corrections, and that additional corrections, although increasing the phenomenal distance from the singular pattern, may still contain the basic pattern as norm, as reference point (Rosch, 1973a). Coding is vastly simplified by coding with reference to some norms, especially if the norms are appropriate. Understanding of the cognitive processes of individuals, peoples, cultures, professional or social groups often involves discovering the norms they apply to the coding of their world.

12. THE GENERAL NATURE OF SINGULARITY

Even friendly critics of gestalt theory complain about the lack of a *general statement concerning the nature of singularity*. The examples given in the preceding sections make it quite obvious what is meant by singularity. But without support from a general theory, such examples could be merely troublesome exceptions, somehow explainable within the framework of established theories like associationism. This problem has been discussed in Wertheimer's early papers (1912, 1920, 1923), as well as in Koffka's (1935) and Köhler's (1940, 1947) more theoretical treatises, and again by Kanizsa (1979), without, it seems, changing many minds. Rather than to summarize, update, and modify their statements to suit the present purpose I give my own answer and do so on two levels.

In the most general sense, singularities *maximize the efficiency of coding* or *minimize the complexities* of cognitive objects. For instance, the triangle in Fig. 42 is best coded as made up of three connected straight lines, which in turn are composed of four equally spaced dots. An inefficient code, by comparison, would be the list of 18 numbers that represent the distances of each dot from, say, the upper and the right edge of the paper. In the case of the random dot pattern of the same figure, no singularity and therefore no coding as efficient as that of the triangle is available. Singularities, in most animal brains, take advantage of the fact that what matters in our world is often as regular as the triangle and not as chaotic as the random dot pattern. For instance, if we see something moving away on a straight line, we need not expect the object to come at us from behind. As a consequence, evolution has equipped these brains with the ability to take advantage of what orderliness there is in the world. Rosch and Mervis (1975, p. 602) and Rosch (1977, 1978) have shown that coding efficiency underlies category formation as well, and Kuhn (1970) comes to similar conclusions in the realm of scientific theorizing. But, as Kuhn also has discovered, coding efficiency or "parsimony" is not the whole answer and not always the answer. In a comparison of Einsteinian and Newtonian mechanics, Kuhn (1957) says:

> Because they provide an economical summary of a vast quantity of information, Newtonian concepts are still in use. But increasingly they are employed for their economy alone, just as the ancient two-sphere universe is employed by the modern navigator and surveyor. They are still a useful aid to memory, but they are ceasing to provide a trustworthy guide to the unknown [p. 265].

58   2. SINGULARITY

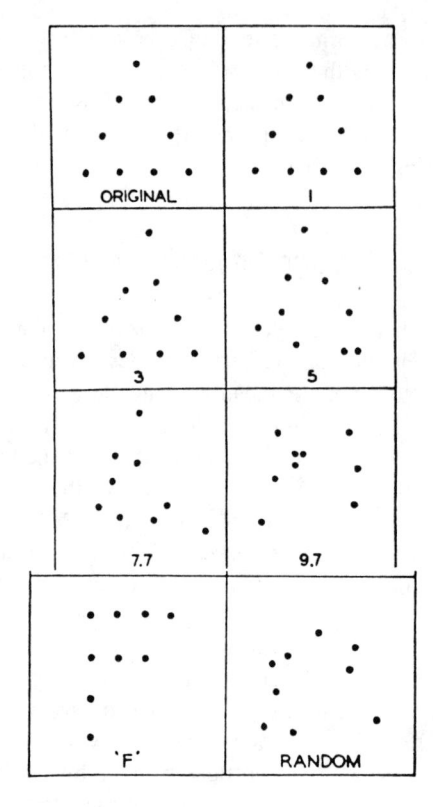

FIG. 42. Patterns from Posner, Goldsmith, and Welton (1967). The numbers 1, 3 etc., indicate degrees of distortion of the "original" triangle.

Kuhn makes the important distinction between a shortcut and a theory, between encoding strategies or mnemonics, which are matters of choice, and singularities, which are appropriate to the intrinsic structure of the object or play the role of cognitive reference points, to use Rosch's phrase. Mnemonics and strategies are *optional* mechanisms. Singularities, be they inborn or acquired, are firmly established, mandatory, "correct" processing frameworks.

Given two codes, it is in general possible to determine which code is more efficient. But, in general, there is no algorithm to construct a code that *maximizes* coding efficiency for a particular domain of objects. Therefore, the characterization of singularities by their coding efficiency does not provide an operational definition of singularity.

Singularities can be identified, however, empirically, by experiment, as has been described in Sections 8 to 11. On an empirical level, singularities are characterized by their sensitivity to change, the regularity, goodness, uniqueness, and self-consistency they impart, and by their normativeness. The most fundamental characteristic of a singular attribute is, however, sensitivity to change. Comparing the triangle and the 7.7 level distortion of the triangle, Fig. 42, there are many changes that would impair the singular attributes of the

12. THE GENERAL NATURE OF SINGULARITY

triangle, whereas the same changes applied to corresponding dots of the nonsingular pattern would change that pattern phenomenally very little or not at all. Because *sensitivity to change* has been used extensively in Sections 8 to 11, it needs no further illustration here. This definition of singularity differs from a general definition in two ways. Singularities have to be discovered, case by case, and they have to be verified by means of experiments like those reported in the preceding sections. This is how Rosch found singular color values, how Metelli (1974 a and b) found self-consistencies that underlie phenomenal transparency, and how Kanizsa (1979) investigated subjective countours. This is also how singularities in verbal and conceptual material have been and will have to be investigated.

Many facts of singularity have long been known. In competing theories, they have been interpreted empiristically, an answer that we can accept only to a degree. Experience does not account for singular color values, or the star map of migratory birds if that turns out to be inborn, or the singularity of circles and squares (Rosch, 1973a, b), or pattern Fig. 34*a*, although it does account for many instances of singularities in concept learning, where it appears as typicality. We can learn the concept of dog only from seeing dogs. But even in their own domain, empiristic explanations encounter fundamental difficulties. The prototype of a concept (see Section 16) is neither an average exemplar nor the most frequent or most familiar. The prototype of a printed A is possibly the block letter A, but the vast majority of typefonts do not use block letters, and we recognize readily the most deviant examples. If one looks for the prototypical teenager, one thinks of many complexions before thinking of acne, even though acne is familiar, frequent, and an "average" trait of that group. Although acne is frequent and familiar, it is not perceived as *normal*. A *clear* skin is singular and most "sensitive to change" toward blemishes. Nor do we deny class membership on the basis of unfamiliarity, as to pygmies, or infrequency, as to chihuahuas. The attributes of real world objects are given by experience alone, yet familiarity, frequency, and averages, or combinations of these do not, in general, produce singular values of traits. A typical American is not necessarily an average American. We understand the statement: True (i.e., prototypical) teachers, like perfect diamonds, are hard to find (i.e., are infrequent, not average). Although there is no formula to define singularity, beware of the empiristic trap of confusing it with familiarity, frequency of occurrence, or statistical mediocrity (see also Section 51).

Ideally, singularity should be defined by some structural characteristic of the stimulus, say, "a continuous line is singular, but a gap in the line destroys the singularity." Several sections in this book, especially Sections 35 to 37, are devoted to show that this statement is false; that a gap can be singular or nonsingular depending on the role of the gap in the design as a whole. Singularity cannot, or not yet, be defined in terms of stimulus structure. It can only be defined operationally and measured experimentally by its *sensitivity to change, self-*

60   2. SINGULARITY

consistency, "aptness," and the like, as discussed in the preceding sections (see also Kanizsa (1979), on the subject of Prägnanz).

Because singularity is a key concept of gestalt thinking, the lack of a structural definition appears to many a sign of vagueness, another reason to remain in the associationistic fold. Still, the same flaw occurs in sciences much more mature than psychology. In physics, for instance, we have a definitive theory of superconductivity. In spite of that, we still have to search more or less empirically for alloys and compounds with a high critical temperature. The theory does not tell which material has the highest critical temperature possible.

13.   ENCODING OF NONSINGULAR FEATURES

The basic data on the encoding of nonsingular patterns are Experiment III of Posner et al. (1967), Experiment II, Table 3, and Experiment III of Posner and Keele (1968), and Experiment I of Peterson et al. (1973). All these experiments use patterns of nine dots, like the three examples in Fig. 42 taken from Posner et al (1967), and distortions of these originals, like the distortions of the triangle shown in that figure. The distortions were produced by applying a statistical rule independently to each of the nine dots. The rule assigns a random direction to the shift and determines the amount of shift randomly, but with the proviso that the average amount of shift reaches a predetermined level, measured either in "bits per dot" or in "average distance per dot" (Peterson et al., 1973; Posner et al., 1967).

The method of a typical experiment is as follows: Each group of subjects is trained on three different distortions of two or more originals. The distortions are all of the same extent on the average: 1 bit per dot for one group, higher levels, say, 5 or 7.7 bits per dot, for others. Each group of subjects is trained until they reliably discriminate between the distortions derived from the various originals. The lower-level distortion groups of course reach the criterion with fewer errors than the groups trained on more severe distortions. All groups then are tested on a battery of patterns that typically includes: the undistorted originals (not previously shown), the three training distortions of each original, three new distortions of each original at the same level of distortion as the training distortions, and three distortions of each original at one or two different levels of distortion. The most dramatic finding by Posner and Keele (1968) was that: "Ss show no significant differences in proportion of errors between the patterns which they had just finished learning and the prototypes which they had never seen [p. 360]." The authors were mainly interested in this aspect of their work, because they felt that it made *abstraction* and *concept formation in general* accessible to experimental investigation. In the present context, their findings are of interest for a different reason. These experiments employed both *regular* (*singular*) and *irregular (nonsingular) patterns*. In Experiment I of Peterson et al., the two regular patterns were a triangle and an "F" (Fig. 42), and the two nonsingular patterns were like the "random" design of Fig. 42. The two types of designs give markedly different results, in Posner and Keele's Experiment II as well as in Experiment I of Peterson et al. The latter experiment is more elaborate and detailed and serves as basis for the following analysis. Three groups were trained, group 1 on level-1 distortions, group 5 on level 5, and a group 7 on level 7.7. Each group was trained on three distortions of all four prototypes just mentioned.

In spite of the statistically equal degree of distortion of all training patterns, the two singular and the two nonsingular patterns differed markedly in this experiment:

1. The subjects trained on level-1 distortions, when tested on (a) the (new) prototypes, (b) the (old) level-1 training patterns, and (c) the (new) level-1 distortions, classified the *regular* patterns with significantly fewer errors (.04 to .09) than the corresponding variants of the two *irregular* ("random") prototypes (.34 to .48 errors of classification).

These results support the notion of *normative effects* of singular values (Section 11). If distortions are slight, if the distortions leave the grouping and the function of individual dots undisturbed, the pattern is perceived and classified as a "prototype-with-modification," to paraphrase Woodworth (1938) and Bear (1974), or "*essentially* the prototype," to paraphrase Rosch (1975a). Therefore, *low-level distortions* interfere little with classification of singular or nearly singular patterns.

Irregular patterns, on the other hand, like the random pattern or the severely distorted (level 7.7 and 9.7) variants of the triangle (Fig. 42), are lacking in "cognitive reference points" (Rosch, 1975a) or *anchoring values* of features. As a consequence, the patterns are not perceived as variants of one prototype and are open to many different ways of grouping, none of which are very compelling. Nonsingular patterns are nondescript, lack salient features, and hence are more confusable. In fact, "lack of salient features" itself becomes an attribute, although an attribute that is not unique, not sensitive to change, the opposite of the sensitivity to change and the uniqueness that operationally defines singular features.

It appears therefore that the distorted triangle and the "F" were perceived, coded, and later recognized as instances of "*essentially*" the prototypes, *with slight imperfections*. The two irregular training patterns were learned as three patterns with somewhat similar but less salient, more vaguely defined, nondescript features. In the case of regular patterns, the normative effect of singularity makes the prototype and the level-1 variants *equivalent,* if not equal. The irregular patterns are not seen as variations of a prototype. They only share a vague resemblance. Hence, they are presumably (their similarity was not measured) more confusable and become less distinguishable when they are presented together with many other irregular test patterns.

This interpretation is supported by another finding. At the end of the classification tests, the subjects were asked to draw "the patterns they thought were associated with the four (answer) keys." The 16 subjects of group 1 drew 15½ "reasonable facsimilies" of the regular patterns but only 10½ reasonable renditions of the irregular patterns, a significant difference. In other words, the subjects did form a usable internal representation of the regular prototypes but were distinctly less able to reproduce whatever they had coded and abstracted from the irregular patterns.

2. Whereas group-1 subjects did well on the slightly distorted variants of the two regular patterns, namely the prototypes, level-1 training patterns and new level-1 distortions, they did poorly on the most severe distortions, at level 7.7 of the regular patterns (triangle and "F"). At level 7.7, they made 2.40 errors of classification compared with only 1.58 errors with the equally distorted irregular patterns. This difference was also reliable ($p < .01$).

Posner and Keele argued that training on low-level distortions does not train the subject in the degree of variability encountered in the test patterns. But their argument applies equally to the regular and irregular patterns and so does not explain the difference between the two types of material.

The explanation lies in the differential sensitivity to random change. Singular features are very sensitive to random, that is, arbitrary or "structure-blind" change of its elements, whereas nonsingular attributes are phenomenally little affected by an equivalent or even geometrically larger shift of individual elements. A large "average shift" applied to the triangle and the "F" disturbs many singular features. It abolishes, for instance, the rectilinearity within the array, the equidistance of the dots along the subparts, and, if large enough, the grouping, and the functions of individual dots in the whole of the singular patterns. Such features hardly exist in the irregular patterns. Judging from the actual distortions shown in Fig. 42, the figural regularities of the triangle are poorly preserved in the level-5 example and lost completely in the 7.7 and higher distortions. Also, the level 5, 7.7, 9.7 distortions of the triangle and the random pattern differ very little from each other. In fact, they appear more similar to each other than to the triangle from which three of them are derived. The same similarity relations prevail between the patterns of Fig. 15. The irregular patterns are more similar to each other than they are to the singular pattern a, contrary to the statistics of dot shift.

In conclusion, unlike regular patterns, the irregular patterns are encoded as chance arrangements of dots. They are hardly affected by shifting the dots in arbitrary ways. They lack features sensitive to structure-blind variations because they lack singular structure.

These findings call attention to a rarely considered aspect of animal perception. In a world of rigid objects, or at most continuously deformable objects, it is biologically adaptive to perceive and remember the spatial and temporal invariants of objects and to be able to "disregard minor perturbations, like "level-1" distortions, *as long as they preserve the grouping and the singular features*. An ability to recognize patterns after disruptions due to *independent* displacements of their elements is useless and wasteful of information-processing capacity, in a world in which the elements of an object in general are *not* independent and do *not* pursue independent trajectories.

3. Peterson et al. found a reliable decrease in accuracy on all test patterns from group 1 to group 5 to group 7.7, for both regular and irregular test patterns. Training group 5 classified the originals, the training patterns, and the level-1 distortions somewhat better than the level-7.7 distortions. Group 7.7, however, made more errors even on the old training patterns (1.06) than group 1 and made reliably more and essentially equal errors on *all* new test patterns (from 1.64 for level-1 test distortions and 1.73 for the originals to 2.07 for level-7.7 distortions). Peterson et al. concluded that whatever group 7.7 learned from the level-7.7 training distortions apparently was *not transferable* to any of the test patterns.

The superiority of the regular patterns, so marked in group 1, also disappeared in the group-5 and -7.7 distortions. This result shows that the grouping and singular features of the two regular patterns, well-preserved in the level-1 distortions, was not present and therefore not perceived, encoded, or "abstracted" from the level-5 and especially level-7.7 training distortions.

Rosch (1975a) reported the same lack of distinctive anchoring in her control experiments, far away from the relevant "cognitive reference points." For example, a line tilted up 100° from the horizontal was perceived as referred to a vertical rather than the vertical to the 100° line. But no such asymmetry was observed in Rosch's two experiments with lines slanted 67.5 and 57.5°. The same distortion, 10° in Rosch's case, which makes a *singular* feature (vertical) into a *nearly singular* one (nearly vertical), leaves a nonsingular tilt little affected.

Whereas the coding of singular attributes is precise, the coding of nonsingular features is only approximate and contains a great deal of indeterminacy. Objects that differ within a nonsingular range of values look "all alike"; "if you have seen one you have seen them all." For this reason, Fig. 15*b* and *c* are more alike than either is to 15*a*. The coding of nonsingular features is approximate; the value of a nonsingular feature is coded only within a relatively broad range.

14. THE THREE REGIONS OF SINGULARITY

In summary, the visual trace is laid down differently for different types of stimulus configurations. We have come to distinguish three cases:

(a) Regular pattern; stable organization; "strong" wholes; features having singular values.

2. SINGULARITY

(b) Regular pattern; stable organization except for *minor perturbations;* features having *almost* singular values.

(c) Irregular pattern; unstable, "weak" organization, often open to more than one grouping none of which is compelling; features having nonsingular values.

Case (a): Singularity. Examples of case (a) are Fig. 15*a,* the triangle in Fig. 42, Fig. 63*d,* or Fig. 68*e.* The organization of the patterns is compelling and unambiguous, the parts are perceived and coded as parts of a single unit. There is a clear hierarchy of parts and subparts and a unique separation of material and form. For example, Fig. 15*a* is seen as a *dotted* (material), straight, and vertical *line* (form). Although these patterns are very sensitive to structure-blind, "random" change, there exist many types of structure-preserving changes. Change can be extensive as long as it leaves the singularity invariant. For example, replacement of dotted lines by solid or dashed lines changes the stimuli markedly but results in the same perceived shape. This aspect of the code was stressed in the gestalt literature under the heading of *transposability,* a term taken from music, where the encoding of a tune is invariant under a change of key. Invariance of the trace under many kinds of transposition is possible only *if the representation codes directly for the invariant "gestalt qualities."* The constituent elements—the dots, dashes, lines, or musical notes—may or may not be encoded as well.

Singular features are *precisely* encoded: The perpendicularity and straightness of Fig. 15*a,* the symmetry and the straightness of the three parts of the triangle (Fig. 42), the horizontal course of its base, the horizontal and vertical symmetry of Fig. 68*e* are all coded with great accuracy. They are also easily learned and accurately remembered. They function as "cognitive reference points" (Rosch, 1975a) for whole families of patterns. Singular features have what Rosch (1971) has called *focal* values.

Case (b): Near-Singularity. Examples are the level-1 distortion of the triangle in Fig. 42, Fig. 63*a,* and Fig. 68*d.* Everything said about case (a) applies *almost* in case (b). The level-1 distortion of the triangle in Fig. 42 is seen as a *slightly irregular* version of the original triangle but has the same parts, subparts, and functions of dots (corner, interior, etc.) as the original. Figure 68*d* is perceived, like *e,* as having two triple curves, *except for* a gap in each side curve. However, the organization of *d* is not always the same as that of *e.* Judging from the reproductions, some subjects see a center curve with a hook at each end plus two, *gapless,* side curves. In this instance, the "contrastructural" gaps introduce an ambiguity that does not exist with the "prostructural" gaps of Fig. 68*e.* Finally, in Fig. 63*a,* there is an *imperfection* of the taper of the triangular shapes that is *inconsistent* with the *perfect* taper of the rectangles.

In all these instances, the pattern is perceived as a modification, a flawed version of a more *perfect* pattern. *This coding is inherent in the pattern; it does not require that the observer has ever seen the perfect pattern.* The features,

14. THE THREE REGIONS OF SINGULARITY   65

although they are not singular, are coded with reference to, as *almost at the singularity*. The sides of the triangle are *essentially* straight, the sweep of the curves is essentially continuous *except* at the gap, the taper is *almost* smooth. The experiments of Posner and Peterson et al. and Rosch (1973a) suggest that this type of pattern is represented by a trace of the perfect pattern with an added modifier to indicate the imperfection. The trace consists of what Woodworth (1938) and Bear (1974) call schema-plus-correction. However, the term schema is too loose to describe clearly the singular aspect of the encoding. The trace in case (b) is organized as in case (a); it has the same parts with the same functions in the whole, the same transposable whole qualities or realized features, *except* that some features are coded as *near but not at* a singular value.

Case (c): Nonsingularity. Examples of case (c) are Fig. 15c, the level-7.7 distortion of the triangle in Fig. 42, the "random" pattern in the same figure, and Fig. 63b. Here, the pattern is more or less irregular and the subgrouping into parts is ambiguous, as with ink blots or cloud formations. Perceived groupings are unstable and arguable. Many perceived features are only approximately encodable and are not anchored on, or related, to a nearby singular value. For example, in the level-9.7 distortion of Fig. 42, three dots form a subunit, but their relationship with the remaining cluster is only approximately encoded, and the number of dots in the cluster and their mutual relationship is not precisely perceived and coded. While it is easy to describe, copy, or reproduce the triangle accurately from memory, a reproduction of the level-9.7 distortion or the random pattern is achievable only in rough approximation. The same is true of the wavy line of Fig. 15c. In contrast to Fig. 15a, it is readily divisible into subgroups, but the subgroups are not compelling or unique. Some regular features are still present: The pattern is still a *line* of dots, still *essentially* perpendicular, and these features are encoded. But the manner in which the dots are *not equidistant* is only vaguely perceived, and the details only approximately coded. Likewise, the manner of deviation from straightness is not precisely perceived and encoded and not accurately reproducible. In Fig. 63b, the relationship of the triangular shapes is perceived as *irregular* and difficult to learn, to reproduce, and to remember. The encoding of this feature is less detailed than the encoding of the regular arrangement of the triangular shapes in Fig. 63d, as reported in Sections 49 and 50.

The infinite variety of possible visual patterns does not always fit smoothly in one of these three types. For instance, ambiguity of grouping is characteristic of case (c), but some ambiguity is found in Fig. 68d, which in other respects belongs as "almost regular" to case (b).

The ambiguity of grouping in case (c) is due to the lack of any one compelling subdivision. None of the many possible groupings is stable. This kind of ambiguity must be distinguished from instances in which more than one grouping occurs and all groupings are stable (e.g., in Boring's young and old woman).

2. SINGULARITY

Attneave (1971) calls these patterns *multistable*. Multistable patterns belong to case (a) in each of their stable versions.

Often a pattern fits in some respect into one category and in another respect into another. For example, the most irregular patterns of Fig. 42 are regular, case (a), at the material level, in having perfectly round and equal dots. Figure 30 has regular *form* with unambiguous grouping into three parts but irregular dot distribution at the material level. The trace then represents the form or, at least, the grouping precisely, but the distribution of the dots along the lines only approximately, as *irregular*.

There are *degrees* of singularity and nonsingularity *within* the three classifications. For instance, in Fig. 42, the level 7.7 has little compelling structure, whereas the level-9.7 distortion, by happenstance, is more easily structured as three dot triples, the middle one tight and the other two forming a pair of parallel lines on both sides of the center triple. In this respect, the 9.7-level distortion is more regular and codable than the 7.7 example.

The remainder of this work leans heavily on the distinction among these three types of encoding, cases (a), (b), and (c). The theory to be developed claims that the fate of the trace differs in specific ways for the three types and that *no trace theory is possible without these distinctions.* It also claims that these distinctions apply to any trace, not just to visual traces. This topic is taken up again in Section 22.

3 Extensions of the Theory

15. EXTRINSIC EFFECTS

The trace of a pattern depends on its hierarchical complexity, its organization into subordinate levels, its parts and their parts, and so on down. But a pattern is also determined, a visual concept (see Section 16) is also shaped, by the "neighboring" and the superordinate context within which it occurs. These influences represent the *extrinsic effects* on pattern perception. The effects can be either figural or due to past experience.

As mentioned in Section 5, Attneave found that a slanted parallelogram is more similar to an oppositely slanted one than to a perpendicular one. I performed two similar experiments (Goldmeier, 1936/1972). Figure 43 shows three small triangles set in a frame consisting of a rectangle and an isosceles triangle. The frame is the same in all three patterns. As in Attneave's experiment, the design with the slanted little triangle, 43a, is significantly more similar to 43c than to the one with the isosceles little triangle, 43b. The frame seems to have added nothing. Figure 44 shows the same three small triangles set in a *slanted frame*. The frame is again the same for all three patterns. The slant of the frame is about midway between the slant of the little triangle in Fig. 43a and 44a and the vertical. But in this new setting, a is significantly more similar to pattern b, containing the isosceles triangle, than to c.

The difference between experiment 43 and 44 raises complex issues in perception, some of which are discussed in Goldmeier (1936/1972). For the present purpose, the experiments demonstrate that the representation of a pattern in one setting differs from the representation of the same pattern in a different setting.

The second experiment, Fig. 45, makes the same point without an *explicit* change in the setting. Figure 45a is symmetrical about the horizontal and vertical axis. In b, the two *right* quadrants are changed; in c, exactly the same changes

68   3. EXTENTIONS OF THE THEORY

FIG. 43. A small triangle in a frame of a large triangle inside a rectangle. In *a* and *c* the small triangles are not isoceles but are mirror images of one another. The little triangle in *b* is equilateral. (From Goldmeier, 1972.)

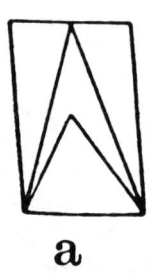

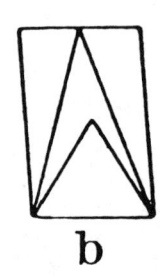

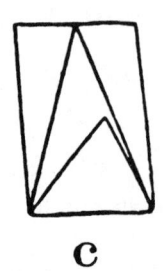

FIG. 44. Here the "frame" is tilted so that its "axis" falls midway between the tips of the little triangles in 43*a* and *b*. Into this tilted frame were inserted the same little triangles as in figure 43. (From Goldmeier, 1972.)

are applied to the two *lower* quadrants. Geometrically, the changes are of equal extent. The change leaves *b* symmetrical about the horizontal only, whereas *c* is symmetrical about the vertical only. Symmetry about the vertical prevails; 45*c* is more similar to *a* for 10 out of 12 subjects ($p < .05$). In a second experiment, all three designs are rotated by 90°. In this orientation, the appearance changes, as the reader can verify by turning the book sideways. Now *b* is symmetrical only about the vertical, *c* only about the horizontal. Nine out of 12 subjects now judge *b* to be more similar to *a* than *c* is to *a*. The reversal of the similarity relations with orientation was confirmed and elaborated by Rock and Leaman (1963), see Rock (1973), see also Corballis and Roldan (1975).

The next and last example, modified from Blesser, Shillman, Cox, Kuklinski, Ventura & Eden (1973), shows that these extrinsic effects act in recognition as well as in perception. If, in Fig. 46, one covers the two left letters and the last letter, then the remaining vertical row reads DAZE. If one covers all but the horizontal row, it reads DANE. The letter at the crossing is either an N or a Z, depending on the setting in which it occurs (Blesser et al., 1973).

15. EXTRINSIC EFFECTS   69

In the first and the third example, the setting is explicitly supplied; in the second case, the difference in orientation is only indirectly given by the relation to the rest of the page. The difference in the first and second example is clearly a *figural* one. In the third example, the difference is also figural, because it is caused by the tilt of the other letters, but it is brought into evidence by evoking two different learned patterns, either Z or N.

If the relationship is reversed, if learning or experience decide which of several figural or semantic aspects are perceived and encoded, we speak of *context* effects or of subjective *set*. For instance, the symbol *0* is a number in 10 but a letter in NO. In these cases, the outcome depends primarily on the previous learning or experience of the observer. Palmer (1975b) has shown that the context created by, say, a kitchen scene influences the identification of subsequently shown drawings of a loaf of bread or a rural mailbox. The two drawings are geometrically similar. But the mailbox is often misperceived as a loaf of bread after the kitchen scene, whereas the loaf of bread is rarely misperceived in this context. The outcome is reversed if either drawing is preceded by a scene appropriate to a mailbox. The scenes create a set in the observer that modulates the figural analysis of a subsequently shown drawing. The effect is strongest if the pictures are difficult to recognize and weakest if the pictures in themselves are rather unequivocal representations of the object. Palmer's experiment is a good

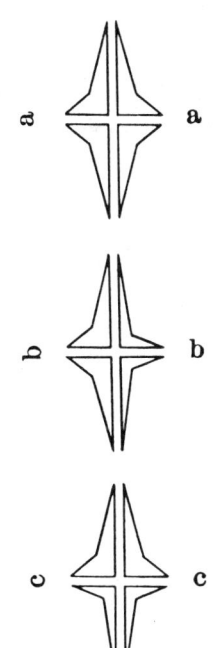

FIG. 45. Figure 45*a* is symmetrical about the horizontal *and* the vertical. In 45*b* and *c* two quadrants are changed to the same extent; in 45*b* the right half is changed, in 45*c* the lower half of the figure is changed. (From Goldmeier, 1972.)

FIG. 46. Covering all but the horizontal row, the letter at the crossing is an N. With all but the vertical covered it is a Z. (After Blesser, et al., 1973.)

model of what is usually thought of as the context effect when it is due to past experience.

Palmer supplied the context in the form of a picture; Carmichael, Hogan, and Walter (1932) supplied it in the form of a verbal label. Figure 47 shows a few examples. To one group of observers, the drawings were presented as showing "Curtains in a window," "Eyeglasses," and "A ship's wheel"; another group received the labels "Diamond in a rectangle," "Dumbbells," and "Sun." The subjects had to reproduce the drawings from memory, and two judges determined whether the reproductions looked more like one or the other of the two objects suggested by the labels. By comparison with an unlabeled control group, the authors felt that the reproductions were influenced by the verbal labels.

The experiments of Palmer and Carmichael et al. show that context is effective in resolving figural ambiguity. In both experiments, the context was not itself figural, as in previous examples. Context here places the object into one or another area of past experience. The two experiments are very much alike. In principle, it matters little whether the connection with past experience is established by pictures or words as long as they communicate the setting. Quite possibly, Palmer's loaf of bread versus mailbox ambiguity could also be resolved *without added context,* if a group of bakers were tested against rural mail carriers. In this case, the two groups bring different mental sets to the task.

If the dependence of the trace on context were confined to ambiguous patterns only, it might not be much more than a laboratory curiosity. However, as Tulving (Craik & Tulving, 1975), Barclay, Bransford and Franks (Barclay, Bransford, Franks, McCarrell & Nitsch, 1974), and other authors have shown, any stimulus, ambiguous or not, together with the context of acquisition, forms a unique event and is coded in a unique "episodic" trace.

The role of past experience goes far beyond resolving ambiguities. Wagner (1978) found that the acquisition of oriental rug patterns among Moroccans varies with experience in the widest sense, including the amount of schooling of the individual, the amount of time spent in an urban rather than a rural setting, and the amount of professional experience as a rug dealer.

Experience in a wider sense plays a still more pervasive role in the everyday perception and encoding of visual data. The effect is related to the inherently hierarchic structure of perception, as Palmer (1977) has pointed out. Whereas shift of attention evidenced by eye and head motion has long been appreciated and used in research (Chase & Simon, 1973), another perceptual process, just as basic, has gone all but unnoticed. This is the process of "selective looking," as Neisser and Becklen (1975) put it, the visual analog of the cocktail-party phenomenon. It can separate two processes, or it can widen or narrow the focus. Looking at a man, for example, an observer can look at a pimple on his nose, at the whole nose, at the face, at the head, at the whole man, or at the group of people of which the man is one. The different percepts so obtained show varying aspects of the scene and vary in detail. The group picture may just show the pimple or at least the nose without giving details of either. There is no question in the observer's memory that the man had a nose and even a pimple on it, but he could not describe them. Artists are aware of this. A painting of the group could show a nose on the man's face without giving details of the nose. Palmer (1975a) has called attention to this trade off between perception of global properties and detail. Figure 48, taken from Palmer (1975a), shows the nose, eye, ear, and mouth as they appear in the sketch of a face, where they lack detail, and in isolation, zooming in, so to speak. In the close-up, greater detail is required,

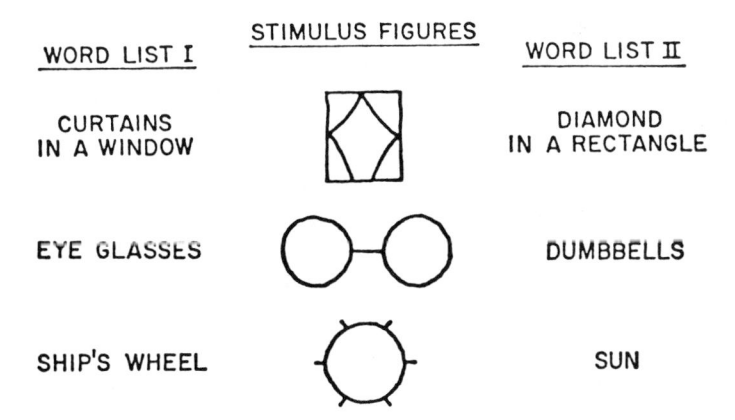

WORD LIST I	STIMULUS FIGURES	WORD LIST II
CURTAINS IN A WINDOW		DIAMOND IN A RECTANGLE
EYE GLASSES		DUMBBELLS
SHIP'S WHEEL		SUN

FIG. 47. The drawings were presented to some subjects with labels from List I, to others with List II labels.

72   3. EXTENTIONS OF THE THEORY

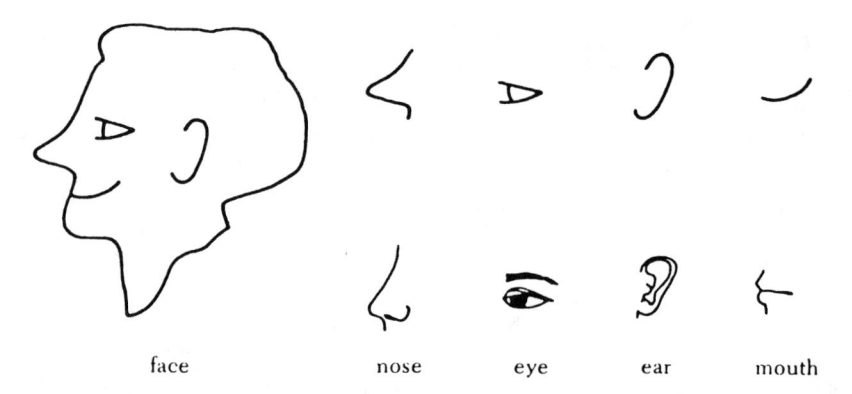

face   nose   eye   ear   mouth

FIG. 48.   The trade-off between perception of global properties of the whole face and of detail. (From Palmer, 1975a.)

perceived, and presumably encoded. The process of "zooming" in and out is not an ad hoc assumption to explain observations like those of Palmer. The process is quite real. It has been studied and even timed (Kosslyn, 1976).

Our "concept" or "schema" of a man potentially includes details of the nose, but, unless the nose is untypical, these details are often not "sketched in" in the trace of a particular man. Similarly, I may not encode and therefore not remember what clothes the man wore when I saw him last; yet, I am certain that he was not nude on that occasion. This phenomenon is akin to the encoding of figure as against the ground. The unencoded detail corresponds to the unencoded features of the background.

Experience is the decisive factor in the encoding of learned patterns. What to the layman is a jumble is to the trained microscopist a particular animal or plant tissue. Wiseman and Neisser (1974) have shown that stimuli that were seen as meaningless patterns were encoded with less detail than the same stimuli seen as faces. Bower, Karlin, and Dueck (1975) showed that nonsense drawings were recalled, recognized, and paired up with each other much better if a title or context was provided. They concluded that the titles induced a schema into which the details could be fitted for encoding.

So much for bona fide, experimentally supported effects of extrinsic mechanisms. Associationism, in its mistrust of intrinsic, structural organization, has chosen without the benefit of experimental verification to assume past experience in the form of frequency or recency of cooccurrence as the universal source of grouping and of attributes. Gottschaldt, in 1926 and 1929, found that as many as 520 previous learning experiences of patterns like Fig. 49a failed to induce recognition or even easily guided perception of a in b, c, d, e, or f.

Figure 50a, by contrast, can be found easily in b, c, and d. Gottschaldt concludes that a in Fig. 49 is not phenomenally realized as a part of b, c, d, e, or f, whereas Fig. 50a can be realized in b, c, or d. Geometrically, both a figures

15. EXTRINSIC EFFECTS   73

are of course present in the larger figures. Gottschaldt provides a number of rules that help distinguish the structure of *a* in isolation and in various contexts. These rules differ from Wertheimer's grouping factors. Bower and Glass (1976) also have investigated this phenomenon. They suggest research efforts toward a "grammar" of visual shapes to complement the linguist's grammar of language (p. 465). Research of that kind could build on the results of Gottschaldt on one hand and on the methods developed by Bower and Glass on the other.

Research in the gestalt tradition, notably the work of Gottschaldt, and of Kanizsa (1979), demonstrates how strongly figural context can affect the trace. Associationism-oriented research has produced evidence that prior experience, supplied either by the experimenter or by the subject's memory, also influences the trace of a stimulus. The experiments quoted in this section suggest that context operates at many levels, for instance:

1. Figural level, Fig. 49 and 50.
2. Reference frames, Fig. 43, 44, 45, 46.
3. Semantic level, where an object is categorized, say, as a loaf of bread or a rural mailbox.
4. "Episodic" level, as an object in a particular setting, say, a loaf of bread in a kitchen or a word in a sentence.

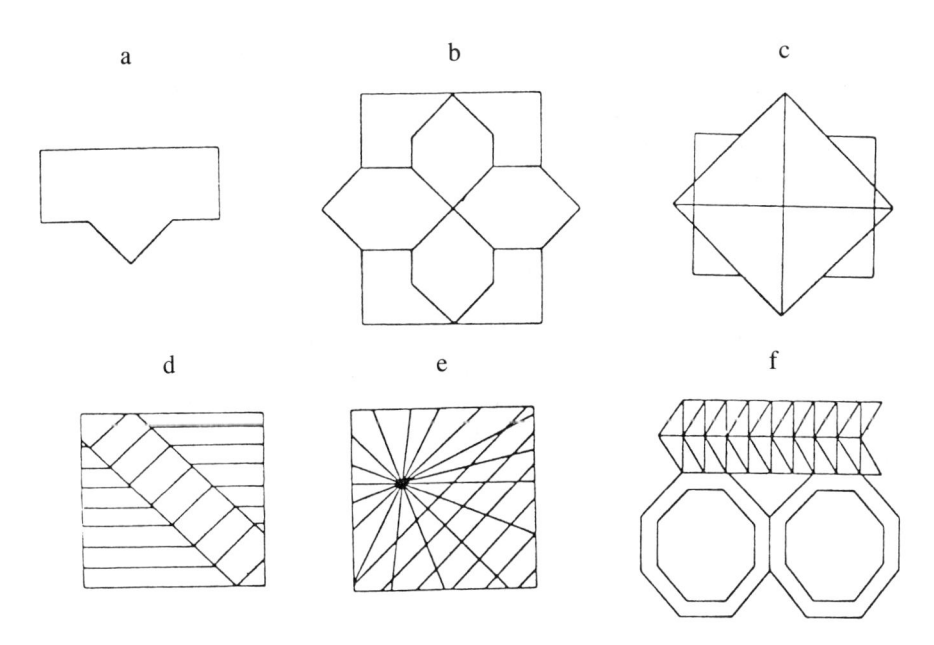

FIG. 49. Pattern *a* is geometrically, but not phenomenally a part of patterns *b*, *c*, *d*, *e*, and *f*. (From Gottschaldt, 1926.)

74   3. EXTENTIONS OF THE THEORY

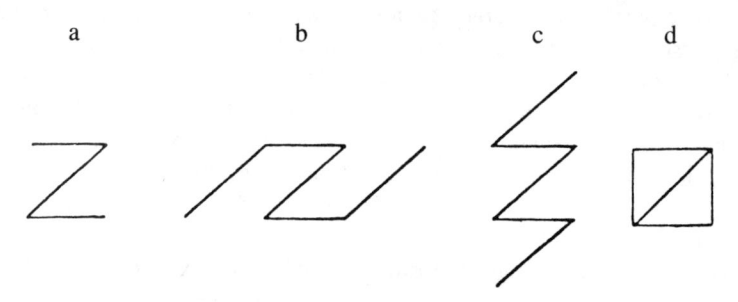

a   b   c   d

FIG. 50.   Pattern *a* is geometrically contained in *b, c,* and *d* and can be recognized within these patterns. (From Gottschaldt, 1926.)

Many other processing levels have been proposed (Treisman, 1979) and isolated experimentally, for instance, the level of "cyclopean vision" (Julesz 1971), or the phonemic, lexical, or syntactic level for words (Lachman & Lachman, 1979; Perfetti, 1979). At every level, there are unlearned effects, say, figural factors for patterns or sound qualities for phonemes, as well as learned determiners that constrain or modify possible attributes. For instance, in the case of phonemes, the setting of a particular language limits the set of phonemes to those permitted in that language: english has no german u-umlaut; german does not have the english "th." For memory theory, it does not matter (as emphasized in Sections 8, 10, and 11) whether the effect is the result of an inborn processing characteristic of our perception, of an acquired processing routine, or of particular types of stored information. To equate all extrinsic effects with learned effects is gratuitous, will often be found in error, and is irrelevant for trace theory. What matters is the organization of the trace, not what did or did not organize it.

16.   VISUAL CONCEPTS

As visual experience accrues, it is condensed into schemata or categories or visual concepts. If the features of a new percept evoke or "make contact" or "resonate with" an already formed visual trace or schema, then the percept is encoded as an embodiment of this schema. If, for instance, a drawing is seen as a human profile, it is perceived and encoded as having two eyes, one visible and the other unseen on the other side. To be complete, a theory of the formation of visual traces must account for the formation of this kind of visual schema or concept.

The most familiar form of the problem is category formation. If one sees a dog one has never seen before, one will probably recognize it as a dog, even if the dog happens to be a very untypical specimen. This feat implies that one possesses, from *past experience,* a schema, an ideal type (Max Weber, 1917), a

16. VISUAL CONCEPTS   75

prototype, a category (Rosch), or a concept (Posner) of DOG. For the purpose of this discussion, we speak of visual patterns interchangeably with what Posner calls concepts (like the "originals" of the experiment of Peterson et al.), what Rosch calls categories (which is not what psychologists from Aristotle to modern associationists call categories, see Rosch & Mervis, 1975), or, to give a concrete example, the notion of the printed capital letter A, a concept investigated extensively by Blesser, Schillman, and others (Blesser et al., 1973). The term here also refers to the special case of visual patterns or categories or concepts containing only one single object; for example, a particular person, the planet Mars, or one single pattern. Sets of one member are potentially as complex as the general case. A particular person looks different lying, sitting, walking, before and after a haircut, dancing, or crying. Mars looks different from different sides, different distances, in winter and in summer, during a dust storm or in calm weather. In order to "know" (in the sense of Garner, 1966) a person, even only by sight, one needs to know the *invariants,* the *underlying pattern* or *concept.* One person may have an ugly, puffed-up moonface and look exactly like another person with a handsome face, afflicted with bilateral mumps. Even a single pattern does have features that *imply* a feature space (Garner, 1974), a feature space that under some circumstances consists of two or more disjoint domains (Attneave, 1971), each with its own invariants (prototypes) and "implied set of equivalent patterns" (Garner & Clement, 1963). The investigation of visual experience in this sense has hardly begun (Metzger, 1975; Palmer, 1977; Rosch, 1973a).

This notion of "visual pattern" or "concept" or category or "visual object" is broader and more general than the one prevalent in experimental psychology (of the Round-and-Blue versus Red-and-Triangular kind) and is also biologically more relevant, or as it is sometimes put, more "ecologically valid." In fact, it describes what humans and higher animals really acquire when they form a concept: a chick's concept of its mother encompassing the hen from front, back, and sidewise, with its feathers smooth or ruffled, sitting, walking, or fluttering. Such concepts have limits. A human child may not recognize its father disguised as Santa Claus. On the other hand, a caricature may reveal the "true self" of a person, whereas a "candid" photograph may not.

What is it that people or machines must learn in order to acquire a visual pattern concept so defined, or even a Posner-type dot pattern, or one of the patterns of Fig. 52, or the letter A?

One theory is the *template* theory that works well for severely constrained sets of patterns. (Selfridge & Neisser, 1960). It assumes that all specimens (dots, dot patterns, letters A) are random variations of a standard (as they actually are in the experiments of Posner & Keele and of Peterson et al.). "Learning the pattern" then means that the subject either learns for each dot or element a "confusion circle," a range of possible locations, or that the subject averages the locations of each dot and arrives at or near the original location of the dot in an "inferred" prototype. This theory ignores the structure of the ensemble. It treats phenome-

76   3. EXTENTIONS OF THE THEORY

nally regular and irregular dot patterns alike. Therefore, it cannot account for the marked difference in the perception and recognition of regular and irregular patterns found by Peterson et al. Evidently, subjects learn the regularities of the features and utilize them if such features are available. Thus, this theory fails even in the domain for which it was constructed by Posner and Keele.

It also fails in naturally given and some artificially created categories. One can hardly conceive of a "template" or a composite sketch of a "generalized dog" or a letter A. In the case of the dog, this composite not only must be representative of dogs but also allow one to reject wolves, foxes, rats, hyenas, and similar animals. As Rosch and Mervis (1975) have shown, natural categories are structured in such a way that this kind of averaging is unrepresentative in principle. Blesser et al., (1973) used Fig. 51 to demonstrate that it is just as hopeless to look for an "average" or a "template" of the letter A.

The alternative approach is based on the insight that visual patterns are *not* perceived and therefore coded as collections of separate elements *plus* their mutual distances and directions, but as organized wholes with parts and subparts, each with *phenomenal* attributes and features. The preceding sections have argued that these partitions and features taken together constitute the representation, whether they are precise and compelling as in strong wholes and good patterns or indeterminate and vague, as in the case of clouds, ink blots, or random dot patterns. In either case, what is learned and remembered, according to this theory, is the organization, the phenomenal parts and phenomenal features, as opposed to *geometric* parts and *geometric* attributes of the pattern. This distinction can be elusive, yet, it is basic for pattern learning. The difficulty arises from the fact that geometric parts in some instances coincide with phenomenal parts, whereas in other cases they differ markedly.

Figure 52 shows a pattern on the left, an inventory of its geometric parts in the middle, and an inventory of its phenomenal parts on the right. The upper row

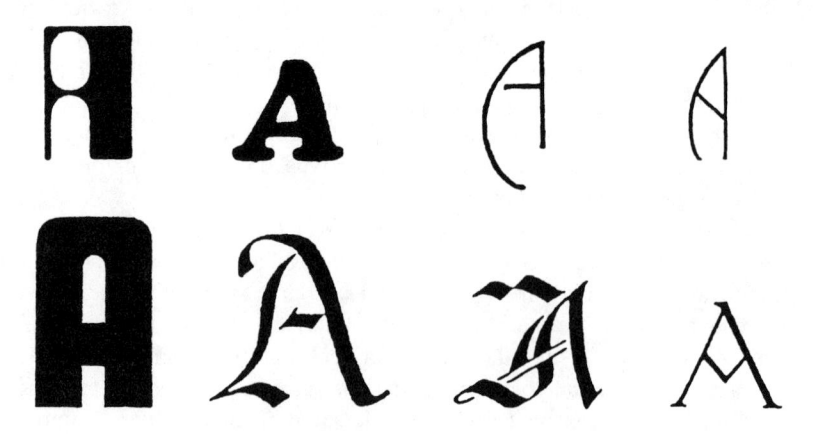

FIG. 51.   A variety of recognizable letters "A." (From Blesser et al., 1973.)

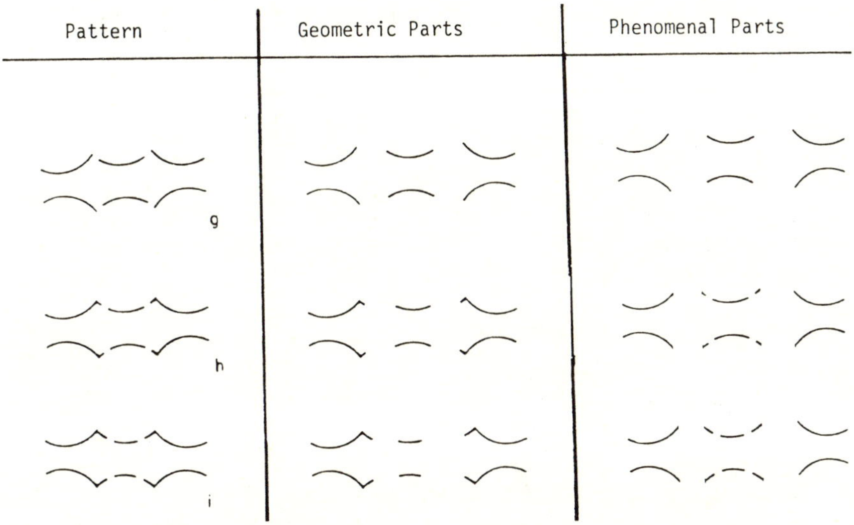

16. VISUAL CONCEPTS   77

Pattern	Geometric Parts	Phenomenal Parts

FIG. 52. Three patterns (Figure 68 *g, h,* and *i*) in the left column, their geometrical parts in the middle and their phenomenal parts in the right column.

shows a pair of three arcs. The pattern is on the left; the arcs separately in the middle represent the geometric parts, which in this case are identical with the phenomenal parts shown on the right. In the second row is another pattern, differing from the first in only one detail: The gaps have been moved by one gap width onto the center curve. The middle column again shows the geometric parts, but in this case, the phenomenal parts on the right differ from the geometric subdivisions. Geometrically, the gaps form boundaries in both patterns. Phenomenally, the gaps bound the parts in the upper pattern, whereas, in the lower pattern, the *cusps* function as boundaries for the arcs. The gaps in the upper pattern are what Wertheimer called *prostructural* (i.e., coincident with the phenomenal part boundaries), whereas, in the second pattern, the gaps are *contrastructural*, interrupting the middle curves, which are the phenomenal subunits.

Pattern *i* in the last row of Fig. 52 is derived from *h* by shifting the gaps by another gap width toward the center. Geometrically (see middle column), the "hooks" of the side curves become longer. Phenomenally (see right column), the gaps move more to the center of the middle curve.

Evidence from copies and reproductions of these patterns suggests that some subjects parse patterns *h* and *i* as shown in the center column, so the following applies only to the majority, diagramed in Fig. 52.

If *h* is taken as the standard pattern, then *g* and *i* represent equal deviations by one gap width from the standard, because, geometrically, the parts of *g* and *i* are changed by equal amounts. Phenomenally, however, *g* has uninterrupted center curves, whereas both *h* and *i* have center curves with two gaps. Disregarding the

78   3. EXTENTIONS OF THE THEORY

concomitant differences in length, direction, etc., both in the geometric and the phenomenal attributes, the following is predicted:

1. In a Posner-type paradigm, Fig. 52i would be better than g as a "learning pattern" if h was the prototype.
2. Pattern i is more similar to h than is g.
3. The locations of the gaps relative to the ends of the curves are *precisely* encoded (as being *at* the ends) in pattern g, but only *approximately* (as *near* the ends), *somewhere within* the center curves, in h and i.

The first prediction has not been tested. But pattern i is indeed significantly more similar to h than is g. A pattern j (Fig. 68), in which the gaps are shifted by one more gap width toward the center, is likewise more similar to h than is g, whereas the difference in similarity to h between i and j does not reach significance (Goldmeier, 1972), supporting hypotheses 2 and 3.

The analysis of these patterns can be cast in terms of visual concepts. One concept is typified by pattern g of Fig. 52 and of Fig. 68. It is characterized by (a pair of) three *uninterrupted* arcs. We conclude from similarity rankings (Goldmeier, 1972, and Section 6) that Fig. 68e and f are also embodiments of this concept but h, i, and j are not. The other concept, by contrast, is exemplified by h, i, or j and characterized by two symmetric gaps in the middle arc.

The differences *within* each concept (i.e., the length and relationship of the three curves in concept e, f, g and the exact location of the symmetric gaps in concept h, i, j) are only loosely or imprecisely coded. The traces are indeterminate in this regard and the corresponding features are nonsingular.

The differences *between* the two concepts, however, are sharply defined. Prostructural gaps in one case, contrastructural gaps in the other. The prostructural arrangement is singular; the contrastructural gap position is nonsingular.

The difference in structure predicts that a subject trained on pattern Fig. 68h will, in a recognition test, choose h, i, or j over e, f, or g. A subject trained, say, on e will, on a test, choose e, f, or g over h, i, and j. But within each of the two concepts, confusions will occur (see section 35).

Every additional phenomenal level in the hierarchy of a pattern concept increases the distance between the geometry of the pattern and its perception. Because templates are derived from the geometry whereas concepts are derived from the phenomenal representation, template theories of concept formation become less applicable as the hierarchical complexity of the pattern increases. In the following example, *two* phenomenal levels arise, *material* and *form*. Figure 70g, f, e, and d, c shows again the two families, or concepts just discussed, except that dotted lines replace the solid lines of Fig. 68. Figure 70 has nothing but gaps, many small ones and a few larger ones. The small gaps are phenomenally the "material" of which the dotted lines are made; the large gaps are "form" features. The material level is subordinate to the form level. The "concepts" are form-based concepts. The grouping is determined by the form, which is only indirectly related to individual dot distances.

If a gap is defined as an interruption of a phenomenal part, then Fig. 68*e, f, g* and 70*g, f, e* do not have gaps, whereas 68 *h, i, j* and 70 *d, c,* do have gaps. These statements are supported by similarity rankings (see Section 6, and Goldmeier, 1972).

Blesser et al., in their work on recognition of printed characters, propose a hierarchy of *three* types of attributes for each character: geometrical, perceptual, and "functional" attributes. All the examples in Fig. 53 deal with the attribute of closure. They are taken from the boundary between the character space of the hand-printed letters *A* and *H*. At the boundary, the attribute of closure is in transition. Geometrically, only *a1* and *b1* are closed. Perceptually, *d1* is also closed; all the other specimens are open. Functionally, for the purpose of assigning the pattern to the letter *A* or *H*, all patterns in column 1 and 2 are "closed," all patterns in column 4 and 5 are "open," and the patterns in column 3 are on the borderline. What Blesser et al. call "perceptual" and "functional" attributes are both *phenomenal* attributes, as the term is used here. Their "perceptual" closure is what we would call a local feature, a property of the top part in isolation, whereas their "functional" closure is a global feature, a *relatively* closed top, taking into account the lower part and the divergence of the two uprights.

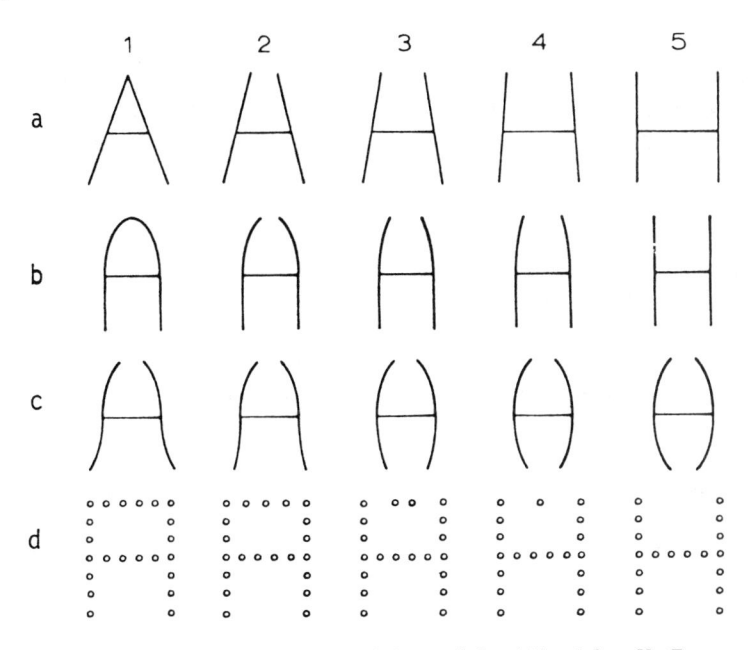

FIG. 53. Geometric versus phenomenal closure distinguishing A from H. (From Blesser et al., 1973.)

The representation of the visual concept A must include functional closure as a characteristic and be immune to mere geometric or local closure. If a child, or a computer, were taught to look for geometric or perceptual closure, they would misclassify most instances in column 2. Just how functional closure is specified is a problem in pattern recognition. Memory theory is concerned with the fact that people readily learn to recognize hand-printed As and therefore must have access to an algorithm for functional closure as part of their concept of A. Whatever the algorithm turns out to be, it is more complex than any proposed so far.

Rosch (1973a) and her collaborators (Rosch & Mervis, 1975; Rosch et al., 1976a, b) have shown that there are *degrees* of membership in a category. As Markman and Seibert (1976) put it: "(Not every) instance of a concept is considered as good as any other.... The evidence strongly indicates that... some instances are clearly better instances (of the concept) than others [p. 562]." To illustrate, in Fig. 53, column 1 contains *better* As than column 2, column 5 *better* Hs than column 4. The center column contains the poorest specimens of either A or H. The letters in column 1 are *typical* letters, close to the prototype, ideal, or schema of an A.

As with individual patterns, there are "good" and "poor" visual concepts. Goodness of a concept often rests on self-consistency, on the fact that the characteristics of the specimens are compatible with each other or predict each other. For instance, in the concept of Fig. 68*e, f,* and *g,* the gaps coincide with change in direction of the arcs; their location is prostructural. In terms of information theory, goodness is redundancy; in mathematical terms, one could speak of overdetermination of the characteristics. A poor concept would be one where the parts of the specimens are independent of each other; have arbitrary relations to each other. This would be true of random dot patterns or random combinations of attributes, like the concept "anything red, round, and small." Until the work of Rosch, research on concepts used almost exclusively such poor concepts. The results of such research tended to be as unrepresentative of actual concept formation as the material it employed. Good concepts, like good figures, are easier to encode or learn than poor ones (Clement, 1964, 1967), easier to remember correctly (Peterson et al., 1973; Rosch, 1973a), and more useful, and indeed preferred, in what Arnheim (1969) has called "visual thinking."

That is not to say that loose or poor concepts do not occur outside the laboratory. For instance, there is no inner reason we know of why a dog *shaped* like a Dalmatian should have *spots* like a Dalmatian, or why a Dachshund should be both elongated and floppy-eared. We don't know why the human chromosome 21 looks the way it does. But unless a microscopist learns to recognize it, he cannot diagnose a trisomy 21, the cause of mongolism. However, the learning of poor categories takes a great deal of practice. Poor, arbitrary concepts are hard to acquire, easy to confuse and to forget. If a poor concept is very well-learned, that is to say, is familiar, like breeds of dogs to many of us, or human chromosomes to a trained microscopist, perceiving and encoding a particular specimen becomes easier. Familiarity and training do *facilitate* perceptual processing and encoding (Postman, 1954). This relation between the effect of familiarity and of goodness *does not mean, however, that goodness is due to familiarity.*

Some confusion exists with regard to the *meaningfulness* of a pattern. There are two kinds of meaning. The roman numerals I, II, and III, the picture of a lady on the ladies-room door, and the arrow indicating a one-way street have *intrinsic, structural* meaning. The numerals 2, 3, 4, or the patterns "one if by land, two if by sea," or the letter A have extrinsic, *arbitrarily assigned* meaning. There is another, derivative kind of meaning, established by myths, scientific explanations, mnemonics, etc. For instance, the symbol 0 "means" the o-sound "because" that is the shape of our lips when we say "oh," or the same symbol "means" zero "because" it is an *empty* circle. The "explanation" supplies a context within which an assigned meaning becomes intrinsic to the structure. The explanation, whether it is correct or false, ad hoc, mythical, or scientific, transforms an extraneous, arbitrary meaning into an "understandable" intrinsic meaning, into the first kind mentioned, in which the structure of the pattern mirrors the meaning. There is a tendency in human cognition to transform extrinsic meaning—lightening followed by thunder—into intrinsic meaning—the anger of the Gods or the sudden release of electric charge.

This is not the place to pursue the psychology of "familiarity" and "meaning" any further. The purpose of developing the two notions this far is to point out an ambiguity in the experiments of Peterson et al. and of Posner and Keele. Figure 42 shows three of their prototypes. The "F" has meaning of the extrinsic, assigned kind, is familiar and regular. The triangle has no meaning except as a greek capital letter but is presumably familiar and regular. The random patterns are neither meaningful nor familiar nor regular. What is missing is a pattern that is regular but is neither meaningful nor familiar. Peterson et al. refer to the F and the triangle as "meaningful." They report that these meaningful patterns behave not like the random patterns. It is probable that the difference was due neither to meaningfulness nor the familiarity of the F and triangle but merely to their regularity. It is likely, however, that familiarity alone (Postman, 1954) or meaningfulness alone can produce very similar results in a Posner experiment *even in the absence of regularity or figural goodness.*

At this point, we are left with *two kinds of goodness.* The *figural goodness,* championed by gestalt theory, systematically investigated by Garner and Clement, Handel and Garner, Bear, Rosch, Palmer (1977), and others; and the goodness in the sense of *typicality,* established by learning the prototype of a concept or category, investigated by Posner and his collaborators (Posner et al., 1967; Posner & Keele, 1968), by Peterson et al. (1973), and also in a series of studies by Rosch and her coworkers (1976a, b).

82   3. EXTENTIONS OF THE THEORY

The notion of figural goodness is often linked to nativism and prototype acquisition to empiricism. The philosophical bias behind these linkages is not pertinent to the present discussion. Whether figural goodness is inborn, preprogrammed, or induced by early experiences, or both is an empirical question, open in each case to research (Held, 1965, 1968). Whether prototypes are acquired by use of inborn processing routines or by random accumulations and associations according to contiguity in space and time or both is again an empirical question (Gottschaldt, 1926/1929; Rosch, 1973a, b; Markman & Seibert, 1976). In either case, the role of goodness and typicality in encoding is the same:

1. Both good patterns and well-learned prototypes are easier to recognize and remember than poorer and less-typical patterns.
2. An *almost* perfect, good, or typical pattern is perceived and encoded as a variant of the good or typical one.
3. A poor or untypical object is hard to perceive and code in exact detail and is difficult to remember accurately. Perception and encoding are either precise, or near-precise, or vague; features are either singular, near-singular or nonsingular (Section 14). The researches of the gestalt school, of Garner and Clement, Bear, and Palmer on figural goodness, and of Rosch and her collaborators on prototypicality converge. Whether the material is new or drawn from prior experience matters little. What does matter is the structure: good, nearly good, chaotic, as discussed in Section 14 for figural goodness; typical, essentially or near typical, untypical, in the case of empirical concepts.

17. THE TRACE VERSUS THE STIMULUS

The preceding sections have set forth what might be called *selection rules,* rules governing which partitions of the elements and which parameters of the whole and of the phenomenal subwholes are selected for coding as phenomenal features, and how accurately the value of a feature is encoded. These rules also decide which possible partitions and features are *not* selected. The section on visual concepts has argued that the trace represents the result of this selection, the phenomenally realized parts and features, as opposed to a list or a template or a "composite sketch" of the stimulus patterns. The present section extends these ideas to *parts and features that have no counterpart in the stimulus pattern at all.*

Figure 36 is seen as a striped pattern with three straight contours and one curved one. Actually, only the right and left contour are geometrically present. The upper and lower contour are supplied by perceptual processes on a higher level. In some settings, the opposite occurs. In Fig. 5, the base of the triangle, although geometrically present and in plain view, is phenomenally absent, merged into the background pattern. In Fig. 54, the two processes occur to-

17. THE TRACE VERSUS THE STIMULUS   83

gether. The oblique sides of the octagon disappear in the overlapping little squares. Instead, the contour of a—partly hidden—larger square is perceived. Dinnerstein and Wertheimer have contributed other types of phenomenal overlap (see Fig. 2), and Metelli (1974a, b) has identified conditions for phenomenal transparency. Kopferman has studied conditions under which two-dimensional patterns appear three-dimensional, and Kanizsa (1979) has investigated so-called subjective contours. Winston (1975) has incorporated three-dimensional overlap into a computer program. All these phenomena exist perceptually but not in the stimulus geometry. In all these examples, we are dealing with parts or features that are phenomenally but not geometrically present, or vice versa. As in all previous cases, one could argue that only the stimulus array itself, a "snapshot," is encoded and stored in memory, and that the same processing routines that supply the elaboration in the original perception are reactivated on the occasion of each retrieval. Alternatively, the pattern could be encoded as it is perceived, overlapping or transparent, with both actual and subjective contours, or with any other elaboration, subtraction, or addition. Some arguments for the second alternative have already been presented. Some persuasive tests could easily be made. For instance, if Fig. 54 is learned, recognition could be tested with an octagon and a square of equal overlap but rotated somewhat so that the oblique sides of the octagon no longer blend into the overlap. Our theory predicts that the square is recognized, not the octagon.

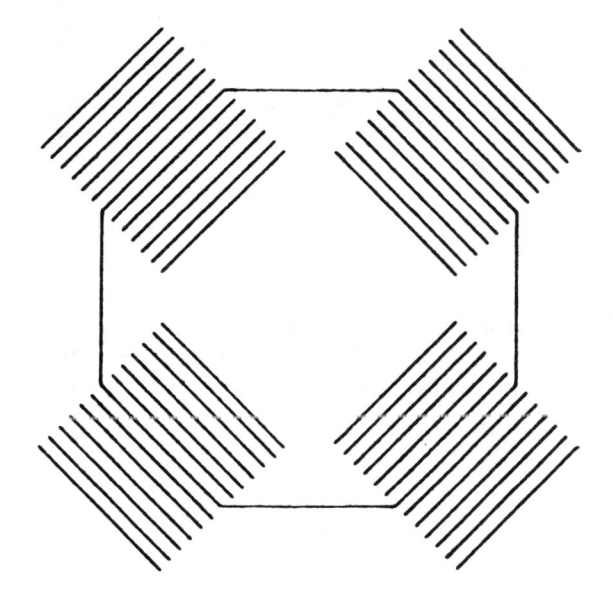

FIG. 54. The octagon geometrically present is usually not seen. Instead one sees a square with corners hidden. (From Galli & Zama, 1931.)

84 3. EXTENTIONS OF THE THEORY

If the elaborations are really part of the internal representation, then they should, in psychophysiological experiments, have the same effect as geometrically present features. This has been confirmed in a variety of ways by Weisstein and her collaborators. One of these experiments (1974) showed that lines occurring in a pattern in which they appear as *not in the plane of the paper* are more accurately localized than if they are part of an equivalent pattern in which they appear in the paper plane. In another experiment (1977), moving subjective contours produced phantom motion and even phantom-motion aftereffects, just like actual contours. Weisstein & Maguire (1978) conclude: "The mechanisms responsible for our effects.... cannot be sensitive only to geometric properties of a pattern. Rather they.... read into the stimulus certain properties that aren't there, such as depth and connectedness [p. 3-18]."

Another instance of subjective additions is due to Winston. Figure 55*a* is seen as two wedges, one on top of the other. Actually, the lower wedge is represented only by the lines shown separately in *b*. Pattern *b* by itself is not seen as a wedge but as two hinged rectangles. Furthermore, the same lines *b* in the context *c* are seen as a brick shape, acquiring again subjective completions, but of a different sort. In both *a* and *c,* the back, top, and bottom of the object is "read into the stimulus."

Unlike the first examples discussed, the unseen part of a scene is in many instances supplied by past experience. We supply another eye when we recognize a drawing as a profile view of a face, because we *know* that people have two eyes. However, little effort has been made to determine how far we are dealing with experience and to what degree figural factors determine what we see in back of perceived fronts. I believe, with Kopfermann (1930), that experience has often been invoked mistakenly. The next example is, however, one in which past experience is undeniable.

A person who is familiar with the statue of Laocoon and his sons, or has seen a picture of it, would describe it somewhat like this: a man in the center flanked by two boys; the serpent entwining them; agony on their faces. Most people could not furnish much more detail, and, given a few tiles from a jigsaw puzzle depicting the statue, they would not recognize it. Yet, the cartoon Fig. 56, although "incorrect" in every detail, readily brings the statue to mind. The cartoonist eliminates the nonsingular features and brings out the singularities of

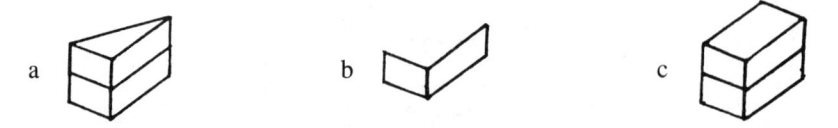

FIG. 55. Pattern *b* is seen as two hinged rectangles. In the context of *a* it is seen as the lower wedge. (Winston, 1975.) In the context of *c* it is seen as the lower "brick."

17. THE TRACE VERSUS THE STIMULUS   85

FIG. 56. Cartoon by Charles Adams. (From the "New Yorker" magazine, April 7, 1975.)

his subject, often transposing them from the heroic or pompous to the banal or ridiculous. The statue and the cartoon share singular properties. These properties must be coded in the trace of the statue and also be part of the representation of the cartoon. Properties like these are difficult to define but nevertheless must be quite real. Testimony to their reality are cartoons like this as well as the many successful imitations, fraudulent or otherwise, of paintings of old masters. A good forgery embodies the *style* of the artist whose work is counterfeited. Style is a set of whole qualities quite remote from the stimulus pattern, yet, an effective aspect of the trace.

How do elaborations, like the three-dimensional coding of Winston's wedges or coding the compositional structure of the Laocoon statue, fit into the theory of coding as data reduction? We have the capability of perceiving three dimensionally. Whenever we do so, there is an infinity of possible completions of the object's hidden aspects. In the case of familiar objects, say, a human profile, the completion occurs from experience. With Winston's wedges or Kopfermann's patterns, the completions are "selected" on the basis of singularity. In the case of the statue, even an observer unfamiliar with the Lackoon myth will perceive the losing struggle of three humans against the long, entangling antagonist. This coding goes beyond the visual data; it summarizes the essence of the data concisely but eliminates much of the nonsingular stimulus detail. The cartoonist takes advantage of the absence of detail in the coding by substituting different and quite inappropriate details into the classical composition. The data reduction that occurs before coding not only saves storage capacity but also allows objects as disparate at the stimulus level as the cartoon and the statue to evoke each other in long-term memory.

The same situation prevails with the coding of stories or proverbs. An instance fitting a proverb can evoke the proverb itself. Honeck, Riechmann, and Hoffman (1975) used stories like this: "A jewel thief was successful for a long time. However, a detective caught him after ten years. But the detective said that if he had not caught the thief someone else would have [p. 411]." This story proved to be an effective prompt for "In due time the fox is brought to the furrier." Honeck et al. (1975) conclude that: "people can encode an abstract characterization of a linguistic input, a conceptual base, which they can then use as a mediating device to recognize specific, conceptually related, instances thereof [p. 414]." Even though the stimuli of the story and the proverb have only the word time in common, the cue value of the story suggests an overlap in the trace structure, the same kind of overlap that connects the trace of the Laokoon statue with the cartoon.

In the quotation from Honeck et al., the key word is "abstract." The trace is, in some respects, so abstract that it spans the proverb and the illustrative features of the story, the original sculpture and the caricature, the work of the master and the imitator.

18. VERBAL MEMORY

Because human memory is preeminently verbal and conceptual, the preceding inquiry would be of little interest if the theory of visual encoding could not be extended to cover verbal material. This section analyzes, out of the abundant research on verbal memory, a somewhat arbitrary selection to show that the same viewpoint applies to verbal memory as well.

1. Parsing

As with visual traces, the first step in acquisition of verbal material consists of parsing, the verbal equivalent of grouping. It partitions a text and assigns functions to the words, phrases, sentences, and paragraphs that result from partitioning. Grouping as a basic problem of perception was recognized by Wertheimer as early as 1923. Parsing as a basic problem in psycholinguistics was recognized much later when difficulties emerged in computer modeling, especially in computer translation of languages. Like grouping, parsing occurs at several levels in a hierarchy, and each level has its own rules. The work of Kintsch (1974, 1976, 1977) and Norman and Bobrow (1976) shows both the progress and the difficulties in this area.

Ancient inscriptions and cuneiform writing did not set off the symbols. The reader had to supply the boundaries. Now, parsing is made easier by spaces between words, punctuation, and paragraphs. But parsing difficulties remain: Stra-phan-ger, a nonword, versus strap-hanger; the lyrics of the song "Marzi doats and dosie doats" versus "mares eat oats and does eat oats" are examples of written and spoken parsing problems. The effect of parsing on memory was demonstrated for numbers and letters by Katona (1940) and, more systematically, by Bower (1972) and his collaborators (Bower & Winzenz, 1969).

2. Selective Encoding

As is the case with visual traces, verbal material undergoes severe data reduction. Psychology was slow to recognize this because the traditional materials, nonsense syllables, numbers, and word lists have essentially no redundancy and therefore do not invite recoding into more economical codes. When recoding does take place, it is not in the service of data reduction but because the perceiver has more than one coding language available, as with bilingual subjects (Kolers, 1966, 1968b) or with people conversant with binary and octal number systems (Cruse & Clifton, 1973). Katona's experiments (1940) that used more structured materials were largely ignored. Only under the influence of Chomsky's ideas (1965), the problem of data reduction in verbal material was rediscovered in a special but important case by Sachs (1967). Sachs found that in connected discourse: "the memory of the meaning is not dependent on memory of the original form of the sentence [p. 437]." The encoding of *meaning* independent of its verbatim expression is the analog of the separate encoding of *material* and *form* (shape) (Section 3, and Goldmeier, 1936/1972, Chapter 3) in visual patterns.

What allows some of the literal surface forms to survive in memory whereas others are quickly forgotten has been investigated for a number of situations: for typographic peculiarities (Kolers, 1979), classroom lecture details (Kintsch & Bates, 1977), and dialogue (Bates, Masling, & Kintsch, 1978). Bates et al. (1978) found that: "the probability that a given surface form will be retained will, at least in part, be a function of the pragmatic role that surface form plays in a given context [p. 196]." Morris, Bransford, and Franks (1977) found that rhyming, a surface feature, can be encoded in preference to meaning, if the testing situation is conducive to perceiving and attending to the rhyme.

88   3. EXTENTIONS OF THE THEORY

The distinction of surface and deep features has limited usefulness, however. Encoding can involve many different aspects of the stimulus, including a variety of surface aspects and an equally great variety of deep or semantic aspects (examples can be found in Bransford, Franks, Morris, & Stein, 1979, and Tulving, 1979). Encoding, it turns out, confines itself to whatever aspects of the stimulus are elicited by the situation, the context, by what Tulving calls the encoding environment and Morris et al. call transfer-appropriate processing. Tulving and Morris et al. are dealing with words. The use of words brings with it the complication that words are not independent entities, that they exist psychologically as parts of texts. These complications are avoided if extended stories are used. In the case of such stories, Kozminsky (1977) showed that biasing titles do for the encoding of text what encoding environments do for words in sentences. Owens, Bower, and Black (1979) manipulated the encoding and subsequent recall of activities by suggesting or not suggesting motives for the actions. The motives were shown to color markedly what was encoded and what was left out. The situation strikingly parallels what Carmichael et al. and Palmer reported for the encoding environment of visual patterns (Section 15).

3. The Function of Parts in the Whole

There is increasing experimental evidence that parsing results in much more than a mere aggregate of words or phrases, all of equal weight. At the level of propositions, for instance, Kintsch and Keenan (1973) found that "superordinate" propositions are remembered better than "structurally subordinate" propositions. This suggests that a proposition is stored differently depending on whether in a given narrative it carries on the main theme or deals with a secondary or tertiary issue. In addition to being parsed as an individual proposition, it acquires a *function* and becomes a part of a *structure* as opposed to an item in a collection, in a disconnected list, of propositions.

After having seen a play, read a book, attended a course of lectures, and assuming that he "understood" what was said, the listener acquires a mental summary, the essence of the contents. A summary is a prime example of data reduction. The elements of a summary correspond to the phenomenally realized parts of a visual pattern. In addition to being phenomenal parts of the summary, the elements have a *function* in the whole, as Section 3 has shown for visual parts. An example from Kintsch (1976, p. 112) illustrates the function of elements in summaries. (The propositions are numbered for later reference). In a story by Bocaccio, a sailor (5) was shipwrecked (6), but he survived (7) by clinging first to a spar (8) and then to a chest. (9) Finally, a woman saw him. (10); she nursed him (11); he found some jewels in the chest (12), so that he could return home (13) as a rich man (items 1 to 4 omitted). Items 5 and 6 are essential story elements. The next two items, 7 and 8, do not advance the story line. Once survival is established, the means are more or less secondary, mere embellishment. Any other object that floats could be substituted for spar and chest. In this story, the spar, item 7, is nonsingular, not predictable from the remainder. The same would apply to the chest were it not for the part the chest plays later, in items 11, 12, and 13. The difference between items 7 and 8 is therefore that 7 is not necessary to advance the story line and not constrained by the plot, hence nonsingular, whereas 8 is an essential link in the chain of events. Items 9 and 10 are not independent: Item 10 implies item 9; thus, item 9 is redundant. Item 9 is also nonsingular. The woman might equally well have *heard* the shipwrecked man or have *been told* about him. Even though items 7 and 9 are part of the chain of events, the information *in general* is implied by items 6 and 10, whereas the details of 7 and 9 are not specifically demanded by the plot. Although the content of item 8 also could be inferred from item 6, making it redundant, the information that the object was specifically a chest rather than a piece of wood or a boat is required by the plot later on, in item 11. This constraint of item 8 by the plot makes item 8 singular. This analysis predicts that items 7 and 9 can be omitted and tend to be forgotten or modified in delayed reproductions as redundant and nonsingular, whereas item 8 tends to be included in a summary and retained in memory. The relationship between the items of the summary is analogous to the relationship between individual dots of a Garner dot pattern, or of the lines in Palmer's line patterns. Experiments with text and story summaries using the methods of Bear's (1973, 1974) and Palmer's (1977, 1978a) investigations should extend the notions of Bear and Palmer to the domain of meaningful discourse.

The analysis suggests that the nonsingular elements are less well-anchored in the structure of the summary than the singular items, the items essential to the narrative. Therefore, singular items should make better cues to the story from which they are taken. This hypothesis was tested in a study by Neisser and Hupcey (1975). Their subjects were 10 members of a Sherlock Holmes Society who had read all 60 of Conan Doyle's stories from one to 12 times over the previous 2 to 10 years, a unique population on whom to study incidental learning. The subjects were presented with sentences taken verbatim from the Holmes' stories. One kind of sentence contained arbitrary details that were independent of the story line, like the *name* ("Good evening, Mr. James Windibank"), or the *appearance* of a character ("His tall, gaunt, craggy figure had a suggestion of hunger and rapacity"), or *general remarks* ("To let the brain work without sufficient material is like racing an engine."), or *specific comments* that were peripheral to or independent of the story line ("each of these mends, done as you observe with silver bands, must have cost more than the pipe did originally"). There were 10 sentences of each of these four more peripheral subtypes. An additional 10 sentences were central, integrally related to the main line of the story ("The gun was made to conceal"). This made a pool of 50 sentences, 40 peripheral to the story line and 10 that contained an essential aspect of the story. Each subject was given about 27 sentences. The subject had to supply: (1) the title of the story; and (2) the context in which the sentence occurred. If an answer was incorrect, the subject was allowed another try. The result was (recalculated from Neisser and Hupcey's (1975) data):

Recall task		Type of Sentence	
		peripheral	central
Title	recalls	52	46
	failures	181	18
Context	recalls	131	57
	failures	130	7

Both titles and context are significantly ($p < .001$) better recalled from story-related cues than from cues extraneous to the theme of the narrative.

If one starts this kind of experiment not with extended narratives but with a lean 30-line story as Bartlett (1932) did, then almost every element carries the story line forward and the marked effect found by Neisser and Hupcey is obscured.

What makes John and Mary so disembodied in "John hit Mary. Mary gives the book to John" is the absence of a function and of a functional relationship between the two. Say, they "meet in the park"; then, substituting functional designations for mere names, we get "the hippie hits the debutante. The debutante threw the book at him." One assumes that is why Anderson and Bower (1973) chose these role relationships rather than the more traditional proper names. It livens up a narrative, even though it does not do much for a computer memory.

4. Context

Gottschaldt has shown (see Section 15) that patterns can "disappear" in a new context. Barcley, Bransford, Franks, McCarrell, and Nitsch (1974) have shown something quite similar for words. Neither Gottschaldt nor Barcley et al. use ambiguous material. The words in the Barkley et al. study have single meanings, like piano, ink, animal. Their thesis, related to Tulvings work (Tulving, 1974b, and others), is that: "the semantic representation of a word may lose its integrity as an independently accessible memory unit when it becomes part of a more complex whole [p. 472]." For instance, the word envelope was presented either in *The secretary put the paper clips in the envelope,* or in *The secretary licked the envelope.* The word envelope was cued in a recall test either with *Something that can hold small objects* or with *Something with glue.* They found that the cue tapping the context in which *envelope* was learned was significantly ($p < .001$) more effective than the cue not related to the context. Nevertheless, among the 20 cues used, there were two that elicited more often the nouns learned in the not-fitting context. Unfortunately, the authors did not identify these two sentences and cues. The exceptions point to an uncontrolled variable. Barcley et al. suggest differences in *saliency* as this variable. If, for instance, tunefulness in a piano is more salient than weight, then *something with a nice sound* might be an effective cue for *piano,* even if the acquisition sentence was *The man lifted the piano,* rather than its counterpart *The man tuned the piano.* The paradigm of Barcley et al. could be used to test this hypothesis. The hypothesis is this: An object or concept, in general, has *central* and *peripheral* features. Given acquisition sentences implying a central and a peripheral attribute and given cues that are based on the two kinds of attributes, *there should be an anomaly:* The central cues should be better than the peripheral ones, over and above the advantage each kind of cue derives from the acquisition context.

Another experiment using the embedding technique employed by Gottschaldt for visual patterns was reported by Britton, Meyer, Simpson, Holdredge & Curry (1979). They embedded the same paragraph in two different narratives. In one, the paragraph was of major importance, whereas in the second context the target paragraph was of minor importance. The critical information was recalled almost twice as well in the context in which it was important as in the other context. The authors believe this to be a retrieval phenomenon. It seems, however, that their experiment has by no means excluded a difference in encoding.

5. Inference

Section 17 dealt with phenomenal parts that have no geometrical counterparts. Evidence was presented there suggesting that "subjective contours" and "hidden edges," for example, are true parts of the trace. Experiments with verbal material suggest that the trace of verbal material likewise contains aspects not explicit in the learned text but *inferred* during acquisition. This has been shown for statements by Kintsch (1977) such as: "The discarded cigarette started the fire," commonly inferred from "A burning cigarette was carelessly discarded. The fire destroyed many acres of virgin forest [p. 337]," even though the first statement is not *explicitly* contained in the second one. Similar results have been reported by Honeck, Riechmann, and Hoffman (1975) for inferences from metaphors and Bransford and Franks (1971) and Barclay (1973) for inferences from statements. Paris and Lindauer (1976) have extended these observations to the encoding of inferences by children. The inferences, whether visual like the back side of Winston's wedges or verbal like inferences from statements, are not arbitrary and are not necessarily supplied by experience as is gratuitously assumed. For instance, nobody would encode the inference that the cigarette was discarded by an adult rather than a 5-year old, or that the fire started not from the cigarette but from a smoldering campfire left unattended, to name some possible inferences just as compatible with experience and logic. The difference between the actual inference and the myriad possible ones is this: The inference that the cigarette started the fire combines with the two explicit statements to form a more

92   3. EXTENTIONS OF THE THEORY

self-consistent whole. The other possible inferences, also available from experience, are gratuitous and ad hoc. Verbal inferences, like perceptual completions, are determined by the tendency of our cognitive apparatus to *maximize self-consistency,* not to accrete random bits of "highly associated" or "familiar" or "frequently experienced" items.

Inferences are so much a part of language use that young children 7 and 10 years of age consistently confuse inferences that are true but had not been learned with actually heard, learned, "old" statements (Paris & Carter, 1973). However, the drawing and utilization of inferences is task related. Adults (Craik & Tulving, 1975) and children about 7 years old (Paris & Lindauer, 1976) may or may not draw inferences, depending on the demands of the situation in which the information is acquired.

6. Levels of Processing

The matter of inferences is related to what has been called "depth of processing." Visual (Bower & Karlin, 1974) as well as verbal material (Craik & Tulving, 1975) can be coded "flimsily" or "deeply." Craik and Tulving (1975) have shown that depth of encoding:

> cannot be considered simply a function of (the number of) encoded attributes; the qualitative nature of these attributes is critically important.... Memory performance is enhanced to the extent that the encoding question or context forms an integrated unit with the target word.... An integrated or congruous encoding yields better memory performance, first, because a more elaborate trace is laid down and, second, because richer encoding implies greater compatibility with the structure, rules, and organization of semantic memory [p. 291].

Although my terminology is different, I believe that the "qualitative nature of the attributes" is what I have called *singular values of attributes.* The "elaborate" trace is what is here called a self-consistent trace, and Craik and Tulving's "compatibility with the structure, rules, and organization of semantic memory" is akin to the *normativeness* of a concept. Craik stated in his "Overview and Closing Comments" (Cermak & Craik, 1979) that undisputedly some encodings lead to better remembered traces than others. The disagreement is over what characterizes the more effective encodings. Within the theory proposed here, the answer is that those traces are most recallable that have the highest degree of internal consistency and singularity. This requires two things: (1) The stimulus must have potential singularities and self-consistencies; and (2) the learner must expend a sufficient processing effort (Tyler, Hertel, McCallum & Ellis, 1979) to discover these singularities and consistencies and encode them. Paris and Lindauer (1976) have shown that 7-year-old children tend *not* to elaborate their encoding of sentences to the extent that 11-year olds do. However, if the 7-year group is instructed to playact the content of the sentences, they do as well as the

11-year olds. Paris and Lindauer have made a good case for assuming that the elaboration of the trace consists of drawing inferences, spontaneous inferences on the part of the 11-year olds, and inferences in the course of playacting by the 7-year group.

Schulman (1974) has shown that incongruous relationships as in "Is a dungeon a scholar?" lead to less stable traces than *congruous,* what is here called *self-consistent,* verbal structures like "Is a corkscrew an opener?" However, it remains to be investigated what memory effects arise from various *degrees* of congruity. Aside from *not being* a scholar, a dungeon *is* harshly confining, an abode, a room, part of some buildings, made of stone, has a floor, can be large or small, and so forth. Some of these features are central to the notion of dungeon, whereas others are quite peripheral. One might expect that central features form more stable and better recallable traces than congruous but peripheral ones.

Since the idea of Levels of Processing was first proposed by Craik and Lockhart (1972), essentially only two levels have been found, formal levels, like upper and lower case print, or rhymes, and the meaning or semantic level. The notion of organization and structure, with parts established by their function in the whole and distinguished by the "strength" with which the parts depend on each other, what we have called self-consistency, suggest that there should be levels of processing *within* the semantic level. The following is an example of processing on three semantic levels: One group of subjects was presented with the numbers 581215192226. The instructions preceding the presentation of the numbers, what we now call the orientation task, were: "I will show you a list of digits. Read it slowly three times so that you can recite it afterward. For example, if the numbers are 390714628, then you read 'three hundred and ninety, seven hundred and fourteen' and so forth." The subjects then read the material as if 581, 215, 192, 226 had been presented to them.

The second group was told: "I will show you a list of digits. Read it slowly three times in order to know it completely and precisely." The subjects were then presented with a card on which was typed: "The Federal expenditures in the last year amounted to $ . . . " followed by a second card with 5812151922.26. (This experiment took place in 1939. The author admits that adding the decimal point flaws the experiment.) Those subjects who were permitted to use pencils marked off triples and read 5 billion, 812 million, 151 thousand, 922 dollars, and 26 cents. Those not permitted pencils read the figure in the same way but more slowly.

A third group was merely told to "try to learn the following series." They then received the same card as the first group.

In an immediate test, all groups did well; the third group was a little slow. In a surprise test 1 week later, the first group did poorly, the second group did hardly better, but some members of the third group made no errors at all. The first group had coded a list of numbers with a minimum of internal structure. Many members of the second group remembered that "the federal debt" was 5.8 billion or more than 5 billion 810 million, which in effect was better than what group one remembered. In the third group, however, many subjects had discovered the inner structural principle of the series, 5(+3)8(+4)12(+3)15(+4)19, etc. This led to the very stable encoding 5 8 12 15 19 22 26, which easily survived a week. The experiment is from Katona (1940/1967) pp. 9-11 and p. 189. Much of Katona's work is directly pertinent to the issue of levels of human processing. Surprisingly, it is not mentioned by any of Cermak and Craik's (1979) symposium contributors.

7. Singularity and Schema

Singularity and its hallmarks, sensitivity to change, self-consistency, and normativeness, increasingly appear in verbal research but often are not recognized because of a strong empiristic bias. Here are two observations in which singularity seems to play an essential part.

In two independent studies, the input was provided to the subjects partly verbally and partly pictorially (Bower, Karlin, & Dueck, 1975; Bransford & Johnson, 1972). Bransford and Johnson supplied an obscure text with or without an explanatory picture. Bower et al. provided obscure drawings with or without explanatory captions. Unfortunately, neither paper tested the explanatory material by itself. Both papers found that the obscure material was not only better understood but also better recalled with the benefit of the explanatory material. Both papers "emphasize the crucial role of semantic contexts" (Bransford and Johnson, p. 725) and report a "unification or knitting together of the disparate parts ... into a coherent whole or schema" (Bower et al. p. 218). In both studies the added material *increases the self-consistency* of the to-be-learned material. Even though item for item the subject has to learn "more" material, self-consistency creates a more stable trace, recall improves, and the memory load actually *decreases,* exactly as in Katonas group three mentioned earlier.

A *schema* is invoked with increasing frequency by Bartlett (1932), Norman and Rumelhart (1975), Neisser (1976), Kintsch (1977), and many others. Schemata serve to *organize experience.* In the work of Bransford and Johnson and of Bower et al., the explanatory material supplied the schema by which the material could be understood. In other situations, the context or the subject's experience provides the necessary schema, or "frame" (Minsky, 1975), or categories (Rosch, 1973a, b), or concepts (Posner & Keele, 1968). Section 15 showed for visual schemata (Palmer, 1975a) that singularities play a major part in establishing a schema. The same arguments apply to verbal or propositional material.

Kintsch, Mandel, and Kozminsky (1977) found that their subjects could summarize scrambled stories as easily as unscrambled ones. They report that in either case, the subjects ended up with a: "macrostructure which corresponded to their *story schema.* If the story is less predictable *from the knowledge of the schema,* this restructuring of scrambled texts is not completely successful [p. 552]." What these experiments do prove is the ability of the subjects to perceive the inner logic or self-consistency of the material, what Kintsch et al. call predictability. What they do not necessarily prove are the parts of their statement quoted in italics; namely, that the story schema that guided the subjects was *learned.* We comprehend a story in such a way that its inner logic, its self-consistency, the predictability of each part from the rest, as Kintsch et al. put it (as Bear, 1973 found for dot patterns), is *maximized.*

This is not to deny that cultural conventions, milieu, upbringing, outlook, and prior experience in the widest sense modulate the perception of texts. In this sense, we certainly use learned schemata to understand and summarize a story. Kintsch and Greene (1978) have shown that to western readers Indian myths are significantly more *bizarre* than stories from the Decameron, even though randomly selected *sentences* from the two sources do not differ in bizarreness. Bizarreness connotes lacking internal consistency, violating conventional norms, and lacking predictability. Without a culture-specific schema, the reader cannot unlock certain macrostructures. He may even perceive a different, unintended structure, as Mandler and Johnson (1977) point out, which makes the story obscure.

Once the macrostructure is established, schemata enter in another sense of that word: How good, self-consistent, logical, well-told, coherent, informative is the story? These aspects also depend on past experiences, on one's schemata in a sense, but they also depend on structural characteristics of the story. The two meanings of "schema" are neither independent of each other nor are they identical. It appears that Bartlett, and later Kintsch, use schema mainly in the sense of a culture-specific framework for understanding, which is clearly a matter of prior experience. To understand Bartlett's ghost story, one has to know for instance what ghosts do at night, what happens when people die, how and when the soul leaves the body, and how ghosts make war. Culture-related schemata govern, say, a 15th century morality play or a classic Greek tragedy. But given the shared conventions of the schema, say, the knowledge or stereotype of a good fairy, a wicked stepmother, or a greedy person, there still are good, well-formed and bad, poorly told stories.

In some stories, details tend to be added or changed or omitted in recall. In the fable of the greedy dog, for instance (Mandler & Johnson, 1977), the dog snaps at the mirror image of the meat in the water, thereby losing the meat already in his mouth. The moral is that greed not only goes unrewarded but ends in a loss instead. One subject renders the ending by saying that the dog lost his balance and fell over, and that was the end of the dog. This kind of substitution illustrates a principle known from the analysis of visual form (Goldmeier, 1972; Section 29; Kopfermann, 1930; Ternus, 1926; Wertheimer, 1923), namely, that the function of a part tends to be encoded and thus preserved, even if the carrier of the function is lost from the trace or is substituted. The function of the last sentence

3. EXTENTIONS OF THE THEORY

of the fable is to illustrate that a greedily hoped-for gain turns into a loss. Either of the two endings serves that function. The macrostructure is encoded and preserved; the microstructure is changed. The change in this case goes beyond what Sachs (1967) found. The change is not merely in the wording; it is substantive. But the change involves a *nonsingular* detail. The *moral* is preserved even though it is illustrated differently, an instance of change of a nonsingular item, case (c), Section 14. This substitution may be called a reconstruction. The reconstruction is not caused by extraneous, strongly associated material, however, but created within the constraint of the function this part of the story has, namely, to *exemplify the moral* of the story.

The picture of text representation advocated here is similar to the model proposed by Kintsch and van Dijk (1978). I list here some major points of agreement with these authors and a minor point of disagreement. According to Kintsch and van Dijk (1978): "Text bases are not... unrelated lists of propositions; they are coherent, structured units. One way to assign a structure to a text base may be derived from its referential coherence [p. 365]." This formulation is the equivalent of what is here called the self-consistency aspect of a whole. The hierarchic structure of more extensive wholes corresponds to the distinction of a "local microlevel" versus a "global macrolevel." Kintsch and van Dijk (1978) stress that *an associative stringing together of local propositions* does not create a meaningful topic of discourse. "Relating propositions in a local manner is not sufficient. There must be a global constraint that establishes a meaningful whole [p. 366]." They stress the role of parsing (p. 378), which they unfortunately have called "cycling." They distinguish micropropositions, our case (c), from macropropositions, our case (a), and find, as we do in Part II of this book, that the rates of forgetting or change with time are much higher in case (c) than in case (a), and that change over a 3-months interval is directed toward the macropropositions, our case (b) of Part II (Kintsch & van Dijk, 1978, pp. 377–378).

We differ with Kintsch and van Dijk in regard to the role of the schema. Although a schema *can be* conventionally imposed, a format prescribed, there is also the alternative, customarily overlooked; that the text creates its own schema intrinsically. The inner logic of a text, of a play, or of a treatise determines the "story line" or the essence of the text. The structure implicit in a well-told story or in a well-reasoned brief or a well-written research report may be *conventional,* but it need not be. Brown (1979) writes: "The use of the term *schema* is widespread, vague, and not always overladen with meaning. One of my favorite games is to remove the word *schema* from a paper written in schemateese and look for changes in meaning.... To be fair [p. 231]." To be fair, there is an inner structure that may well be called a *schema,* but the gratuitous suggestion that a schema is always imposed from without, normative, and above all *learned* is another vestige of the pervasive empiristic bias that has plagued psychology for far too long.

8. Macrostructure of the Trace

In their analysis of short stories, Mandler and Johnson (1977) found many counterparts of the trace structure posited here for visual material:

1. The more a story conforms to an "ideal structure," the better it will be recalled. Specifically, recall is better if "all the basic nodes of an ideal structure" are there and are in the "expected sequence." Like Kintsch and his group, Mandler and Johnson suggest that "ideal" and "expected" structures are acquired *from experience,* in conformance with the prevailing empiricist climate. But experience should not be uncritically invoked. The "ideal structures" and "expected sequences" are precisely those that maximize self-consistency and inner logic. Actually, the goings-on in most fables, where animals expostulate and sermonize, or Alice's adventures in Wonderland, or Captain Ahab's adventures, are neither *familiar* nor *frequently encountered* nor *expected* nor predictable from past experience. But, intrinsically, they are self-consistent and are possessed of their own inner logic.

2. Information that does not carry the story line tends to be forgotten. This applies to mere elaborations, such as clauses explaining how or why something is done, or temporal bridges, like "when he got home," or propositions that are deletable from the text without disturbing the flow of the narrative. All these will be less well and less accurately recalled than the items subserving the structure of the story.

3. Episodes will be recalled better if they are causally (i.e., logically) connected with the rest of the narrative, than if the connection is merely a temporal coincidence, a juxtaposition, what Wertheimer called an *and-sum;* in short, the stuff associations are made of.

4. The same event is recalled better or worse, depending on its *function* within the structure, the context in which it is embedded.

5. If the propositions of a story are presented in improper sequence, then the proper sequence tends to be restored in recall. This is an instance of case (b) of Section 14, the change of near-singularity toward a singularity.

9. Singularity of Category Members

Singularity of features has been addressed in the verbal domain only gingerly and infrequently. Exceptions are, however, becoming more numerous. Rosch (1973a, 1975a, c) has extended the investigation of singular values of colors, directions, and patterns to members of categories. Among category members, singularity means typicality (Rosch et al., 1976a, b); the prototype of a category possesses a preponderance of the core features of the category (feathers, wings, beak, for birds). *Typically,* the feature cluster is self-consistent (a bird typically

3. EXTENTIONS OF THE THEORY

has wings *and* can fly) and normative (a newly hatched bird is not prototypical, a broken tricycle is not a typical toy).

Rosch has found that categories, or concepts, are formed around attributes that singularly characterize a class. According to Rosch et al. (1976a), these attributes are *ideally* present, are typical but: "need not be true of all items classifiable as members of the category [p. 433]," as, for instance, the ability to fly, typical for birds but not found in every bird. Rosch and Mervis (1975) have stated:

> Division of the world into categories is not arbitrary. The basic category cuts in the world are those which separate the information-rich bundles of attributes which form natural discontinuities.... Formation of prototypes of categories appears to be likewise nonarbitrary.... Prototypes appear to be just those members of a category which most reflect the redundancy structure of the category as a whole.... Categories form to maximize the information-rich clusters in the environment and, thus, the cue validity of the attributes of categories [p. 620].

Categories tend to be perceived as discrete entities, even when they actually shade continuously into neighboring categories. This cognitive separation is achieved by coding the category around singularities in the continuum of characteristic attributes. Categories are coded around "good" examples or prototypes. A typical adult is neither aged 16 nor 91; a typical tree is neither a bonsai tree nor a giant redwood. These examples should not be taken to mean that typical is the same as average. Justice Oliver Wendell Holmes may be the prototype of a judge. He certainly was well above average as a judge. The prototype represents a *singular combination of features and of parts,* which together have properties different from the features separately. Icarus plus feathers, even in mythology, does not quite make a bird. Max Weber (1917) has based his research in sociology on prototypes, which he called "ideal types." The prototypical constellation of attributes creates a singular object. All that applies to singularity in perception also applies here. If an item is typical, it is readily identified as a member of the category. Slight deviations from typicality, case (b), Section 14, are conspicuous (say, a dented fender on an otherwise perfect new car). Prototypes can become stereotypes (also case (b)) as in "Mother knows best," "the roaring twenties," "birds can fly." Rosch et al. (1976a) speak of "exaggeration of structure [p. 434]" and point out that this kind of simplification makes it easier to deal with the infinite variability of our experience. The misleading inaccuracy of the stereotype is the price we pay for imposing more order on our world.

In general, the encoding of near-singular items, case (b) of Section 14, causes an asymmetry in the trace structure, as these items are coded close to the singularity. As Rosch found "exaggeration," so Bock and Brewer (1974) found a "recall bias" in the direction of the preferred form of two alternative sentence forms. They compared prompted recall of sentence pairs like "The magician touched the girl and the girl disappeared" and "The magician touched the girl and she disappeared." With most such pairs, one version "sounds better" or is "more natural." They obtained preference ratings for the sentences and found that the preferred version is recalled unchanged in 51% of their cases and changed to the lower rated alternative in only 5%. The nonpreferred versions were recalled unchanged in only 31% of the trials and changed to the preferred version in 27% of otherwise correct recalls. (The remaining 44 and 44%, respectively, were incorrect or unsuccessful recalls.)

If a category member is far from typical, say, gelatin as a food or a person as an animal, we have the nonsingular case (c) of Section 14. In this case, category membership predicts very little about the item; hence, features and their values are hardly constrained by knowing that the item is within the category. This case is exemplified by points 1, 2, 3, and 4 of Mandler and Johnson's analysis in (8) earlier.

10. Encoding Specificity

Gottschaldt's paradigm (Section 15) is to train the subject with a target pattern, then to test for recognition of this same pattern embedded in a larger complex. He finds that in some of the instances recognition fails, even though the target pattern in isolation is recallable. Tulving and his collaborators, in a series of papers (Tulving & Thomson, 1973), used the *reverse paradigm* to show what amounts to the verbal analog of Gottschaldt's results:

> target words T (e.g., CHAIR) were presented at input in the company of cue words C (e.g., *glue*). Subjects expected to be tested for recall of T with C as a cue. When, instead of presenting C as a cue, the experimenter provided another word X (e.g., *table*)—which was a close semantic associate of the target word T but which had not appeared anywhere in the list—as an extralist retrieval cue, subjects could not readily use it as an aid in recall of T [p. 778].

Tulving and Watkins (1977) conclude from such studies: "that the target words... were specifically encoded with respect to, and as an integral part of, their study contexts, and that the resulting memory traces were sometimes more readily accessible through retrieval information extracted from one type of cue, for instance the context phrase, than another, for instance the copy of the nominal target [p. 520]." The implication is that the nominal target (the word itself) is not independently coded. An increasing number of other studies are coming to similar conclusions. All these authors are discovering for words what Gottschaldt had found for isolated patterns: Both verbal material and patterns tend to behave like chemical radicals. They are highly reactive. In a suitable environment, they combine with other words or materials to form molecules, become parts of larger entities, and lose some or all of their identity as they are incorporated into larger units. An isolated pattern, syllable, word, or even sentence often is coded only within the trace of the larger unit but not by itself. There is no trace of arbitrary elements, as there is no trace of EMBER in the trace of November and no trace of COIN in the trace of coincidence.

A related area of research is *encoding specificity,* a phenomenon identified by Tulving and his collaborators (summarized in Tulving & Watkins, 1977). Encoding specificity is not so much a principle as it is a postulate, an axiom of memory theory. To put it epigrammatically and somewhat cryptically, the axiom states: *We encode what we perceive and remember what we encode.* Initially, the axiom was invoked in situations of outright ambiguity. (Tulving worked with words, but the axiom applies universally. I use here visual examples.) Anybody who sees Fisher's (1968) ambiguous picture as a girl *only* will encode a girl and will recognize a less-ambiguous girl picture but not a less-ambiguous picture of the man, and vice versa. Encoding specificity makes the center in Fig. 46 an N or a Z. The trace incorporates only those features that were part of the percept but not the features that define the alternatives inherent in the stimulus configuration.

This concludes this sampling of verbal memory research. It has demonstrated, I trust, that the encoding theory developed here is applicable to memory for verbal and conceptual material as well as for the visual memory from which it originated.

19. SYNOPSIS OF ENCODING

The theory of encoding proposed here originated in a trace theory for visual data. However, it is intended to apply to all human encoding. This generalization is founded on the belief that human information processing is an offshoot of the visual stimulus processing of higher mammals and organized along the same lines.

Be that as it may, visual as well as verbal and conceptual traces are regarded in this theory as the end product of a drastic data reduction. The reduction is accomplished in three ways: by establishing a hierarchy of subdivisions, by establishing a limited number of parts and features at each level of subdivision, and by providing only a limited degree of accuracy of most values of these features. As to the hierarchy, it should be stressed that there is no one global hierarchy as assumed in some memory theories. Rather, the hierarchies are local and often would not fit together if pursued to their ultimate logic. Also, they are often only temporary, to bring order to some limited domain of experience and subject to rearrangement as new material accrues.

The subdivision of the world starts as a top-down process. It leads to as few subdivisions as possible, while still allowing to understand, organize, and appreciate the world. For example, in antiquity, the material world was subdivided conceptually into four elements: earth, air, fire, and water. Contemporary lore

19. SYNOPSIS OF ENCODING   101

has it that there are 92 elements plus a few more man-made ones. The former subdivision is the more parsimonious one and, at least in the account of Heraclitus, the more persuasive. Today's version, on the other hand, has greater self-consistency, considering all we now know in chemistry. Neither subdivision is a mere list. According to Thales of Miletus, earth, air, and fire are ultimately made of water. Bertrand Russell (1945) regards this: "as a scientific hypothesis and by no means a foolish one. Twenty years ago, the received view was that everything is made of hydrogen, which is two thirds of water [p. 26]." Heraclitus did not share the view of Thales and Russell, believing that of the four elements, fire is the principal one. The modern Table of Elements also is more than an unstructured list. The table is "periodic" in an intricate way. There are subgroups including, among others, alkali metals and "noble" gases. Rosch et al. (1976a) propose that in general, subgroups are so formed that membership in a group carries: "the most information, possesses the highest. . . . cue validity and. . . . thus (keep the subgroups) the most differentiated from one another [p. 382]." The result is maximum discriminability of a minimum of entities, characterized by their function within any one level of the hierarchy.

Each object so conceived is endowed with features. The features are so assigned as to conform to a minimum principle, depending not only on the object itself but also on the group of which the object is a member. Garner (1974) writes "The properties of the single stimulus cannot be specified except in relation to the properties of the sets within which it exists [p. 9]." As one's universe enlarges, more features are psychologically activated, and the depth of processing increases apace. A good example, too involved to relate here in detail, is the increase in the ability to remember and discriminate oriental rug patterns. This ability increases as a function of schooling in general and of professional experience with rugs in particular (Wagner, 1978). The more one needs to know, the more features are activated, but only "relevant" features. What is relevant depends on the situation of the organism. In the psychological laboratory, it often depends on an "orienting task."

Finally, the memory load is minimized by admitting only few values for each feature, values called here *singular*. If a feature happens to have a nonsingular value, then it is coded only coarsely, within an approximate range of values measured by its approximate deviation from singularities. This achieves precise coding in a few areas of biological importance at the expense of vague coding in most others. For instance, when memorizing how to find the way to a destination, one focuses on a few "landmarks" leaving many other features along the way only vaguely characterized. If the shortest way lacks singular features, easily codable landmarks, one may even choose a less-direct path, provided it is "easier to remember." Similarly, people who live in an apartment know related aspects of the floor plan, like the relation of the living room to the adjoining balcony. However, even after years of occupancy, they do not encode unrelated aspects like the relation of the balcony to the nearby bedroom, a bedroom that is

3. EXTENTIONS OF THE THEORY

neither visible nor accessible from the balcony (Norman & Rumelhart, 1975, p. 21-23). *Encoding is selective and parsimonious.* If there is a concise formulation of the proposed coding theory, it is: *The world is coded in such a way that a maximum of information is represented by a minimum of psychological objects, with a minimum of parts, with the parts represented by their functions within the whole and possessing a minimum of features, and the fewest values of these features.*

II THE FATE OF THE TRACE

some widely held views have to be completely discarded, and none more completely than that which treats recall as the reexcitement in some way of fixed and changeless 'traces'.
—Bartlett, 1932

4
Theory of Memory Change

20. MEMORY CHANGE

Part II deals with the fate of the trace after it has been formed. The very notion that the trace could change after being safely deposited in a memory bank runs counter to conventional memory theories. The implicit assumption of these theories is that the whole purpose of memory is: (1) to preserve information *intact;* and (2) to retrieve the correct piece of information on demand. The ideal embodiment of that kind of memory is a computer memory. It is an anxiom of both computer design and association theory that information in memory is in dead storage. Any change that occurs is a mishap, an *error*. Because people are not as perfect as computers, memory theorists see their task in devising models explaining the errors humans make, where "errors" includes wrong answers as well as no answers. Consider two examples. The first is the list of letters, T, T, T; C, C, T; A, T, T; G, A, G. There are 12 items formed from four kinds of letters, A, G, C, T. *One* error might be a replacement of the second T by a C. The second example is a paraphrase of a proposition in Anderson and Bower's (1973) book: The Hippie and the Debutante Kissed in the Park. This sentence contains four items of information. The following might be an example of *four* errors: The boy and the girl embraced on the lawn. In the first example, there was an 8% error rate (1 in 12), in the second, 4 in 4, or 100% errors. Now look at the two examples differently. Let each of the four letter triples stand for a codon on the DNA molecule. The first one, TTT, codes for phenylalanine. The wrong one, TCT, codes for serine; a 25% error, but a substitution that can be 100% fatal. For instance, substituting the amino acid valine for glutamic acid changes normal

4. THEORY OF MEMORY CHANGE

hemoglobin into sickle-cell hemoglobin. What in the memory code may be a negligible error, 8%, can in the genetic code lead to an irreparable error.

In the other example, the opposite is true. Whereas in some contexts, it might matter that the boy was a hippie, the girl a debutante, and precisely what they did where; for many purposes, the 100% erroneous statement preserves all the information that matters. What is preserved is quite central to the original, what is left out (what kind of boy) or substituted (lawn for park) is peripheral. Admittedly, there are cases where the exact and complete information is needed. An "approximate" identification of the accused would not do in a court of law. A telephone number known to a 1% accuracy would not help very much. But, in general, our memories would be hopelessly cluttered if traces could not change in the direction of gist and simplification (Kintsch & van Dijk, 1978). Part II gives a theoretical and experimental account of memory change, consistent with the notions of trace structure developed in Part I.

Memory change is of course a matter of every day experience. Conventional memory theories account for it by a combination of fading, reconstruction, and extrinsic effects on the trace. Fading and reconstruction is an extrinsic mechanism if the reconstruction uses materials extrinsic to the trace. Extrinsic causes for memory change have been proposed ever since Wulf's (1922) proposal of intrinsic change, of change due to stress within the trace, was made. Hanawalt (1937) retested Wulf's designs in a study using improved procedures but was unable to confirm Wulf's claims. So, he and Woodworth (1938) concluded that the changes they found were best described by a theory of fading-plus-reconstruction, where the change occurred either at the time of acquisition or of reproduction of the designs. The material for the reconstruction phase was assumed to be extrinsic, to consist of familiar objects or words that somehow became associated with the memorized pattern. As the trace of the pattern faded, the association would become increasingly effective and dominate the reconstruction. Most theorists felt that Hanawalt's monograph and a subsequent paper (Hanawalt & Demarest, 1939) furnished a convincing alternative to the Wulf-Koffka hypothesis ascribing change to stress within the trace, or *intrinsic* stress. The Hanawalt-Woodworth explanation of fading-plus-reconstruction was more in tune with the associative memory theories then and now prevailing (Woodworth, 1938; Anderson & Bower, 1973) and is widely accepted. I felt then and believe still that both extrinsic and intrinsic mechanisms play a role in memory change. This is not to deny that both fading and reconstruction do occur. As to fading, any theory of memory change must assume some mechanism of weakening of the trace once the stimulus is no longer active. There is also no doubt that some changes of the trace are due to importation of associated material. Reconstruction in that sense has, however, been shown only under special circumstances. Carmichael et al. and Hanawalt and Demarest used *ambiguous* patterns and gave biasing verbal labels suggesting one of the two objects represented by the drawing (Fig. 47). Hanawalt (1937) used Wulf's patterns, many of which were weak wholes, in many ways nonsingular and with little inner stress to begin with. They showed random changes that were almost unclassifiable. There were few instances of obvious, identifiable reconstruction, just as there were few clear-cut changes in the direction of intrinsic stress. The most convincing evidence for extrinsic effects on the trace and reconstruction of memory content comes from the much more recent research of E. F. Loftus (1979b). It shows how eye witnesses can be misled by being given false information after they have witnessed an event. In these experiments, extrinsic change is achieved by adding contradictory information to an existing trace. As Loftus indicates, it remains undecided whether the new information changes the trace or merely suppresses or supersedes it (Loftus 1979a). Extrinsic changes represent that part of the processing of the trace that assimilates the new trace into the existing system of traces. This fitting-in can result in a change of the new trace, but sometimes it is accomplished by changing old, existing traces, as Loftus has demonstrated. Whether or not the trace changes depends on whether the new information can be incorporated without destroying the self-consistency of the old representation. If the misinformation is too "blatant," the old trace will not change (Loftus, 1979c). The role of extrinsic changes in our theory is described in Section 64. Having agreed that extrinsic material interacts with a trace so that memory is changed, the question arises: Can change also occur from intrinsic or autochthonous stress, from stress entirely within the trace? This alternative is often not envisaged, because association theory assumes an atomistic picture of the trace, a trace devoid of inner structure. In association theory, it matters little whether one uses syllables, words, dot patterns, phrases, or sentences. "The lan and the pum" is in association theory equivalent to "the hippie and the debutante" used by Anderson and Bower, and the computer that models their theory would accept pum as easily as debutante. In the absence of inner structure, associationism is committed to consider *all memory change* as extrinsic. Hanawalt and Woodworth came to that conclusion and no other associationistic explanation of the phenomenon has appeared since. The explanation is based more on associationistic doctrine, which requires that similar and familiar objects and words associate themselves spontaneously to the trace, than on experimental fact. I have argued the case for intrinsic change in a 1941 paper, summarized by Riley in 1962. The arguments are these:

1. The fact that extrinsic material *can* change memory, especially memory for ambiguous (Carmichael et al., 1932; Hanawalt, & Demarest, 1939) or poorly integrated, nonsingular material (Gibson, 1929; Hanawalt, 1937) or memory for irreconcilable "facts" (Loftus, 1979b), does not prove that the organization of less ambiguous patterns *is* guided by outside influences, nor does it leave outside affiliations as the only possible source of material for change.

108   4. THEORY OF MEMORY CHANGE

2. It is difficult to see why the outside material supposedly associated to the trace during learning should not fade along with the trace and become less and less effective as time passes. Change, on the other hand, increases with time.

3. If the outside material accrues later, then it is less and less able to contact the trace because the trace has faded so much.

4. The activities of organizing and data reduction that lead to the formation of the trace are unlikely to cease abruptly when the stimulus subsides. It is more probable that the reworking of data continues, processing the trace to deeper and deeper levels, to use Craik and Lockhart's phrase, until is has reached the maximum of stability of which it is capable and fits as best it can into the body of already stored information.

5. The notion of reconstruction is vague. If it means a random association akin to guessing, it is testably different from intrinsic change, as is shown later. If reconstruction follows the intrinsic stress of the trace, then there is no difference between the two theories except in terminology.

This puts the debate on an experimental basis. Chapter 4 describes a theory about the nature and the effect of internal stress and develops specific, testable hypotheses. These predictions are tested in Chapters 5, 6, and 7. Fading theory is discussed in more detail in Section 24.

21. INTRINSIC STRESS

In the passage quoted in Section 2, Wertheimer makes the point that an observer is not free to impose an arbitrary grouping on a given stimulus array. On the contrary, there are powerful forces that compel particular groupings and exclude most of the infinitely many others. Likewise, some features in the stimulus array are salient; they are what is here called *singular*. Other features are *close to* a salient value, *nearly* singular, whereas still other relationships or potential attributes are only *approximately* coded. Finally, the vast majority of conceivable attributes are not psychologically represented at all.

The process of trace formation is comparable to the writing of a historical account. Many documents and artifacts exist; many of these are evaluated, some are discarded, others are condensed, and eventually a few are organized into a coherent description. The final result incorporates only a fraction of the raw data, but it organizes the data into a whole in as logical a fashion as the material permits. Encoding is a process in which as much order as possible is imposed, given the material and given the capabilities of the processor. Stress arises when the stimulus material does not permit a maximum of regularity or simplification, when it falls short of complete inner logic or has features that lack perfect singularity. As the trace forms, the stresses toward complete consistency and singularity remain in the trace and are "frozen in," like the stresses in a piece of glass as it cools from the melt. The stress persists long after the stimulus array has subsided. The stresses in the trace represent: (1) imperfections in the way the trace is organized into parts; and (2) deviations from singular values of features.

A theory that postulates a system of stresses must specify where in the trace the stress is located, how severe it is, and in which direction it acts. Again, as in connection with feature values, Section 14, three situations occur and must be distinguished.

Case (a). If the partition into parts is perfect and cannot be improved with a given material or if features have singular values, then the trace contains no stress at all. Examples of maximally perfect partitions are Fig. 34a and b, given the limited domain of 5-dot patterns in 3 × 3 matrices. Each part has a function, each function is represented by a part. In the domain of journalism, a perfect report would be a report that is well-organized, leaves no pertinent questions unasked, and leaves no posed questions unanswered. A perfect report would be free of irrelevant details and asides but would account for all parts of the topic. Similar specifications can be drawn up for an ideal psychological research report or for stories (Kintsch & van Dijk, 1978). At a lower level of verbal expression, the choice of words and phrases can be felicitous, communicate meaning well or do so poorly, as Edwin Newman (1975) has demonstrated so well. If words express meaning perfectly, then there is no stress at that level of the trace. If two sentences express the same meaning, then the version that is more apt has less intrinsic stress, more stability, than the version judged less apt (R. C. Anderson, 1974).

Case (a), singularity, includes those features that have singular values. For instance, in Fig. 36a, the upper border is a smooth curve; its trace has no stress. The dot positions of the triangle in Fig. 42 likewise are singular, and therefore without stress. In a well-constructed narrative, everything eventually "falls into place," no "loose ends" remain. The story line is as smooth as the upper border of Fig. 36a, although, like the border, it may have ups and downs.

Case (b): Near-Singularity. The strongest stress occurs if the organization of a pattern is *almost* right, the set of parts *nearly* perfect. With feature values, the strongest stress occurs if the value is *close to but not quite at* a singular point. The stress can be so strong that a missing part is mistakenly perceived as present, or a superfluous part as absent, or a nearly singular value mistaken for singular, especially if perception is impaired, as for instance in brief tachistoscopic exposures.

Pattern Changes in Case (b). Bear (1973) presented 4-dot subpatterns of Garner's 5-dot patterns to his subjects with the instruction to place an additional dot into the matrix in a cell "implied or suggested" by the dots already present. In each of the three patterns of Fig. 57, the demand character of one position was so strong that 97, 93, and 93%, respectively, of all subjects chose that one

110 4. THEORY OF MEMORY CHANGE

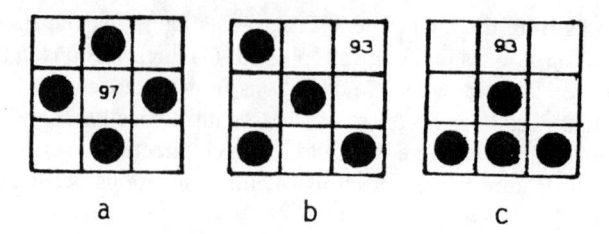

FIG. 57. Three 4-dot patterns used by Bear (1973). The number in each array indicates the percentage of Bear's subjects who chose that position for placing a fifth dot.

position out of the five available placements. The other four cells were practically never chosen (see Fig. 57). This kind of completion experiment can also be performed with words, phrases, sentences, and extended stories. The recognition experiments of Sections 52 and 59 likewise illustrate near-singularity, case (b). The stress in these cases is measured by the tendency toward certain pattern changes and by avoidance of others.

Feature changes illustrating case (b) originate from *nearly* singular values. The level-1 or -3 distortions of the triangle are representative. They are moderate distortions of the equilateral triangle of Fig. 42 and are perceived as the triangle with *slight imperfections,* judging from the findings of Posner et al. (1967). The strong tendency to perceive nearly singular feature values as "referred to the singularity" has led Rosch (1975a) to designate singularities as *cognitive reference points*. Rosch showed that *nearly* singular colors, *almost* vertical and horizontal lines, and *nearly* round numbers are perceived, or thought of, as slight variations from the singularity. Rosch performed two experiments. In the first one, the subjects were presented with a singular and a nearly singular color, line, or number and given a sentence like "x is essentially y." There was a highly significant preference for inserting the nearly singular item into the x position and the singular item into the y slot. For example, "103 is roughly 100" was significantly more common than "100 is roughly 103." In control experiments like "167 is roughly 164," there was no such preference. We return to the controls, which are relevant in themselves, in the discussion of case (c).

In a second experiment, Rosch used the same materials to determine the *phenomenal distance* of nearly singular items from the singular ones, and vice versa. The nearly singular item was perceived as significantly closer to the singular item than the singular item was to the almost singular one. In other words, there is an asymmetry in the perception of distance. The distance is longer when measured from the singular member to the near-singular member of the pair, shorter from the nearly singular member. Again, the asymmetry was absent in control pairs, in which neither member was close to having singular values. The asymmetry is in effect a measure of the existing stress.

Asymmetries were also reported by Handel and Garner (1966). These authors asked their subjects to find for a given 5-dot pattern (from the set described in Sections 9 and 10) another pattern similar to it. The choice tended to be a pattern with a goodness rating *above* the rating of the stimulus. In terms of stress, there seems to be a stress in the representation of the stimulus toward a "better" pattern.

Stress in the direction of a better pattern and the resulting asymmetry has also been demonstrated in the domain of syntactic choices. Bock and Brewer (1974) used sentence pairs like "The magician touched the girl and the girl disappeared," versus "The magician touched the girl and she disappeared," or "Tarzan heard the jungle drums at sunset," versus "At sunset, Tarzan heard the jungle drums." In an experiment based on cued recall, the authors found "speech-output biases in favor of certain surface forms." Specifically, 51% of the preferred sentence forms were recalled unchanged, compared with only 31% of the unpreferred versions. Furthermore, 5% of the preferred forms shifted at recall to the unpreferred form, whereas 27% of the unpreferred sentences shifted in recall to the preferred form. Both results were highly significant ($p < .0005$). In stress terminology, there is a strong stress or a weak resistance to stress, which makes one permissible sentence form better or more singular than another also permissible form.

R. C. Anderson (1974) made a similar observation in an experiment mentioned earlier. His material consisted of 16 pairs of equivalent sentences, for example: *The princess ran after the thief. The princess chased the robber.* The pairs were rated for equivalence of meaning and aptness or wording. Memory was cued by the common subject of the two sentences and tested either immediately or after 24 hours. One of Anderson's results was that substitutions that preserved the meaning were less common in the sentences judged as aptly worded, what we call singular, case (a). In the sentences judged to be less felicitous, meaning-preserving substitutions were more common, our case (b).

In the conceptual domain, an asymmetry was found by Tversky (1977) between "prominent" countries and less-prominent ones: "For example, 66 subjects selected the phrase 'North Korea is similar to Red China' and only 3 selected the phrase 'Red China is similar to North Korea' [p. 334]." The same asymmetry appeared in similarity ratings. The similarity of the less-prominent to the prominent country was rated significantly higher than the similarity of the more prominent country to the lesser member of the same pair ($p < .01$).

Tversky attributes the asymmetry to a difference in saliency, which is what Rosch calls prototypicality, what Garner and many others call goodness, what Kintsch and many followers of Bartlett call conformance to a schema, and what is here called singularity.

Kintsch, Mandel, and Kozminsky (1977) examined summaries of stories presented to the subjects either scrambled or in proper order. They found: "that subjects reorder scrambled stories . . . so that the end product of comprehension is a macrostructure for the story that is not discriminably different from the macrostructure derived from the same story in its natural order [p. 552]." The stress in this case acts in the direction of the "unscrambling" of the text. Kintsch et al. (1977) believe that text comprehension is guided by a culturally determined story schema, rather than by the plausibility or inner logic or self-consistency of the story itself. Be that as it may, traditional schema or inner logic, there is an asymmetry. The unscrambled story is summarized unchanged, the story that is sequentially perturbed is restored to an unperturbed state. The restoration only occurs if the scrambled story is close to the schema, nearly singular. "If the story is less predictable from the knowledge of the schema, this restructuring of scrambled texts is not completely successful." We then approach case (c).

Case (c): Nonsingularity. This category includes poorly organized wholes, with unclear subdivisions, questionable borders, like the items in a lost-and-found department or the rubble after a tornado. In the semantic domain, snatches of conversation, irrelevancies, lists of syllables or words, and aimless rantings exemplify the nonsingular case. Among feature values, case (c) includes those values that are neither singular nor even nearly so (e.g., lines that are oblique, patterns that are irregular, like the level 7.7, 9.7 distortions, the random pattern of Fig. 42, and the poorest of Palmer's (1977) 6-line patterns). The nonsingular features of Figs. 21, 22, 23, and 24 are also examples of case (c). Case (c) includes poorly structured, irregular, "random" patterns and structureless lists of syllables, words, and sentences.

Nonsingularity is characterized by the absence of stress. The asymmetries found in case (b), which are a consequence of stress, are lacking in case (c). Rosch (1975a) examined nonsingular stimulus pairs, for instance, lines tilted at 22.5° and 32.5°, and found that about equal numbers of subjects chose the two possible orders in a sentence like "x is sort of y." Nonfocal colors and not-round numbers also were assigned to the two possible orders with about equal frequency. Rosch's second experiment, it is recalled, demonstrated marked asymmetries in judged distances, depending on whether they were measured from the singular to the nearly singular object or in the opposite direction. In the case of the nonsingular controls, case (c), no asymmetries appeared in the judged distance between colors, pairs of tilted lines, or number pairs.

Because the patterns of case (c) are neither regular nor singular, there is no stress, or at most very little stress. Irregular forms are not distinctive, do not suggest particular improvements, and do not demand or lead to further processing. The nonsingular attributes of case (c) are not sensitive to change, say, in similarity experiments, as shown in Fig. 21 or 22.

Stress is peculiar to case (b), the nearly singular features. Stress is absent in case (a) as well as in case (c), although for quite different reasons.

22. A MODEL OF STRESS

The following model illustrates the distinctions among case (a), (b), and (c). Imagine a ball, B in Fig. 58, on a surface with a cross section like the curve in Fig. 58. If the ball is placed in the bottom of the well, at (a), it is in a position of no stress and of maximal stability. It will have no tendency to move, but if it is even slightly displaced, then gravity strongly tends to return it to (a). This resistance to change is the defining characteristic of *singularity*. In this model, position *a* represents a singular value, case (a) of Sections 14 and 21.

If the ball is placed at (b), which is *near* but not exactly *at* a singular value, there will be a strong tendency to move in the direction of the singularity, at (a). This tendency corresponds to the strong stress of case (b) of the preceding section. It models the asymmetry between nearly singular values, which tend toward the singularity, and singular values, which are stable.

Finally, the ball placed at (c_1) or (c_2) also is under no stress, just like the ball at (a). But, unlike the situation at (a), even a large displacement causes neither stress nor a tendency to return to the original value at (c).

Two more features are needed to complete the model. The surface on which the ball rolls must provide something equivalent to friction, so that the position of the ball, which represents the trace, does not permit the ball to move so easily as to "forget" its position rapidly. The other feature is some form of random gaussian noise, say brownian or thermal motion or some vibration, which tends to push the ball slightly and randomly in either direction along the curve. Together, the two features introduce a time factor into the model, a relaxation time or annealing time, the time required for momentum to dissipate.

These various components of the model add up to the following: A singular feature, modeled by the ball at (a), is subject to three influences; the random vibration that causes displacement; a restoring force that increases monotonically and steeply with the displacement; and frictional damping that holds down oscillations. The result is little uncertainty of position at any time and no drift over the long term, corresponding to a stable, singular value of the feature represented. In terms of memory, the model predicts that singular aspects of traces do not change, even over very long time periods; they are stable.

FIG. 58. The ball (B) at position (a) is stable, not under stress. At position (b) there is a strong tendency for the ball to go to position (a): strong stress. At (c_1) or (c_2) the ball is under little stress to return to its initial position if it is displaced. Position (a) models singularity, (b) models near-singularity, (c) models nonsingularity. The roughness of the line models the friction slowing the ball down.

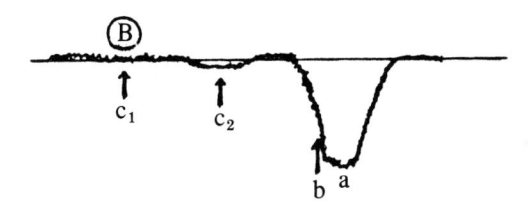

4. THEORY OF MEMORY CHANGE

A nearly singular feature, modeled by the ball at (b), is subject to the same random vibrations and damping as the ball at (a), but because of the steep slope at (b), gravity is a displacing, not a restoring, force. In case (b), gravity causes the ball to drift in the direction of (a). The rate of drift is inversely related to the friction and directly related to the vibratory energy and to the slope. As the ball approaches (a), the slope and therefore the rate of drift decreases and eventually the ball comes to rest at (a). In terms of memory, this behavior of the ball corresponds to a long-term change of nearly singular traces toward singularity.

Nonsingular features, modeled by the ball at (c_1) or (c_2) on the large horizontal region of the curve, are subject mainly to the vibration and the friction. These two factors combine to induce a random walk that is slow if friction is sufficiently high. The ball may drift in either direction with equal probability. If the curve is not completely horizontal, gravity comes into play. At (c_2), for instance, gravity tends to confine the ball within a shallow bowl in this particular curve. But, since the vibrations are gaussian, an occasional strong vibration may drive the ball over the edge toward (b) and eventually to (a). The ball could also go away from (b) and end up on the adjoining horizontal segment at (c_1). The most probable location of the ball is somewhere on the horizontal branch of the curve, not too far from where it was originally. At (c) as at (a), there is little stress because in both locations the curve is essentially horizontal. But unlike the situation at (a), there is no slope near to (c) that would confine the ball to a precise location. Consequently, after a long lapse of time, the position of the ball has considerable uncertainty. In terms of memory, the model predicts for nonsingular features a great deal of long-term change. The change can go in either direction; the exact value of nonsingular features is poorly preserved in memory, only vaguely or imprecisely remembered. As time goes by, information is increasingly lost.

What has been said for features applies also to wholes and their parts, the strength of wholes, the goodness of patterns, and the partitioning into parts. Case (a) refers to a stable grouping, case (b) to a nearly perfect partitioning with a strong tendency to change in storage toward perfection, and case (c) includes more or less poorly organized wholes, loose aggregates, typefied by random dot patterns, lists of syllables, letters or words, and a storage shed full of disordered items.

The curve on which the ball is placed represents the internal environment. This environment is initially preformed by heredity and subsequently modified and enriched by experience. The shape of the curve is therefore subject to wide variations, which form subgroups of the three main cases. Some of these are shown in Fig. 84. Figure 84*a* shows a variant of case (a) in which the singularity has a "fine structure." In this case, the ball is confined to the well with a high probability. Within the well, however, the ball could be found in any one of the three compartments, more likely one of the outer, deeper ones, less likely in the middle, not so deep one. We return to this variant in Section 63. Figure 84*b* shows a "potential well" divided into two compartments by a fairly high barrier. If the ball rests in one compartment, it tends to remain there unless one of the infrequent vibrations of higher energy helps the ball to jump into the other compartment, to "tunnel through the barrier" in the parlance of quantum physics. We return to this variant also in Section 63. Figure 62 (solid line) portrays a weaker singularity, with more gentle slopes. In this situation, the ball is less narrowly confined to the bottom point of the well, whether it was placed originally *close to* [case (b)] or *at* [case (a)] the lowest point. This is the situation described in Section 29. Figure 58 shows another kind of fine structure, namely, the irregularities that account for the friction mentioned before. Depending on the slope and on the scale of the irregularity relative to the average vibration, the drift along the surface will occur continuously or stepwise, and slowly or rapidly. These differences represent variations especially important for case (b) and (c), the near-singular and nonsingular case.

The horizontal part of the curve models the tabula rasa of Locke, the realm of nonsingular information, of trivial, ununderstandable knowledge and sundry experiences (case (c)). The horizontal is the locus of storage of such items as the position of dots in a random pattern, one's telephone number, or shoe size, or the names of the moons of Saturn. If a person remembers the moons of Saturn, then the curve is no longer flat but develops an indentation representing each moon. If this memory is poor, the identations are shallow. In the mind of an astronomer who specializes in the moons of Saturn, the identations are deep, with detailed inner structure, indistinguishable from the wells representing case (a). Nonsingular features are coded only approximately in case (c). The approximate coding includes an extended range of values, for instance, if a person is coded as "tall" rather than as of a specific height. Tallness is represented in the model as a very shallow bowl, without definite margins. In other instances, there are definite limits, as in the case of "frozen" against "liquid." There is a sharp border between liquid and frozen, but the regions extend far and almost level on the other side.

23. PREDICTED RESULTS

The brain is not populated by little balls any more than by arrays of Julesz' (1971) magnetic dipoles. But the model of the little ball in, or near, or far away from the "potential well," as it is called in physics, represents the relevant aspects of stress theory even for one unfamilar with potential theory. The model suggests a number of testable predictions. We begin with memory not for complex traces but for individual features, say, the slant of a line or the organization of a pattern at one particular level of the hierarchy, like the form in Fig. 6, as opposed to the material (dots) of which the form is made. The predictions will depend on whether the feature or organization falls under case (a), (b), or (c).

116   4. THEORY OF MEMORY CHANGE

If the feature is singular, say, the line is vertical, or the form is a perfect circle, or the inner dot exactly at the center (Fig. 6a), we have *case (a)*. Because there is no stress, the model predicts no memory change of this feature: (1) The trace is stable; it will be remembered unchanged; (2) the trace remains unchanged even after long periods of time.

In terms of remembered values of the feature, there will be few changes and no increase in changes with time. The distribution of recalled values approximates a Dirac δ function (Fig. 59a). Neither the mean nor the width of the distribution will change with time.

If a feature is *nearly* singular, say, a line is almost but not quite vertical, or there is a small irregularity at the "material" level, like the short fourth line in Fig. 36b, we have *case (b)*. In this case:

1. Marked change is expected.
2. The change is progressive over time.
3. The change is not random; it occurs only in the direction of the nearby singularity. For instance, the line becomes vertical; Fig. 36b changes to *a*.

In terms of remembered values (see Fig. 59b):

1. The mean of the distribution of remembered values shifts from the learned value *b* toward the singular value *a*.
2. This shift of the mean progresses with time.
3. There is little shift *away from* the singularity, in other words, the shift is *directed,* not random.

If a feature is *nonsingular,* say, the line is far from vertical or horizontal, or a pattern is poorly organized in a particular respect like the pattern of Fig. 71, where the line is tacked onto the triple arch, we have *case (c)*. Here, as in case (b), we expect: (1) high incidence of change; (2) Degree of change increasing with time; (3) unlike case (b), the change in case (c) is not unidirectional, but (4)

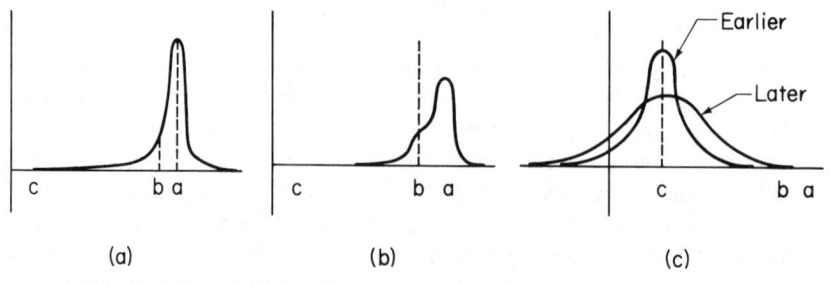

FIG. 59.   The distribution of remembered values, if the learned value was singular, *59a,* near-singular, *59b,* or nonsingular, *59c.*

as in case (a), the mean of the remembered values is unchanged; (5) unlike case (a), the width of the distribution of values increases with the passage of time. In other words, as the trace changes, it spreads out to more and more adjacent values. The number of changes, the extent of change, and the spread over possible values all increase with time, but the average of the values shifts very little. The whole distribution of values (Fig. 59c) flattens and widens with time, the standard deviation increases, and the mean stays near its original value. Because of the wide spread of values, ceiling and floor effects can intervene in case (c), especially after very long time intervals. Figure 59c shows two curves. The higher and narrower curve represents an earlier stage of change, the lower and wider curve a later stage.

This model and its predictions were formulated with features and feature values in mind. For parts and their functions within the whole, the same concepts apply, however. A strong whole with self-consistent structure, in which each part has a well-defined function, is stable, case (a). A whole with an imperfection, the situation investigated by Baer, Section 11, tends to change in memory from "schema plus correction" to the "schema" itself, from nearly typical, case (b), to the prototype, case (a). Finally, weak wholes, mere aggregates, will be poorly remembered. "Loose ends" will be lost; parts without function, embellishments, will be forgotten, case (c). Complexities of structure will decay into simpler structures or will become irrecoverable. After sufficient time has elapsed, only the strongest and clearest structures will survive unchanged; others will deteriorate, fragment, or become irretrievable.

There are many variations on this outline. Some of these appear in the context of the experiments reported in later chapters. Two points should be made now, however. First, we assume that the features, groupings, or organizations under discussion can vary *independently*, that they are, in vector terminology, orthogonal to each other or are separable, to use Garner's (1974) word. Separability implies an orthogonality axiom that may be stated as follows: *Any phenomenal feature or any partitioning is, at least locally (i.e., over a limited domain of values), orthogonal to all others.* This is not the place to discuss the axiom at length. Suffice it to say that this axiom is a corollary of Sections 6 and 7, dealing with dimensionality and realized parameters. This axiom also tacitly underlies Tversky's (1977) feature theory of similarity and Rosch's (1978) feature theory of categorization. For the present work on memory, the axiom legitimizes the experimental procedure of comparing memory for individual features, or parts, or for grouping of patterns employed in the experiments of Chapters 5, 6, and 7. We assume for instance that in a particular pattern, one feature may be singular, another feature nonsingular, and yet another nearly singular, and that the trace will change or be stable, independently, in all three respects. Because of the Orthogonality Axiom, the outline of trace changes presented in this section for *individual features* is all that needs to be said about the fate in memory of the entire trace.

4. THEORY OF MEMORY CHANGE

The other point to be made concerns the boundaries between the three proposed degrees of singularity: (a) singular; (b) near-singular; and (c) nonsingular values. In Fig. 58, two steep slopes sharply localize the singularity at (a) between them. A steep slope indicates the narrow region (b) representing near-singularity. The large region of almost zero slope represents (c), nonsingularity. The three regions are sharply separated by abrupt changes in slope. Actually, similarity relations often suggest much gentler slopes and more gradual transitions between the three regions. A good example is the solid curve of Fig. 62, representing the relationship between the patterns of Fig. 61 a to h. The singularity well is so wide and the two slopes bordering it are so little confining, that both c and d can be considered as being at the bottom of the well and therefore singular. The slope on the right is so gradual that a change from c to e is not impossible, although not as likely as a change from c to d. While e is near-singular, being on the slope, f is on the borderline between nearly-singular and nonsingular. In a memory experiment, see Section 29, the trace of f should behave as near-singular by changing toward e and d, but, being so near to the horizontal, nonsingular part of the curve, f should also have a small probability of climbing up the incline to g and h. If we call c singular, it should be stable in the sense that it does not change to a or b on the steep side and have only a small probability of going beyond d on the less-steep side of the well. Pattern f can be called nonsingular because the slope is almost horizontal, so that f could drift to either side, to g and h or e and d. But f can also be classified as near-singular because the drift should preferentially go down the slope to e and d and only rarely up to g and h.

In general, singularity means stability, but the region of stability can be narrow, as pictured in Fig. 58, or wide, as in Fig. 62, where it includes patterns c and d. Further descriptions of the fine structure of singularity are found in Section 63.

The boundary between near-singularity, case (b), and nonsingularity, case (c), also is not as sharp as Fig. 58 suggests. It can be so gradual that in a given instance either classification can apply in part. Instead of three completely separate situations, the experiments in Chapters 5, 6, and 7 illustrate a whole spectrum of change. But, in spite of the existence of transitional cases, I hope to show that the three types of change proposed here bring order and understanding to what up to now has seemed to be random decay of the trace.

24. STRESS VERSUS FADING THEORIES

Memory theories customarily assume that a trace does not change at all once it is established. This is a useful and remarkably successful assumption. Moreover, it is correct to a first order of approximation, for instance, over short retention times, and with unstructured and unstructurable materials like, say, a word–number list. But, in general, memory change occurs and must be dealt with in

24. STRESS VERSUS FADING THEORIES 119

theory. The associationistic theory for this purpose is the theory of fading-plus-reconstruction mentioned in Section 20. Fading theory assumes that with the passage of time accuracy is lost and "errors" increase for all traces indiscriminately. Fading theory also assumes—as proposed for instance by Hanawalt (1937) and Woodworth (1938)—that the trace associates with itself during learning; in storage, and at retrieval, familiar material, objects, or words. These associations then participate in the reconstruction phase along with the faded trace.

Fading or some equivalent is found in most memory theories, including stress theory. In stress theory, the gaussian random vibrations of our model cause fading by changing the position of the little ball. This in turn causes loss of information about the balls original position, the position of which represents the value of a particular feature. Thus, with the passage of time, the value of the feature, say, the position of the gaps on Fig. 72b, becomes more and more uncertain. However, in stress theory, this uncertainty occurs only in the case of nonsingular values, in case (c). *Nearly* singular values drift toward the singularity and stop there, and singular values do not change at all. Association theories in general and fading theory in particular do not take into account the internal structure of the traces, such as degree of "goodness" or singularity; they are structure-blind. A memory change in association theory is due either to pure fading, in which case the change is undirected, random, exactly as in our nonsingular case (c). Or, the change is guided by associated objects or words, in which case the outcome depends on what material happens to be associated. Associations can mimic a change from near-singular to singular, our case (b), if most subjects have associations pointing in the same direction, or if a particular item tends to be associated strongly with a specific other item. But, in general, the guiding associations, either familiar objects or words, are not likely to be more singular than the learned item or to differ from it all in one direction. Associations can be quite idiosyncratic, and they can be very unlike the learned items. If the trace fades with time and then these associations prevail, the result is not necessarily a more singular response, as in our case (b). The response may be bizarre or it may be less singular, leading on the average of many subjects to random variations, as in case (c). Finally, if the original trace is singular, a "strong" unit, a "good" pattern, it should fade and deteriorate in fading theory, whereas stress theory predicts no change, our case (a).

In summary, fading alone without guiding reconstruction predicts random change, increasing with time, in a gaussian distribution of values. To be more concrete, if a large group of subjects remembers the value of a feature, say, the size of the gap in Fig. 75, some will remember the gap too small, some too large; the errors in both directions will increase with the time elapsed, but the average of all answers will be close to the true value. Fading theory makes this prediction whether the feature is nonsingular, as in the example of the gap in the circle, or nearly singular, say, a slant of 95°, or singular, as in a line exactly vertical. Stress theory, it is recalled, makes this prediction only in case (c) (the nonsingular value, exemplified by Fig. 75) but predicts directed change in case (b) (nearly singular values) and no change in case (a) (singular values).

Because fading is not influenced by the trace structure, it affects singular values as well as nonsingular and near-singular values. As a consequence, in a fading theory, singular values are just as unstable as nonsingular ones; for example, a perpendicular line is just as likely to become slanted as a slanted line is to become more slanted, or less slanted, or, perchance, even perpendicular.

As to reconstruction, pure reconstruction has no place in a memory theory. If I remember a clock but not the numerals on the clock face, I may *conclude* that it "must have had" roman numerals. But a conclusion is not a memory; a memory theory is not required to predict conclusions. The same reasoning applies to idiosyncratic perceptions. For example, a subject in Gibson's (1929) study associated with one pattern "footprints on the sands of time." If idiosyncratic associations occur at the time of acquisition, we are simply dealing with a differently perceived stimulus, like the difference in perception produced by manipulations of the stimulus context in the experiments of Carmichael et al. (1932) and of Palmer (1975b). This phenomenon is relevant to the theory of perception and was discussed in Section 15 on trace *formation,* but it, too, does not concern memory theory. Unusual associations are sometimes formed in an effort to remember an item by means of mnemonics. These can be quite unrelated to the structure of the trace. An example is the ancient "method of loci" (Neisser, 1976).

If associations accrue to the trace during storage or at recall, whether by way of extrinsic "suggestions," as retrieval clues, or spontaneously, fading theory predicts change in the direction of these extrinsic influences. The work of Tulving and his collaborators (Tulving & O. Watkins, 1977) and of Barclay, Bransford, Franks, McCarrell and Nitsch (1974), on the other hand, suggests that a trace once formed is endowed with a "specificity," as Tulving terms it, which strongly resists extrinsic change. If change from suggestions or clues can be demonstrated, the mechanism is either extrinsic independent of trace structure, as discussed in Section 15, or related to the trace structure, say, to an ambiguity or a nonsingularity, in which case it is an intrinsic change. A fading theory admitting intrinsic change becomes in effect a stress theory.

The predictions of stress theory and fading compare as follows:

1. In the case of a strong whole, a singular feature, our *case* (*a*), stress theory predicts a stable trace. Fading predicts change, either random, undirected fading or change toward associated objects or words, by way of reconstruction.

2. In case of a nearly singular feature, an almost well-organized whole, our *case* (*b*), stress theory predicts long-term drift toward singularity. Fading predicts again random, undirected change or assimilation to randomly associated objects or words, which may in some instances all point in one direction.

24. STRESS VERSUS FADING THEORIES 121

3. In the case of nonsingular features or poorly organized wholes, our *case* (*c*), stress theory predicts random, undirected change and so does fading theory.

Fading theory always predicts undirected random change except that a direction can be simulated by change in the direction of extrinsic, associated material. The memory changes predicted by fading are independent of the structure of the trace. Stress theory predicts intrinsic changes specific to the structure of the particular trace. In some circumstances, case (a), stress theory predicts the *absence of change*, whereas fading implies indiscriminate degradation of all traces without regard for the trace structure.

Fading theory holds that *all* changes are either due to fading alone, or directed toward an object or word association. Fading theory ascribes all change to an *extrinsic* mechanism, namely fading (= noise) or fading plus reconstruction. Stress theory accepts the possibility of extrinsic changes if they can be validated experimentally but proposes additionally, also subject to experimental validation, the *intrinsic* mechanisms set forth in Sections 22 and 23.

The role of time also is different in the two theories. While both theories assume a random deterioration with time, the deterioration afflicts *all* aspects of the trace *uniformly* in fading but affects *selectively* certain aspects more than others in stress theory. Because the deterioration is acting continuously, it will lead to loss of information in both theories. Ultimately, even in stress theory, traces will become impoverished. In stress theory, impoverishment can cause restructuring at a less-complex level, or it can make a trace incomplete and defective. When my monograph (Goldmeier, 1972) was published, I showed it, separately, to two of my cousins, a housewife, and a stockbroker. Both cousins started to leaf through it, noticed the illustrations and asked me if these were the pictures I had shown them in 1935, when I did the experiments. The subjects were 8 and 12 years old then and evidently still remembered something about the patterns. They had forgotten the individual patterns but remembered enough to bring to mind the test episode 36 years earlier. By that time, I had forgotten that they even served as subjects. (For examples of deterioration, fragmentation, and impoverishment, see Chapter 6 and Sections 53, 55, 56, 57, and 58 of Chapter 7.)

Over the short term, little change is predicted by either theory. Over the very long term, both theories converge. The decision between the two theories requires experiments over the period of time after change has had time to occur but before traces have deteriorated severely. The time of onset of decay varies with the complexity of the trace, the "level of the original processing," the kind of processing, the context of acquisition, and the conditions of storage, matters that are beyond the scope of this investigation.

Fading of wholes and their parts follows rules similar to those for attributes. If the organization of the whole, be it a visual pattern or verbal material, is weak, then in both theories, parts or items drop out, are forgotten. If the whole is strong

4. THEORY OF MEMORY CHANGE

enough so that the parts tend to be more interdependent, as in some of Garner's better dot patterns or in a well-formed narrative, then only fading, being structure-blind, predicts loss of parts. Stress theory, in the case of stronger, near-singular wholes, predicts either added or lost parts, whichever is required to achieve greater singularity. In singular wholes, where stress theory predicts stability or absence of change, fading predicts random loss of parts. In stress theory, fading is relegated to a minor role, to the special case of weak wholes, as for instance in the loss of the horizontal line in Fig. 71a, Section 42.

Fading alone cannot easily explain the *addition* of parts, for example, the addition of little Vs to Fig. 64g, Sections 31 and 44. In an effort to repair this defect within the associationistic framework, Hanawalt and Woodworth (1938) proposed a combination of fading with an associative form of *reconstruction*. In the nonsingular case (c), reconstruction is unnecessary; both theories coincide. In the near-singular case (b), stress theory predicts change toward the singularity, whereas reconstruction adds associated material, especially familiar objects or frequently co-occurring items to the trace. The added material may accrue either at the time of acquisition, during storage, or at the time of retrieval. The mechanism of reconstruction has been shown to exist (Carmichael et al., 1932; Hanawalt & Demarest, 1939; Palmer, 1975b). Stress theory claims that, in addition to the—extrinsic—reconstruction, there is also—intrinsic—stress on the trace that changes the trace toward singularity. Hanawalt and Woodworth assumed, parsimoniously, that the extrinsic mechanism was the only one, especially after their diligent efforts failed to discover intrinsic change (Hanawalt, 1937). Chapters 5, 6, and 7 of this book attempt to demonstrate that intrinsic change does occur as well. The difference between the two theories appears in case (a) and (b). In case (b), intrinsic change is *directed* toward singularity, whereas reconstruction can occur in all directions. In the singular case (a), the expectations of the two theories are reversed. Stress theory predicts no change. Fading, being blind to singularity or internal consistency of the parts of a whole, leads to decay, especially loss of parts. Sooner (at acquisition) or later (at retrieval) or during storage, the loss is filled in by reconstruction.

As Riley (1962) reported, the long dispute over the interpretation of memory change has been inconclusive. Change, whether produced by reconstruction or by intrinsic stress often looks very much alike. The strategy adopted here is therefore not only to analyze the singularities of the material but to examine two versions of the same pattern, one singular the other near-singular or nonsingular. If the trace is subject to fading-plus-reconstruction, the two versions should change to the same degree and should change in many different ways, depending on the extrinsic material associated. If the change obeys stress theory, then the singular version should be stable, the near-singular version should change to the singularity, and nonsingular versions should show undirected change. Even if there is dispute about singularities and about the direction of change, under fading all versions should change equally, whereas if stress theory applies, they should differ markedly in the incidence of change.

The purpose of the preceding picture of fading theory is not to impute this theory to anyone nor to set up a strawman to be easily vanquished. The purpose is merely to elaborate an associationistic alternative to stress theory by which the data to be presented can be judged.

As regards the mechanism of change, fading-plus-reconstruction suggests reconstruction to occur at the time of retrieval, whereas for stress theory, a more natural assumption is gradual change of the trace during storage. Some of these possibilities are examined in Chapter 8.

25. EXPERIMENTAL CONSIDERATIONS

The main difference between the two theories, although not the only one, is the progressive change of nearly singular features toward a singular value. The reason why this kind of intrinsic change was not found more readily lies in the experimental arrangements that customarily favor extrinsic change. The following points need consideration in experiments aimed to distinguish between the two viewpoints.

Time Intervals. Most memory research employs very short time intervals, minutes or hours. The experimental demonstration of intrinsic changes with material like that used here requires much longer periods; days, weeks, even months. Hebb and Foord (1945) tested the circles A and B of Fig. 75 for closure of the gap. They failed to find closure. Admittedly, the gap is contrastructural and therefore a candidate for closure, but memory was tested after only 5 minutes and 1 day, rather short periods for so deep a structural change. Longer test periods might have resulted in closure. The experiment had other imperfections as well. The recognition material by which change was tested offered 23 circles with a gap, but only one without (Fig. 75). This may have biassed the outcome against closure. At any rate, the fact that a particular experiment fails to demonstrate a change like closure over the short term does not exclude the possibility of long-term change.

Experimental Design Favoring Intrinsic Change. Intrinsic change on the one hand and forgetting and extrinsic change on the other compete with each other. Intrinsic change is observable only if extrinsic change and forgetting are minimized. This requires: (1) a small number of experimental designs; (2) the greatest possible differences between designs; and (3) designs incorporating strong and unambiguous stress. As to (1), length of series, Hanawalt used eight designs, Goldmeier (1941) used six, and the present study uses three patterns or

124   4. THEORY OF MEMORY CHANGE

tasks for each subject. As to (2), variety, the three studies rank in the same order. Finally, the need for strong stress in an unambiguous design seems obvious. These aspects of the experimental design are discussed in more detail in Goldmeier (1941), p. 501.

Problem of Circularity.   The original gestalt proposal was that traces change toward a better gestalt and that these changes progress with time. (Wulf, 1922; Koffka, 1935; Goldmeier, 1941). In an attempt to disprove these claims, Hanawalt (1937) reinvestigated the question using Wulf's patterns together with an improved experimental procedure of his own. He found nothing that he could not explain by fading-plus-reconstruction, making the gestalt explanation appear superfluous. Hebb and Foord (1945), in response to Goldmeier (1941), set out to disprove the notion of *progressive, directed* change. They used the patterns of Fig. 75 and showed that neither patterns A and C nor B and D changed progressively in one direction, say, in the direction of closure of the circle or "sharpening" or "leveling" of the arrowhead. These two influential papers seemed to settle the question of memory change for a whole generation of psychologists. But, as Riley's (1962) account shows, the question did not remain settled. Hanawalt had assumed, understandably, that Wulf's patterns would show intrinsic changes better than any pattern an opponent could devise. Actually, Wulf's paper was a pioneering effort, a pilot experiment; his patterns were not analyzed beforehand, and he made no effort to predict specific changes. As a consequence, no recognition material could be prepared. Wulf took the changes observed in reproductions as evidence of the assumed tendency to greater goodness, but such evidence is anecdotal and therefore arguable.

Hebb and Foord presumed that the directed changes, either leveling or sharpening claimed by Wulf and Koffka, were meant to apply to any pattern at all, and that a tendency to closure was claimed for any gap whatever. With that in mind, they devised the patterns of Fig. 75, A, B, C, D. Both designs have little intrinsic stress. Whereas a gap in a circle indeed goes against the structure of a circle, placement of the gap in the top center gives the design the preferred vertical symmetry. Hebb and Foord further imputed to gestalt theory that large gaps tend to become smaller. But whereas a gap itself can in some designs be contrastructural, the size of the gap is in general a nonsingular attribute. The gap in Fig. 75 A is about as contrastructural as the one in B. Likewise, the angles in Fig. 75 C and D are about equally nonsingular. Hebb and Foord worked with nonsingular feature values, our case (c). As might be expected in case (c), they found no directed change. They did find an increase in the variability with time. Their results confirm the prediction of stress theory for case (c). Unfortunately, case (c) does not discriminate between fading and stress theory, as pointed out in the preceding section.

The controversy just described could arise only because the reports of pattern changes by Wulf (1922) and also by later authors, for example, Bartlett (1932) and Paul (1959), are descriptive but not predictive. Unless the strength and the direction of the intrinsic stresses or the purported extrinsic factors for a given pattern are established independently, that is, without reference to the outcome of the memory experiment, the hypotheses suffer from circularity. In the experiments to be presented in Chapters 5, 6, and 7, independent structural information comes from many sources, ranging from an appeal to plausibility to separately established aspects of goodness, symmetry, parallel course, self-consistency, congruity (Schulman, 1974), factors of grouping (Wertheimer, 1923), similarity rankings (Goldmeier, 1972, Chapter 7) to a pairing method of two related patterns in memory experiments. The method of paired experiments was used in some instances in Goldmeier (1941) and is used systematically in the present study. Each member of the pair serves as control for the other.

Experimental Procedure. Wulf, Bartlett, and other early investigators (Perkins, 1932) simply presented the material and subsequently tested the same subject repeatedly after various time intervals, by means of reproduction or free recall. This procedure is open to several objections. First, if a change appears in pattern reproduction, the change may not be a memory change but instead could have occurred during perception or be due to the limitations of the subject's drawing skill. Hanawalt (1937) met this problem by having the subjects *copy* the whole series of stimuli twice. The second copy is taken as the end result of the learning phase. The reproductions from memory are considered as changed only to the extent to which they differ from each subject's own second copy. Hanawalt also eliminated the custom of testing a subject repeatedly. Instead, he used a separate group of subjects for each time interval examined. Both these improvements in method were adopted by Goldmeier (1941) and by the present study.

26. RECOGNITION VERSUS REPRODUCTION

If the theory of the changing trace is valid, then changes should be detectable in recognition as well as in recall or reproduction. In fact, as a test for memory change, recognition is in many ways complementary to reproduction. However, either method fails if the principles of stress theory are ignored. Stress theory affects different aspects of the two testing methods differently:

1. Whereas reproductions furnish a great variety of changes, recognition tests show only the changes that the experimenter has anticipated by preparing suitable variants of the standard to choose from.

2. Whereas reproductions generally show changes of several kinds and in several dimensions simultaneously, the recognition material can be confined to the variation of a single parameter. The method of one-dimensional variation was introduced by Hebb and Foord (1945) and adopted here. Failure to use this

4. THEORY OF MEMORY CHANGE

method contributed to the inability of some previous experimenters to demonstrate directedness in memory changes in recognition. On the other hand, the method is not mandatory. Goldmeier (1941) reported two instances of change in recognition toward a more singular pattern, using "multidimensional" recognition choices (Sections 31 and 34), whereas Hebb and Foord (1945) failed to demonstrate directed change in spite of using this method.

3. Whether the recognition material presents one-dimensional or multidimensional choices, it must correctly anticipate the changes of the traces. Only if the experimenter succeeds in doing this can changes be detected. If they are anticipated, the evaluation of the results is trivial.

The converse is true of reproduction tests. No material needs to be prepared, but the analysis of the reproductions is complicated, whole dimensions of change can be overlooked, and classification of individual reproductions is often doubtful.

4. Whereas reproductions show any changes that the subject is able to portray, recognitions show only the changes represented in the recognition material. This difference applies to intrinsic and extrinsic change alike. Therefore, the recognition method lends itself to *filtering out extrinsic changes and to observing intrinsic change* (*i.e., change* due to stress *within* the structure of the trace), *in pure form,* simply by providing only material reflecting the anticipated intrinsic change.

5. There is a marked difference between the two methods in the number of responses, especially if the test interval amounts to several weeks. Almost all subjects will be able to make a choice from recognition material even after 6 to 8 weeks, indicating that there is very little complete forgetting. Reproductions, on the other hand, decrease or become fragmentary after even a few days, demonstrating decreased and partial availability of the trace. *Recognition tests tend to underestimate forgetting; reproduction tests overestimate it.*

6. In either method of testing, some changes are missed. This is obvious in the case of recognition. If the prepared recognition material does not contain an example of a particular change, then that change is suppressed. But, because *some changes are mutually exclusive* even in suitable reproduction material, one change can hide another. This occurred in the case of the gaps in Fig. 68. There are two possibilities; either the gaps shift within the design or they close. In many reproductions, they were closed. The recognition material, however (Fig. 68), did not provide for closure, so that the recognition test answered, in effect, the question: Where does a gap go if it does not disappear by closure?

7. Some changes, for instance, "degree of curvature" or "angle of divergence of curved lines," are difficult to measure on reproductions. Some qualities of reproductions cannot be reduced to numerical form at all except indirectly by judgments of some sort. Recognition tests easily solve that problem. All one needs is a series of designs with graded variations of the curvature or divergence or other attribute from which the subjects may choose. The choices

26. RECOGNITION VERSUS REPRODUCTION 127

determine the degree of change to any required accuracy without need for judgments or difficult measurements.

Keeping in mind the peculiarities of recognition tests as well as the theory of stress, the reasons why so many investigators failed to find intrinsic changes by this method become understandable. O. L. Zangwill (1937), Hanawalt (1937), Hebb and Foord (1945), and Rock and Engelstein (1959) all used designs with some strongly singular features, producing no change, and other features so far from singular that they would change randomly. They then prepared variants of their designs by varying one or a few features. Because the tendency to a good gestalt is active in the experimenter, too, their variations usually left singular features unchanged, while making random combinations of changes of nonsingular features. Consider now just two of the many features of a standard (St, Fig. 60), feature x and feature y. The patterns A, B, C, D, E, created by varying x or y or both, are members of a two-parameter family in a two-dimensional feature

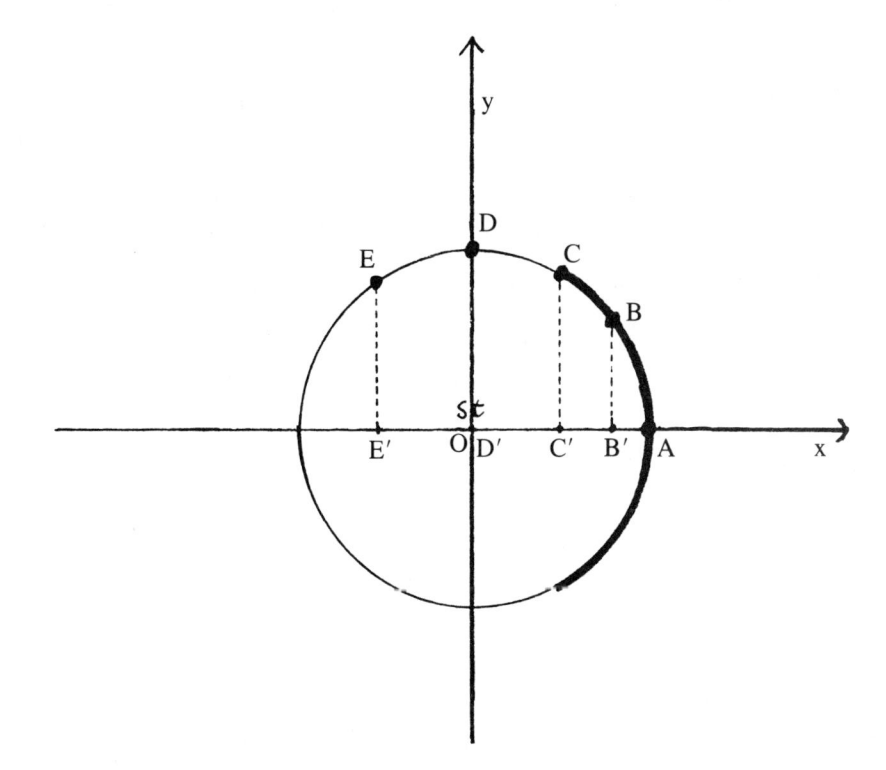

FIG. 60. Diagram of the abstract feature space of a two-parameter family of patterns. Points designated by the capital letters indicate the location of the various patterns in this abstract space. The standard, marked St and also D' is at the Origin O.

128   4. THEORY OF MEMORY CHANGE

space that is diagramed in Fig. 60. Suppose now that the trace has changed from St to A (Fig. 60) and that the material provided for recognition contains design C, D, and E as well as the standard, but not designs A and B. All the variants are equally distant from the standard and therefore equally similar to it. They differ only to the extent to which features x and y are changed, as measured by the respective x and y coordinates. The trace, on the other hand, has changed—to A—with respect to feature x and not at all with respect to feature y. So, in balance, even though variants C, D, E are equally far from the standard—all lying on a circle in similarity space (Goldmeier, 1972, Chapter 7) around St—the observer chooses the standard in recognition because the standard is closest to the changed trace A. Only choices within the heavily drawn segment, like A or B, if they are offered, are preferred to St. But that segment is only one third of the full circle, so the likelihood of offering such a comparison figure by a random guess is only 0.33.

But that is not all. If three features are varied, x, y, and z, the similarity space is 3-dimensional and the choices lie on a spherical surface. The similar and preferred choices then have to lie within the circular cap of which the heavy segment of Fig. 60 is a cross-section, whereas all the remaining parts of the 3-dimensional sphere around St are less similar to A than the standard. But that cap on the sphere is a much smaller part of the whole sphere than the segment is of the circle. So the standard is even more likely to be chosen than any randomly selected point on the sphere. The more features, the less likelihood that anything but the standard is chosen. This leads to the mistaken conclusion that the trace has not changed.

Hebb and Foord (1945) avoided this pitfall by varying only one feature. However, they picked a feature so far from singular (gap size) that random variation rather than directed change is expected, our case (c). Zangwill (1937), on the other hand, labored under an additional handicap. Neglecting the hierarchical structure of traces and the peculiarities of reproductions just outlined, he took his recognition material from each subject's own reproductions. Hence, the choices he offered were impoverished compared with the trace when pitted against the standard.

One-dimensional variation of the recognition material, as first used by Hebb and Foord, even though it has advantages, does not guarantee success. If the standard is varied along the linear dimension A-St (Fig. 60) and assuming again the trace has changed to A, then A is chosen in recognition over all other designs, including the standard. B' is next, then C' then D' or St, then E'. But if D-St (= the y - axis) is used as the single dimension along which the recognition patterns are varied, and again assuming that the trace has changed to A, the subject would then choose the standard, because it is *closest to A* along the line D-St and is least likely to choose D.

There just is no substitute for anticipating the stresses for the various features, through informed guesses, possibly pretested and validated by experiments like those reported in Goldmeier (1972), Chapter 7. On the other hand, awareness of the stresses enables the experimenter to construct recognition material that demonstrates the changes expected from the theory and the absence of changes where none should occur. Construction of suitable material requires detailed analysis of the design with regard to expected intrinsic changes. In Goldmeier (1941), some explicit analyses of this kind were omitted in the interest of brevity. This ommission has no doubt contributed to many misunderstandings of that paper. Therefore, such analyses have become an important part of the present report, see, for example, Sections 32 and 46.

5 Intrinsic Change in Recognition

27. EXPERIMENTAL DESIGN

The work of Hanawalt (1937) and others working in the 1930s (Riley, 1962) demonstrated that the memory traces of patterns presented together in the same experiment interact, leading to the effect called figure assimilation. For instance, the reproduction of a pattern may consist of the material (say, dots) of one design combined with form features of another design (say, the line drawing of a cross like that in Fig. 64). (Examples are shown in Goldmeier, 1941, Fig. 3, samples 6-9.) Figure assimilation is an effect extrinsic to the individual trace and therefore highly undesirable in experiments intended to bring out intrinsic changes. In the present study, the incidence of figure assimilation was held down by: (1) limiting each experiment to lists of three patterns or tasks and; (2) making the three patterns as dissimilar as possible. For instance, designs 70i, 70d, 68d, 68h, and 68e, which are similar to each other, were never in the same list. Sixteen tasks or designs were used with 24 independent groups of subjects. Each group received three tasks. Four groups comprise Experiment I, 16 groups comprise Experiment II, and 4 groups Experiment III.

Subjects. The 20 independent groups of Experiments I and II were students of Westchester Community College, Valhalla, N.Y.; all were in one of the sections of the Introductory English course; each section included 20 to 30 students; each experimental group was made up of one of these sections. The experiments were conducted by the English teachers who had been briefed on the experimental design. Experiment III, using four groups of students of Pace College, Pleasantville, N.Y. was conducted by myself, using the same procedure

27. EXPERIMENTAL DESIGN   133

The recognition material in Experiments I and II and the last pattern of Experiment III was the same regardless of whether the groups had memorized the patterns in one or the other of the two related learning booklets. The same material could be used for both groups because the designs memorized in Experiment I, for instance, were merely two different members of the series of designs shown in Fig. 70, 61, and 63. Similarly related materials were used in Experiment II and in the last design of Experiment III. In the case of Experiment III, the first design was identical for the two subgroups, but the second design was different. Two independent groups learned Fig. 65, the other two learned Fig. 66, necessitating four different test booklets in Experiment III to accommodate the related but not identical recognition series for Fig. 65 and 66.

The Instructions.   The booklets contained a running set of instructions, most of which have been quoted previously, so that the booklets were largely self-administering. However, in large-scale experiments, redundancy is desirable and was provided by means of *instruction sheets* that told the teacher verbatim what to say and when, and precisely what to do. In Experiment III, which I conducted myself, I also used the instruction sheets, although I did not adhere to them to the letter. For example, the instruction sheets for the learning booklets began as follows:

Read the portion of the instruction in quotation marks to the class. Keep an eye on the class and repeat any instructions that are not followed.

"This test will not be used in your grading. It is a research project in which the college is cooperating and we hope that you do not mind being a part of it. Do not open the booklets until I tell you, please."

Distribute the booklets and pencils and say: . . . etc.

The purpose of the learning period was disguised by the final instruction that read:

"This was a test to see how difficult it is to copy things correctly and how much improvement is possible on the second try. Thank you . . . etc."

The standard instruction, used for most copies, is exemplified by the instruction for Fig. 61c and 61f, first copy:

"Turn to page 5 and study the figure very carefully but do not draw as yet, just study the figure very carefully."

Wait a few moments until everyone has studied the figure and say:

"Now copy it on the bottom half of the page."

5. INTRINSIC CHANGE IN RECOGNITION

For the dot Fig. 70*i* and 70*d*, the sentence "You need not count the dots accurately" was added to the instructions each time. For the "bar and triangle" designs, Fig. 63*b* and 63*d*, the sentence "It is enough if you just draw it, do not fill it in black" was added.

The purpose of copying the designs is threefold. On the one hand, the copy provides an indication of what the subject had actually perceived. Secondly, as Hanawalt first proposed, each subject's own second copy rather than the present standard is properly the base line from which change in later reproductions is measured. Thirdly, copying the designs induced the subjects to attend to the design in detail so as to form an enduring trace, without being instructed explicitly to commit it to memory. Copying, we felt, is an "orienting task" that increases what has come to be known as "depth of processing" (Cermak & Craik, 1979). With the third aim in mind, the instructions for copying were varied for different designs. Particularly, we wanted the option of *copying from memory*. Therefore, in preparing the booklets, the specimen sheets for Fig. 61*c*, 63*b*, and 63*d* were sawed in half, except for the last half inch, so that the standard could be first studied, then folded over and "drawn from memory." In the actual experiments, this feature was used only for the *second copy* of Fig. 63*b* and 63*d*. The instructions for this page, for both Fig. 63*d* and 63*b*, were:

"Please turn to page 12 and then to page 13 and again study the figure without copying it.
THIS TIME YOU WILL BE ASKED TO DRAW FROM MEMORY."

This procedure, on the second copy at least, would prevent the subject from copying piece by piece without ever building up a mental image of the whole design. I have no data to decide whether this precaution was really necessary.

The instructions for the memory-test period were all quite similar. The pertinent instructions for Experiment I, reproductions first, recognition test second, were:

"Now try to remember the three problems you copied on the first test. Please reproduce all three from memory on this page as best as you can and as many as you are able to recall."

And then

"Please turn to page 5 and circle the figure most like the one you copied on the first test. Circle only ONE figure, please."

and so on for all three figures.

As this description shows, all three experiments were alike. We therefore discuss the results pattern by pattern, regardless of which of the three experiments contained the particular pattern.

28. COROLLARIES OF THE EXPERIMENTAL DESIGN

1. All three experiments test reproduction as well as recognition. For some groups, the reproduction test was followed by a recognition test; for the others the order was reversed. Thus, we have two kinds of reproductions: (1) reproductions made "from memory"; and (2) reproductions made after having seen the recognition materials, thus, "cued reproductions." Obviously, these two types of recall are different and must be treated differently.

2. We also have two kinds of recognitions, those that were and those that were not preceded by an attempt at reproduction. Turner and Craig (1954) suggested that a recognition test is more likely to demonstrate memory change if it is preceded by a test of reproduction. They drew this conclusion from an experiment using a single pattern and time intervals of up to 4 days. Their pattern and their recognition material is incorporated in Experiment III as the first of the three designs on all four learning booklets. This extends the time interval of the Turner and Craig study to 6 weeks. Even after 6 weeks, their findings were strongly confirmed. However, some of the other patterns in the present study changed less when the reproductions test preceded recognition. More importantly, with either test sequence, the observed changes occurred in the same direction. Because our interest lies in the kind and the direction of change, which is unaffected by the test sequence, we have combined the results of parallel recognition tests whenever that seemed expedient. We have, however, in most cases, tabulated the recognition tests separately as well, to make the data available.

3. The experiments here reported deal with the degree and direction of change of certain features of a design. Following Hanawalt, the word change is *not meant as change from the printed specimen or standard presented to our subjects but as deviation from each subject's own second copy*. Reproductions and recognitions from any subjects whose second copy of a design deviates from the standard with regard to a feature reported on are *excluded from consideration*. Thus, all reported changes are differences between a reproduction or recognition and that *same subject's second copy*. This procedure is quite in tune with Tulving's notion of "encoding specificity."

4. The theory of memory change proposed in Chapter 4 requires information about singularities in the patterns used in memory experiments. In the case of the patterns shown in Fig. 61, 63, 68, and 70, some information of this kind was obtained by means of similarity rankings (see Section 6, and Goldmeier, 1972.) The method and those results of interest here are the following:

If the patterns of Fig. 61 are ranked by their similarity to pattern c, the rank order obtained from 15 subjects is:

```
                  b              a
   c     1.3   (2.3  2.7)   (4.5 [4.8] 5.7]    6.9
         d       e           f        g        h
```

The numbers are average rankings. The parentheses and brackets (sometimes overlapping) enclose any rankings that do not differ significantly from each other. Reading the top row from right to left, then c, then the bottom row from left to right, the sequence of similarities is a b c d e f g. The tabulation shows that d and e are closer to c than is b; that a is farther from c than are b, d, e, and f; and that g and h, in that order, are still farther. Another ranking by 15 subjects, with pattern f as the standard, contributed additional order information. In the same notation as before the rankings were:

```
              e            d         c    b    a
  f  (1.2  2.1)        (3.5  3.8)   (5.0 [5.9) 6.6]
              g            h
```

Reading again from a to f to h, the brackets and parentheses indicate that e is less similar to f than is g (not reaching significance) but is significantly more similar than is h; c–b and b–a are not significantly different in rank, but c and a differ significantly. Of course, these are only rank orders, not measured distances in similarity space. Shepard (1963) has shown, however, that even limited ordinal information can lead to tight constraints on the relative distances. Together, the two rankings suggest the distances shown on the abscissa of Fig. 62. The points are not uniquely determined, but they are narrowly limited. If one takes the height of the apex of the middle pair of lines in Fig. 61 or the apex angle as the varied parameter, the eight patterns are roughly equidistant. The similarity rankings, on the other hand, Fig. 62, result into three separate groups: a and b, c and d, and f, g, h, with e intermediate. The relatively large distance of c and d from the other two groups indicates that in the region of c and d the pattern is sensitive to change and therefore singular, whereas near a, b and f, g, h, roughly equivalent changes produce smaller phenomenal changes. Because pattern e is intermediate, it is considered nearly singular.

The singularity in this case is not narrowly localized. Two similar patterns, c and d, both occupy the well of the curve of Fig. 62 and differ very little in singularity (Sections 29 and 63).

29. CHANGE TOWARD SINGULARITY—DESIGNS 61C AND F

The recognition material for this experiment is shown in Fig. 61. The variation consists in an increasingly flat course of the middle pair of lines as these lines pivot about a point at the base. The lines are steepest in 61a, flattest in h. The pivot point is off center, nearer the outer lines. Therefore, the design can not become both "parallel" (61c) and "balanced" (61d) in the same design. Rankings of similarity (see Section 6 and preceding Section 28) show that the most

29. CHANGE TOWARD SINGULARITY—DESIGNS 61C AND F   137

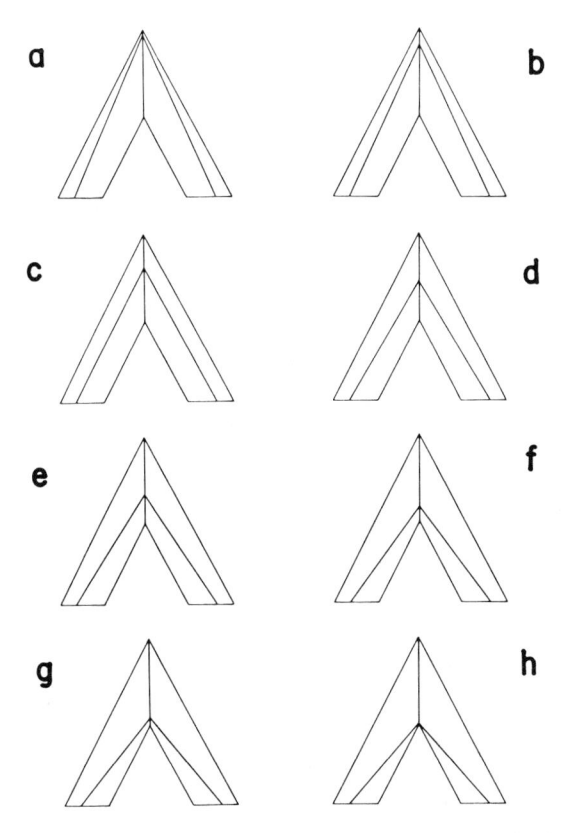

FIG. 61. Recognition material for Experiment 61. The subjects were shown this array in the recognition test without the letters *a* to *h*. Either pattern *c* or *f* had been memorized.

singular designs are *c, d,* and *e,* with maximal singularity near *d*. Two factors seem to contribute to the singularity, parallelity of the middle pair of lines relative to the other two pairs in 61*c,* and a more even subdivision of the space between the outer and inner pair of parallel lines, as in 61*d*. With the type of variation used in this series, the singularity does not peak sharply at one single design but in the broader range of variation extending from 61*c* to *d* and even *e*.

Fig. 62 is a diagram of the singularity drawn in the manner of Fig. 58. One dotted curve represents parallel course, peaking narrowly at *c*. The other curve represents balanced partition of the space between inner and outer lines, peaking broadly near *d*. The two dotted curves add up to the solid curve that represents the resultant singularity. The dip in the solid curve (i.e., the singularity) extends from *c* to *e* and is deepest between *c* and *d*. The spacing of the designs along the abscissa reflects the similarity rankings of the designs, their phenomenal distance from each other in similarity space (see Section 28). Note particularly the cluster-

138 5. INTRINSIC CHANGE IN RECOGNITION

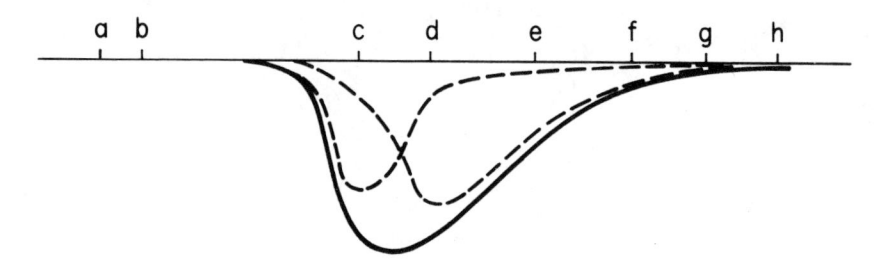

FIG. 62. Diagram of the singularity relations between the patterns of figure 61 a to h. The diagram is drawn in the manner of figure 58. One of the dashed curves peaks narrowly at c. It represents parallelity of the lines. The other dashed curve peaks broadly near d. It represents balanced partition of the space between inner and outer lines. The two dashed curves add up to the solid curve which peaks between c and d and represents the total singularity.

ing together of Designs 61c and d. This clustering is, according to Krumhansl (1978), an indication of singularity. Because the singularity well is so shallow compared with the well in Fig. 58 at point a, it accommodates the two patterns c and d, on each side of the deepest point. The two patterns are both singular and should be easily confused with each other, but not with patterns a, b, and f, g.

Given the constraints imposed by the recognition material (Fig. 61), what are the expected results when either 61c or 61f are memorized? Designs 61c and 61f differ greatly in "goodness," "Prägnanz," or singularity. Whereas in 61c all three line pairs are parallel, putting it within the singular region 61c-d, 61f is unequivocally outside that region, although close to it. The "closeness" is indicated in Fig. 62 by the fact that at f the solid curve begins to slope perceptibly toward c-d. The theory predicts very little memory change for 61c. What change there is should be in the direction of d rather than b and go no further than to e. This prediction indeed summarizes the recognitions after 6 weeks (Table 1, last line). The majority of subjects choose the design they had memorized (28 of 41

TABLE 1
Experiment I, Designs of Fig. 61, Recognition.
Choices of Designs 61a–h

Design memorized:			c				f			
Designs chosen:	N	c	d	e	N	d	e	f	g	h
Reproduction first	22	**16**	5	1	15	2	8	**3**	1	1
Recognition first	19	**12**	7	—	10	2	8	—	—	—
Combined	41	**28**	12	1	25	4	16	**3**	1	1

Note that 61a and b were never chosen.
Boldface indicates choices of the standard.

29. CHANGE TOWARD SINGULARITY—DESIGNS 61C AND F 139

subjects), 12 choose *d,* and one chooses *e.* Designs *a* and *b* and *f,g,h* were never chosen. In the case of 61*f,* the theory predicts change *toward* the singularity: (1) Change should be *frequent;* (2) what change there is, should be in the direction of *e* and *d* rather than toward *g* and *h,* even though *g* and *h* are more similar to *f* than *c* and *d.* The similarities are expressed as distances of *f* from *g* and *h* and from *e,d,* and *c* in Fig. 62; (3) because *f* is not singular, its trace should be indeterminate, not sharply defined, and therefore the changes should spread over a wider range of variants than is the case with the singular pattern 61*c.* Table 1, last line, shows that only 3 of 25 subjects select 61*f* in recognition; the majority, 16 of 25 subjects, select *e,* 4 even go as far as *d,* and only 1 each remember *f* as *g* or *h.* The difference between 61*c* and 61*f* in the occurrence of unchanged recognitions, 28/41 versus 3/25, is highly significant ($p < 0.005$). In fact, there is no significant difference between *f* remembered as *e,* 16/25, and *c* remembered as *c,* 28/41 ($X^2 = .13$ 1df, $p < .8$). In other words, the frequency with which the singular design 61*c* is remembered unchanged is about the same as the frequency with which the nonsingular design 61*f* is changed in memory to the more singular 61*e.* The table also shows the expected scatter of recognitions of 61*f* over 5 designs, *d-h,* whereas those of 61*c* are confined to 3 designs, *c-e,* even though more subjects are involved, 25 versus 41. This spread is difficult to quantify because there is no direct measure available for the distances c-e or d-h. Using, however, similarity as a yardstick, the distance *d-h* in Fig. 62 is twice the *distance c-e.*

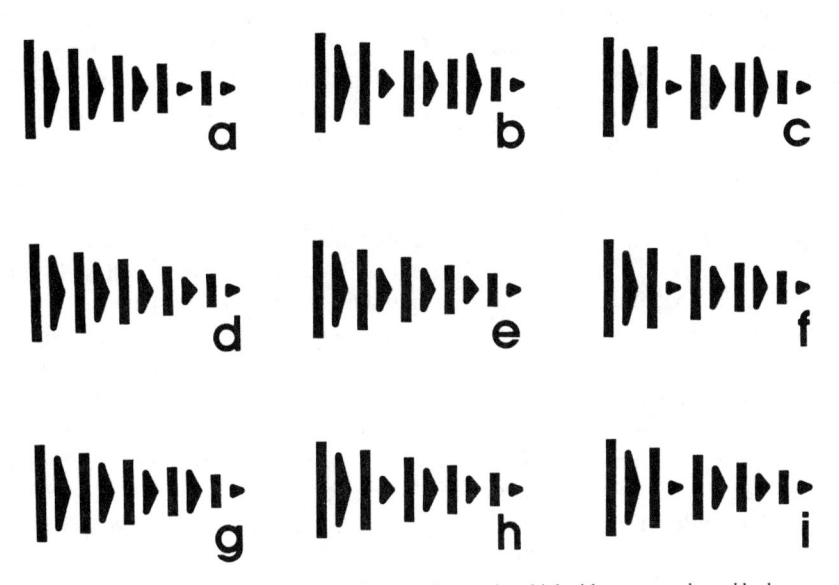

FIG. 63. Recognition material for experiments in which either pattern *b* or *d* had been memorized.

5. INTRINSIC CHANGE IN RECOGNITION

30. CHANGE TOWARD SELF-CONSISTENCY—DESIGNS 63D AND B

The recognition material for the experiment with standards 63d and 63b is shown in Fig. 63. Each design consists of the same five bars alternating with triangular shapes. We designate the triangles by size, as indicated on Fig. 78a as 9,7,5,3, and 1. Only the size of the second and the fourth triangle is varied, according to the following key:

design	a	b	c	d	e	f	g	h	i
size of 2nd triangle	7	3	1	7	5	1	7	3	1
size of 4th triangle	1	7	7	3	3	5	5	3	3

The letter designations (a, b, etc.) of the designs are merely labels; their alphabetical sequence is not related to a sequential variation of any attribute of the designs. The nine patterns are arbitrarily chosen from the 16 possible combinations of 1,3,5, and 7 in ordered pairs of two. Of these nine patterns, 63d is the most regular with the combination 7-3, so that the triangular shapes decrease monotonically in size: 9-7-5-3-1, just like the bars. On the other hand, 63b, with the reverse combination, is very irregular: 9-3-5-7-1 (i.e., the size of the triangles first decreases, then increases, then decreases again).

Omitting design 63i, which was never chosen, the remaining eight designs of Fig. 63 were analyzed by similarity rankings. Although their similarity relationships are apparently complex, they can be fairly well-ordered in the sequence a-d-g-e-h-b-f-c. This dimension of similarity space may be termed the monotonic-reversal axis. In the first four designs, a-d-g-e, the triangular shapes decrease monotonically, that is to say, they never increase from left to right. In the other four patterns, the sequence reverses, from decrease to increase and back. Because the bars decrease evenly in all the designs, the monotonically decreasing triangles make for an *internally consistent structure* of the pattern as a whole, as in *a,d,g,* and *e,* whereas reversals make for a clash between the regular decrease of the bars and the irregular sequence of the triangles. In this respect, *d* is "better" than *b,* and the monotonic designs (a,d,g,e) are better than those with reversals (h,b,f,c). In view of these differences between the designs, the expectations are: (1) The trace of 63d should be resistant to change, stable, whereas by comparison that of 63b should have a tendency to change; (2) any changes that occur in the trace of 63d should be restricted to other "monotonic" designs (a,e,g) rather than go in the direction of the designs h,b,f,c with their intrinsically less consistent structure. Conversely, the trace of 63b should tend to change in the direction of the structurally more consistent monotonic designs; (3) the changes occurring with the relatively singular pattern 63d should have a narrower *range* of distribution (i.e., involve fewer patterns and patterns quite similar to 63d, compared to the *range* of changes encountered with 63b).

30. CHANGE TOWARD SELF-CONSISTENCY—DESIGNS 63D AND B 141

Table 2 shows the recognition choices 6 weeks after the patterns were memorized. Line 3, which gives the combined figures, demonstrates the first point mentioned, that 22 of 28 subjects remember 63*d* unchanged, whereas only 14 out of 35 remember 63*b* unchanged. The difference is highly significant ($X^2 = 9.45$, $p < .005$), proving the trace of 63*d* to be much more stable than that of 63*b*.

Point 2 deals with the *direction* of change (Table 2, last line). In the more stable pattern, 63*d*, what changes there are remain within the *same type* (monotonic) as the standard. On the other hand, of the 21 subjects who do not choose the memorized design 63*b*, which contains reversals, only 8 stay with the *same type* (reversals) as the standard, whereas 13 choose the *other*, more self-consistent type instead. To summarize line 4 of Table 2: Of subjects who change and who memorized 63*d*, 6 choose *same* type, 0 *other* type. Of those who memorized 63*b*, 8 choose *same* type, 13 *other* type. The difference is significant ($X^2 = 7.16$, $p < .01$). And, recall that all subjects had unchanged copies. (As stated in Section 25, a change in the second copy of the learning phase disqualifies a reproduction or recognition with respect to the feature under investigation.) This comparison demonstrates a strong trend to monotonicity, confirming point 2. The trend would be still more pronounced if it were not partly obscured, for reasons related to point 3.

The range of changes (point 3), in the case of 63*d* (Table 2, line 3), is limited to the three monotonic patterns *a*, *g*, and *e*. Most changes, four of the six, go to the most similar design, 63*g*. On the other hand, with 63*b* as standard, the changes range over six of the eight designs, from 63*d* to 63*c*, including three of the four designs in the monotonic group. Measured by the number of designs included (three designs against six), the range of change for the singular pattern

TABLE 2
Experiment I, Designs of Fig. 63, Recognition.
Choices of Designs a–h*

	Design d Memorized					Design b Memorized						
Designs chosen	N	a	d	g	e	N	d	g	e	h	b	f	c
Reprod. first	15	1	11	3	—	18	1	1	3	1	9	—	3
Recogn. first	13	—	11	1	1	17	1	1	6	—	5	1	3
Both combined	28	1	22	4	1	35	2	2	9	1	14	1	6
		a,e,g		h,b,f,c**			a,d,g,e**				h,f,c		
Same data, changes only, collapsed	6	6		0		21	13			8		

*63i is omitted. It was never chosen.
**a,d,g,e are "monotonic," h,b,f,c contain "reversals" as explained in the text.

63*d* is much smaller than that for the less stable, nonsingular pattern 63*b*, confirming point 3.

This tendency of the nonsingular design to spread the choices over a wider range *competes* with the tendency toward greater singularity of the trace and, statistically speaking, dilutes it. The results represent a superimposition of the two tendencies, a random scatter away from 63*b* in *both directions* and a *unidirectional* tendency toward monotonic designs.

31. SYMMETRY—FIGURE 64*G*

In 1932, Perkins demonstrated a tendency of unsymmetric designs to become more symmetrical in later reproductions (see Section 62). There were objections to his method of repeated reproductions that resembles that of Wulf. Actually, the method is not unlike that employed by Bartlett (1932), who is only rarely faulted on such grounds. Regardless of any criticisms, it seemed desirable to repeat such an experiment with Hanawalt's method, the method used in the present study, and to establish the tendency to greater symmetry in recognition as well as reproduction. This was done in Goldmeier (1941) as part of a larger experiment. The procedure differed from that described in Section 27 in the following minor points: (1) No booklets were used. In the learning period the designs, drawn on cardboard in sizes between 3 and 10 inches, were shown to a whole class of college students; (2) there were four independent subgroups, one tested immediately, one after 3 days, one after 2 weeks, and one after 6 weeks; (3) all subjects had the reproduction test first; (4) the recognition material, a series of numbered drawings, was shown to the whole class; (5) a series of six designs was memorized by each group. The design reported on in this section was fourth in order of presentation.

The recognition material is shown in Fig. 64 *a–h;* the design memorized was 64g. Table 3 gives the results (recalculated from Goldmeier, 1941, Table V). The top line lists all eight designs. The 3rd, 4th, and 5th rows of the table list the symmetry axes of each design. This list shows that all the designs have some symmetry. Even the standard 64*g* is symmetrical, but only about a 45° oblique axis. However, psychologically, symmetry is strongly realized only if the axis is vertical, less so if it is horizontal, and symmetry about an oblique axis is phenomenally nearly dormant (Goldmeier, 1936/72, Chapter 6; Rock & Leaman, 1963). This means that phenomenally Fig. 64*h* is the most strongly symmetrical design, followed by 64*b*, and finally by *a* (and *f*); 64*d* ranks still lower, with *c* and *e* lowest. Note further that the standard *g* and *c* are mirror images of each other, reflected in the vertical, which makes them very similar to each other. Surely, there are additional features of the design that play a role, but those connected with symmetry seem to matter most.

The outcome of the recognition tests (Table 3, rows marked 6 weeks) parallels the phenomenal strength of symmetry of the various recognition designs. Of the

31. SYMMETRY—FIGURE 64G

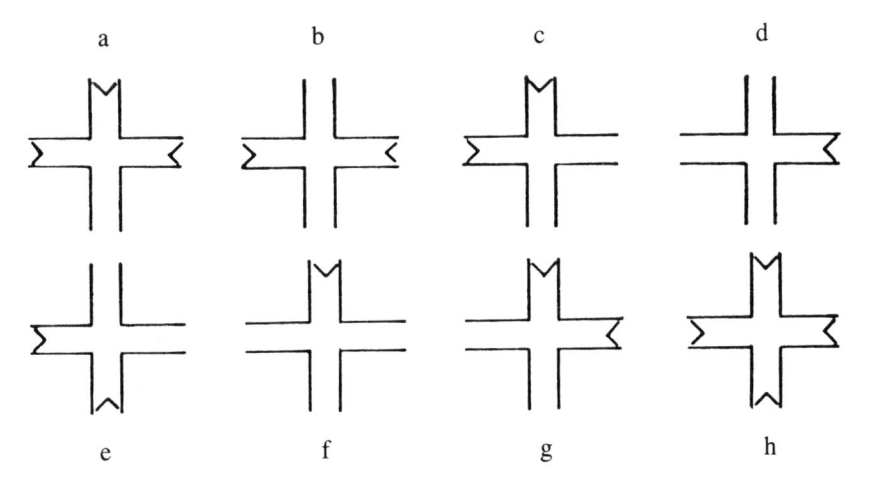

FIG. 64. Recognition material for experiments in which pattern g had been memorized. (From Goldmeier, 1941.)

TABLE 3
(From Goldmeier, 1941, Table V)
Recognition, Design Fig. 64

Design chosen		h	b	a	g	c	f*	d*	e*
Position of Vs**		·+·	·+·	·+·	+·	·+	+	+·	·+
axes of symmetry***		v	v	v			v		
		h	h					h	
		2ob			ob	ob			ob
	N								
3 days	30	0	0	0	30	0	—	—	—
2 weeks	42	5	3	1	33	0	—	—	—
6 weeks	47	17	10	1	14	5	—	—	—

| | | SAME CONDENSED | | |
Designs chosen	N	vertically symmetric	standard	mirror image of standard
		(h,b,a)	g	c
3 days	30	0	30	0
2 weeks	42	9	33	0
6 weeks	47	28	14	5

*Designs d,e,f were never chosen.
**The position of the Vs is diagrammed by a dot near the crossbar bearing the "V" in Fig. 64.
***v = vertical; h = horizontal; ob = 45° oblique.

47 recognition choices, 33 represent a change. Of these only five choices went to 64c, the design very similar to the standard and sharing its oblique symmetry. The remaining 28 choices went to three designs with better symmetry. A majority of 17 went to the best design, 64h, (four axes of symmetry including the vertical), 10 to the next best, b, (vertical and horizontal), and one choice to 64a (vertical only). Thus, of 33 changes, 28 went in the direction of greater symmetry, as understood here, versus five changes to the same degree of symmetry but greater similarity to the standard. The difference is highly significant ($p < .001$). Incidentally, the tendency to better symmetry is already noticeable to a significant degree after only a 2-week interval (nine choices out of nine, $p < .001$, see Table 3).

The recognition material was planned so as to allow the predictions of fading to manifest themselves. The material includes two designs, d and f, in which one of the two V's of the standard is missing; it also includes one design, a, with an additional V and one, h, with two additional V's. If fading implies loss of detail, choices of d or f, the designs that have only one V, should be most common, whereas choices of a with three V's, should be rare and choices of h with four V's still rarer.

The recognition material also includes two designs in which one V is "misplaced," the vertically symmetric Design 64b and Design 64c that does not have vertical symmetry. Because both of these designs agree with the standard in the placement of one V and disagree on the other V, they should be equally favored under fading. Finally, there is Design 64e, in which both V's are misplaced. This design has only oblique symmetry and therefore is an unlikely choice under either theory.

In terms of fading theory, the results are these: (1) *Two* V's are never misplaced (i.e., 64e is never chosen) as expected from either theory; (2) of the two instances of *one* misplaced V, the symmetric design 64b is chosen much more often than the mirror image of the standard, 64c. Fading would predict the two variants to be equivalent. However, the difference, 10 choices of 64b, five choices of 64c, falls short of being significant; (3) if the V's fade they should tend to be "forgotten," as Hanawalt (1937) has argued. Fading and reconstruction cannot easily account for added V's. The opposite actually occurs. The two designs with one missing V are never chosen, and 64h with two added V's accounts for 17 of the 33 changed recognitions.

The results militate against fading theory, although they fit an explanation by a "tendency toward increased (vertical) symmetry."

32. SELF-CONSISTENCY AS FIGURAL INTEGRATION—EXPERIMENT FIG. 65

Whereas fading fails as an explanation, the tendency toward increased (vertical) symmetry is not necessarily established as the complete explanation by the experiment with Fig. 64. As I have pointed out previously (Goldmeier, 1941):

32. SELF-CONSISTENCY AS FIGURAL INTEGRATION EXPERIMENT FIG. 65

FIG. 65. In a companion experiment to figure 64 this pattern was memorized. Subsequently recognition was tested with an array like that of figure 64, except that the regular cross of figure 64 was replaced by the cross of figure 65. The patterns *a* to *h* had respectively the same arrangements of the little Vs as in figure 64*a* to *h*.

> The 'tendency toward symmetry'... is conditioned by the principle of increased integration.... Evidently, Design 64*g* becomes not only more symmetrical, but in so doing, more integrated.... An easy way of testing this interpretation would be to create an asymmetric modification of Design 64*g* which could achieve integration without becoming symmetrical [p. 497–498].

I have now designed and tested two asymmetric modifications of 64*g*. One of these is shown in Fg. 65. Figure 65 is the second of the three designs presented to two groups of Experiment III and tested by a reproduction-before-recognition group and by a recognition-test-first group. All eight recognition designs consist of the "double-curved cross with a thick line," shown in Fig. 65, and have little V's, arranged as in the corresponding designs of Fig. 64*a–h* (e.g., the top left recognition design for Fig. 65 consists of the double-curved cross of Design 65 and little V's in all but the bottom arm of the cross). We refer to the eight designs by the *letter* of the corresponding design of 64 *a–h* with the *number 65*. The standard, (Fig. 65) is referred to as 65*g*, the design with V's in all four cross arms as 65*h*, etc. As in the recognition material for 64*g*, the eight choices offered for 65*g* differ only in regard to the little V's, whereas the double-curved cross is common to all eight variants.

Even though the cross part of Fig. 65*g*, is not symmetric and consequently none of the eight arrangements of V's make the design symmetric, the results of the recognition tests (Table 4, line 2) very much parallel those obtained with the symmetric cross of Fig. 64*g* (Table 4, line 1). In both experiments, design *h* (V's in all four arms) and *b* (V's in both horizontal arms) account for over half the changed recognitions. In both experiments, few subjects recognize the standard *g* or designs *c* or *e* (similar to the standard, 2 V's), and still fewer choose the two designs with one V, which is what fading and "forgetting" predict.

What, if not symmetry, explains the outcome of the two experiments? The explanation must lie in structural properties shared by Designs 64 and 65. In both designs, opposite crossarms are strongly grouped together into two subunits, the

146 5. INTRINSIC CHANGE IN RECOGNITION

two crossbars. This grouping occurs according to Wertheimer's (1923) factor of "good continuation" and is a potent organizing principle in both designs. The organization into *two* cross*bars* is independent of symmetry, but, like symmetry, it makes some placements of V's more consistent with the structure of the cross than others. Overall consistency increases if a V is placed into *both ends* of one cross bar or *both ends* of both crossbars, instead of into one but not the other end of either bar. In both Design 64 and Design 65, the V's in the standard *g* are inconsistent with the subgrouping of the cross into two crossbars. The inconsistencies are similar to the inconsistency between triangles and bars in 63*b* (Section 30). In the case of variations *c,f,d* and *e* of 65*g*, the placement of V's is just as inconsistent with the cross structure as in the corresponding variations of 64*g*. In the case of 65*a*, it is somewhat more consistent and most consistent in 65*b* and 65*h*. The notion of increased self-consistency therefore explains the prevalence of choices of *h* and *b* and the scarcity of recognitions of *c,d,e,* and *f* and of the standard of *both* Designs 65 *and* 64.

Now for the differences between Designs 65 and 64. Fading, of course, predicts that there are no differences in the recognitions, because the V's fade independently of the cross. Actually, differences do occur because of the structural differences between the two crosses. The four crossarms of Design 64 are equal. This equality is *most consistent* with placement of V's in all four arms, Design 64*h*, less so with placement into the horizontal arms only, Design 64*b*, and least with placing V's in three of the four equal arms, Design 64*a*. In this respect, 64*a* is at great disadvantage in spite of its vertical symmetry. Table 4 shows 64*h, b,* and *a* recognized by 17, 10, and 1 subjects, respectively. The equality of the four arms in Design 64 favors a grouping in which all arms are equivalent. This grouping competes with and somewhat suppresses the grouping together of each set of opposing arms into a subgroup, a *crossbar*. In Design 65, on the other hand, there is: (1) *no equality;* Wertheimer's factor of good continuation has free rein to produce the subgrouping into a vertical and a horizontal crossbar; (2) the equality of the two arms of the vertical bar is weakened by the phenomenal differences between "up" and "down" (as opposed to the near

TABLE 4
Number of Recognitions, Design 64g, 65g, 66g

Position of Vs (as in Fig. 64)		h	b	a	g	c	f	d	e
Standard	N								
64g	47	17	10	1	**14**	5			
65g	65	16	21	7	**10**	5	3	2	1
66g	54	5	3	2	**31**	4	2	4	3

Boldface indicates the standard.

equivalence of "right" and "left") (Goldmeier, 1972, proposition 3, p. 93). Therefore, in Design 65, the structural equivalence of the ends of the horizontal arms is stronger than the equivalence of the upper and lower arm.

Compared with Design 64, the cross structure of Design 65 is less compatible with placing V's in all four arms (Design *h*) and more consistent with having V's in the two horizontal arms (Design *b*). Again, the placement of V's in Design *a* is the least consistent, but the inconsistency is less in *a* than in 64*a* because Design 65*a* has two V's in the horizontal arms, like 65*b*, plus one V in the upper arm, which in Design 65 is functionally (i.e., as concerns subgroupings) more independent than in the cross of Design 64, where it is one of four coequals. Instead of four equivalent arms favoring the arrangement 64*h* over 64*a*, Design 65 has, functionally and phenomenally, the horizontal pair of arms, the top arm, and, thirdly, the bottom arm. This grouping, although compatible with arrangement *h*, is more amenable to arrangement *a*, which leaves out the V in the bottom arm.

The recognitions reflect the differences between the two designs. In the case of Design 65, arrangements *b* and *a* have gained frequency over *h*.

The following comparisons, based on the number of subjects selecting Designs *h* over *a* or *b* (from Table 4) bear this out.

Arrangement chosen	*h*	*b*
Design 64	17	10
Design 65	16	21

The difference is suggestive ($p < 0.2$).

Arrangement chosen	*h*	*a*
Design 64	17	1
Design 65	16	7

The difference is significant ($p < .05$). Finally, choices of *h* versus choices of *a* or *b*:

Arrangement chosen	*h*	*a* or *b*
Design 64	17	11
Design 65	16	28

a significant ($p < .05$) difference, preference for *h* with Design 64, a preponderance of *a* or *b* over *h* for Design 65.

33. SELF-CONSISTENCY CONTINUED—FIGURE 66G

The experiment with Design 65*g* disposes of the explanation of Experiments 64*g* and 65*g* by symmetry, unless one argues that the cross of 65*g* is so nearly

148   5. INTRINSIC CHANGE IN RECOGNITION

symmetric that the symmetry explanation carries over to 65g. To answer this criticism, an experiment was performed with the design shown in Fig. 66. The recognition material for the experiment with 66g consists of the cross of 66g with the same arrangements of V's as those in Fig. 64a to h, applied, however, to the cross with the "bent left arm" of Fig. 66. Geometrically, the cross of Design 66 is *more* like 64 than is 65. If 65 is nearly symmetric, the cross of Design 66 is even more like the symmetrical cross of 64g. On the other hand, the phenomenal grouping of the arms is drastically different from either cross, 64 or 65. By Wertheimer's factor of equality—straight versus bent—the arms are grouped 3 to 1. By the factor of good continuation, the arms are grouped 2 and 2 into two crossbars. These two groupings compete with each other; no unique, compelling, grouping is available. However, the arrangement g of the V's, as in Fig. 66, *resolves the ambiguity in favor* of the 2 and 2 grouping. A V in the "upper" arm of each bar *stabilizes* the pattern as a "cross with a V in the top end of each crossbar." The V's increase the self-consistency of Design 66g. The increased self-consistency is analogous to the enhancement of the plain cross by the four V's in 64h, of the double curved cross by the arrangement 65b, and the increased compatibility of cross and V's in 65a compared with 64a. By this reasoning, the arrangement 66g should be stable and therefore preferentially recognized. Taking the figures from Table 4, unchanged recognitions of 66g compare with those of 64g and 65g as follows:

	recognitions unchanged (g)	changed (non-g)
Design 66	31	23
Design 64	14	33

The preference for arrangement g in Design 66 over that in Design 64 is significant at the 1% level. Comparing 66 with 65:

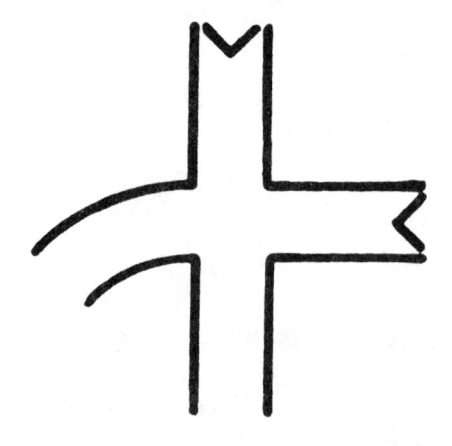

FIG. 66. This pattern also was used as standard in a companion experiment to 64g and 65g. The recognition array featured the cross shown in figure 66 with the arrangement of little Vs as in figure 64a to h.

	recognitions	
	unchanged	changed
	(g)	(non-g)
Design 66	31	23
Design 65	10	55

Again the difference is significant ($p < .001$).

None of the other seven arrangements of V's (see Fig. 64 and the top symbols in Table 4) enhance the structure of the cross design of Fig. 66.

To push this analysis further soon becomes speculative in the absence of further experimental data. For instance, the cross of Fig. 66 should be well-stabilized by three V's, placed in the top, bottom, and right arm (i.e., into the three straight arms). Three V's in this arrangement should resolve the ambiguity in the cross structure in favor of a 3 to 1, or straight versus bent, grouping of the arms and a standard with this arrangement of V's should be even more stable in a recognition experiment than 66g, whereas the same arrangement in the setting of the cross of Fig. 64 or 65 should be just as unstable as 64g and 65g proved to be. However, I have not made experiments with these designs.

Taken together, the three cross experiments 64, 65, 66, demonstrate that the apparent "tendency toward symmetry" in Experiment 64 is mediated by the more general principle of increased integration of the design features, by what we call here self-consistency, and what is also called goodness or regularity.

Taken by itself, experiment Fig. 66 contains a lesson for those who report and theorize on the absence of memory change. If Hebb and Foord (1945), for example, had used 66g as their standard design instead of their own (Fig. 75), they would have "proved" the absence of memory changes. Had they used 64g—which was published in 1941 and available to them—they would have disproved their thesis. The contention (Koffka, 1935; Wulf, 1922) that traces change in the direction of a "better" gestalt has the important corollary that *an already optimal design fails to change* [case (a) of Section 23].

34. SLANT—FIGURE 67D

The standard for the next example of recognitions is Fig. 67d. It has many nonsingular features. One of them, the slant of the left upright line, is examined for tendencies to a more singular design. The reason for selecting the slant is the relative ease with which slant can be measured in the copies and reproductions.

The line looks slanted if it forms an angle of 87° or less with the horizontal. In the standard, Fig. 67d, the angle is 85°. If the angle measures 88–92°, the line looks perpendicular; if the angle is larger, the line looks slanted to the right. If either of the latter two changes occurs, the design is more singular; If the left line is perpendicular, it falls into the singular vertical; if the line is slanted to the right,

150   5. INTRINSIC CHANGE IN RECOGNITION

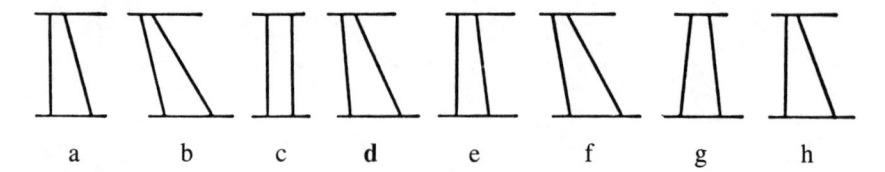

   a   b   c   **d**   e   f   g   h

FIG. 67.   Recognition array for 67*d* as standard. (From Goldmeier, 1941.)

the figure as a whole is closer to symmetry (as in 67*g*). The two kinds of change, one toward perpendicularity and the other toward symmetry, both happen to involve a change toward larger angles, so they can be lumped together in the tabulations (as "over 87°"). Both represent change toward a more stable configuration. In Fig. 67, "over 87°" includes Designs *a, e,* and *h* (90°), Design *g* (96°), which is quite close to symmetry about a vertical axis, and 67*c,* which is both vertical and symmetric.

This experiment is also taken from Goldmeier (1941). The standard 67*d* was the sixth and last design memorized. The procedure is described in connection with Experiment 64 (Section 31).

In tabulating the results (Table 5), the data are subdivided according to the slant of the left upright bar in each second copy. If the second copy had a slant of 87° to the left or if it was *more slanted* (i.e., if the angle was *less than 87°,* as in the standard), it was classified as "2nd copy slanted to the left"; if more than 87°, as "over 87°." Presumably, over 87° second copies indicate that the design was seen and memorized in a more stable form. A recognition choice of over 87° would then not represent a change. In fact, these subjects should preferentially choose over 87° (i.e., *there should be little further change*). On the other hand, those who memorized the standard as a design with the left bar slanted to the left, *as attested by their own second copies,* should tend to change to the more stable designs as a consequence of the stresses in the trace.

Even though only one standard was used, the situation is comparable to the experiments with Designs Fig. 61, 63, 64, and 66, where a stable variant of a design was compared with a less stable one. The subjects with a second copy over 87° effectively memorized a more stable variant, whereas those with slanted copies memorized a less stable variant.

The results after the 6-week interval are shown in the last line of Table 5. Of the subjects who copied the design as "slanted," only 10 chose one of the slanted designs, whereas 23 changed to an over 87° design. This difference is significant at the $p < .05$ level. Conversely, a significant majority of those who had copied the standard as over 87°, 12 out of 15, ($p < 0.05$) chose one of the designs over 87°. Again, a significant majority chose the more stable designs.

What would a fading theory predict in this experiment? For those who "correctly" copied the slant to the left there should be errors of increasing magnitude as time goes by. The errors should randomly go either to more slanted designs (i.e., *same* as learned or to designs over 87° that we call "changed"). There is no reason why fading should lead to more changed, as it significantly does. For those who copied the design as over 87°, fading likewise should impartially lead to choices of same (in this case, over 87°) and of changed (i.e., "slanted to the left"). So it should not make any difference what the subject memorized; the distribution of same and changed should not significantly differ in the two cases. Comparing the data (from the last line of Table 5):

	remembered as "same"	as changed
copy with left slant	10	23
copy over 87°	12	3

The difference is marked ($\chi^2 = 10.26$, $p < .01$). Diffuse and undirected fading would produce this result in less than 1 of 100 instances.

The idea of measuring memory change from the second copy instead of from the given standard was conceived by Hanawalt (1937) to separate spurious, *perceptual* change from the true *memory* changes (if indeed there were any). Because Hanawalt's distinction here favors the gestalt point of view, there might be second thoughts about its validity. I think it is valid, but abandoning it in this case still leads to the same conclusion. Dropping the distinction between the "slanted" and the "over 87°" copies and combining the two groups, 13 subjects choose designs slanted to the left as much or more than the standard, compared with 35 who change to over 87°. This deviation from a half and half distribution

TABLE 5
(Recalculated from Goldmeier, 1941, Table VI)
Recognition, Design Fig. 67d

	Number of Ss whose 2nd copy is			
	slanted to the left* and who chose designs		over 87°* and who chose designs	
Interval	slanted to the left**	over 87°**	slanted to the left**	over 87°**
3 days	16	3	4	7
2 weeks	19	7	3	13
6 weeks	10	23	3	12

*The second copies were carefully measured as to the slant of the left upright. If this angle measured 87° or less, it was classified as "slanted to the left," if more, as "over 87°."
**"Slant to the left" includes the standard 67d as well as 67b and 67f. The remaining designs, a, c, e, g, and h, are "over 87°."

152   5. INTRINSIC CHANGE IN RECOGNITION

is significant at the 1% level of confidence. But from fading theory, it should not even be half and half because the memorized design was not midway, but slanted to the left.

35. MEMORY FOR GAPS—I. DESIGN 68*E* VERSUS 68*H*

The last group of experiments in this chapter deals with a number of related designs containing *gaps* (Fig. 68). A discussion of the widespread misunderstanding of gestalt theory to the effect that "all gaps tend to close" is left to the next chapter, on reproduction. The recognition experiments in this chapter deal with gap *position* as it affects the structure of the design. Closure is excluded by the simple expedient of not providing recognition material with closed gaps.

The designs of Fig. 68 (except 68*l*) contain four symmetric gaps. The gaps are shifted, by one gap width, from the side curves to the cusps and from there to the center curve. Geometrically, the variation from Fig. 68*a* to 68*l* is one-dimensional. Psychologically, there are two dimensions of change. Designs 68*a*

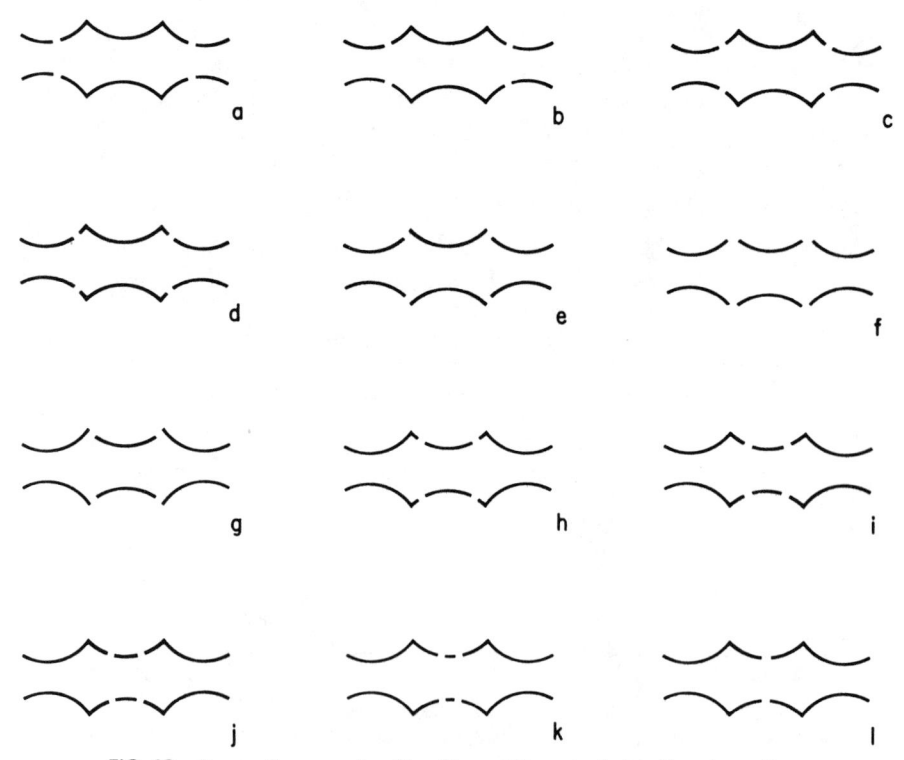

FIG. 68.   Recognition array for either 68*e* or 68*h* as standard in Experiment II.

TABLE 6
Experiment II, Designs of Fig. 68, 4 Week Interval.
No. of Ss Choosing Designs a–l* in Recognition

Design memorized		e						h					
Design chosen	N	e	f	g	N	a	b	c	d	g	h	i	j	l
Reproduction first	11	**8**		3	18			5	5	1	**3**	2	1	1
Recognition first	18	**16**	1	1	13	2	4	1	2		**2**	2		
Both combined	29	**24**	1	4	31	2	4	6	7	1	**5**	4	1	1
Same condensed		e	f–g				a–d			e–g	h		i–l	
	29	**24**	5		31		19			1	**5**		6	

Boldface indicates standard design.
*68k is omitted. It was never chosen.

to 68d and 68h to 68l have gaps *within the curves* whereas Fig. 68e, f, and g have gaps *at the cusps*. This is evident from the similarity rankings described in Section 6 (and Goldmeier, 1972). In addition, the rankings show that the designs are very sensitive to change from Fig. 68d to e and from h to g. This sensitivity to change defines singularities (see Section 8, especially the comments to Fig. 31, 32, and 33). In the case of the patterns of Fig. 68, the rankings indicate that the *cusps* of these designs are *singular gap locations*, whereas gaps within the curves (as in 68d and 68h) are nonsingular. The singularity at the cusps implies in our theory that: (1) singular patterns, like 68e, show *few instances of memory change* [case (a) of Section 23], whereas a nonsingular pattern, such as Design 68h, shows comparatively many changed recognitions [case (c) of Section 23]; (2) if 68e does change, it changes to Designs 68f or 68g, which also have the gaps at the cusps, whereas the choices of subjects who memorized 68h (or d, Section 36) range widely over most of the available designs; (3) Because a strong singularity can create two separate dimensions of change (see Section 6, this section earlier, and Attneave, 1950), the ranges of variation of the two designs 68e and 68h should be mutually exclusive (i.e., changes of 68e should fall into the range 68e to g; changes of 68h should involve the remaining designs, to the exclusion of Designs $e, f,$ and g).

Either Design 68e or 68h was first on a list of three tasks given in Experiment II. Four independent groups were tested at each of four time intervals (details of the procedure in Section 27). The following discussion is based on the four groups tested after 4 weeks. Recognition was tested with the full array of 12 designs shown in Fig. 68. This array, which shows 68e in the upper center spot and 68h in the lower center, was used for the two groups who memorized 68e as well as for the two 68h groups.

Table 6 shows, on the first two lines, the recognition choices made by the four groups. The third line contains the sum of the results of line 1 and 2. The last line

FIG. 69.

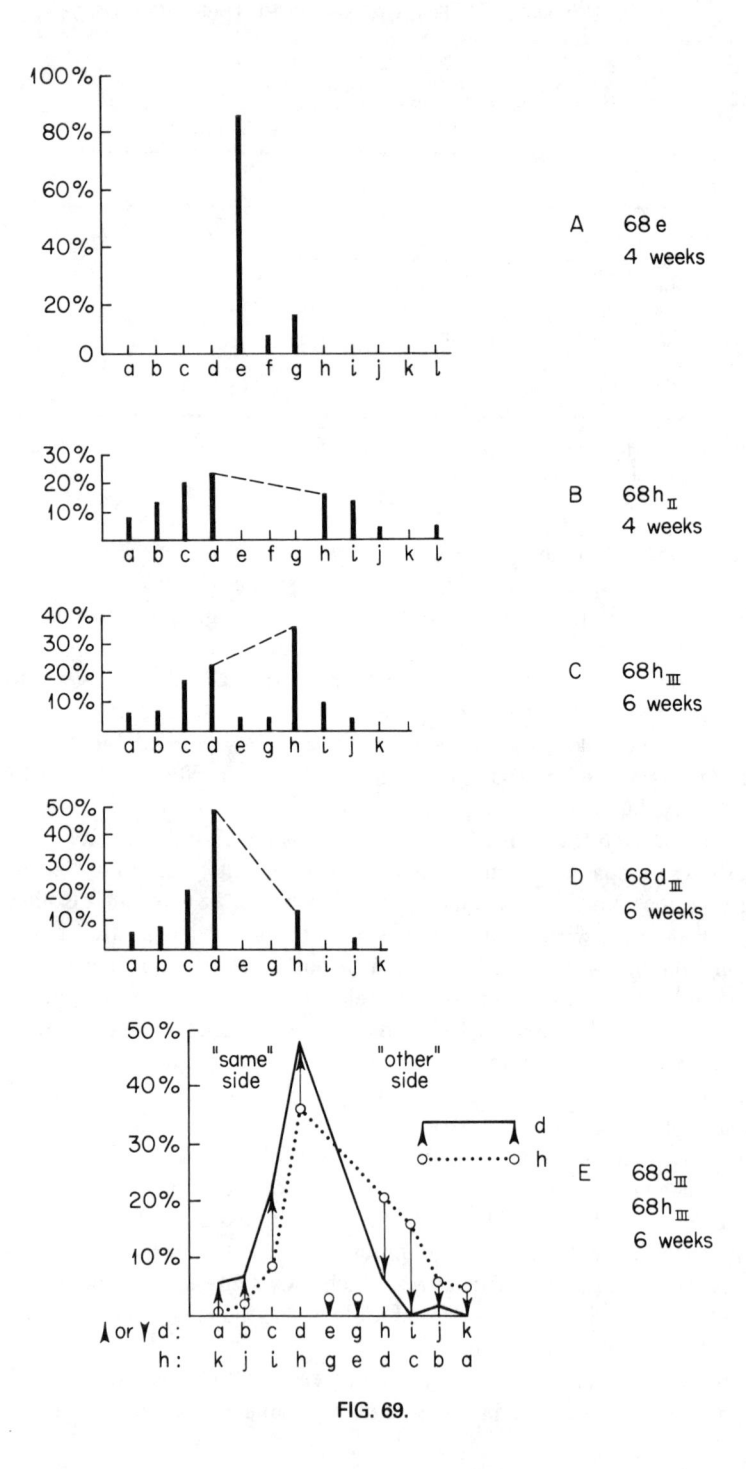

gives the data of line 3 in condensed form. The content of line 3 is graphically displayed in Fig. 69A and B.

1. Fading should weaken the trace of 68*e* to the same extent as that of 68*h*. Therefore, fading theory predicts the same amount of "error" (choice of designs other than the standard) for the recognitions of both designs. The result, from Table 6, line 3 or 4, is that: if 68*e* is memorized, there are 24 unchanged, 5 changed; if 68*h* is memorized, there are 5 unchanged, 26 changed recognitions. This difference between two geometrically nearly identical designs is highly significant ($p < .001$). Because fading predicts the opposite result, the difference must be a consequence of the *intrinsic structural differences* between the two designs and their traces. The gap locations of 68*e* are intrinsically *stable;* those of 68*h* are indeterminate, only vaguely fixed by the structure of the design.

In statistical terms, fading theory calls for the same percentage of "correct" recognitions for both 68*e* and 68*h*, because both have been "learned to the same criterion." Figure 69A and B (and C) show graphically the great difference in correct choices between the two designs.

2. The gap locations of 68*e, f,* and *g* are *prostructural,* hence, in the singular range. All the remaining locations are *contrastructural,* and therefore in the nonsingular range. Accordingly, changes of 68*e* are confined to the two neighboring, singular variants, 68*f* and *g,* whereas changed recognitions of 68*h* include (Table 6, line 3) eight of the 11 variants of 68*h* offered. This difference is another measure of the marked *stability* of 68*e,* and the indeterminacy of 68*h,* with respect to gap location.

In terms of error curves, fading theory predicts that the curves of two equivalent designs should have the same width. (This applies when, as in this case, one distribution completely overlaps the other. With disjoint distributions, the metric of the sample space requires consideration.) Figure 69 demonstrates the disparity in width of 69A compared with 69B (and 69C and D).

3. The designs of the recognition material (Fig. 68) are the result of the *variation of a single parameter* (gap location) *in graded steps* (in most instances, steps of one gap width) from 68*a* to 68*l.* The standard Designs 68*e* and *h* are four or more steps away from the ends of the series. In such circumstances, fading theory predicts an error curve that *monotonically decreases* from the standard in both directions.

FIG. 69. Graph A shows the recognition of $68e_{II}$ after 4 weeks. Graph B shows the recognitions of $68h_{II}$ after 4 weeks. The subscript II indicates Experiment II. Similarly, subscript III in C, D, and E signifies Experiment III. Graph C shows the 6-week recognitions of $68h_{III}$. Graph D shows the 6-week recognitions of $68d_{III}$. Graph E shows C and D superimposed and *h* charted backwards, so that the "same side" and the "other side" can be compared. Solid line indicates d_{III}, dotted line indicates recognitions of h_{III}.

5. INTRINSIC CHANGE IN RECOGNITION

In comparing the actual plots (Fig. 69), we disregard: (a) the small secondary peak at g in Fig. 69A (it is discussed in Section 63); (b) the choices of e and g (for h) in Table 6 and in Fig. 69B and C (they are not significantly different from zero); and (c) the fact that the curves for 68h, Fig. 69B and C, are skewed in favor of Designs a, b, c, and d (as discussed in Section 36). With these three simplifications, we find that the "error curve" of 68e (Fig. 69A) is monotonically decreasing from the maximum (disregarding the choices of 68g, (see Section 63), whereas the plot of 68h and 68d (Fig. 69B, C, and D) is strongly bimodal. The bimodality is caused by the virtual absence of recognitions of e, f, and g on the part of subjects who memorized the nonsingular Designs 68h (and 68d). Bimodality usually indicates the presence of two different populations in a sample. Here, this explanation is unlikely. The reason for the bimodality is the fact that the variation of the gap position is *phenomenally two-dimensional* (even though it is geometrically one-dimensional), as shown by similarity studies (Section 6). Exclusion of the intruded dimension represented by 68e, f, and g is indicated by the dashed lines in Fig. 69B, C, and D. It transforms the graph into a unimodal distribution. This interpretation of the bimodality is supported by the fact that the recognitions of 68e vary only within the interspersed dimension encompassed by 68e, f, and g. "Fading" is quite unable to account for this *mutual exclusion of recognition choices.*

We conclude that psychologically the variation from 68a to b, c, d, *and from there directly to* 68h, i, j, k, and l represents a single dimension of change. An error curve should therefore proceed from point d to h and skip points e, f, and g. If this reasoning is correct for the choices with 68h as the standard, it also applies if 68d is memorized. Figure 69D shows the curve obtained when 68d is memorized (see next section). This curve, too, conforms to a typical error curve if points e, f, and g are left out (dashed line).

36. MEMORY FOR GAPS—II. TENDENCY TO CONSISTENT STRUCTURE: DESIGNS *D* AND *H*

Fading does not explain the almost complete absence of choices of 68e, f, and g by subjects who memorized 68h and therefore does not explain the bimodality of Fig. 69B. The question arises, can fading account for the curve Fig. 69b if the bimodality is patched up by the dashed line? This question is investigated by the following experiment, which forms part of Experiment III. Figures 68d and 68h serve as standards, each for two independent groups. Figures 68d and 68h each are the third of three designs presented in Experiment III. The time interval between memorizing and testing is 6 weeks. The recognition material differs from the array shown in Fig. 68 by the absence of Designs 68f and 68l. The remaining 10 designs are presented in the two different arrangements in the

36. MEMORY FOR GAPS—II. TENDENCY TO CONSISTENT STRUCTURES 157

following diagram, one for the two groups who memorized 68d, the other for the two groups who memorized 68h. (Boldface indicates the design memorized by the group.)

Arrangement of the 10
recognition designs
for testing the subjects
who memorized

68h	68d
a b	k j
c d e	i h g
g **h** i	e **d** c
j k	b a

In both arrays, the design memorized occupies the center bottom position, so that neither one of the standards has a positional advantage (if indeed position within the array matters). The arrays are related to each other by a 180° rotation.

1. Although fading treats 68d and 68h alike, structurally, the two designs are *not* equivalent. In 68d, *two* gaps are on *two* side curves, whereas in 68h, *two* gaps are crowded on *one* center curve. The relation of gaps to curves leads to a *more consistent structure:* In 68d, each side curve has "its" gap; in 68h, *four* gaps on two (center) curves, *no* gaps on four (side) curves. The *Tendency to a Self-Consistent Structure* predicts a tendency to favor the side curves (i.e., to favor recognitions of Designs 68a, b, c, d over 68h, i, j, k, regardless of whether Design 68d or 68h is memorized. Therefore, those who memorized 68d should choose gaps on the *same* curves, whereas those who memorized 68h should choose gaps on the *other* curves. ("Same" curve means the curve on which the gap appeared in the standard. "Other" curves are the curves that in the standard did not have a gap. In the case of 68d, the *side* curves are the *same* curves and the *center* curves are the *other* curves. In the case of 68h, the reverse is true; the center curves are the *same* curves, the side curves *other* curves.) Fading, on the other hand, predicts a preference for the same curves in the case of *both* designs. The results (Table 7) show the same kind of change whether a reproduction test precedes recognition (first line of Table 7) or the recognition test is given first (second line of Table 7). Because the conclusions follow from both experiments separately, the following analysis uses the combined figures only (third and fourth line of Table 7). Stress theory predicts that the gaps in 68d tend to remain on the same (side) curves, whereas the gaps in 68h tend to the other (also the side) curves. Line 4, Table 7 gives the recognition choices of the gap locations on the same and other curves for both designs:

5. INTRINSIC CHANGE IN RECOGNITION

TABLE 7
Designs of Fig. 68, Recognition
Choices of Designs a–j*
Experiment III, 6 Weeks

		Design d Memorized				Design h Memorized			
		"Same" (Side) Curves	Cusps	"Other" (Middle) Curves		"Same" (Middle) Curves	Cusps	"Other" (Side) Curves	
Gap On	N				N				
Designs chosen		a b c d	e g	h i j		j i h	g e	d c b a	
Reproduction first	29	1 2 5 15	6		35	1 4 12	1	10 5 2	
Recognition first	29	2 2 8 14	2	1	30	2 12	1	4 6 4 1	
Both combined	58	3 4 13 29	8	1	65	1 6 24	1 1	14 11 4 3	
Both combined and condensed	58	a–c d 20 29	e–g 0	h–j* 9	65	i–j* h 7 24	e–g 2	a–d 32	

Boldface indicates the standard.
*Design k was never chosen.

Number of subjects choosing gap locations on the

	"same" curves	"other" curves
68d memorized	20 (49)	9
68h memorized	7 (31)	32

The numbers in parenthesis include *all* choices on the same curves, the smaller numbers represent only *changed* ("incorrect") recognitions. The difference between the two designs is significant at the .0005 level for either set of numbers.

The failure of fading theory is graphically illustrated in Fig. 69E. Fading predicts the same percentage of correct recognitions for 68h and 68d and the same percentage of one-step errors, two-step errors, and three-step errors on the same side and the same percentage of errors for the various designs with gaps on the other side. In other words, the graphs should be mirror images of each other. As the graph demonstrates, those who memorized d have an excess of recognitions of each of the designs on the same side and a consistent deficit on the other side. Instead of being mirror images of each other, both graphs are skewed toward the side curves (Designs a, b, c, and d).

2. Fading predicts that a recognition error should be as likely toward one side of the standard as in the opposite direction and regardless of whether the standard happens to be 68d or 68h. For instance, with 68d as standard, choices of 68c and 68h should occur with the same frequency as choices of 68i and 68d, respectively, if 68h is the standard. The comparison seems fair by the rules of

fading theory: 68c is as close to the standard d as 68i is to h. Likewise, whatever measure of change one assigns to the error of choosing h instead of d, it is as large as the reverse error of choosing d for h. Yet, (line 3, Table 7):

with standard   d, we have   13 choices of 68c,   8 choices of 68h;
with standard   h, we have   6 choices of 68i,   14 choices of 68d.

The ratios of 13/8 for d and 6/14 for h differ significantly ($p < .05$). The change is *directed* toward c and d, toward the side curves, toward greater self-consistency.

3. Fading predicts that smaller errors are more frequent than larger ones. We present therefore another comparison involving only 68c and 68i. A choice of 68c is a larger error for subjects who memorized h than for subjects who memorized d. (The meaning of "large" and "small" is inherently vague. Fading theory lacks a noncircular way to measure the "size" of errors in nonoverlapping ranges.) Conversely, a choice of 68i is a larger error if d was memorized than if h was memorized. Line 3, Table 7 gives the number of choices:

	"smaller error"		"larger error"	
standard 68d	(choice of 68c)	13	(choice of 68i)	0
standard 68h	(choice of 68i)	6	(choice of 68c)	11

The 68d result is compatible with fading, but, in the case of 68h, there are more large errors. The difference is highly significant ($p < .0005$). Regardless of which design is memorized, the more self-consistent Design 68c is more often chosen than Design 68i.

37. MEMORY FOR GAPS—III. GAP STRENGTH: FIG. 70 VERSUS FIG. 68

Figure 70 shows a series of designs like Fig. 68, but they are composed of dotted lines. The gaps are created by the omission of two dots and are wider than those of Fig. 68. The experiment of the preceding section, with 68d and 68h, is replicated with the dotted designs of Fig. 70. Design 70i has the gaps on the side curves like 68d, and Design d corresponds to 68h, having the gaps on the center curves. Designs 70i and 70d are, respectively, the first of the three designs in Experiment I. The experiment uses four independent groups, two groups for Design 70i and two groups for 70d.

Line 4 of Table 8 gives the recognition choices of gap locations on the same and other curves for 70i and 70d. Again, same means the same as the standard with respect to the curves on which the gaps are located. A choice of 70i,j,k,l is called a choice on the same curves if 70i is memorized; a choice of 70a,b,c,d is

160   5. INTRINSIC CHANGE IN RECOGNITION

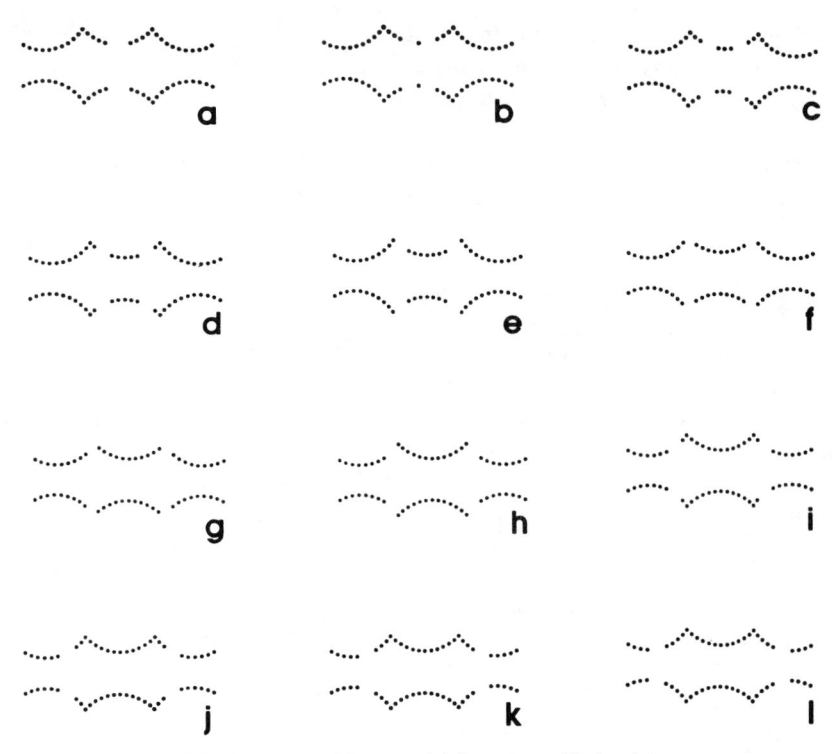

FIG. 70. Recognition material for patterns 70 *d* and *i*.

called a choice on the same (in this case the center) curves for those who memorized 70*d*. The other curves for 70*i* are 70*a,b,c,d;* for 70*d*, they are 70*i,j,k,l*.

Number of subjects choosing gap locations on the

	"same" curves	"other" curves
70*i* memorized	8 (19)	4
70*d* memorized	4 (18)	11

The numbers in parenthesis include *all* choices on the same curves, the smaller numbers represent only changed recognitions. The difference between the two designs is significant ($p < .05$) considering the changed recognitions only, short of significance ($p < .2$) if all recognitions of designs with gaps within curves are considered. In the case of both designs, five choices fell on gap positions *at the cusps* (Figs. 70*e,f,g,h*). These choices, being neither on the same nor the other curves, are excluded.

TABLE 8
Recognition Choices of Designs 70b*–l
Experiment I

		Design i Memorized													Design d Memorized									
		"Same" (Side) Curves			Cusps					"Other" (Middle) Curves				"Same" (Middle) Curves			Cusps					"Other" (Side) Curves		
Gap located on:	N	l	k	j	i	h	g	f	e	d	c	b	N	b	c	d	e	f	g	h	i	j	k	l
Designs chosen																									
Reproduction first	15	1	2	1	**8**		1	1				1	16	1	1	**3**	1	1	2		1	3	2	1
Recognition first	13		2	4	**3**	1	2			3			18		2	**11**		1		1	2	1		1
Both combined	28	1	2	5	**11**	1	3	1		3		1	34	1	3	**14**	1	2	2	1	3	4	2	2
Combined and condensed	28	j–k 8			**i** 11	e–h 5				d 3	b–d 4		34	b–c 4		**d** 14	e–g 5				i–l 11			

*Design 70a was never chosen and is therefore not listed in the table.
Boldface indicates the standard design.

162   5. INTRINSIC CHANGE IN RECOGNITION

The results of Experiment 70*i* and 70*d* parallel those of Experiment 68*d* and 68*h* but are weaker. This weakness is not merely a matter of statistics but is due to the weak organization of the pattern. The relevant design features and the gaps are not very salient; therefore, the tendency for change is weak, even though it is in the predicted direction. Specifically, the weakness is a matter of *low gap strength*. The gaps in Fig. 70 are enlarged distances between dots. They differ from regular distances only in degree, not in kind. Similarity experiments with these designs and with the same designs drawn in solid lines (Fig. 68) show the gap effect to be much weaker with the dotted patterns (Goldmeier, 1972, Section 57, 58). The present experiments, Fig. 70 versus Fig. 68, demonstrate that memory changes, like similarity, depend sensitively on the *strength* of the perceptual organization, in this case, on the saliency of the gap.

The three-gap experiments show:

1. Memory for prostructural gap locations (68*e*, gaps at cusps) is *stable* compared with memory for contrastructural locations (68*d*, 68*h*, 70*i*, 70*d*, gaps within curves) that is *imprecise*. (The trace is *indeterminate* with respect to contrastructural features.) As in physics, the word "stable" carries the connotation that there is always some uncertainty but that the *range of uncertainty* can be small—stability—or large—indeterminancy—and is in either case subject to laws.

2. The difference between prostructural and contrastructural locations is twofold. If the gap location is contrastructural: (a) More recognitions fall on *changed* designs (*more errors*); and (b) the range of recognition choices is larger (*errors more widely scattered*).

3. Some contrastructural gap locations are more compatible or consistent with the overall structure of the design than others. With the designs used in this study there is a *significant tendency for change to side curves*.

4. Gap effects depend on the *gap strength*, as shown in the case of the tendency to a consistent structure. This tendency is more pronounced with the strong gaps of Fig. 68 than with the weak gaps of Fig. 70.

38. THE EVIDENCE FOR DIRECTED CHANGE IN RECOGNITION

Past efforts to demonstrate directed change in recognition have suffered from several defects. If there was no directed change (Hebb & Foord, 1945, and many others), the experiment proved nothing. If directed changes were found, as in the case of Experiments 64 and 67, which were reported in 1941, there did not seem to be any way to prove that the change was directed toward an intrinsically more singular and self-consistent design. At most, one could appeal to plausibility or the results of independent ratings of "goodness." This defect is overcome here.

38. THE EVIDENCE FOR DIRECTED CHANGE IN RECOGNITION

For each unstable design in Fig. 61, 63, 68, and 70, a stable variant was identified; in some instances, independently, by means of similarity rankings; in all cases by memory experiments and subjected to the same recognition tests. The question is no longer: Is there a change in the direction of what hopefully everyone will accept as stability? Now the experiment with the stable variant furnishes a standard of stability for each design from which to measure the change. Fading can not explain stability in one and lack of it in the other *of two closely related designs,* pairs like 70*i* and 70*d*, 61*c* and 61*f*, 63*d* and 63*b*, 64*g* and 65 or 66*g*, and the subgroups of Design 67*d*.

In order to prove the existence of directed change or, for that matter, the existence of anything, it suffices to exhibit a single positive instance. Having done so six times, the case can well rest here. Whatever interpretation one wishes to place on the results of the recognition experiments, he cannot deny:

1. The existence of directed change.
2. The failure of fading theory to account for it.

6 Intrinsic Change in Reproduction

39. CHANGE IN SEVERAL DIMENSIONS

In recognition tests, the observable changes are limited to the variants provided by the experimenter. In recall, they are limited only by the subject's ability to express them. In recognition, the theory has to account only for the frequency of the several choices. In recall, it has to explain the infinite variety of reproductions encountered.

The recognition material can be intentionally restricted in such a way as to examine only *one or a few dimensions* of possible changes, for instance, the consistent or inconsistent placement of the gaps in Fig. 68. Any other dimensions of change, for instance, changes in the number or mutual relationship of the curves, cannot manifest themselves; they are, in effect, excluded. *Identification and analysis of each dimension of change separately is required in recall just as in recognition,* but it is a much more difficult task.

The investigation of changes in recall of the designs Fig. 72a and b, taken from Goldmeier (1941), well illustrates this point. There were, as always, many dimensions of change. Any one of them might be tabulated, and if there are enough of that kind, a statistical increase of changes with time might be demonstrated. For instance, some subjects draw the lines more curved; others draw them less curved than in their second copies. Riley (1962) objected to the omission of information on these changes of curvature (p. 437). There are, however, good and quite generally valid reasons for such omissions. Firstly, because the *degree* of curvature is nonsingular, random changes either way are expected from stress theory as well as from any decay or fading [see Section 23, case (c)]. Thus, the information does not discriminate between the two theories. Secondly,

166   6. INTRINSIC CHANGE IN REPRODUCTION

needs specific features of the curves or one of the two symmetric halves, in short, the features at the base of the hierarchy, whatever they happen to be in the particular design.

If the subject omits the design, this interpretation remains conjectural. But some subjects *reconstruct* a design, grafting the features remembered onto an ad hoc base. Reconstruction seems to account for the "reproduction" of 68e shown in Fig. 80q. The drawing embodies the features mentioned, yet, it is totally dissimilar to the standard. Recall of isolated features as in Fig. 80q or Fig. 79, b14, or d8 is rare in our material even though common in everyday life. Because of their dissimilarity to the standard, such reproductions are easy to detect. They are not due to "extrinsic" changes in the customary sense of this misleading term, although they have some resemblance to such extrinsic mechanisms as the so-called verbalizations (changes in the direction of associated verbal material) and figure assimilations (changes in the direction of another design from the same list) or object assimilation (change in the direction of a familiar object). Reconstruction uses knowledge from outside the trace and is therefore an extrinsic mechanism. But the outside material is not associated with the trace by pure coincidence in time or space but selected by virtue of *structural affinity*. For instance, the cross patterns, Fig. 64g, 65g, and 66g, often evoke the associations "crucifix" and "street" intersection," both of which appear sometimes in the comments from the subjects. An example of a reproduction that seems guided by the association with crucifix is Fig. 73g. An object assimilation based on street intersection may be found in Fig. 74a. The subject who reproduced Fig. 66g as Fig. 74a furnished the one word comment intersection in the learning period.

41. PROCEDURE AND SOURCES OF EXPERIMENTS

Twelve of the 24 groups involved in Experiments I, II, and III were given a reproduction test first, a recognition test second. Only these twelve groups are considered in this chapter on reproduction. The experiments reported in the present chapter have in common that reproduction was tested before the subjects were exposed to any recognition materials. The features analyzed in this chapter are selected for their relevance to the theoretical issues and for ease of classifying and quantifying the changes unequivocally.

In addition to Experiments I, II, and III, one experiment taken from Hanawalt (1937) and three experiments from Goldmeier (1941) are discussed in this chapter.

Compared with the tidy and objective scoring procedures possible with the recognitions, the scoring of the reproductions is often subjective and in individual cases open to serious question. Because of the difficulties of measurement inherent in evaluating reproductions, I have in several instances reported the whereas it is easy to distinguish a hand-drawn straight line from a line meant to be curved, it is difficult to specify, or measure, the degree of curvature and still harder to do this for the *change* in degree of curvature between the second copy and the later reproduction. Finally, the designs of Fig. 72 contain six curves that can change independently, further complicating the evaluation of this kind of change. With all this in mind, the analysis of the reproductions in this chapter is guided by the following considerations:

1. Any reproduction may show many different dimensions of change concurrently, in the same reproduction.
2. The investigation of change must deal with each kind or dimension of change separately, independent from all others.
3. From a theoretical point of view, only those changes deserve investigation that permit decisions among competing theories.
4. From a practical point of view, the method of testing memory changes by means of recall rather than, say, recognition is best suited to those types of change that are easy to measure, count, or otherwise quantify, In the case of Fig. 72*a* and *b,* for instance, this applies to changes in the *number* of curves, *number* of gaps, or change in *direction* of the curves (concave versus convex) (Goldmeier, 1941, p. 491 and later, Section 43). The features selected for statistical analysis are in each case chosen on the basis of what can be quantified.
5. In some instances, only one feature is analyzed; in other cases, there is enough information to analyze more features.

40. FRAGMENTARY REPRODUCTIONS AND RECONSTRUCTIONS

If the trace of a design is only partially accessible, if certain key features are irretrievable or forgotten, reproduction may be impossible, even though other features are remembered. Therefore, the number of reproductions obtainable is a good deal smaller than the number of recognitions from an equally large group of subjects.

A large amount of remembered information may be insufficient to reproduce a design. For example, a subject may remember that Fig. 68*e* is a line drawing (rather than a dot pattern or a solid area), that it is made up of disconnected, equal curves, and that it is symmetrical about the horizontal and about the vertical. Even though this is a considerable amount of information, it is not of the right kind to make a drawing. A subject may omit the design for want of the necessary details, where verbal recall or recognition might have elicited at last some of the information.

The features of any design are interrelated in a *hierarchy*. For example, one cannot draw a symmetric, curvilinear, disconnected design *as such*. One first

42. "FORGETTING" IN HANAWALT'S FIG. 17 (HERE FIG. 71A)

complete set of reproductions (Fig. 79 in Section 49, the Symbol Task, Section 55, and the 2-week and 6-week reproductions of the Story Task, Section 53). This enables the reader to judge for himself the evidence for the theory proposed.

42. "FORGETTING" IN HANAWALT'S FIG. 17 (HERE FIG. 71A)

In reproductions of the design of Fig. 71a, Hanawalt observed that the horizontal line was often omitted. He published (Hanawalt, 1937, p. 85) all the reproductions of this design for each recall period and many samples of second copies. The following analysis is based on this material. There is no denying the observation. All the second copies have the horizontal; 24 of the 25 "immediate" reproductions have it. Of the "later" reproductions (1, 4, and 8 weeks later), 11 of 23 have it; 12 lack the horizontal. The difference between immediate and later recalls is highly significant ($p < .001$). Hanawalt explains this result as "simple forgetting" (1937, p. 41). If one calls omitting the horizontal "forgetting it," what can he mean?

Forgetting is often considered as due to "interference." This idea works well for material made up of unconnected words, syllables, letters, or numbers, collected into long lists of "items" that by assumption have no relevant internal structure. If some of these items are similar to each other, they interfere with each other and are forgotten. If we consider Design 71a as one of the eight items of Hanawalt's "list," interference could only explain forgetting of the whole design, not of a specific part. Interference theory and any of its many equivalents is then not applicable.

Although strictly atomistic theories admit only two possibilities, an item either is or is not recalled correctly, one could, ad hoc to be sure, relax the notion of item and consider the design as composed of four items, one horizontal line and three arcs. Because the arcs are so similar, they should tend to interfere and be forgotten, whereas the horizontal, being dissimilar, should be remembered. The opposite is true. Of 23 late reproductions, 12 lose the horizontal and 2 lose an arc or two.

Going further away from interference theory, we come to theories of trace decay, exemplified by Hanawalt and Woodworth's fading-plus-reconstruction.

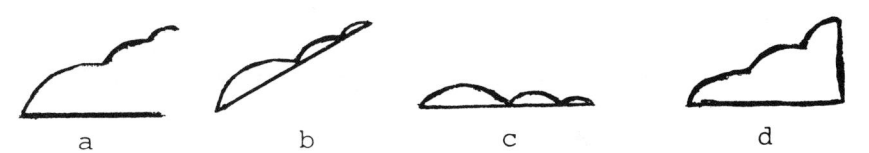

FIG. 71. Pattern 71a was used by Hanawalt (1937). Patterns b, c, and d are variants of a discussed in the text.

168   6. INTRINSIC CHANGE IN REPRODUCTION

As has been mentioned, this theory assumes diffuse or random fading, followed by a reconstruction of what remains. Fading would have to assume that randomly, in some instances, the horizontal decays. But, if this decay really occurs in a random location in the design, it should again randomly involve the other parts of the figure as well, say, one of the arcs. Of the 1, 4, and 8-week reproductions, 11 have a horizontal base line, 12 do not. Of the same reproductions, 20 have three arcs, 3 do not. (One reproduction has one arc, one has two, and one has four arcs.) In tabular form:

	unchanged	changed
Horizontal line	11	12
No. of arcs	20	3

The difference is highly significant ($p < .005$).

Why should fading attack the horizontal line and spare the arcs? How would random fading account for the instance of four arcs instead of three? To explain findings like these, it is necessary to take account of the internal structure of Design 71a. The proposed structure is based on my own impressions, supplemented by Wertheimer's (1923) factors of grouping. It is rather subjective but could be validated by experiments using variants of the design in question. Yet, the fact that the intrinsic structure I am proposing explains the result of the memory experiment argues in its favor. Besides, I expect the reader to find it easy to agree with my phenomenological description.

The three arcs form a rhythmic, well-articulated, clearly structured subunit, held together by its iterative regularity (Wertheimer's factor of similarity). The arcs decrease monotonically in size. The whole subunit is perceived as tilted out of a horizontal direction. A base line in harmony with this part of the design would connect the two ends and touch the two cusps between the arcs, as in Fig. 71b. Such a base line would have the same tilt as the triple arc unit and would supply closure to the design. By contrast, the horizontal line in Fig. 71a is functionally irrelevant to the rest of the design, *merely added on* tacked on to one end of the arcs. *Phenomenally,* the line has no "base" function. (For further discussion of phenomenal obliquity and phenomenal base function, see Goldmeier, 1972, Section 44.) The organization of the entire design is, then, quite weak, whereas the two subunits, the horizontal line and the three arcs, are relatively strong subwholes, with the arc unit representing the dominant part and the horizontal line forming a subordinate part, an "appendage," not integrated into the whole pattern.

Omission of the line means that the figure has rid itself of an inconsistency, of a base line without base function, of a detail not part of the main design. This change is comparable to the achievement of greater intrinsic consistency in Fig. 70i versus 70d or 68h versus 68d.

The proposed interpretation of the result is that loss of the horizontal is "prostructural," enhances the structure, whereas changes in the number of arcs, particularly omissions, disrupt the structure, are "contrastructural." Specifically, the three arcs are *consistent* with each other, whereas "three arcs and 1 line at a different angle" are less so.

The assertions are testable, for instance, by control experiments with a design like 71*b* or *c*, in which the straight line should not be so easily lost, or by an addition as in 71*d*, which gives the design closure and ties the "dangling" horizontal into the design. Either of these modifications should stabilize the straight line and make it less easy to "forget" it. This prediction in the case of 71*d* derives support from the fact that the variant 71*d* is not my invention but is an actual 8-week reproduction by one of Hanawalt's subjects (1937, p. 85).

It might be argued that the explanation proposed here is not different from fading-plus-reconstruction. The random vibration mentioned in Section 22 corresponds to fading, and the preservation of the arcs with dropping of the horizontal line is a form of reconstruction. But, there is an important difference. The "random vibration" is a source of diffuse change like fading. But, as explained in Sections 22 and 23, diffuse change actually occurs only in case (c), with nonnonsingular features or weak structures. Consequently, the relation between the horizontal and the "main part" of the pattern is *selectively* weakened, whereas the strong subunits, the three arcs and the line itself, are not degraded. Reconstruction also does not blindly restore some pieces, say, of the line but improves the structure, as in Fig. 71*d* or, more often, by dropping the entire line. If these differences are considered, the present theory involves neither (diffuse) fading nor (structure-blind) reconstruction. If these differences are ignored, then fading and reconstruction are in effect redefined to accommodate the experimental result. Fading selectively attacks the horizontal line, and reconstruction fails to restore it.

Woodworth has proposed the coding paradigm of schema-plus-correction. In Fig. 71a, the three arcs would be the unperturbed schema and the horizontal would be an added correction. Fading would attack preferentially the "correction," preserve the "schema," and so cause the loss of the horizontal. This explanation, too, seems to differ only semantically from stress theory. With the same logic, one might consider the horizontal plus the two lower arcs as the schema and the small top arc as the correction and predict, wrongly, loss of the top arc. Schema-plus-correction is predictive only if it is defined in terms of near-singularity: Schema means singularity; the correction specifies a small perturbation of the singularity.

43. PROSTRUCTURAL AND CONTRASTRUCTURAL FEATURES—DESIGNS 72a AND B.

The explanation of "forgetting" in Fig. 71*a* as due to a tendency toward greater self-consistency rests on a structural analysis of Design 71*a*, specifically, on the assertion that the arc unit is a strong and dominant subunit. The properties are

170   6. INTRINSIC CHANGE IN REPRODUCTION

        a   **b**

FIG. 72.   Two patterns used in reproduction tests. (Goldmeier, 1941.)

only asserted, not independently established. The analysis of the structure of the following designs, 72a and b, rests on a firmer and less-arguable foundation. In this case, we consider only the *difference in structure of two designs* that are—geometrically—almost identical. The gaps and the curves in Fig. 72a and b are exactly alike. The only difference between the designs is that the middle pair of curves is flipped about its end points, so that in 72a the curves are concave outward, in 72b concave inward. Two types of change are investigated. One type, change of gaps, includes only: (1) closure of some or all gaps; (2) increase in the number of gaps with preservation of the curvature of the lines. The other type of change investigated, change of the curves, includes only: (1) change from concave to convex (facing inward or outward); (2) change in the number of curves; and (3) both types of change together. Degree of curvature, size of gaps, and *any other changes aside from those specifically listed* are excluded from consideration, for the reasons given in Section 39. The example is taken from Goldmeier (1941) (Designs 1a and 1b, p. 490).

    Association theories and fading theories do not predict any particular change of the gaps or curves in the two designs. Both theories would find it difficult to explain a decrease and even more an increase in the number of gaps or curves, or closing of gaps, or an inversion of the curvature of some curves. If they succeeded in doing so, they could not explain why any of the changes should affect one of the designs significantly more often than the other, because the designs have exactly the same parts, the same size of gaps, and the same shape and size of the curves. The only difference lies in the structure, the phenomenal organization of the two designs.

    Actually, there is a marked difference in the reproductions. After 6 weeks, Design 72a shows no change of the gaps as defined earlier, whereas four out of 12 reproductions of Design 72b show changes of gaps. In tabular form, after 6 weeks (recalculated from Goldmeier, 1941, Table I):

	Design 72a	Design 72b
changes of gaps	0	4
no change of gaps	13	8

43. PROSTRUCTURAL AND CONTRASTRUCTURAL FEATURES 171

This is a significant difference ($X^2 = 5.16$, $p < .025$) between the two designs. In the same material, also after 6 weeks, there were

	in Design 72*a*	in Design 72*b*
changes of curves	8	0
no change of curves	5	12

In words: None of the curves of Design 72*b* changed, but in eight out of 13 reproductions of Design 72*a*, there were changes of curves as defined earlier. This difference is highly significant ($p < .001$).

Both of these results become understandable if one takes the phenomenal organization, the structure of the two designs, into account. Phenomenally, 72*b* consists of one top and one bottom curve, each perceived as a unit. The three partial curves are grouped into one unit by the agency of Wertheimer's "factor of good continuation." In this setting, the gaps are perceived as fortuitous, brief interruptions of one smooth curve. The gaps are contrastructural. They disturb the design rather than articulate it. Their number and location along the curve is arbitrary and, except for symmetry, unrelated to the structure of the design. The gaps in this setting are out of context, accidental, nonsingular interruptions and therefore change readily in various ways: more gaps; fewer gaps; closure of gaps. Conversely, in Design 72*a*, the partial curves do not continue each other smoothly. Upper and lower half of the design each consists of three separate curves. The gaps are precisely at the hiatus between the curves; they are prostructural and even articulate the design. To close the gaps, to increase their number, or to locate them elsewhere on the curves would disrupt the design. Hence, no changes of gaps in 72*a*, but a significant amount of change in 72*b*.

As for the curves, Design 72*b* has, phenomenally, only one curve in the upper and one in the lower half, whereas 72*a* has three independent curves in each half. The three curves in 72*a* form a weak ensemble. Changes in arrangement, in orientation, and even in number are possible without destroying any singular whole qualities (e.g., symmetry), whereas, in the case of 72*b*, some very small changes destroy the unity, the even flow, of the overall curve. For example, a slight up or down displacement of the middle curves is destructive in 72*b*, producing a misalignment, but it is inconsequential for 72*a*. The arrangement of the three curves in 72*a* is weak, nonsingular, an example of case (c) of Section 23. Hence, the changes are expected and are expected to occur in a variety of ways, not tending in one specific direction. *In 72b, changes of the partial curves are prevented by the strong grouping of the partial curves into one smooth overall curve.* Changes in the number and orientation of partial curves are indifferent to the structure of 72*a*, but contrastructural within the context of 72*b*. Consequently, many changes of curves occur in 72*a*, none in 72*b*.

The experiments with Designs 72*a* and *b* demonstrate that in reproduction, as in recognition, prostructural features of a design resist memory change; features that are indifferent to the structure, or contrastructural, tend to change.

6. INTRINSIC CHANGE IN REPRODUCTION

The changes of indifferent and contrastructural features are *not directed* and do not occur in only one direction. In this respect, they resemble the random changes predicted by fading.

44. DIRECTED CHANGE IN FIG. 64G

Omissions, discussed in connection with Fig. 71*a,* and lack of change, observed in the experiments with Design 72*a* and *b,* did not generate nearly as much controversy as Wulf's (1922) assertion that traces change in the direction of a better structure, here called case (b) of Section 23. Cases of this type discriminate most clearly between gestalt theories and fading or associationistic theories.

The first example of *directed* change in reproduction, Design 64*g,* is taken from Goldmeier (1941). The procedure and the design features are described in Section 31 in connection with the recognition tests. The only kind of change considered in the reproductions is the presence or absence of the little V's in the crossarms. The results after 6 weeks are listed in the last line of Table 9. Of the 37 reproductions obtained, 10 are unchanged (5th column, Table 9), 27 are changed. Mathematically, there are 16 different possibilities of placing V's in the cross of Fig. 64. A "V" can go either in all crossarms (one way), or in three crossarms (four possible ways), or in two arms (six ways), in one arm (four ways), or in none (one way). Only six of these 16 ways were utilized by our subjects, as diagramed in line 1 of Table 9. Of the eight ways in which an odd number of V's (1 or 3) can be placed, none was used. Of the six ways of using two V's, four are symmetrical about a *single oblique axis.* One of the four is the standard, Fig. 64*g,* another is 64*e.* The standard is reproduced unchanged in 10 instances, arrangement 64*e* in one. The two arrangements with two V's symmetrical about the opposite oblique axis are never used. The two arrangements with

TABLE 9
(From Goldmeier, 1941, Table III)
Reproduction, 6 Weeks Only, Standard Fig. 64g

Placement of Vs*	.+.	+	.+.	+.	+.	.+
See Fig. 64**	h	—	b	—	g	e
axes of symmetry***	v	v	v	v		
	h	h	h	h		
	2ob	2ob			ob	ob
size of "equivalent set"	1	1	2	2	**4**	4
37 reproductions:	15	6	1	4	**10**	1

*The dots indicate placements of Vs in relation to the crossarms of the standard 64g.

**The letters refer to designs in Fig. 64. The second and fourth arrangement was not provided in the recognition material of Fig. 64.

***v = vertical; h = horizontal; ob = oblique.

two V's having vertical *and* horizontal symmetry occur in five reproductions. The remaining two possibilities, V's either in none or all four arms, account for 21 of the 27 changed reproductions. The most frequent change, the placement of V's in all four arms, occurs in 15 of the 27 changed reproductions.

A fading or decay theory leads one to expect forgetting as the main type of change, which, in this case, leads one to expect either one V or no V at all. If one admits Hanawalt's (1937) modification of the theory, "fading-plus-reconstruction," then the reconstruction part of the theory can also account for reproductions that contain two V's, as in the standard, but in the wrong places. A suitably modified fading theory allows, therefore: (1) *Two V's, misplaced,* (five possible ways), *or one V* (four possible ways), *or no V's* (one possible way), with the "smaller" changes more frequent than the larger ones; (2) added V's can be explained by "reconstruction," but it is difficult to see how fading leads to it. Three V's (four possible ways, *one* V added in reconstruction) should be more frequent than four V's (one possible way, *two* V's added in reconstruction); (3) finally, fading or decay or forgetting theory predicts loss of V's to be more frequent than an increase in the number of V's.

As Table 9 shows, the results run counter to all predictions suggested for fading: (1) Misplacement or loss of V's account for only 12 of the 27 changed reproductions, not for most of them; (2) three V's, far from being more frequent than four V's, do not occur at all; four V's are the most frequent single change (15 of 27 changed reproductions); (3) loss of V's occurs in six reproductions, an increase in V's occurs in 15, difficult to explain by fading or forgetting.

Symmetry, or internal consistency—the two explanations cannot be differentiated by this experiment (see Section 32)—account for most of the findings. The symmetry axes are listed below the symbol for each distribution of V's. The first two columns of Table 9 list the reproductions with four V's (first column, as in Fig. 64*h*) and no V's at all (second column). These reproductions have the largest number of symmetries and the most consistent relationship between V's and arms: All arms are treated on an equal basis. Together, the two designs account for 21 of the 27 changed reproductions. The remaining changed reproductions include five with two axes of symmetry and with two V's placed in a related pair of arms, and only a single reproduction like 64*e* with one oblique axis and two V's in unrelated arms of the cross. In short, *of the 27 changed reproductions, 26 changed toward greater self-consistency.* Statistically, this result is highly significant.

45. SYMMETRY AS SELF-CONSISTENCY IN FIG. 65*G*

The recognitions of Fig. 64*g*, 65*g*, and 66*g* and the reproductions of Fig. 64*g* have been discussed only in terms of placement of V's, the only change permitted by the recognition material and the main change observed in the reproductions of 64*g*. The cross of 64*g* is phenomenally stable and perceived as a

6. INTRINSIC CHANGE IN REPRODUCTION

"strong" subwhole with little tendency for change (cf., the discussion of strong subwholes in Section 42, in connection with the triple arches of Fig. 71). The cross of 65g is, like the cross of 64g, a strong subwhole, but it is much less stable than the cross of 64g or the triple arch of Fig. 71. Therefore, the cross is: (1) expected to change *independently of the V's;* and (2) expected to change *toward a more stable* form.

Stress theory predicts two types of change for the cross part of 65g. The difference in thickness of the lines forming the horizontal arms is an *inconsistency* of the cross design. Consistency requires that two lines coordinated by being parallel become equal in such material qualities as thickness (in the meaning of "material," as in Goldmeier, 1972, Chapter 3).

Other expected changes concern *the curvature* of the horizontal arms: (1) The curvature is inconsistent with the straightness of the vertical arms; (2) the curvature is inconsistently applied to the right and left arm inasmuch as the two curved arms are curved in opposite directions; (3) The degree of curvature is *nonsingular,* the singular value for curvature being zero curvature (i.e., straightness).

Therefore, the changes expected for reproductions of 65g include:

1. Changes of the cross: (a) Loss of the thickening of the lower contour of the horizontal arms; (b) change to more singular and more consistent curvature, particularly straightening and other equalizations.
2. Changes of V's: (a) changes in the *shape* of V's (not investigated for 65g); (b) changes in placement of V's (or equivalent closures), including omission of V's.

1. Changes of the Cross

(a) Loss of Thickening. The thickened lower contour of the horizontal arms is a feature so arbitrary, contrastructural, and out of step with the rest of the design that three subjects did not even include it in their second copies. Because we define change as deviation from the second copy, the lack of thickening eliminates these three reproductions. The other 15 out of 18 subjects who furnished reproductions did copy the thickening in 65g. A significant number of these, 12 of 15, ($p < .05$) omitted the contrastructural feature in their reproductions. The remaining three reproductions *with* evidence of thickening did not portray it unchanged. One reproduction is only thickened on the right arm, one (Fig. 73f) shows thickening on both lines of the left arm, the left side of the vertical bar, and omits thickening on the right arm. The third reproduction replaces the thickening by a double contour and doubles the *upper* border of the horizontal arms instead of the lower one (Fig. 73c). Not one of the 15 reproductions renders the thickening exactly as in the standard and the subjects own second copy.

45. SYMMETRY AS SELF-CONSISTENCY IN FIG. 65G   175

(b) Change to a More Self-Consistent Curvature. All second copies of 65g have two straight vertical arms and two oppositely curved, horizontal arms. Three of the 18 reproductions preserve these features (e.g., Fig. 73b and c). In another reproduction, the self-consistency of the cross is markedly *decreased* (Fig. 73a); in the remaining 14 instances, self-consistency is more or less increased: Two reproductions increase the self-consistency of the cross, one by equalizing the curve of the right and left cross arm, the other, Fig. 73d, by directing both side arms up. This change makes one reproduction symmetrical and the other one (Fig. 73d), which features a slight curve of the upper arm, nearly so. Four reproductions increase self-consistency by curving all four arms (e.g., Fig. 73e and f). The remaining eight reproductions have four straight arms. In one reproduction, the arms continue through the center (Fig. 73k). In

FIG. 73. Samples of reproductions of figure 65g.

176 6. INTRINSIC CHANGE IN REPRODUCTION

three of these eight reproductions, the cross looks just like the cross in Fig. 64, a change that represents the ultimate increase in self-consistency of the cross part. In two other reproductions, the lower arm is longer. One of these is definitely a case of verbalization ("crucifix," see Section 40), the other (Fig. 73*g*) probably is not. Finally, two straightened crosses have slanted up-and-down arms; one of these also shows an elaboration (Fig. 73*h*).

Summarizing changes with respect to *self-consistency of the cross part in reproductions of 65g,* we find:

Decrease in self-consistency	1 case (Fig. 73*a*).
No change	3 cases (Fig. 73*b,c*).
Increase in self-consistency	14 cases
Curvature or direction of horizontal arms equalized	2 cases (Fig. 73*d*)
All four arms curved	4 cases (Fig. 73*e,f*)
All four arms straight	8 cases (Fig. 73*g,h,i,k*)

In 14 of the 15 changed reproductions, self-consistency increased. The difference is highly significant ($p < .001$). The increase in Fig. 73*d* is arguable. Removing this case, self-consistency is increased in 13 of 15 cases ($p < .01$).

2. Changes of V's

(a) Changes in Shape. Figure 73 shows that the V's are often reproduced as straight lines, little single or double curves, facing in or out, completely or partially closing the ends of the arms, and in still other ways. This extreme variability of shape contrasts with the stability of *position in the arm* and *intrinsic symmetry.* All V's in all reproductions of 65*g* (and in all but one of 66*g*) are placed at the end of an arm and are reasonably symmetric with respect to the long axis of that arm. Obviously, symmetry is a *singular feature* of the V, whereas the V-shape otherwise is nonsingular. Furthermore, the V's are perceived in the *function of closure* and remembered as closure, which confers stability on placement at the end but not on preservation of the exact angle. (For the important distinction between function and function carrier, see Section 3 and Goldmeier, 1972, Section 29.) To pursue this argument further would require control experiments with V's placed away from the ends, inside or outside of the cross, V's with different angles, etc.; experiments that were not performed.

(b) Changes of Placement. The recognition experiments with Figs. 64*g*, 65*g*, and 66*g* and the reproductions of 64*g* show that the placement of the V's, or their equivalents, or omissions of V's is governed by self-consistency of the resulting design. Self-consistency may or may not take the form of symmetry. In

45. SYMMETRY AS SELF-CONSISTENCY IN FIG. 65G   177

64g, self-consistency is indistinguishable from symmetry; in 65g and 66g, an asymmetric variant of the cross makes the distinction possible in recognition. However, when it comes to reproduction, many crosses of 65g revert to a symmetrical arrangement (for example the cross in Fig. 73g,i, and k). (One reproduction, similar to Fig. 73h but without the asymmetric center, is symmetric about an oblique axis but classified as asymmetric. It has no V's. Actually, reclassifying this case as symmetric slightly improves the statistics. But, because oblique symmetry is psychologically not very effective (Goldmeier, 1972, Section 43), this reproduction is counted as asymmetric.) The crosses of eight reproductions are classified as asymmetrical. Of these, three have V's or equivalent closures in all arms, two have no V's ("h^{-1}"), one has V's in both verticals ("b^{-1}"), one has one V at the top ("f"), and only one lacks (vertical) symmetry (Fig. 73i). None has V's placed as in the standard and second copy. Altogether, in seven of the eight reproductions with symmetry of the cross, the V's are placed more symmetrically, a significant change in the direction of symmetry and self-consistency ($p < .05$). (See Table 10 for results, and for the meaning of symbols h^{-1}, b^{-1}, f, etc.)

In 10 reproductions, seven of which appear in Fig. 73, the cross is not symmetric. In four of these, V's, or closures, occupy all arms ("h",) including one reproduction with five arms, Fig. 73a. In five cases, there are *no V's or closures* ("h^{-1}"), including Fig. 73d, f, h. One reproduction has an asymmetric cross together with inconsistent placement of V's (Fig. 73b). This is the only reproduction that portrays both cross and V's *unchanged*. In other words, a

TABLE 10
Reproductions of 64g, 65g, 66g

Vs or closure*		h	h^{-1}	b	b^{-1}	g	e (g^{-1})	f	d	—
Symmetry of cross	N									
Fig 64g symmetric	37	15	6	1	4	10	1	0	0	0
Fig 65g symmetric	8	3	2	0	1	0	0	1	0	1
Fig 65g asymmetric	10	4	5	0	0	1	0	0	0	0
Fig 65g total	18	7	7	0	1	1	0	1	0	1
Fig 66g symmetric	11	3	5	1	1	0	0	0	0	1
Fig 66g asymmetric	7	1	5	0	0	0	0	0	1	0
Fig 66g total	18	4	10	1	1	0	0	0	1	1

*As Fig. 73 shows the Vs took many shapes in the reproductions. The placement of the Vs or closure is indicated by the dots near the cross and by the letter of the corresponding arrangement in Fig. 64. The last arrangement has no counterpart in Fig. 64. h^{-1} and b^{-1} (and g^{-1}) are related to h, b (and g) of Fig. 64 by exchanging Vs and empty places.

significant fraction of changed placements (nine of nine, $p < .01$) increase the consistency between cross and V's; even in the absence of symmetry, one reproduction is unchanged. Taking symmetric and asymmetric crosses together and accepting only placement of V's into all or none of the arms (h or h^{-1}, Table 10) as evidence for increased consistency, the experiment furnishes 14 reproductions with increased self-consistency, three without increase and one unchanged reproduction. Fourteen increases out of 17 changes in placement of V's is a significant ($p < .01$) increase in self-consistency. In this case, the result means a more consistent relation between V's and arms.

Recapitulating the reproduction findings with $65g$:

1. The inconsistent, contrastructural thickening of two lines of $65g$ tends to be dropped or changed in a significant majority of reproductions.
2. In a significant number of reproductions, the cross part of $65g$ increases in self-consistency.
3. The reproductions of the V's show great variability in nonsingular attributes and great stability in the two features relating to their function as closure.
4. The relationship between cross arms and V's becomes significantly more consistent in the reproductions through changes in number and placement of V's.

46. SELF-CONSISTENCY IN REPRODUCTIONS OF FIG. 66G

Stress theory predicts an increase in self-consistency for reproductions of $66g$ as it does for $65g$. The cross part of $66g$ can increase in inner consistency by equalizing the curvature of the arms in pairs of two instead of having one odd, curved arm and three equal straight arms, by equalizing all four arms or in still other ways. Because straightness is a singular degree of curvature, zero curvature or straightening of the curved arm should be a frequent change. It is difficult to *see how fading can predict such changes, or how fading could avoid predicting* changes that do not occur, like forgetting an arm or *forgetting one of the four separate, continuous, L-shaped lines that make up the cross.* None of these four "items" is ever "forgotten," no *interference here.*

With respect to changes of the cross part, the 19 reproductions of $66g$ fall into three groups:

1. *Decrease* in self-consistency of the cross part, one case, shown as Fig. 74a. This reproduction may well represent an instance of an extrinsic mechanism (Section 40).
2. *No change* of the cross part, four cases.
3. *Increase* in self-consistency, 14 cases. In nine of the more self-consistent crosses, all four arms are straight, and the cross looks like that of $64g$. Two of

46. SELF-CONSISTENCY IN REPRODUCTIONS OF FIG. 66G   179

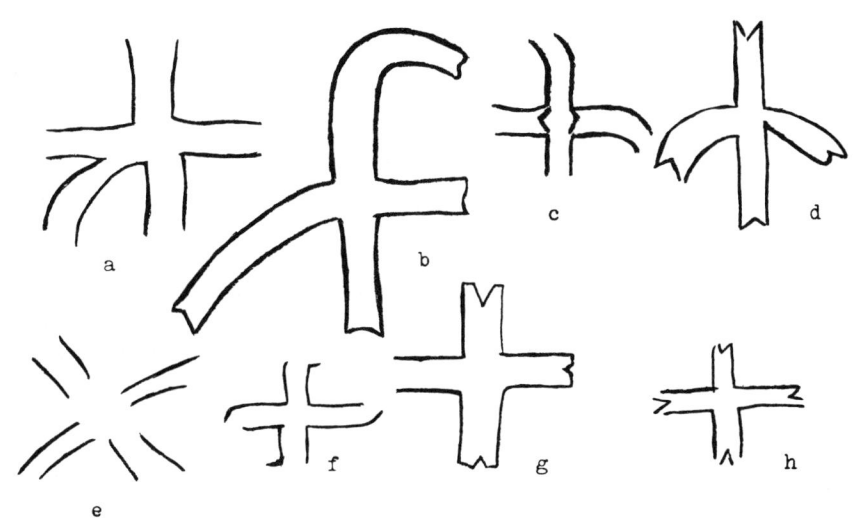

FIG. 74. Sample reproductions of figure 66g.

these are shown as Fig. 74g and h. Two other crosses have four straight, mutually perpendicular arms. They are shown in Fig. 74e and f; Fig. 74e possibly represents a verbalization. One cross has acquired vertical symmetry without straightening, shown in Fig. 74d. In the remaining two instances, two *bars* of the cross are equalized by rendering each bar as consisting of one curved and one straight arm. These two reproductions are shown in Fig. 74b and c. In all, of the 15 reproductions of 66g changed with regard to the cross, only Fig. 74a is in the direction of decreased self-consistency, whereas, in 14 instances, the change amounts to increased inner consistency of the cross part. The ratio of 14 to 1 is highly significant ($p < .001$).

Point 3 at the end of Section 45, about the positioning of V's relative to the arms and the shape of the V's, applies equally to the reproductions of 66g and need not be repeated. The only instance of V's *not* placed at the ends of arms, shown as Fig. 74c, probably represents a verbalization (Section 40).

One of the 19 reproductions of 66g belongs to a second copy that features the cross part unchanged but contains only one V, placed as in Fig. 64d, instead of the two V's as in 64 or 66g. This reproduction, shown as Fig. 74e, is properly included in the statistics of cross changes but, because of the change of V's in the second copy (see Section 25), it is ineligible for statistics on changes of V's. The remaining 18 reproductions qualify for consideration of changes in placement of V's, including omission of V's. The results are tabulated on the last line of Table 10. All the 18 reproductions are changed with respect to V's; that is, the arrangement with one V in the top arm and one in the right arm, as in 66g, does not occur. The most frequent changes are V's in all four arms (four cases, "*h*") and V's in none of the arms (10 cases, "h^{-1}"). The h^{-1} group (no V's) includes the

6. INTRINSIC CHANGE IN REPRODUCTION

reproduction Fig. 74f, which one might classify under h, and 74c, which one might include in the arrangement "b." All other classifications are straightforward. There is one instance each of V's in both horizontal arms ("b"), both vertical arms ("b^{-1}"), the right arm (d), and all but the left arm (Fig. 74g).

In order to decide whether the changes increase or decrease intrinsic consistency, the concomitant changes of the cross have to be considered. If the cross has changed to a symmetric form, particularly vertical symmetry as in Fig. 74e,f,g, and h, then the arrangements or omissions, h, h^{-1}, b, b^{-1}, are consistent with the changed cross, and the change away from the standard g represents an increase in consistency. By this argument, 10 of the 11 reproductions with a symmetric cross (including Fig. 74d and h) have increased self-consistency; one (Fig. 74g) shows a decrease. The increase in 10 of 11 reproductions is statistically significant ($p < .01$).

Of the seven nonsymmetric crosses, four are unchanged, the other three are shown as Fig. 74a, b, and c. One reproduction has V's in all arms (Fig. 74b), five have no V's (Fig. 74a and c and three with unchanged crosses). This placement of V's seems more consistent with these crosses than the arrangement in the standard (and the second copies). One reproduction has an unchanged cross and one V in the right arm (as in 64d). The V is in the "odd" one of the three straight arms, an arrangement that seems to be at least as consistent with this particular cross as the arrangement in the standard 66g. In fact, in the recognition test arrangement, d does reasonably well; only the standard and arrangement h are chosen more often. However, we conservatively count this reproduction as *not increased* in self-consistency. Of the seven reproductions with asymetric crosses, the placement of V's is then more consistent than the second copy in at least six instances. In five of the six cases, all V's are omitted (e.g., Figs. 74a and c; in one instance, all arms have V's, Fig. 74b). Combining the reproductions with symmetric and those with asymmetric crosses, the placement of V's is changed so as to result in increased consistency with the cross in 16 of the 18 eligible reproductions, a highly significant increase ($p < .001$) in internal consistency of the pattern.

To summarize briefly the changes of 66g in reproduction, we find:

1. Changes of the cross of 66g occur in 15 reproductions. In 14 of the 15 cases, the change *increases* self-consistency of the cross.
2. Changes of individual V's parallel those reported for the V's of standards 64 and 65g.
3. Changes of placement of V's in relation to cross arms make *the V's more consistent with the cross* in 16 of 18 instances.

In most experiments, the changes in reproduction parallel the changes in recognition. In the case of 66g, however, all reproductions show changes of V's, whereas over half the recognitions are unchanged. This kind of result led

Hanawalt (1937) and Rock and Engelstein (1959) to propose that: "the trace... does not change (but) becomes unavailable [p. 229]." This question was discussed in Section 26, in general. Here is an example showing why, in the case of 66g, reproduction and recognition should diverge.

The recognition material contains only the "bent" cross, which is quite consistent with the standard arrangement "g" of the V's. But only four of the 18 reproductions contain the bent cross of the standard, therefore only the four reproductions with a bent cross can properly be compared with the recognitions. Three of these four reproductions omit the V's completely (h^{-1}), a change that circumvents the consistency dilemma and that, quite aside from consistency, is not represented in the recognition material and for this reason cannot be matched by the recognition results. That leaves one reproduction with both a bent cross and a placement of V's represented in the recognition material, namely, a change classified as "d" (one V in the right arm). The frequency of this particular change, 1 in 18, matches the frequency of the same change in the recognition tests, 4 in 54 (see Tables 4 and 10) reasonably well.

What the comparison of recognitions and reproductions teaches in the case of 66g is that the most important inconsistency resides in the structure of the cross, and that the V's are either so irrelevant to the design as to be omitted (10 of 18 reproductions, Table 10) or are integrated into the design as closure of all four arms or of a pair of opposing arms (6 of 18 reproductions). Because the inconsistency of the bent cross is imposed on the recognition material, the somewhat matching inconsistency of the V's is maintained. This explains the discrepancy between the two tests of the state of the trace.

47. BALANCE AND RECTANGULARITY—DESIGN 67D

The procedure of the experiment with Fig. 67d is the same as that with Fig. 64g described in Section 31. The left upright line of the standard is inclined to the left, making an 85° angle with the horizontal. This angle was carefully measured in all second copies and in all reproductions. Copies and reproductions were then divided into those in which the left upright is inclined to the left by 87° or less, and those in which this angle measures more than 87°. If it measures 87° or less, the design as a whole looks slanted, as, for instance, the standard, Fig. 67d. If the angle measures 88 to 92°, it looks perpendicular, as, for instance, Fig. 67a or 67h. If it is still larger, the design approaches symmetry and looks more balanced, as, for instance, Fig. 67g. Thus, drawings with a left slant, "87° or less," are less singular and so less stable than are those with the angle "over 87°."

As mentioned in Section 34, about one third of the second copies render the left upright as over 87° rather than slanted to the left, 87° or less, as in the standard. The change in copying attests to the strength of the tendency to larger

6. INTRINSIC CHANGE IN REPRODUCTION

TABLE 11
(From Goldmeier, 1941, Table IV)

	No. of Subjects Whose 2nd Copy Is			
	slanted to the left* and whose reproductions are		over 87°* and whose reproductions are	
Time Interval	slanted to the left	over 87°	slanted to the left	over 87°
Immediate	25	1	1	10
3 days	13	1	1	10
2 weeks	12	6	3	7
6 weeks	3 (1**)	10	0	4

*The second copies were carefully measured as to the slant of the left upright. If this angle measured 87° or less, it was classified as "slanted to the left," if more, as "over 87°."

**There was one reproduction in this group which was too deteriorated to be classified.

angles in this design. The subjects who copied the design as over 87° perhaps perceived and probably *memorized a changed and more stable version of the standard 67d*. Stress theory of intrinsic change predicts that those whose copies are over 87° will reproduce the design in this more stable form, and those whose copies are slanted to the left (like the standard) tend to change in later reproductions to over 87°. Fading theory predicts that some subjects will draw reproductions more slanted than their copies and others, randomly, less slanted. Thus, for those who copied the standard as slanted to the left, both theories predict some change to over 87°, but stress theory predicts that as time goes by there is more and more change to over 87°. Fading predicts that eventually about half will change to over 87°, the other half will remain slanted to the left (i.e., 87° or less). For those who copied the design in the over 87° form, fading predicts that some reproductions randomly revert to a slanted angle, whereas stress theory predicts that the over 87° form is more stable in memory and therefore does not change back. We call a reproduction "unchanged" if it agrees with its second copy as to slant (i.e., either left slant or over 87°); otherwise, we call the reproduction "changed." In this terminology, stress theory predicts a majority of changed reproductions with copies slanted to the left, a majority of unchanged reproductions with copies over 87°. Fading predicts an equal distribution of changed reproductions regardless of the slant in the second copies. Since in both theories the change increases with time, the difference should be most evident with the 6-week interval (Table 11, last line). As the tabulation shows, of the reproductions with slanted second copies; 10 are changed, only 3 are unchanged, whereas of the 4 reproductions with second copies over 87°, all are unchanged. This difference is significant at the .01 level. The result is consistent with the

48. PARALLEL LINES AND SELF-CONSISTENCY

assumption of intrinsic change of the unstable trace and absence of change in the more stable trace. There is change, but it occurs in one direction, not randomly as predicted by fading theory.

In this case, only the 6-week interval shows enough change to discriminate between the two theories. In general, experiments with short intervals (e.g., those of Hebb & Foord, 1945, using 24 hours) are unsuited for the issues raised here.

48. PARALLEL LINES AND SELF-CONSISTENCY

A. Changes Common to 61c and f

The designs of Fig. 61 consist of three nested isoceles triangles, with an incomplete base line. The intermediate triangle is the varied part of the designs. The variation is similar to that of the arrowhead design, Fig. 75C and D, used by Hebb and Foord (1945). The intermediate triangle, like Hebb and Foord's arrowhead, varies with respect to the angle at the apex. Predictably, Hebb and

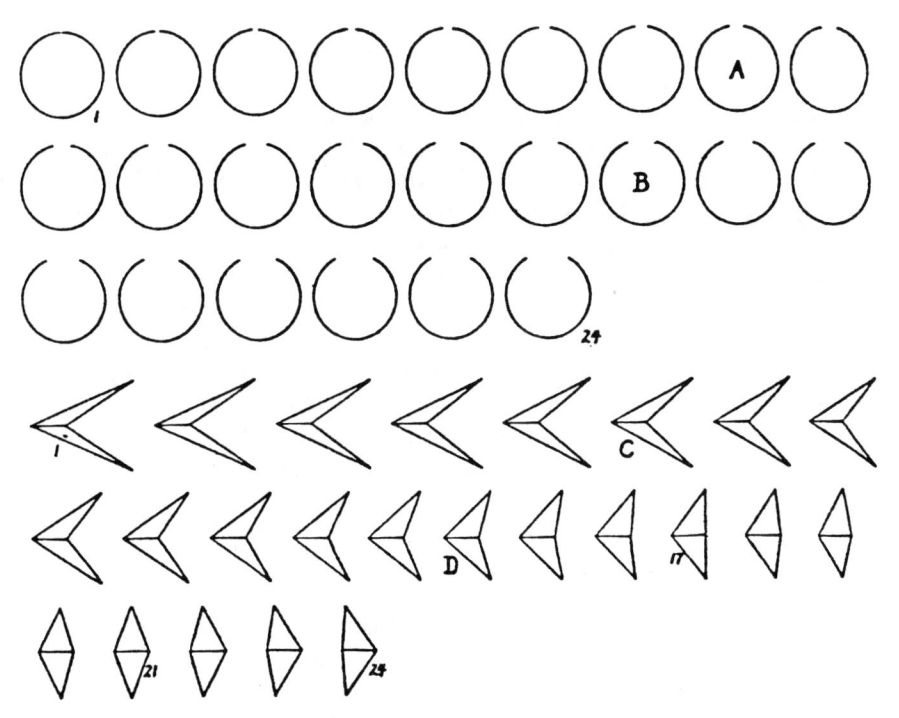

FIG. 75. Material used by Hebb and Foord (1945) to test recognition of patterns 75 A and B, and C and D.

Foord found no tendency to change, because they varied a nonsingular feature (the angle at the apex) within a nonsingular range of values (oblique directions). The intermediate triangle in Fig. 61, unlike Hebb and Foord's arrowhead, is embedded in a larger design. The innermost and the outermost triangle are parellel to each other and form a box or frame. This frame singles out a direction in space that in itself is nonsingular. However, as the recognition experiments, Section 29, show, this setting creates a strongly singular direction for the enclosed triangle. The recognition results further suggest a tendency for the three triangles to *become more coequal* (e.g., in their relative spacing).

Analysis of the reproductions is complicated by the many unconstrained dimensions of change and the smaller numbers of reproductions. Two of the 22 subjects failed to reproduce 61c, 4 of 15 subjects failed to reproduce 61f, leaving only 20 reproductions of 61c and 11 of 61f.

The designs of Fig. 61 were devised to test a nonsingular feature of a pattern, like Hebb and Foord's arrowhead, embedded in a frame making one version singular, whereas leaving the other version nonsingular. The design as a whole has, of course, many features besides the direction of the middle lines, many of them common to both versions. Common features include: (1) a vertical symmetry (singular, always preserved, at least in the overall configuration); (2) an open base line, which is nonsingular. The base line is closed in 9 of 20 reproductions of 61c and in 2 of the 11 reproductions of 61f. The difference between 61c and 61f in this respect is not significant ($p < .2$); (3) it has long been established that an enclosed object takes the enclosure as a frame of reference with regard to such things as induced motion (Duncker, 1929; Oppenheimer, 1934) and direction in space (Asch & Witkin, 1948a; Goldmeier, 1972, Section 52, and Fig. 43 and 44, this volume, Section 15). *The experimental strategy, which is to establish a strongly singular direction, is served by enclosing the intermediate triangle between the other two triangles.* But the resulting designs are not structurally improved or made more singular by having three, rather than only one or two triangles. Having three triangles is in itself not a singular feature. Therefore, a decrease in the number of triangles is a common, although unintended, change. Only 10 of the 20 reproductions of 61c and 7 of the 11 reproductions of 61f have three triangles (8 of 61c and 4 of 61f have 2, and 2 of 61c have only one triangle). This difference between 61c and 61f is also not significant ($p < .5$).

B. Differences Between 61c and 61f

Figures 61c and 61f both contain three sets of nested triangles. We compare the two related designs with respect to change in direction of the intermediate triangle. For this purpose, we count a reproduction of 61c as unchanged if the three triangles are parallel and consider 61f as unchanged if the intermediate triangle is *not parallel* to the enclosing triangles. In the case of both designs, we

48. PARALLEL LINES AND SELF-CONSISTENCY

require that in unchanged reproductions the outermost and the innermost triangles are parrallel. A changed reproduction of 61c is shown in Fig. 76a; examples of changed reproductions of 61f are Fig. 76b (the enclosing triangles are not parallel) and Fig. 76e (intermediate triangle parallel to enclosing triangles). Our criteria are applicable only to the 10 reproductions of 61c and the 7 reproductions of 61f containing *three* triangles. Out of all qualifying reproductions of 61c, 9 are unchanged, 1 is changed; of 61f, 2 are unchanged, 5 are changed. The difference in the incidence of change is striking (and statistically significant, $p < .01$): Ninety percent of the reproductions are stable if the three triangles of the standard are parallel, as in 61c, but only 29% are stable if the intermediate triangle departs from parallel course, as in 61f. If fading can explain the changes, it certainly cannot explain the marked difference in the incidence of change in two so similar designs.

The definition of change used here includes two separate kinds of change: (1) *The enclosing triangles* can change from parallel to convergent, as in Figs. 76a and b; (2) the intermediate triangle can change from parallel to nonparallel in 61c, or from nonparallel to parallel in 61f. Only the second type, the change of the intermediate triangle, was examined in recognition, and, in this respect, 61c was found more stable than 61f (Section 29). It is, therefore, of interest to analyze the reproductions for this more narrowly defined change. The definition of "unchanged" remains the same as before; "changed" now means only that the intermediate triangle changes to *not parallel* to the enclosing triangles in a

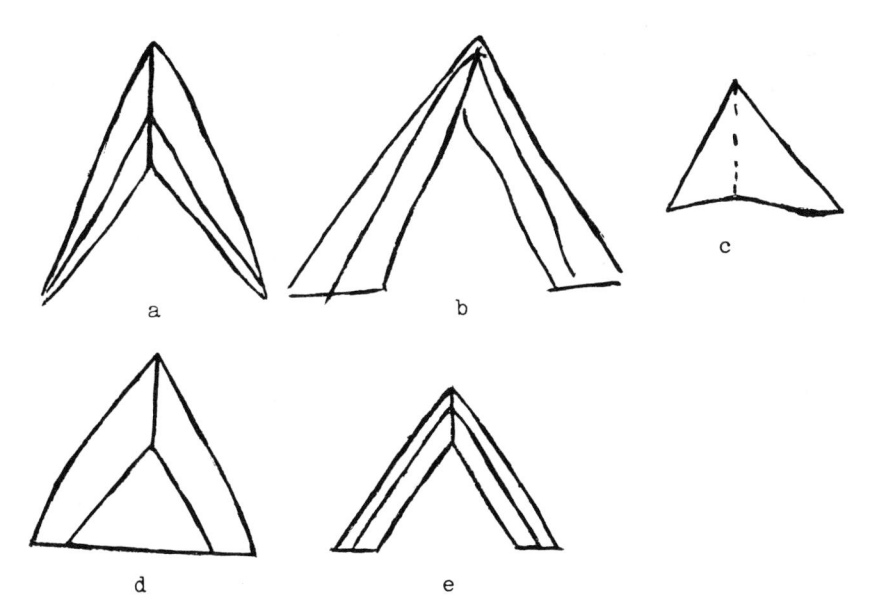

FIG. 76. Sample reproductions of pattern 61c (a and c) and 61f (b, d, and e).

186   6. INTRINSIC CHANGE IN REPRODUCTION

reproduction of 61c or that it changes to *parallel* in a reproduction of 61f (Fig. 76e).

With this narrower definition of change there are: 9 unchanged, 0 changed reproductions of 61c; 2 unchanged, 3 changed reproductions of 61f.

In other words, no change of 61c but marked change of 61f toward a parallel course of the intermediate triangle. The difference in incidence of change between the more stable pattern 61c (0% change) and the less-stable pattern (60% change) is in the same direction as the change in recognition and is quite significant ($p < .01$).

The similarity experiment (Section 6), the recognition experiment (Section 29), and the analysis of the reproductions all indicate that 61c is more stable than 61f. The reason for the difference lies in the structure of the two patterns: The parallel course of the three triangles of 61c is singular; 61f lacks this singular parallel course. But, more general structural features than parallel course are involved. It is easy to invent designs analogous to 61c and 61f using curved or angled lines instead of straight ones (Fig. 77).

Blum (1967) has generalized parallel course to a relatedness or correspondence with the same psychological cogency as parallelity. What makes parallelity so effective in the context of these designs is the fact that the lines have *"parallel" functions,* play the same role, even if they are not actually parallel: They originate and end on the same short line segments, and the two extreme lines are parallel lines. So, ultimately, singularity (i.e., Prägnanz) becomes a matter of self-consistency: Consistency requires of three lines that begin together and end together and of which two are parallel to run on parallel (or corresponding) paths. Memory changes occur in the direction of greater internal consistency. In the particular case of the family of designs of Fig. 61, self-consistency amounts to parallel course.

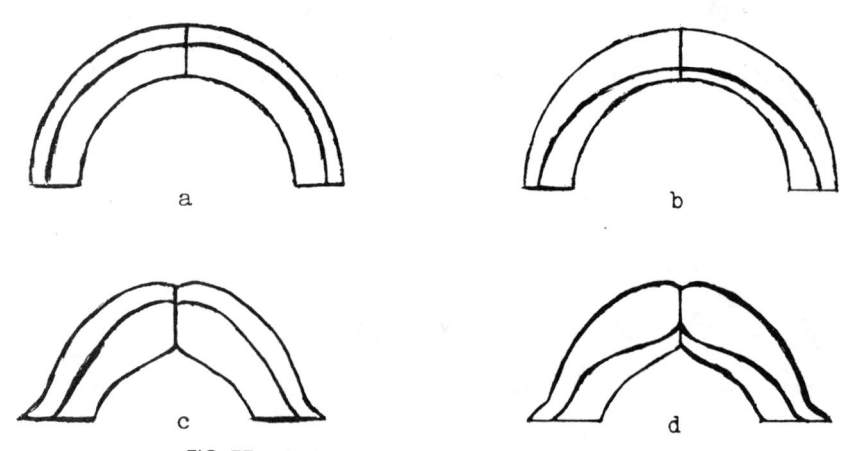

FIG. 77.   Analogues to 61c and f using curved lines.

The reader may wonder whether he/she would apply the same distinctions that I applied, and whether he/she would consider my distinctions valid, if all reproductions were before him/her. Let me state, therefore, that the samples given illustrate not the average reproduction but those most likely to be questioned (e.g., two of the three reproductions of Design 61 excluded as not having parallel enclosing triangles, Figs. 76a and b). Still, I feel, as apparently Hanawalt (1937) did, that the reader needs examples of complete, unselected sets of reproductions to appreciate what is involved in classifying various types of change. Therefore, *all* reproductions of Designs 63b and d that had unchanged second copies are presented in Fig. 79(b and d). They are discussed in the following section.

49. DESIGNS 63B AND D—CHANGE OF TAPER

Figures 63b and 63d are congruent with respect to the 5 bars and 3 of the 5 triangular shapes. The remaining two triangular shapes, also common to both patterns, are in reversed order in the two designs. If the bars are designated by the letters E, D, C, B, A and the triangular shapes by the numbers 9, 7, 5, 3, 1, as in Fig. 78a, then

              b is E9D**3**C5B**7**A1
   and   d is E9D**7**C5B**3**A1

The two designs differ only in the order of shapes 3 and 7 (printed in boldface).

From the point of view of associationism, the designs are equivalent: the same parts in nearly the same sequence. Neither prior experience nor differences in ease of associative bonding (say, between D-3-C and D-7-C, etc.) can be invoked.

Phenomenally, there are marked structural differences of self-consistency and simplicity. In 63d, the monotonic, regular taper of the bars is repeated by the taper of the triangular shapes. The decreasing arrangement of the bars *parallels* the arrangements of the triangles, resulting in a relatively regular and simple structure. In 63b, the arrangement of the triangles is out of step with the monotonic taper of the bars, resulting in a structure that is more complex (even though regular and lawful on the more complex level, see Fig. 78b). Phenomenally, the difference of the two patterns is expressible in terms of *taper*. Pattern b has three tapers, first to the right, then to the left, then again to the right (Fig. 78c). Pattern d has one left-to-right taper.

This section deals with the taper of the reproductions. *Fading predicts random changes of individual elements,* eroding the taper and affecting both patterns equally. From the point of view of stress theory, Pattern b should be *more variable,* showing increase as well as decrease in the number and direction of tapers [case (c) of Section 23]; Pattern d should be more stable.

188   6. INTRINSIC CHANGE IN REPRODUCTION

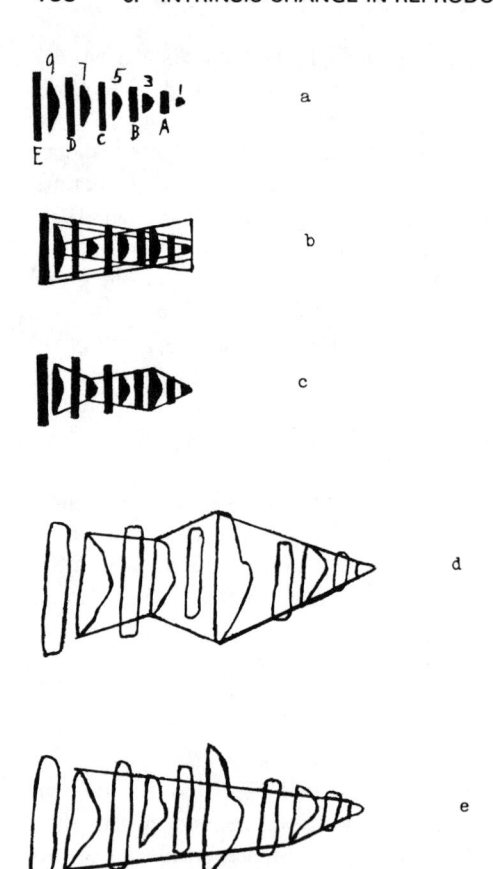

FIG. 78. Figure 78*a* shows pattern 63*d*. The bars are coded by letters, the triangular elements by numbers. Figure 78*b* and *c* show the 3 tapers of 63*b* by means of auxiliary lines. Figure 78*d* and *e* show auxiliary lines applied to an actual reproduction.

Stress theory further suggests that the number of tapers should decrease rather than increase in Pattern *b,* because identical taper of both triangles and bars is the most self-consistent configuration. For the same reason, the number of tapers of Pattern *d* should remain at or near one, rather than increase through random changes of elements as their traces undergo fading separately.

Many of the reproductions are changed with respect to the type of elements, the bars, and triangular shapes. Some have only one kind of elements; in others, the two kinds do not alternate as in the standard. These changes make the classification of tapers difficult and sometimes open to challenge. The changes of elements form the topic of the next section. This section classifies the reproductions by taper and by regularity into categories from the most irregular, 1, to most regular, 8, and a "fragmentary" group 9:

1. Three reproductions are irregular, with three or more tapers; *b*1, *b*8, *b*17 (Fig. 79*b*). In reproduction *b*1, a case could be made for only three tapers as

follows: elements 1-2-3, 4-6-8, and 5-6-7, numbered from left to right. The first two groups taper to the left, the third to the right. The fewest tapers I can see in $b8$ is four: two groups of elements, 1-3-5-7 and 2-4-6-8, both first increasing, then decreasing. Reproduction $b17$ is difficult to divide into subgroups. Taking the large elements 1-3-5-6 as one group and the small ones 2-4-7-8 as another, the large elements first decrease, then increase, making two tapers; the small elements also increase and then decrease a little, resulting in either two tapers if the small increase is counted, or one taper (equality) if the differences are discounted. These three reproductions are the most irregular ones, regardless of how many tapers are assigned.

Next in number of tapers and in regularity is a group of four reproductions, Fig. 79, $b2$, $b7$, $b9$, $b18$. Each of these reproductions has three tapers, if one counts a group of equal-sized elements, like the first three and second three elements of $b18$, as one taper with zero convergence. By degree of regularity, this group can be further divided into the more irregular subgroup 2, consisting of $b9$ and $b18$, and the more regular pair 3, $b2$ and 7.

4. Next in order of increasing regularity are $b5$ and $b21$ (Fig. 79b). These two reproductions come close to being unchanged reproductions of Pattern b. Both have regularly decreasing bars interspersed with triangles that first decrease, then increase, then decrease again, as in the standard. Yet, these reproductions are more regular. In the standard, the middle taper, which runs counter to the taper of the bars and the two other triangle tapers, is prominently formed by three triangles (Fig. 78c). In $b5$ and $b21$, the interruption of the taper consists of only *one* triangle, resulting geometrically in three tapers, right-left-right, as shown in Fig. 78d. But, phenomenally and geometrically, these reproductions can also be considered as having *one continuous left-to-right taper,* interrupted by a single larger triangle as diagramed in Fig. 78e. Of the two geometrically correct diagrams, Fig. 78d and $e,$ diagram $e,$ expresses the psychological appearance of the reproductions more adequately. Reproductions $b5$ and $b21$ are thus more regular than the standard b and are better characterized as having "one, interrupted taper" (Fig. 78e) than as having three tapers as in the standard (Fig. 78c and d).

5. Reproductions $b11$, $b12$, $b13$, and $b19$ have only two tapers, one less than the standard. This classification is unambiguous for $b11$, 12, and 13 and applies to $b19$, if one considers elements 1-3-5-6 as forming one taper and elements 2-4-5 as forming the other, opposite taper, with the fifth element participating in both tapers.

6. Still simpler, almost monotonically decreasing, are reproductions $d2$ and $d10$. In both cases, only one element, the middle or fourth triangle in $d2$ and the end triangle in $d10$, is smaller and larger, respectively, than required by the slant of the remaining triangles, spoiling the otherwise uniform taper. I am inclined to think that this irregularity was not intended, but the reproductions are definitely changed in this respect relative to the second copies by the same subjects.

190   6. INTRINSIC CHANGE IN REPRODUCTION

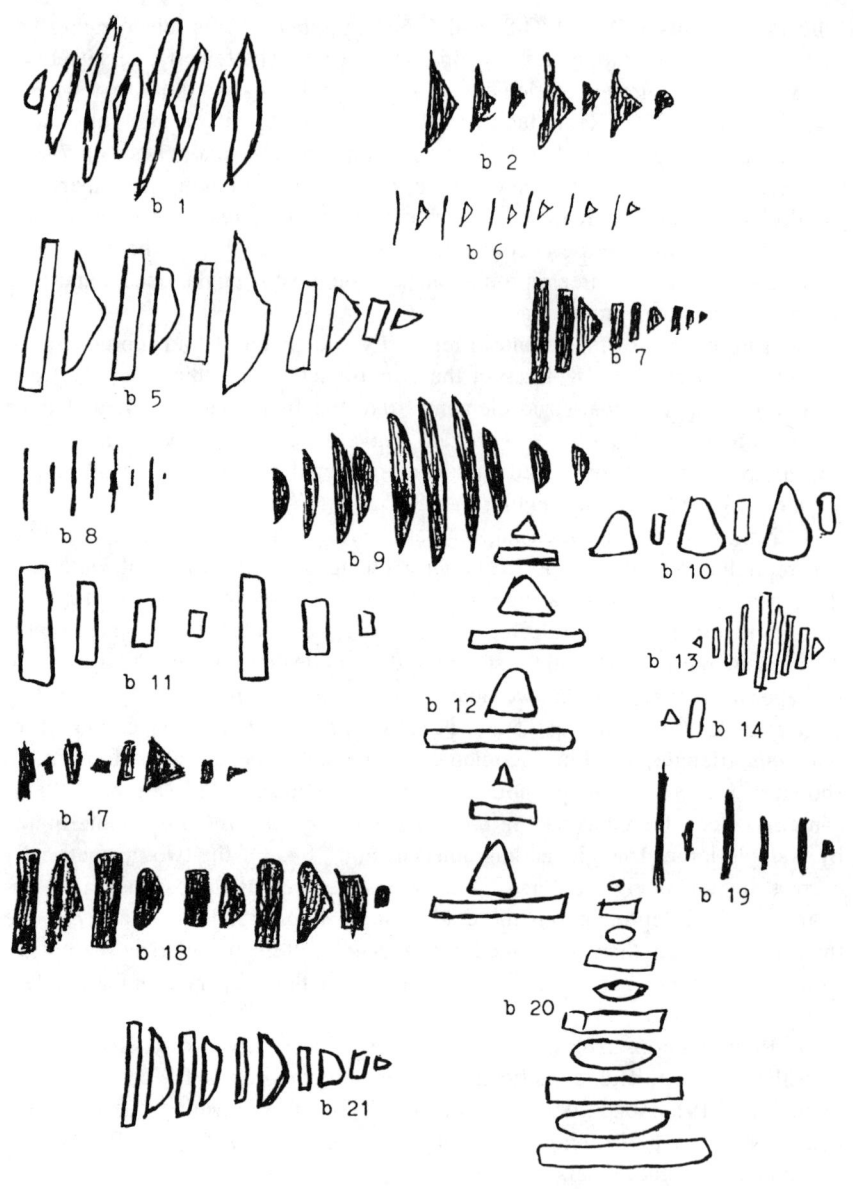

FIG. 79-B

7. Next in order of simplicity of structure and fewer tapers are reproductions $b10$ and 20 and $d3,4,5,6,12,14,15$. $B10$ looks like a simplified version of $63d$, even though it is a reproduction of $63b$. Figure $79b20$ could pass for an unchanged reproduction of $63d$. Actually, both are reproductions of $63b$ that have

49. DESIGNS 63B AND D—CHANGE OF TAPER 191

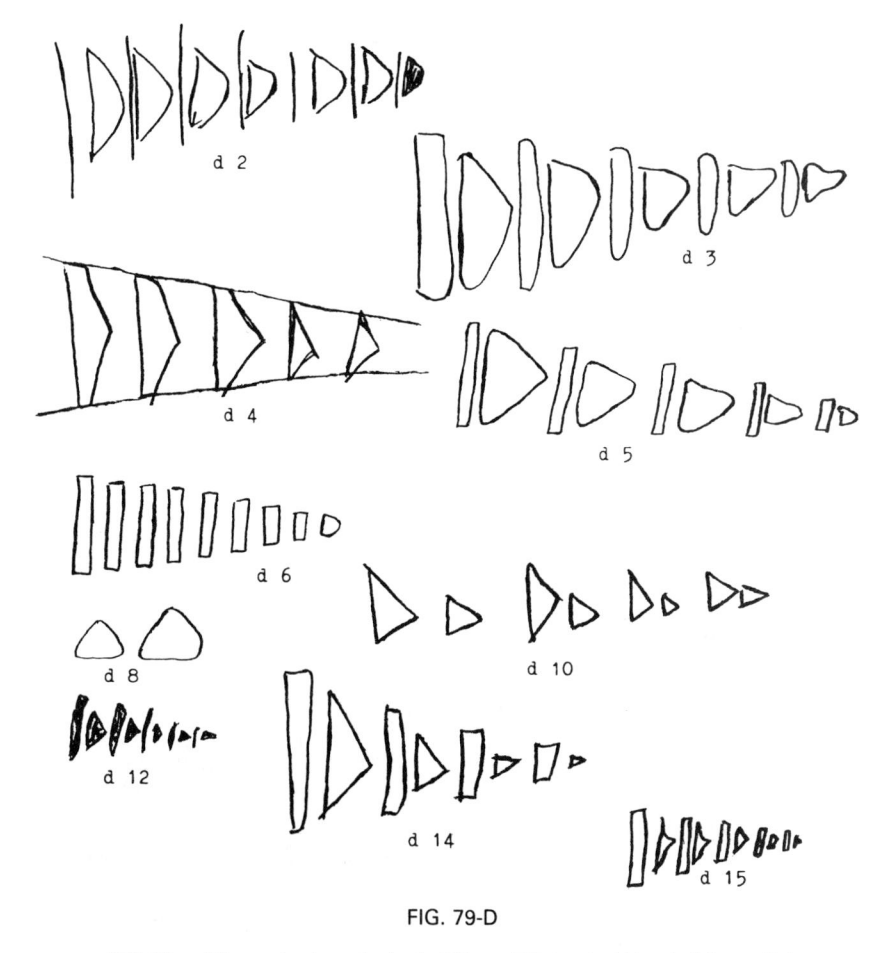

FIG. 79-D

FIG. 79. All reproductions obtained of Figure 63b (marked b) and of figure 63d (marked d).

changed, like many recognitions of 63b, to a single monotonic taper. Reproductions d3,4,5,6,12,14,15 represent reproductions of 63d with unchanged taper.

8. The triangles of reproduction b6 decrease in size so slightly that they might be intended as equal, so that this reproduction was classified as "zero taper." Alternatively, it could be added to the "1 taper" group. In either case, reproduction b6 is markedly simpler and represents the ultimate in regularity, although still preserving the basic structural principle.

9. A subject who remembers only the material, the kind of elements composing the pattern but not the structure, may omit the pattern entirely. In the case of reproductions b14 and d8 (Fig. 79), the subjects seem to have set down tentatively two elements without being able to complete the structure. We classify

192   6. INTRINSIC CHANGE IN REPRODUCTION

these two reproductions as fragmentary. One cannot meaningfully assign a taper to these reproductions.

The result of this discussion is the following rank order of reproductions by overall regularity:

Categories	listing b	N	listing d	N
1. 3 or more tapers, irregular	b1, 8, 17	3	—	
2. 3 tapers, irregular	b9, 18	2	—	
3. 3 tapers, better ordered	b2, 7	2	—	
4. 3 tapers, equivalent to 1 interrupted taper	b5, 21	2	—	
5. 2 tapers	b11, 12, 13, 19	4	—	
6. 2 tapers, almost one			d2, 10	2
7. 1 taper	b10, 20	2	d3, 4, 5, 6, 12, 14, 15	7
8. 0 taper, elements nearly equal	b6	1	—	
9. Fragmentary	b14	1	d8	1
Totals	Pattern b	17	Pattern d	10

In comparing the two patterns, we consider all but the fragmentary reproductions, category 9, of the list. This leaves 16 reproductions of 63b and 9 reproductions of 63d. Of the 16 reproductions of 63b, seven have 3 definite tapers (categories 1,2,3), but none of these has the succession of right–left–right taper characteristic of the standard. By contrast, 7 of the 9 reproductions of Pattern d preserve the single left-to-right taper of that pattern. Even if the two reproductions in category 4 are counted as unchanged, the difference in the preservation of taper is still highly significant (2 of 16 versus 7 of 9, $p < .01$).

The *range* of different tapers includes seven categories in the case of Pattern b, two in case of d.

The deviation from regularity in two reproductions of Pattern d (category 6) is minimal. Conversely, 11 of the 16 reproductions of Pattern b (all categories except 1 and 2, omitting 9) increase the regularity of the pattern compared to the standard. Specifically, in category 3, the three tapers are all in the same direction not right–left–right as learned. The two reproductions of category 4 have phenomenally only one interrupted taper. In category 5, the number of tapers is simplified from three to two. Reproductions b11,12,13 contain two *successive* tapers, b11 and 12 in the same direction and b13 in opposing directions with a novel change to symmetry. B 19 features two opposed, *interdigitated* tapers.

50. DESIGNS 63B AND D—CHANGE OF ELEMENTS

Interdigitation is not novel or added. It is present in the standard between bars and triangles. In the case of reproduction $b19$, interdigitation is *transposed,* from bars and triangles to longer and shorter lines. The maximal possible regularity is represented by categories 7 and 8 with one and no taper, respectively.

With regard to regularity, the two patterns compare as follows:

Regularity	decrease	no change	increase
Pattern b	5 (1,2)	0	11 (3,4,5,7,8)
Pattern d	2 (6)	7 (7)	—

(The numbers in parenthesis refer to the categories in the preceding listing.)

This comparison closely parallels the findings in the recognition experiment with Patterns 63: (a) Pattern $63d$ is significantly more stable than $63b$ (7 unchanged out of 9 versus none of 16 unchanged); (b) pattern $63b$ shows marked change toward more regular structure (11 more regular, 5 less regular), a change not possible for $63d$, which is maximally regular (1 taper); (c) change to a less-regular structure is significantly rare in both patterns, 7 out of 25 reproductions ($p < .05$).

50. DESIGNS 63B AND D—CHANGE OF ELEMENTS

The structure or the form of Patterns 63 is determined by the taper, by the alternation of two distinguishable types of elements, by self-consistency, in short by global features. But the global structural principles do not necessarily *reach down* within the hierarchy of features to the level of the *material* of which the patterns are composed, in this instance, the bars and triangles. As far as the structure is concerned, Patterns $63b$ and d could equally well be made of red and green ovals, or dots and circles, or other kinds of material. The exchange of one kind of material for another, without changing the structure of the pattern, is the analog of paraphrasing an idea by the use of different words or sentences. Nothing in the structure of the two patterns specifically requires them to consist of bars and triangles. The situation is akin to case (c) (Section 23), although not identical with it. The consequences for memory change are similar, however: The bars and triangles can change, whereas more structure-dependent features remain stable. Variability of the material features, which are not structure-dependent, is equally likely in *both* patterns. We examine some changes of the material and analyze their relationship to the overall structure.

Discrete Elements. Even when the structure is quite changed or impoverished, the patterns are still rendered as composed of *discrete,* unconnected elements. This—global—feature is preserved in all 27 reproductions (Fig. 79).

194 6. INTRINSIC CHANGE IN REPRODUCTION

Shape of Elements. In some reproductions, the bars have been simplified, "leveled" to mere lines ($b6, b8, b19, d2, d12$) or evolved into a cigar shape, midway between a bar and a triangular shape, a case of so-called figure assimilation ($b1, b9$). The triangles become more pointed to the right ($b2, d4, d14$, and others), or broad based ($b10, d8$), or both ($b12$).

One Kind of Element. Eight of the 27 reproductions are composed of only one kind of element. $B2$, $d4$, $d8$, and $d10$ contain triangles only. $B11$ contains bars only. $B8$ is composed only of lines, and $b1$ and $b9$ contain cigar shapes only. In spite of this drastic change at the material level of the hierarchy, global aspects are preserved and expressed: three tapers in $b2$, two tapers in $b11$, one taper in $d4$, for example. Fading would have to explain why in these reproductions alternate elements fade.

Another four reproductions, $b7$, 13, 19, and $d6$, fall in this category, if we allow for a small triangle at the end of a taper in reproductions otherwise composed of bars only ($b7$, 13, and $d6$) or lines ($b19$ of Fig. 79).

With the addition of the four "mixed" cases (bars with triangles at the end of tapers) to the eight "pure" cases, the subgroup of reproductions with only *one* type of element stands at 12 members. However, in three of these reproductions, the global feature of possessing two kinds of material is actually preserved, even though all elements have the same shape. In $b8$, $b19$, and $d10$, the *two shapes are replaced by two sizes of one shape.* Using the concepts elaborated in Goldmeier (1972, Chapter 4, Part B), we say that in $b8$, $b19$, and $d10$ large lines or triangles have taken on the *function* of the bars; small lines or triangles have assumed the *function originally carried by the triangular shapes.* The memory trace has preserved the *function,* whereas the *carrier of the function* is changed or lost. (This is a common experience of daily life: "The boss, or whoever was in charge, I think it was Joe, or Jim, said. . . ." The function "boss" is remembered; the carrier of the function is lost or changed.)

With the addition of the mixed cases and the deletion of the three reproductions having two types of element distinguished by size instead of by shape, the subgroup with one type of element finally consists of 9 reproductions, 6 "pure" cases, $b1$, 2, 9, 11, $d4$, 8, and 3 mixed cases (with small-end triangles), $b7, b13$, and $d6$.

Number of Elements. Both standards, $63b$ and $63d$, contain 10 elements. Fading theory predicts that forgetting leads to fewer elements. Table 12 agrees roughly with this prediction (see last line of Table 12). Only two reproductions exceed 10 elements, 15 have fewer than 10 elements, 10 reproductions are unchanged with 10 elements.

In our theory, the number of elements in itself is irrelevant. Instead, we look for structural features that have consequences at the level of the "material," in this case the elements. A pervasive feature of the two patterns is the alternation

50. DESIGNS 63B AND D—CHANGE OF ELEMENTS

TABLE 12
Number of Elements in Reproductions of 63b and 63d
(Each Number in the Design Columns
Identifies One of the Reproductions in Fig. 79)

No. of Elements	Design b	Design d	No. of Cases
2	14	8*	2
5	—	4*	1
6	10, 19	—	2
7	2*, 11*	—	2
8	1*, 8, 17	10, 14	5
9	7*, 13*	6*	3
10	5, 9*, 12 18, 20, 21	3, 5 13, 15	10
12	6	—	1
14	—	2	1
			Total 27

*This reproduction contains only one type of elements as defined in section 50.

or pairing of two kinds of elements. To the extent that this feature is preserved in memory, reproductions with an *even number of elements* should predominate. Table 12 lists 21 reproductions with an even number of elements and 6 with an odd number. The significant ($p < .01$) predominance of even numbers is difficult to interpret in terms of fading. The obvious argument for fading, pair-wise association between bars and triangular shapes, is not sufficient to explain $b6$ and $d2$ with added pairs or $b5$, $d8$, and $d10$, where the pair associations have held, but the pairs have undergone changes that are far from random. If one member of a pair has faded, how can it still evoke its associate? The predominance of even numbers of elements requires a very selective kind of fading.

The explanation based on the singular feature of alternation or pairing is strengthened, if it is restricted to the 18 reproductions in which two kinds of elements are present, to the 18 reproductions in Table 12 without asterisk. *All 18 reproductions with two types of elements, no matter how much the whole pattern or individual elements have changed otherwise, have an even number of elements* ranging from two to 14 elements.

In the remaining nine reproductions, those with one type of element, an even number of elements should be as likely as an odd number, unless the global structure of the pattern imposes special constraints. Of these nine reproductions (marked with an asterisk in Table 12), seven are unconstrained in this respect. $B1$, $b9$, and $d8$ have an even number; $b2, b11, d4$, and $d6$ have an odd number of elements, a 3-to-4 ratio consistent with either fading or stress theory.

The remaining two reproductions, $b7$ and $b13$, represent unique changes of Pattern b toward greater self-consistency and regularity. In reproduction $b7$, the

196   6. INTRINSIC CHANGE IN REPRODUCTION

feature of three tapers is preserved, but the middle taper is turned into the same direction as the others. The overall taper of the bars is also preserved. The inconsistency between the three tapers of the triangles and the one taper of the bars is eliminated by using triangles only as the pointed ends of each taper. The three subtapers tighten up the structure of the whole pattern by forming one overall taper, by facing in the same direction, and by containing the same number of elements each, two bars and an end triangle. These changes make the structure so self-consistent that it leaves no room for further change and by its nature requires an odd number of elements: three (tapers) times three (elements) is odd.

A different approach to self-consistency leads to reproduction $b13$. One of the three tapers of Pattern b is dropped, leaving two tapers that preserve the original one left-one right directions. The stability of the resulting two back-to-back tapers is improved, as in the previous instance, by an equal number of elements in each taper. The equality makes possible the symmetry, which further stabilizes the opposite direction of the tapers. The new configuration, consisting of one central bar with two equal tapers to both sides, inherently requires an odd number of elements: One plus two times anything is odd.

The changes of Patterns 63 illustrate that memory changes occur simultaneously at several levels, that the intrinsic changes serve to make the pattern more self-consistent, and that the changes occur in large measure independently, exemplifying the orthogonality axiom proposed in Section 23. For example, reproduction $b10$ drastically simplifies the three opposing tapers to one, on the global or form level. At the same time, and independently, the number of elements is reduced to six, or three pairs, not enough to express three tapers but sufficient to form one taper. The bars have been simplified to being equal; the taper is carried by the triangles only. On the level of material, the bars and triangles have become broader. The triangular shapes have become more triangular and turned "base down," a more singular position than "standing on end," as in the standard (see Goldmeier, 1972, Section 50, on singularity of position). The reproduction is the result of these various changes on several levels simultaneously.

51. CLOSURE IN FIGURES 68 AND 70

According to a well-known tenet of gestalt theory, a local feature of a well-integrated pattern is largely characterized by the role it plays in the whole of which it is a part. For example, a musical note is psychologically defined by the tune in which it occurs (as "lead in," "tonic," not as "f sharp").

A notorious misunderstanding of gestalt theory—in contradiction to this tenet—is the notion that all gaps tend toward closure, irrespective of the whole design in which they occur. This section aims to clarify this misunderstanding

51. CLOSURE IN FIGURES 68 AND 70

and at the same time contribute to the understanding of *closure as a means to increase self-consistency*.

In reporting on the gaps in reproductions of Design 70*d*, 70*i*, 68*h*, *d* and *e*, we use the following categories (Table 13):

1. "Unchanged" means gaps in the same relation to curves as in the standard and the second copy. In the case of 70*d* and 68*h*, unchanged means that two gaps are *within* the upper middle curve and two *within* the lower middle curve. In the case of 70*i* and 68*d*, it means that there is a gap *within* each of the four side curves. In the case of 68*e*, it means that there are gaps *at the cusps (i.e., between the curves)*. Hence, as far as the gaps are concerned, the reproductions of 68*e* shown in Fig. 80 *p* and *q* are unchanged. Figure 80*e* shows a reproduction of 70*i*, which is unchanged by our definition. Figure 80*l* shows an unchanged reproduction of 68*h*.

2. "Closed" means that there are no gaps within the curves and none at the cusps between adjoining curves. A reproduction is listed as closed if no gaps are open. Thus, Fig. 80*g*, *m*, and *n* are closed reproductions of 68*h* and Fig. 80*o* is a closed reproduction of 68*e*. Figure 80*f* is a reproduction of 70*i*, in which the gaps in the upper curves are unchanged and those in the lower curves closed. It is listed as "other," because it qualifies neither as unchanged nor as closed.

3. "To cusps" means that the four gaps drawn within the curves of the second copy have changed to gaps at *all cusps between the curves* of the repro-

TABLE 13
Gaps in Reproductions of Figs. 70*i* and *d*, 68*h*, *e*, *d*

Design	Interval	N	Closed %	#	unchanged	to cusps	To side curves	other	unclassifiable
70 i_I	6 weeks	15	87%	13	1	0	—	1*	0
d_I	6 weeks	20	75%	15	0	2*	0	3*	0
68 d_{III}	6 weeks	18	67%	12	1	1	—	4	0
h_{III}	6 weeks	12	42%	5	3	2	0	2	0
68 h_{II}	Immed.	13	0%	0	12	0	1	0	0
	2 weeks	13	15%	2*	7	1	0	3*	0
	4 weeks	18	56%	10	4	1	0	2	1*
	6 weeks	12	25%	3*	4	4	1	0	0
68 e_{II}	Immed.	22	5%	1	21	—	0	0	0
	2 weeks	14	0%	0	14	—	0	0	0
	4 weeks	12	0%	0	12	—	0	0	0
	6 weeks	7	29%	2	5	—	0	0	0

*Some of these reproductions are shown in Fig. 80.
The subscripts I, II and III indicate that the result is part of Experiment I, II or III.

198   6. INTRINSIC CHANGE IN REPRODUCTION

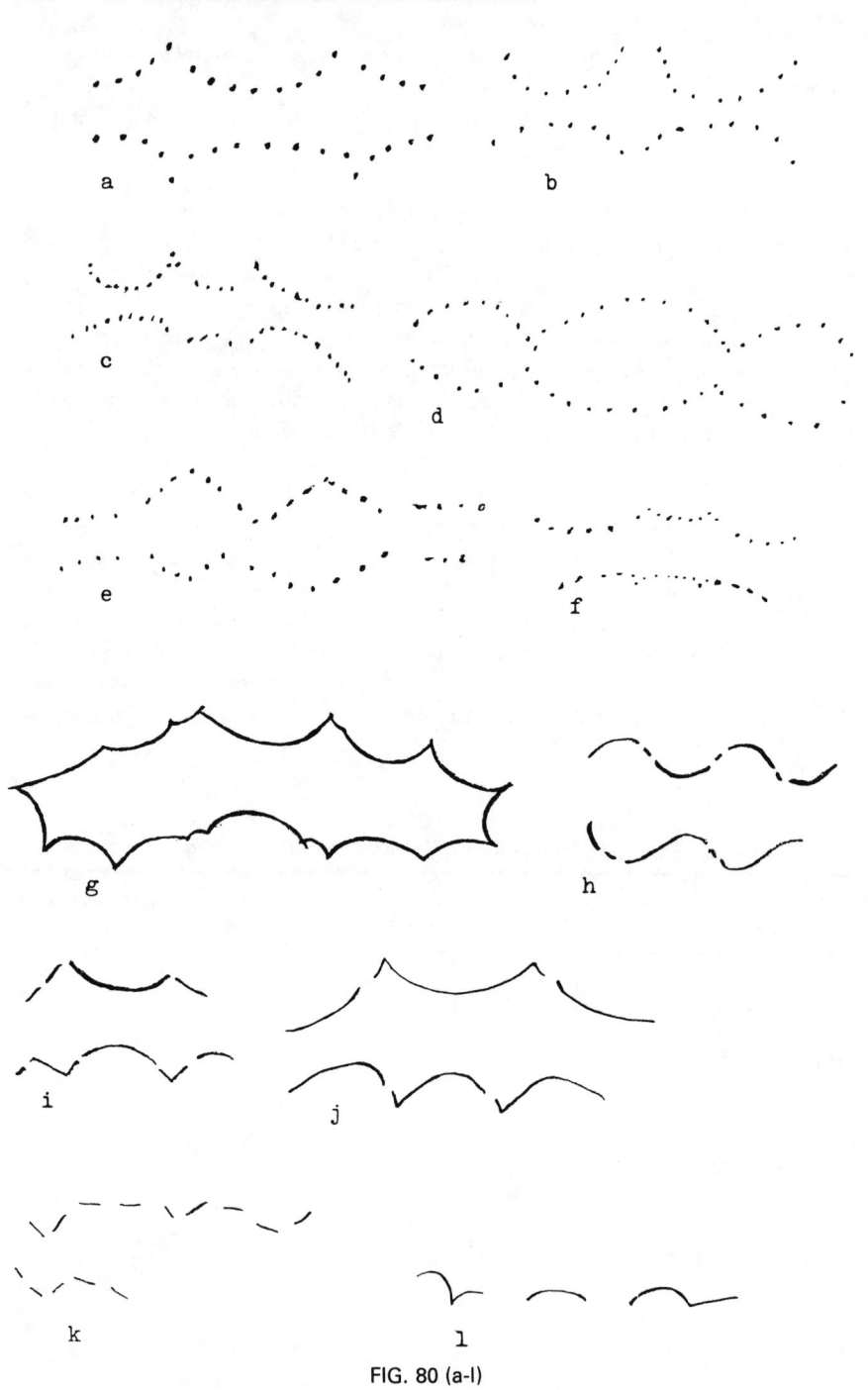

FIG. 80 (a-l)

51. CLOSURE IN FIGURES 68 AND 70   199

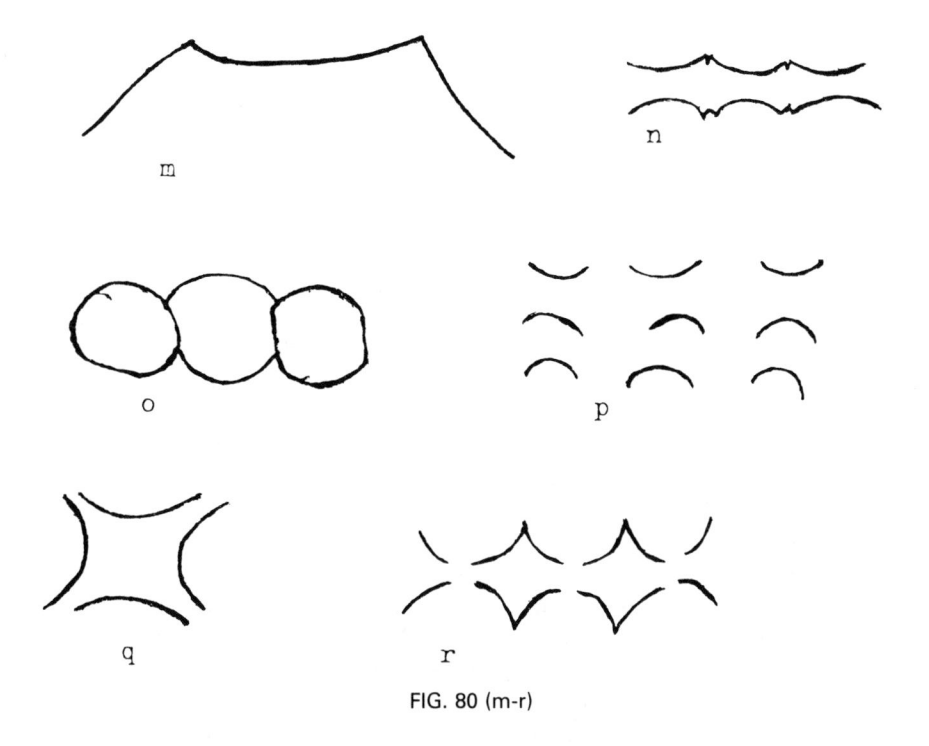

FIG. 80 (m-r)

FIG. 80. Selected reproductions of pattern 70 *d* (*a, b, c*), Pattern 70 *i* (*d, e, f*), 68 *h* (*g, h, i, j, k, l, m, n, r,*) and Pattern 68 *e* (*o, p, q*). These examples were classified as "to cusps," "closed," etc. They illustrate extremes of each class. They should not be taken as typical. A typical "unchanged" reproduction looks very much like the standard. The following lists for each sample the standard, the time interval between learning and reproduction, and the classification. *a*: 70*d*, 6w, to cusps. *b*: 70*d*, 6w to cusps. *c*: 70*d*, 6w, other. *d*: 70*i*, 6w closed. *e*: 70*i*, 6w unchanged. *f*: 70*i*, 6w, other (2 gaps closed). *g*: 68*h*, 2w, closed. *h*: 68*h*, 2w, other. *i*: 68*h*, 2w, other. *j*: 68*h*, 2w, other. *k*: 68*h*, 4w, unclassifyable. *l*: 68*h*, 4w, unchanged. *m*: 68*h*, 6w, closed. *n*: 68*h*, 6w, closed. *o*: 68*e*, Imm., closed. *p*: 68*e*, Imm., unchanged. *q*: 68*e*, 6w, unchanged. *r*: 68*h*, restructured, 6w.

duction. Figure 80*a* is an example. It is a reproduction of 70*d*, has no gaps within curves, and the distance of the end dots between the curves is sufficiently greater than that within curves to indicate gaps. Figure 80*b,* also a reproduction of 70*d,* also qualifies as changed to cusps. It has no gaps within the curves and gaps at *all* cusps, even though there are only two cusps instead of the original four. Figure 80*i* is not an instance of to cusps, even though there are gaps at the two upper cusps. Not only are the lower cusps closed, but there also are gaps within several of the curves.

To cusps as a category of *change* obviously does not apply to Design 68*e*.

4. "To side curves" means that a reproduction has two upper and two lower side curves and gaps *within* these. Obviously, this category of change does not apply to Designs 70*i* and 68*d*.

5. "Other." There were 15 reproductions that did not fit into one of the preceding categories. Most of them were mixed cases (e.g., one reproduction of 70*d* had two gaps closed and two at cusps). Other instances are shown in Fig. 80, *c,f,h,j,k*. Thirty-six subjects did not furnish reproduction of these designs, 2 of 70*d*, 7 of 68*d*, 7 of 68*e*, and 23 of 68*h*, all in 6-week groups.

Analysis of the five designs, 70*d*, 70*i*, 68*d,e*, and *h*, illustrates well the fallacy of treating a local feature, such as a gap, in isolation, out of the context of the remainder of the design. The incidence of gap closure in 6-week reproductions of these designs ranges from 87% to 25%, and in the 4-week reproductions of 68*e*, it goes down to zero (Table 13).

Gap Strength. The most obvious difference is that between the dot figures 70*d* and 70*i* and the line drawings 68*h,d*, and *e*. Even though the gaps in Fig. 70 are wider than those in Fig. 68, they stand out less. In Fig. 70, the gaps differ from the lines only in degree, as one larger distance between dots in a row of many smaller distances. In Fig. 68, gaps and lines differ in kind, forming discontinuities within otherwise continuous lines. In Fig. 68, the gaps are more salient, more intrusive, or as we say, *stronger* than in Fig. 70. The greater strength of the gaps in Design 68 compared with Design 70 is also brought out by similarity experiments (the rankings were like those described in Sections 6 and 35, but weaker). Given a comparable interval of time and assuming that the tendency to closure is insensitive to the actual size of gap, as long as the gap is relatively small, *the difference in gap strength makes closure of the gaps more probable in the designs of Fig. 70 than in those of Fig. 68.*

The reader is reminded that each row of Table 13 reports on a different group of subjects, and that the changes reported are the differences between each subject's own second copy and his or her reproduction.

Both 70*i* and 68*d* have gaps in the side curves. The incidence of closure is 87 versus 67%. Designs 70*d* and 68h_{III} (Design 68*h* was used as standard in Experiments II and III. The subscripts II and III indicate which experiment is discussed.) have gaps in the center curves. Closures occur in 75 versus 42%. Both results are in the expected direction (i.e., closure occurs more often with the dot design than with Design 68, but when tested by chi square, the differences are at most suggestive, ($p < .2$ and $p < .1$, respectively). On the other hand, the difference between the two dot figures is small ($p < .5$) and likewise the difference between the two solid figures is not statistically significant ($p < .2$). Therefore, it seems permissible to add up closures of the two dot figures and compare them with the total closures of the two solid figures. The combined tally is 80 versus 57%, and this difference, 70*i* + *d* versus 68*d* + h_{III}, is statistically significant, $p < .05$.

Elimination of the 6-Week Groups of 68h and 68e. All memory theories predict that changes *increase* over time. However, in the 6-week group of Experiment $68h_{II}$, there are *fewer* closures than in the 4-week group with $68h$ as the standard. Not only is this result the opposite of what one would expect, but it approaches statistical significance ($p < .1$). A like reversal occurs in the recognition results. The changes of both recognition groups of $68h_{II}$ are smaller than those at the 4-week interval. The reproductions of $68e$ at the 6-week interval also show relatively more closures than those of the 4-week group. Here, the difference is smaller and statistically not significant. In the case of this $68e$ group, the recognitions also are severely affected. Only two recognitions were valid. The other nine subjects circled more than one of the recognition choices that eliminates the test as ambiguous. The suspect 6-week recognition results were sidestepped (Section 35) by using the 4-week recognitions of both $68h_{II}$ and $68e$, instead of the 6-week groups.

After talking to the teachers conducting the tests, I discovered that the test period for these groups fell into the earliest morning class on the day of a heavy snowstorm. This cut attendance and caused students to straggle in after the test had begun. Apparently, the instructions did not reach all students right away. I believe that major deviations from the protocol occurred, specifically with the Designs $68h$ and $68e$. The second and third task in the same test (reported in Chapter 7) are not affected. Apparently, by then the late comers had caught up.

Rather than suppress these results, I decided to report them in the pertinent tables and graphs but to discard the 6-week results with $68e_{II}$ and $68h_{II}$ from further consideration or identify them as suspect wherever they are mentioned.

The Structural Role of Gaps. The gap *strength* is related to the *material* of the design, in this instance, dotted versus solid lines. (For the distinction between material and form, see the previous discussion on gap strength). A second relevant characteristic of gaps stems from the role of the gap in the structure of the design. The gaps in $70d$, $70i$, and in $68d$ and $68h$ *interrupt* the flow of the lines in which they occur; they are *contrastructural*. The gaps in Design $68e$ separate different curves and serve to *articulate* the design; they are *prostructural*. The gaps in Fig. $70e$, $70d$, $68h$, $68d$ are in nonsingular locations, case (c), Section 23; those in $68e$ occupy the singular cusps. The consistency of the nonsingular designs is enhanced by closure of the contrastructural gaps (as well as by various other possible changes), whereas Design $68e$ is under no such stress. Because $68e$ is a line drawing, the gaps are not only prostructural but also *stronger* than the gaps in the dot figures $70i$ and $70d$. Both features tend to stabilize the gaps. Accordingly, there are significantly more closures, in 28 out of 35 reproductions of the dot figures, as against 2 of 7 closures in the (discarded) 6-week group of $68e$ ($p < .01$), and none in 12 reproductions by the 4-week group of $69e$ ($p < .001$).

The stronger gaps in $68d$ and $68h$ resist closure more strongly. Comparing the

6-week group of $68d_{III}$ with the (discarded) 6-week group of $68e_{II}$, the difference in closures is suggestive, $p < .1$. A comparison of the 6-week closures of $68h_{III}$ with the (discarded) $68e_{II}$, 42 versus 29%, also lies in the expected direction without being statistically significant. If either $68d_{III}$ or $68h_{III}$ is compared with the *4-week* test of $68e$, the differences are statistically significant, but the incidence of closure of Design $68e$ after only 4 weeks is not directly comparable with *6-weeks* changes of $68d$ or $68h$.

Fortunately, the 4-week groups of Designs $68h_{II}$ and $68e_{II}$ afford a valid comparison over a like time span. After 4 weeks, 56% of reproductions of $68h_{II}$ have closed gaps, whereas none of the reproductions of $68e_{II}$ after the same time interval are closed. This difference is highly significant, $p < .005$.

Gaps on Side Curves Versus Gaps on Center Curves. The 6-week experiments with the dot figures $70i$ and $70d$ and the line drawings $68d$ and $68h$ have a curious result: The incidence of closure is higher in the variants with gaps in the side curves $70i$ and $68d$ than in the center curves $70d$ and $68h$. For Design 70, the incidence is 87 versus 75%; with Design 68, closure occurs in 67 ($68d_{III}$), versus 42% in $68h_{III}$, and 25% in the (discarded) $68h_{II}$ group. Only the latter (discarded) difference is statistically significant.

There is no compelling explanation for this difference in terms of either fading or increased self-consistency of the design. The question therefore has no direct bearing on the problems of the present research and was not further pursued.

7 Change of Nonvisual Traces

A. THE STORY TASK

52. THE EMPIRISTIC FALLACY—RECOGNITION

Stress theory, like fading, undertakes to explain all of memory, not just memory for form. But unlike fading, stress theory requires a thorough knowledge of the structure of each memory content. For instance, investigation of memory for chess positions requires familiarity with the intricacies of chess on the part of the investigator, the subjects, and the reader. Memory for chess positions (mainly over the short term) has been investigated with results both intriguing and seemingly compatible with stress theory by Chase and Simon (1973). Because of the requirement for detailed structural information, I chose nonvisual memory tasks from fields less demanding than chess, less specialized than music, less-defying analysis than emotional experiences, and less ambiguous, subjective, and lacking in unique connotations than Bartlett's (1932) ghost story. This is not to disparage these fields as unsuitable. Investigation of memory contents in these and other fields, from the viewpoint of stress theory, would be of great intrinsic interest. In the case of memory for *events that an individual has witnessed,* the interest would also be immensely practical. Traditional memory theories throw little light on the memory performance of witnesses before the courts of law. The few existing investigations, like those of Loftus (1979b), deal mainly with the effect of biasing context, an important problem, certainly, but not the only possible source of error. In addition to intentionally introduced contradictions, intrinsic changes, too, can color and alter the memory for events.

7. CHANGE OF NONVISUAL TRACES

One of the two nonvisual tasks tested here is a *story*. The story was the second of the three tasks in Experiment II. It was presented in two versions, each version to eight independent groups. Each version was tested in two groups "immediately," in two after two weeks, in two after 4 weeks, and in two groups after 6 weeks. The procedure is that described in Section 27 and is identical with that followed for the visual tasks, particularly Designs 68e and 68h, which constituted the first of the three tasks in Experiment II. The story task appeared in one of two versions:

Second Task

"This is the story about three brothers who bought stock in the stock market. The youngest brother invested $8000, and when he sold his stock later he got $16,000 for it. The next brother invested $10,000 and sold it for $22,000. The oldest brother invested $12,000 and sold his stock for $24,000. All three did very well indeed."

The story in the other version was identical with this story except for the single number 22,000, which was replaced by the number 20,000. The reader should reread the story now, substituting 20,000 for 22,000, to appreciate the restructuring of the entire story as a consequence of this isolated change.

Recognition was tested by reprinting the beginning of the story verbatim up to "... next brother invested..." then continuing as follows: "... next brother invested $10,000 and sold it for

$12,000
$14,000
$16,000
$18,000
$20,000
$22,000
$24,000
$26,000
$28,000
$30,000

The oldest brother invested $12,000 and sold his stock for $24,000. All three did very well indeed."

This recognition test form was used for both versions. It includes every word of the story except the proceeds received by the middle brother, for which it offers 10 choices.

Fading predicts that the recognition choices for either version of the story form a gaussian error distribution centered on the number memorized, somewhat like this fictitious example (suppressing hereafter the last three zeros):

52. THE EMPIRISTIC FALLACY—RECOGNITION

number chosen		12	14	16	18	20	22	24	26	28	30
version "20"	N = 26	—	1	3	4	**10**	4	3	1	—	—
version "22"	N = 32	—	—	2	3	5	**12**	5	3	2	—

(Boldface in each case indicates "correct" choices.)

The actual choices (from the two 6-week groups of version "20" and the two 6-week groups of version "22") are distributed as follows:

number chosen		12	14	16	18	20	22	24	26	28	30
version "20"	N = 26	—	—	—	—	**26**	—	—	—	—	—
version "22"	N = 32	1	1	1	2	15	**11**	1	—	—	—

(For both versions, boldface indicates the number of recognitions of the standard.) By any statistical test, the results with the two versions differ significantly, from each other as well as from the typical gaussian distribution, contrary to what fading would lead one to expect. The 20 version is without error. As an error curve, it is extremely peaked. In fact, it is a δ-function as suggested for the singular case (a), Section 23. The 22 version peaks at the wrong point, nearer to 20 than to the zero error at 22.

Apologists for empirism and fading can invoke "familiarity" of the number 20,000 to explain why there are no "errors" in the "$20,000" story as against 21 out of 32 errors in the story using the less familiar number 22,000. The recourse to familiarity (i.e., frequent prior experience) is one of several versions of the empiristic fallacy that has plagued memory theory and that bears on the notion of singularity so central to stress theory.

1. To begin with, the assumption of familarity is often too glibly made. Is the number 20,000, or this dollar amount, really so familiar? Possibly, it is more familiar than 19,998, but it also is possibly less familiar than, say, 22 or $22, or $19.98. Probably the experimental outcome would have been the same if all the numbers had been multiplied by 10 or 100. Should the amount of $200,000 or $2 million also be accepted as familiar, compared with $220,000 or $2.2 million? I suggest that: (a) None of these numbers or amounts are very familiar; and (b) that differences in unfamiliarity are negligible. In any event, the burden of proof that our subjects are more familiar with $20,000 than with $22,000 lies with the empirist.

2. The—intuitively obvious—difference between the 20,000 and the 22,000 version rests on the difference between the singularity of a *round* number contrasted with one that is not so singled out. This matter is discussed in Wertheimer's seminal paper of 1912 on "Numbers and Number Concepts" (see also Rosch, 1975a). We think, perceive, and remember numbers by anchoring them to round numbers in a quasi-spatial fashion (e.g., 22 is *in the "low" twenties*). Round numbers act as reference points just as in Fig. 68*e* the ends of the curves act as anchor points for the gaps. The fact that 20 is a round number and 22 is not

7. CHANGE OF NONVISUAL TRACES

is a consequence of the decimal system. In an *undecimal* system, one based on the number 11, for instance, 20 appears as 19, and 22 becomes the "round" number 20. Admittedly, the decimal system is familiar and well-learned. But the greater singularity of 20 compared with 22 is not a consequence of the *familarity* of the decimal system but of the *structure* of the decimal system. There are situations in which 144 becomes a round number: an even gross; a dozen dozens; or 3.14159... in goniometry where angles are measured in multiples of π. The advantage and the distinction of 20 or 20,000 is structural, not learned in itself, except inasmuch as the decimal system is learned.

3. In some situations, familarity does create singularities (e.g., in imprinting or overlearning), but in other situations, sometimes characterized as "cognitive dissonances," long familiarity by itself fails to override an ordering anchored on the singularities inherent in the situation. Examples are "clues" in plain view but "overlooked" by all but the expert, or discoveries consisting of reordering long familiar facts. The most famous instance of the latter kind is Einstein's appreciation of the equivalence of inertial and ponderous mass, "familiar" to physicists since the time of Newton 200 years earlier, but not "understood."

The preceding 6-week recognition tests show that:

1. Version "20" is *unchanged,* where many recognition choices of version "22" are changed and *widely* scattered, ranging over seven of the 10 alternatives offered.

2. The difference between the two versions in the *number of unchanged recognitions,* 26 of 26 versus 11 of 32, is highly significant.

3. The median choice of the 20 version is *unchanged at* 20; that of the 22 version has *changed to* 20. The means are also both at 20 (20 and 20.13).

Stress theory accounts for these findings on the basis of (1) singularity and (2) self-consistency.

Singularity.   The findings conform to stress theory if we agree that $20,000 is a singular amount for subjects operating in the decimal system, therefore unchanged, whereas $22,000 is the near-singular case (b), Section 23, causing both scatter and a strong trend toward the singularity.

Self-consistency.   The singularity of 20,000 by virtue of being a *round number* compared with 22,000 is only one factor in the outcome of the experiment. The stability of the number 20 depends also on the internal consistency confered on the 20 version by the *principle of exact doubling of all three amounts.* This hypothesis is testable by an experiment not performed here, using the same story but different key amounts; for example:

```
    9 — 18              9 — 18
   11 — 22   versus    11 — 20
   13 — 26             13 — 26
```

and tested after 1 to 4 weeks. (All numbers are "harder"; therefore, the outcome should be less clear-cut and changes should occur earlier.) In this proposed experiment, the doubling feature favors the number 22, not the round number 20. In the present experiment, the increased internal consistency, conferred on the 20 version by the consistent doubling, is lacking in the 22 version. Probably, both factors play a part in the recognitions.

53. SELF-CONSISTENCY IN REPRODUCTION

In order to report on the reproductions concisely, we use the following notation: The unchanged "22" story (see preceding section) is coded as:

```
    8  -  16
   10  -  22
   12  -  24
```

giving only the amounts (in thousands) invested (left column) and obtained from sale (right column) of the youngest brother (top line), middle brother (middle line, and oldest (bottom). The unchanged "20" version of the story in this same notation is:

```
    8  -  16
   10  -  20
   12  -  24.
```

All 6-week and *all* 2-week reproductions are reported here.

The 6-Week Reproductions

Fading theory affords little guidance in analyzing the reproductions. After 6 weeks, there is only one "correct" reproduction of the 20 version from 12 subjects and no correct reproduction of the 22 version from 11 subjects.

Differences emerge if the reproductions are judged by the degree of self-consistency. That means in this case the "consistent doubling" of the 20 version and the "two doublings and one near doubling" of the 22 version.

The 20 version is more integrated or coherent because of its greater self-consistency and therefore easier to recall. Only 2 of the 12 subjects omitted the story completely, whereas 8 of the 11 subjects who had memorized the 22 version gave up on setting down at least a fragment.

208   7. CHANGE OF NONVISUAL TRACES

Of the three partial responses obtained from the 22 version, only one is numerical:

"$12000
$18000
$24000"

The other two are without numerical structure. They are: "3 brothers invested money" and "three fellows invested money in a bank which were different amounts." The ten 6-week reproductions of the 20 version include one non-numerical and one vaguely numerical one: "3 brothers" and "one brother bought land for $18000, other brother bought land for . . . older." The remaining eight reproductions of the 20 version consist of one unchanged reproduction and seven that preserve the mathematical structure to various degress. One starts "There were three brothers" and ends "The profit was the same proportionally" without giving numbers. One report is:

```
 6 - 12
 8 - 16
10 - 20,
```

a clear instance of what, in music (and in gestalt theory), is called *transposition*. This response preserves not only the doubling feature but also the increase of the three investments in steps of $2000. Fading theory would have to call the six numbers "wrong" (e.g., the middle pair was learned as 10–20, not 8–16, as this response explicitly states). The remaining five responses recall only initial amounts. In our notation, the five reports are:

(a)	(b)	(c)	(d)	(e)
"made"				
8	8–	10–	8–	8–
10	10–	15–	12–	16–
12	20–	20–	10–	20–

In (a), "made" may refer either to the profit or the selling price. In the former case, it is unchanged. Correct or incorrect, these subjects recall a *true part* of the story as opposed to a random fragment, by recalling the fact of three investments. This kind of recall is unexpected from fading. The numbers are presented to the subjects in the order 8, 16, 10, 20, 12, 24. According to the proudest achievement of fading theory, the bowed learning curve, the first and last number, 8 and 24, should be recalled in preference to the middle numbers, 10 and 20. Looking at the five reports, we find that 10 or 20 or both occur in all five reproductions, and 24, which has the "recency" effect in its favor, is missing entirely. Reproductions (a) and (b) correctly include every other item in the serial learning order.

Within fading theory, this result would argue for a new, zig-zag-shaped, learning curve.

All five responses, the two "correct" ones as well as the incorrect ones, indicate that the structural feature of buying-selling is preserved in memory; that the numbers are not lost randomly but as members of a conceptual subunit that is or is not recalled as a whole. Within the subunit of "buying prices," two responses (a,d) are unchanged, one response (c) preserves—in transposed amounts—the singular "equal step increase" feature, even though the figures themselves, *which are nonsingular in the original,* have changed. Two responses (b,e) preserve at least the "increase" feature. Finally, the responses 10-15-20 and 8-16-20 probably reach across subunit boundaries for a source of the figures 16 and 20. The inclusion of 16 and 20 on the buying side therefore probably represents *structural weakening* of the distinction between buying numbers and selling numbers, rather than a *randomly wrong* response. The figure 15 in response (c) seems to be a change serving the preservation of the equal step structure.

At the 6-week interval, the less-stable 22 version of the story has become so degraded that some of the stress-induced changes are no longer evident.

The 2-Week Reproductions

Because the 2-week reproductions are less severely changed and more numerous than the 6-week reproductions, the changes appear more clearly and are more instructive. Also, the 22 version is better preserved so that it can be compared with the 20 version.

After 2 weeks, the incidence of changed reproductions of the story is as follows:

	unchanged	changed
version "20"	9	3
version "22"	4	10

Change is significantly ($p < .02$) more frequent in the 22 version of the story, revealing it to be less stable in reproduction as well as recognition.

In our code, the three changed reproductions of the 20 version are:

(a)	(b)	(c)
5 — 10	100 — 200	12 — 16
8 — 16	200 — 400	14 — 16
10 — 20	300 — 600	

(The numbers in (a) and (c) are thousands; those in (b) are the actual numbers). Reproductions (a) and (b) preserve two important singular aspects of the 20

7. CHANGE OF NONVISUAL TRACES

version, namely, the doubling of all amounts and the increase from pair to pair. Adding these 2 reproductions of the 20 version to the 9 unchanged ones, we find that 11 out of 12 reproductions preserve the "doubling" and the "increase" feature of the story. Other changes of reproductions (a) and (b) are discussed later. Reproduction (c) is too fragmentary to identify changes due to stress unambiguously.

The 22 version, even though less self-consistent, has a number of singular features that are preserved in some of the 10 changed reproductions. Four of the 10 preserve the somewhat complex "Two exact doublings and one near doubling" feature of the 22 story. They are, in our notation:

(d)	(e)	(f)	(g)
8 — 16	5 — 10	6 — 12	5 — 10
10 — 23	8 — 16	10 — 22	8 — 16
12 — 24	10 — 22	8 — 16	10 — 24

Together with the 4 unchanged reproductions, this adds up to 8 out of 14 responses that preserve this complex structural characteristic of the 22 story.

Three exact doublings, as in 20, is more self-consistent than Two exact doublings and one near doubling, as in 22. Therefore, the former principle confers more stability (i.e. less memory change) than the latter. The following table gives the number of responses that preserve the respective *principles* regardless of changes in the specific *amounts:*

	principle preserved	principle violated
version "20"	11	1
version "22"	8	6

The structural principle of the 20 version is significantly ($p < .05$) more stable than that of the 22 version.

Aside from the four unchanged reproductions of the 22 story and the four that preserve the structure but not all numbers (d, e, f, and g), there are four changed reproductions that can be understood as having changed in the direction of greater self-consistency:

(h)	(i)	(j)	(k)
8 — 16	5 — 10	10 — 12	8 — 10
10 — 20	—	16 — 18	10 — 12
12 — 24	12 — 24	20 — 22	12 — 20

and two fragmentary responses:

53. SELF-CONSISTENCY IN REPRODUCTION   211

```
    (l)              (m)
 8 — 16       "... prizes now unknown."
10 — ?
 ? — ?
```

Reproduction (h) achieves increased intrinsic consistency by changing from the memorized 22 version to the more consistent 20 version. Reproduction (i) avoids the inconsistent middle pair by omitting it, leaving only two doublings. Reproductions (j) and (k) both have changed from multiplying by two to adding two (thousand). The principle of adding two is part of the original structure, embodied in the sequence 8, 10, 12 of purchase prices. In the case of reproduction (j), the addition of two is applied to all three pairs, thereby increasing consistency. In (k), it is applied to two pairs with a larger addition to the third one, *transposing* the multiplicative 22 scheme to an additive "two regular + one irregular" principle. This response (k) further increases consistency by a change from the *overlapping* intervals of the standard to *contiguous* intervals: The sale price of one brother becomes the purchase price of the next brother.

In both versions of the Story Task, the purchase prices are, in our notation,

```
 8   -
10   -
12   -.
```

The number triple is composed of round numbers. This is a singular feature. On the other hand, the numbers straddle the number 10,000, which in our decimal system separates the thousands from the ten thousands. This is a nonsingular feature. Stress theory predicts changes which tend to preserve singular features, while making nonsingular features more singular. There are five changed purchase price triples in the 2-week groups, namely:

"20" version		"22" version		
(a)	(b)	(e)	(g)	(j)
5-	100-	5-	5-	10-
8-	200-	8-	8-	16-
10-	300-	10-	10-	20-

All five still represent round figures but all five no longer straddle the 10. A change in five out of five cases is statistically respectable ($p < .05$). This change also occurs in the 4-week and 6-week reproductions but is less prevalent. Presumably, decay has made further inroads into the structure, so that even approximate numbers are lost. As decay advances, more types of restructuring became compatible with the more and more impoverished trace. The interplay between decay and restructuring was mentioned in Section 24 but is not investigated here systematically.

B. THE SYMBOL TASK

54. STRUCTURE OF THE SYMBOL PATTERNS

The second nonvisual memory task consists of a sequence of letter and number symbols. This task is the last of the three tasks given to the 16 independent groups of Experiment II. Everything said about the procedure of Experiment II in Section 27 and about the story task in Section 52 applies to the symbol task as well. The symbol task has two versions. One version is the symbol pattern

E9D7C5B3A1,

which we call d, because it is so labeled in the recognition array, Section 59. This pattern was memorized by the eight independent groups who memorized the 22 version of the story task. The other eight groups, who memorized version 20 of the story task, memorized the symbol pattern

E9D3C5B7A1,

called b, being pattern b in the recognition array.

Item by item, the two patterns are very much alike. Both patterns consist of the same 10 symbols; eight of the symbols occur in exactly the same serial position within the two patterns. The patterns differ only in the position of the numbers 3 and 7. Where pattern b has a 3, d has a 7, and where b has a 7, d has a 3.

Because both versions contain the same elements, neither pattern can be said to be more familiar on that account. Whereas the sequence 1, 3, 5, 7, 9 and possibly also 1, 7, 5, 3, 9 may be considered familiar, and familiar to a different degree, neither sequence or its reverse actually occurs in the patterns. Rather, the patterns contain sequences like E9, 9D, D3, or D7, 3C, or 7C, which presumably are equally familiar or unfamiliar. The same degree of familiarity attaches to the trigrams, like 5B7 and B7A contained in b, compared with 5B3 and B3A in d. Nor can the longer subsequences or the entire patterns claim any particular familiarity. Finally, if there is anything familiar about the *patterns,* as distinguished from the letters and numbers, the differences in prior experience between the two patterns must be very small.

There is then no relevant difference between the two patterns with respect to elements, associative bonds between the elements, and familiarity of the elements or of the subsets or sequences of elements. Fading, therefore, predicts the same percentage of correct reproductions for both patterns. The results from the

54. STRUCTURE OF THE SYMBOL PATTERNS

TABLE 14
Unchanged Reproductions, Symbol Task

	Pattern b			Pattern d		
		Unchanged			Unchanged	
Interval	N	No	%	N	No	%
Immediate	12	12	100%	21	20	95%
2 week	11	1	9%	13	9	69%
4 week	13	0	0%	9	4	44%
6 week	8	0	0%	3	0	0%

eight groups are shown in Table 14. At the "immediate" test interval, both patterns are remembered unchanged by practically all subjects. At the 6-week interval, neither pattern is remembered unchanged. But after 2 and 4 weeks, Pattern *d* is significantly better remembered than Pattern *b* (by 69% and 44% of subjects for *d*, compared with 8% and 0% for *b*). Fading does not account for the marked difference between *b* and *d* at the 2-and 4-week intervals.

Stress theory undertakes to account for the difference in the number of unchanged reproductions and for the kind of change observed in the changed reproductions, and to do so on the basis of the structure of the two patterns. Before analyzing the changes, we list therefore five structural features common to both patterns and two features that distinguish Pattern *b* from *d*:

1. Both patterns consist of two kinds of material, *letters* and *numbers*. The word material is used in the technical meaning introduced in Goldmeier (1972), Chapter 3: In the case of visual forms, the term is illustrated by a dotted circle; the dots are the "material," the circle is the "form" of the pattern. In the case of sentences, the words are the material; in connected discourse, sentences could be material, and the meaning or gist is the form or object composed of the sentences.

2. By Wertheimer's grouping factor of similarity, the letters tend to form one subgroup, the numbers another, coequal subgroup.

3. Letters and numbers alternate but tend to be perceived either as *interdigitated or as forming a matrix or background one for the other*. If such a perceptual relationship exists, then grouping into digrams and trigrams like 5B or D3C, even though they are contained in the patterns, is unlikely. These groupings are *psychologically not realized* as subgroups (in the sense explained in Section 2), whereas for instance "EDCBA" or "ABCDE in reverse" is perceived as a *true* or *phenomenal* or *natural* part of the pattern (i.e., it is a *psychologically realized* subgrouping).

214   7. CHANGE OF NONVISUAL TRACES

4. The letters are psychologically represented, or coded, *specifically as members of the alphabet*. The letters are experienced not as "an E *and* a C *and* etc." but as "the first few" or "the first five," or as "the letters from A to E," or in some other way *as based on* the alphabet.

4b. The *order* of the letters is psychologically related to the alphabetical order, specifically, "the reverse."

The empirist should keep in mind that although the alphabet is indeed *familar*, the information characterizing the subsets as EDCBA is *structural*. The ordered set EDCBA rates high on singularity for subjects accustomed to perceive disconnected capital letters as members of the alphabet, but the set rates below the ordering ABCDE.

5. The numbers are a subset of the set of positive integers. The subset has *five* members, which is a manageable size for memory purposes. The set consists of *odd* numbers only, of only the *lowest* odd numbers, and, in the familiar decimal system in which our subjects think, of *all* odd one-digit numbers in the whole set. They are the *only* five, odd, lowest, one-digit numbers. Far from being randomly chosen, the numbers obviously belong to a rather *singular* subset. But the five lowest, odd, one-digit, positive integers do not constitute the most singular set of whole numbers. By removing "odd" from the specifications of the set, we obtain the still more singular set 1, 2, 3, 4, 5, which, being more singular, should (and indeed does) occur as a memory change.

The two patterns *differ* in two important aspects.

(a) They differ in the *order of the numbers*. The numbers in Pattern *b*, 9-3-5-7-1, ascend in the middle and descend at the two ends, whereas in Pattern *d*, the numbers, 9-7-5-3-1, descend throughout. The ordering in Pattern *d* is singular, whereas in Pattern *b* it is nonsingular. The structure of Pattern *d* is perspicuous, whereas the sequence 9-3-5-7-1 of *b* is difficult to conceptualize. The numbers of pattern *b* can be thought of as: "two reversals," or as "9-5-1 with 3-7 in between," or as "9-7-5-3-1 with the 7 and 3 exchanged," or as "1-3-5-7-9 with the 9 and 1 exchanged," or on a lower "level of processing" as "irregular." By contrast, Pattern *d* is easily perceived as: "1-3-5-7-9 in reverse," or as "first five odd numbers in descending order," or as "all the way down from 9 by steps of two." It should be easy to document the singularity of the ordering in *d* compared with that in *b*, although I have not performed experiments to support that claim.

(b) The two patterns differ in self-consistency. In pattern *d*, the regular reverse order of the numbers echoes the reverse order of the letters. In pattern *b*, the numbers follow each other in an irregular way, whereas the letters follow each other in a regular order. In *d*, one rule governs the order of both numbers and letters. In Pattern *b*, one simple rule governs the letters, another complicated rule, the numbers. The simple rule leads—in both patterns—to a singular order. The complicated rule in Pattern *b* not only makes the order of the numbers less singular but decreases the self-consistency of the whole pattern. Consequently,

55. REPRODUCTIONS OF THE SYMBOL PATTERN

the tendency to greater self-consistency can change the numbers of Pattern *b* to an ordering like in *d*, but *d* should not tend to change to the ordering of Pattern *b*.

55. REPRODUCTIONS OF THE SYMBOL PATTERN

All "immediate" reproductions of Pattern *b* and all but one immediate reproduction of Pattern *d* were unchanged. The analysis is therefore based essentially on the reproductions obtained from the 2, 4, and 6-week groups, in which the changes were numerous. The following is a complete list of the reproductions of both patterns.

A total of 32 reproductions of

Pattern *b*, E9D3C5B7A1

were obtained at the 2, 4, and 6-week intervals. One 2-week reproduction was unchanged; the 31 changed reproductions are listed here:

test interval	list number	reproduction	recognition choice (see Section 59)
2 weeks	$b1^a$	9E3D5C7BA7	*b*
	$b2^a$	E9D5C3B1A7	*b*
	$b3$	E9D7C5B3A	*d*
	$b4^a$	9E7D5C3B1A	*d*
	$b5^b$	9E8D7C6B5A	*d*
	$b6$	D7C5B6A1	*b*
	$b7$	E3F7C5D3B9	*b*
	$b8$	E9 5B 73A	*b*
	$b9$	A 7B1	*c*
	$b10$	"The large number"	*b*
4 weeks	$b11$	E2D7C3B1A5	*h*
	$b12,13$	E3D5C7B1A	*b,b*
	$b14$	1D7C5B1A	*d*
	$b15^b$	E1D2C3B4A5	*d*
	$b16$	D9 C5 B3 A1	*d*
	$b17^b$	E5D4C3B2A1	*d*
	$b18$	A1B2C5D7	*g*
	$b19^a$	A9B7C5D3E1	*d*
	$b20$	E235941A	*b*
	$b21$	426987	*g*
	$b22$	A1I6U5	*b*
	$b23$	B1	*e*

216 7. CHANGE OF NONVISUAL TRACES

6 weeks	$b24^a$	"similar to E9D7C5B3A1"	d
	$b25^a$	E9D7C5B3A1	d
	$b26^a$	1E3D7C5B9A	d
	$b27$	E9D1C5B3A1	i,c
	$b28^b$	0, 1, 3, 2, 5, 4, 7, 6	d
	$b29$	DGCFBEA	d
	$b30$	"Remembering order of numbers 35794623"	b
	$b31$	"9 numbers"	c

The following *changed* reproductions of

Pattern d, E9D7C5B3A1

were obtained at the test intervals indicated:

test interval	list number	reproduction	recognition choice
"immediate"	$d1$	E9C7-5	h
2 weeks	$d2^b$	7E6D5C4B3A21	d
	$d3^a$	F9E7D5C3B1A	d
	$d4$	E 7D 5C 3b 1A	d
	$d5^b$	5E4D3C2B1A	d
4 weeks	$d6^b$	5E4D3C2B1A	d
	$d7^b$	A5B4C3D2E1	d
	$d8^b$	E5D4C3B2A1	d
	$d9^a$	F9E7D5C3B1A	d
	$d10$	A2B4D8	g
6 weeks	$d11,12^b$	E5D4C3B2A1	d,d
	$d13^b$	A9B8C7D6E7	d

[a] Set of numbers unchanged.
[b] Set of numbers consecutive.

56. CHANGES OF THE NUMBER SEQUENCE

The numbers of Pattern *b*, 9-3-5-7-1, have three important structural characteristics: (1) two *reversals,* one at 3 from down to up, and one at 7 from up to down; (2) an overall *downtrend,* 9-1, with an interspersed, shorter and smaller *uptrend,* 3-7; and (3) *the inconsistency* between the uninterrupted downtrend of the letters and the alternating and opposing down–up–down trend of the numbers.

Analysis of the number sequence is inapplicable to responses *b,* 10, 23, 29, and 31 (Section 55), leaving 27 changed and one unchanged reproduction of Pattern *b* and 12 changed and 13 unchanged reproductions of Pattern *d* for consideration. These reproductions of *b* and *d* include the responses from the 2, 4, and 6-week groups but not the immediate groups.

Reversals

An outstanding characteristic of the number sequence of Pattern *b* is the existence of the reversals at seven and at three. Table 15 shows the number of reversals in the 28 pertinent reproductions of Pattern *b* and in the 25 pertinent reproductions of Pattern *d.*

Increase in Range of Number of Reversals. Reversals are nonsingular, an instance of case (c) (Section 23). As the table shows, there are reproductions of Pattern *b* with 0, 1, 2, 4 and 5 reversals. In the case of Pattern *d,* the range is much narrower, either no reversal or one reversal, with the latter occurring in only one instance.

Familiarity cannot explain this marked difference in range of changes because fading and its counterforce, familiarity, apply to *the entire string* E9D7... versus E9D1..., not selectively to structurally grouped and abstracted subunits, like the numbers. Nor does fading distinguish between such *structural features* as the different frequency of reversals within the number subunits.

Consistent with stress theory, reproductions of Pattern *b* range over 0, 1, 2, 4, and 5 reversals, whereas those of Pattern *d* range only from 0 to 1. The one instance of 5 reversals in Pattern *b* is open to a different interpretation (see Section 58), which would classify this response as 0 reversals and decrease the range to 0, 1, 2, 4.

Tendency to Fewer Reversals. A sequence with many reversals is more nonsingular than a sequence with few reversals, which in turn is less singular than a sequence without reversals. Therefore, an increase in the number of reversals should be rare, decreases should be frequent. Table 15 shows an increase, from 0 to 1 reversal, in 1 of the 25 reproductions of Pattern *d* and to 4 or 5 reversals in 2 of the 28 reproductions of *b.* A decrease is not possible with Pattern *d* because it has no reversals, but, in the case of Pattern *b,* the number of reversals decreases in 17 reproductions, remains unchanged in 9, and increases in 2 cases. The difference between decreases and increases, 17 versus 2, is highly significant ($p < .001$). According to fading theory, increases in Pattern *b* are as likely as decreases. In Pattern *d,* fading provides for random "errors" in the numbers, and *random* errors inevitably introduce reversals. But, whereas many

218 7. CHANGE OF NONVISUAL TRACES

errors occur, only *one* of the 25 reproductions contains any reversals, and this reproduction contains only one reversal. *"Freedom from reversals" is a very singular and therefore stable feature of Pattern d, a decrease in the number of reversals a very frequent change of Pattern b.*

Self-Consistency and Reversals. The letters in both patterns are in a (reverse) alphabetic sequence, free of reversals. Absence of number reversals is consistent with the unreversed order of the letters. Self-consistency is an additional reason for the nearly complete absence of reversals in reproductions of Pattern *d* (one reversal in 25 reproductions). In the case of Pattern *b*, which contains two number reversals, the situation is more complicated. Self-consistency is enhanced by an *absence* of reversals but not by a mere reduction to one reversal from the memorized two. Self-consistency, therefore, favors a change from two reversals to none over the "smaller" change from two to one reversal. The change of Pattern *b* support this argument. Table 15 shows six reproductions with one reversal and 11 reproductions without reversals. If response $b28$ is considered as having zero reversals (see Section 58), the number of zero reversals increases from 11 to 12. Fading predicts the opposite; more one-step changes than two-step changes.

Trend

Overall Trend. In both patterns, the numbers have an overall downtrend. In Pattern *d*, the numbers decrease uniformly; in Pattern *b*, the overall downtrend of the numbers is interrupted by an uptrend. The mixed downtrend in Pattern *b* is less singular than the uniform downtrend in Pattern *d*. The preservation of the downtrend in the reproductions parallels the difference in singularity between the two patterns. Twenty four of the 25 reproductions of Pattern *d* but only 18 of the 28 pertinent reproductions of Pattern *b* preserve the overall downtrend (see Table 15). The observed difference between the patterns is highly significant ($p < .005$).

Downtrend and Reversals. The downtrend is better preserved in *d* than in *b*, in agreement with stress theory. However, fading likewise accounts for this difference. Unlike *d*, Pattern *b* contains an uptrend, 3-5-7, so that fewer random errors are required to convert the *partial uptrend* into an overall uptrend than are required to turn the *consistent downtrend* of Pattern *d* into an overall uptrend.

Indeed, in the 17 reproductions of Pattern *b with reversals,* 9 trend down, 2 are level, and 6 trend up, consistent with the random error distribution expected under fading. However, in this nonsingular subgroup of trend reversals [case (c) of Section 23], stress theory *also* predicts random changes. In the absence of

56. CHANGES OF THE NUMBER SEQUENCE

TABLE 15
Reversals and Overall Trend of the Number Sequence
in 28 Reproductions of Pattern b and in 25 Reproductions of Pattern d.
2, 4, and 6 Week Reproductions Combined.
Italics Indicate Uptrend of Letters,
"0" Indicates Original Set of Numbers

Number of Reversals Broken Down by Trend	Number of Reproduction in List in Section 55	Trend Down	Level	Up	Totals
PATTERN b					
5 { down / level / up	28			1	1
				1	
4 { down / level / up	30		1		1
2 { down / level / up	1₀, 6, 8, 27, X₀*	5			9
	7, 11, 21, 26₀			4	
1 { down / level / up	2₀, 12, 13, 20	4			6
	14		1		
	22			1	
0 { down / level / up	3, 4₀, 5, 9, 16, 17, *19*₀, 24₀, 25₀	9			11
	15, *18*			2	
	Totals Pattern b	18	2	8	28
PATTERN d					
1 down	*13*	1			1
0 { down / up	2, 3₀, 4, 5, 6, 7, 8, 9₀, 11, 12, X₀**	23			24
	10			1	
	Totals Pattern d	24		1	25

*One unchanged reproduction.
**13 unchanged reproductions.

reversals (i.e., in the 11 reproductions of Pattern *b* that have changed to the singular zero-reversals order), fading predicts random errors, either an uptrend or a downtrend. Stress theory considers the change to zero reversals as an increase in singularity [case (b) of Section 23]. Therefore, in this case, the theory predicts greater stability of the memorized overall downtrend. As Table 15 shows, 9 of the 11 reproductions with zero reversals have a uniform downtrend; 2 show an uptrend. If reproduction 28 is counted as without reversals (see Section 58), the statistics change to 9 out of 12 with downtrend.

57. GENERALLY PRESERVED FEATURES

In their preoccupation with errors and forgetting, memory theorists often pay little attention to the changes and errors that do *not* occur. We turn here to the analysis of the more stable features.

Material. The "material," in this case letters and numbers, is rather well-preserved, even when little of the "form" aspects of the two patterns is recalled. All reproductions of Pattern *d* and all but six of the 32 reproductions of Pattern *b* include *both* letters and numbers. Five of the remaining 6 reproductions (10, 21, 28, 30, 31) refer to or include numbers but not letters; one reproduction (29) consists of letters only. Both kinds of material are preserved in 51 of the 57 reproductions and one kind in the remaining six. The 3, 6 and 12 subjects who after 2, 4, and 6 weeks, respectively, failed to furnish any reproductions may well have remembered one or both kinds of material without giving an indication of it. Under the circumstances of this experiment, the material tends to be well-preserved even if the form changes. This is the reverse of what the level of processing notion suggests. "Material" corresponds to such features as numbers, letters, and rhymes. "Form" relates here to global features of a pattern. The experiment supports the contention of Morris et al. (1977) that "depth" of a level is a relative thing, relative, that is, to the learning and testing environment. Also, the level idea relates to material as against *meaning*. These patterns, however, although they have structure, have no meaning or gist. They resemble nonsense syllables in this respect.

Alternation. The regular alternation of letters and numbers is preserved in 24 of the 25 reproductions of Pattern *d* and in 23 of the 32 reproductions of Pattern *b*. Alternation is significantly better preserved ($p < .02$) in Pattern *d* than in Pattern *b*. Undoubtedly, the reason is the greater singularity of Pattern *d*. Fading could not account for this difference between the two patterns.

Number of Symbols. The average number of symbols in the 25 reproductions of Pattern *d* is 10, 5 numbers and 5 letters unchanged from the standard. The 31 reproductions of Pattern *b* (Response 10 is excluded) contain an average of 5 numbers and 3.5 letters, for a total of 8.5 symbols. The number of both kinds of symbols and the frequency with which each combination occurs is plotted in the bar graphs of Fig. 81. The 5-numbers and 5-letters combination of the standard occurs more frequently than any other combination; in 20 of 25 reproductions of Pattern *d* and in 13 of the 31 pertinent reproductions of Pattern *b*. The number of symbols is significantly better preserved in the more self-consistent and singular Pattern *d* ($p < .005$). The *spread* of responses also is wider for Pattern *b* than for the more singular Pattern *d:* The 31 responses for

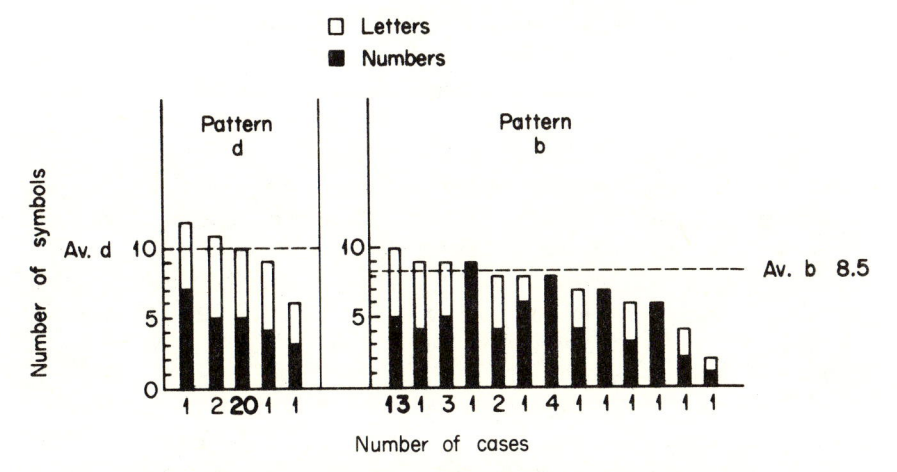

FIG. 81. Number of symbols in reproductions of patterns 63*b* and *d*.

Pattern *b* are spread over 13 combinations; the 25 reproductions of Pattern *d* fall into only five groups (see Fig. 81).

Preservation of the Original Set of Symbols. Preservation of the original symbols is studied here regardless of the order in which they occur. From the point of view of fading, both letters and numbers are members of a vastly "overlearned" set; therefore, these symbols should be retained in both patterns to the same degree. This argument, based on the familiarity of the letters and numbers and on associative bonds, was previously rejected on theoretical grounds. Here, it is tested experimentally. Stress theory predicts different degrees of retention, based on the structure of the entire pattern and of the subsets of letters and numbers. Three specific, testable, conclusions follow from stress theory:

1. The letter set, which consists of *consecutive* letters, should be more stable than the number set, which is less coherent consisting of nonconsecutive numbers. This difference between letters and numbers applies to both patterns.

2. Because the *ordering of the numbers* in Pattern *d* is more singular (regularly down) than the ordering of the numbers in Pattern *b* (down–up–down), the original numbers themselves, *disregarding the order,* should be preserved more often in Pattern *d* than in Pattern *b*.

3. The regularly descending letter set is more consistent with the regularly descending number set of Pattern *d* than with the irregularly descending number set of Pattern *b*. Even though both patterns contain the same letter set in the same positions and in the same order, self-consistency of the pattern as a whole confers

better retention on these same letters in Pattern d than in the context of Pattern b. Self-consistency, in other words, is a *reciprocal* relation: Regular numbers stabilize regular letters; irregular numbers decrease the stability of even regular letters.

These three conclusions were indeed confirmed. The original *set of letters* (disregarding the order of the letters) occurs in 22 of 25 reproductions of Pattern *d* and in 16 of 32 reproductions of Pattern *b*.

The original *number set* is indicated by a small o after the list number in Table 15 and by a superscript *a* in the listing of Section 55. The original numbers are preserved in 15 of 25 reproductions of Pattern *d* and in 8 of 32 reproductions of Pattern *b*.

Based on these figures: (1) The original set of letters is significantly better retained than the numbers; $p < .05$ for Pattern *b*, $p < .025$ for Pattern *d*: (2) the original number set is significantly better preserved in Pattern *d* than in Pattern *b*, $p < .01$, even though both patterns contain the same sets of numbers; (3) the original letter set is significantly better retained in Pattern *d* than in Pattern *b*, $p < .005$, even though both patterns contain the same letter set, in the same serial order, and in the same position.

Consecutive Symbols. Letters and integers both have a *natural order*. A group of such symbols therefore gains internal consistency, singularity, and stability if it consists of consecutive members of the series. The letters in the two-symbol patterns are not only consecutive but also start at the beginning of the series, in this case, the beginning of the alphabet. In the midst of much change, consecutiveness is well-preserved in memory. Even a reproduction as changed as DGCFBEA (*b*, 29) contains the consecutive letters of the alphabet from A to G, in a changed but, as we show (Section 58), by no means random order. The feature of consecutiveness of the letters is lost in only three reproductions of Pattern *b* (8, 20, and 22), and one of Pattern *d* (10), and in the only changed reproduction of an immediate test (*d*, 1).

If the letters tend to *remain* consecutive, the numbers tend to *become* consecutive. Consecutiveness, being singular and therefore stable, occurs *as a change* of the number sequence, memorized as a nonconsecutive set. Four reproductions of Pattern *b* (5, 15, 17, 28) and eight of Pattern *d* (2, 5, 6, 7, 8, 11, 12, 13) are changed to consecutive numbers. The change occurs in 8 of 25 reproductions of Pattern *d* but in only 4 of 29 pertinent reproductions of Pattern *b*. This difference, although statistically not significant, at least suggests that the regular order of the numbers in Pattern *d* is more conducive to a change to consecutive numbers than the irregular arrangement in Pattern *b*.

The change to consecutive numbers takes three forms. In eight reproductions, the change occurs to the most singular set, 1-2-3-4-5, either in ascending order (reproduction *b* 15) or descending (*b* 17, *d* 5, 6, 7, 8, 11, and 12). In two

57. GENERALLY PRESERVED FEATURES   223

instances, the consecutive number set goes as far as 7, starting either at 0 and ascending (*b*28) or descending to 1 (*d*2). In another two cases, both descending, the set starts at 9, as in the standard, and goes down as far as 5 (*b*5) or 6 (*d*13). This last case of change to consecutive numbers is the only reproduction in which one digit is repeated.

Tendency to Anchor.   There is a strong tendency to *anchor* the symbol series, whether or not it is consecutive, at a "natural" starting point. All but two reproductions with letters contain the letter A (the two exceptions are *b*23 and *d*1). The number sets preserve, through many changes, either the 1 or the 9, often both. One begins with 0.

Ascending Order.   If symbols have a natural order, they also have an intrinsic foreward direction. Alphabet and number system are both learned. Once a series is learned, its structural features of order and direction are established as well and create "restoring forces," stresses toward the norm. In Patterns *b* and *d,* both letters and numbers are in "reverse" or "descending" order. Table 15 shows that in nine reproductions (eight of Pattern *b* and one of Pattern *d*) the order of the numbers changes to "up." The table also identifies, by means of italics, seven reproductions in which the letters have changed from down to up. Self-consistency seems to demand that the two changes facilitate each other and occur together. However, in only three reproductions (*b*18, *b*22, *d*10), both letters and numbers ascend. Possibly, letters and numbers tend to be perceived separately, as figure and ground (see Section 54), and for that reason to change independently. The figure-ground relationship is suggested by the scarcity of responses written in the form of digrams or trigrams (exceptions are *b*8, *b*9, *b*16, *d*4). A figure-ground relation is facilitated if the ground surrounds or "frames" the figure. This leads us to the next category of change.

Framing.   If equally many letters and numbers alternate, the pattern either starts with a letter and ends with a number, or vice versa. In either case, the pattern is "unsymmetic," the letters "stick out" at one end and the numbers at the opposite end. Patterns like *b* or *d* cannot have both symmetry *and* equality of numbers and letters. Some reproductions become symmetrical in this sense by bracketing or framing the numbers with letters or the letters with numbers. Framing as a change to symmetry occurs in reproductions 1, 3, 8, 12, 13, and 20 of Patterns *b* and 2, 3, 4, and 9 of Pattern *d*. Framing is accomplished by extending the memorized set of letters to include F (*d*3, *d*9), or by omitting some letters (*b*8, *b*20) by increasing the number set (*d*2) or curtailing it (*b*3, *b*8, *b*12, *b*13, *d*4), and in other ways less transparent and understandable.

Numbers First.   There is no structural reason why the patterns should start with a letter, as in the two standards, rather than with a number. Reproductions

224   7. CHANGE OF NONVISUAL TRACES

1, 4, 5, 14, and 26 of Pattern b and 2, 5, and 6 of Pattern d change from the nonsingular "letter first" to the equally nonsingular "number first" arrangement, while (with one very minor exception, $d2$) preserving the singular feature of alternation of letters and numbers.

58.   IS THERE LAW AND ORDER?

Fading holds that memory changes occur randomly. Stress theory tries to establish memory change as an orderly process governed by laws. But even the lengthy analysis of the symbol patterns presented here leaves many details of change unaccounted for. Perhaps the most frustrating instances of unexplained change are reproductions 28 and 29 of Pattern b,

    01325476
    and
    DGCFBEA.

These reproductions appear to have changed randomly, in an idiosyncratic manner. The changes run counter to well-established tendencies. Each preserves only one kind of material; there is no alternation of letters and numbers. Both reproductions have five reversals of direction, even though by and large reversals tend to decrease in number or remain unchanged. These are the only responses with five reversals.

Further problems are posed by impoverished responses, like A 7b1 ($b9$) or E9 C7-5 ($d1$) or B1 ($b23$), which are difficult to interpret because they are so fragmentary.

This residue of unexplained features and obscure reproductions prompts two remarks. First, whenever one deals with natural, unrestrained occurrences like reproductions from memory, some events remain inaccessible. One can test the aerodynamic behavior of profiles in the controlled environment of a wind tunnel but be unable to apply the laws derived from wind-tunnel tests to the fall of a dry leaf in the autumn breeze. My other remark is that sometimes persistent inquiry yet yields the explanation of a puzzling finding. The two reproductions of Pattern b mentioned before, 01325476 and DGCFBEA, serve as an example. The structure of the two reproductions beomes understandable if they are rewritten as follows:

    $0^{13} 2^5 4^7 6$ ($b28$)
    $D^G C^F B^E A$ ($b29$)

The upper and the lower symbols form two interdigitated subgroups. The *alternation* is completely preserved in $b29$ and almost preserved in $b28$. Both patterns turn out to possess *two kinds* of material, odd and even numbers in $b28$, and the first 4 letters of the alphabet versus the following 3 letters in b29. Contrary to first appearances, there are zero reversals, not five. The statistics on reversals are amended accordingly to show a still stronger trend to zero reversals. In b28, both the even and the odd series have changed to an uptrend; in b29, the downtrend is preserved in both series.

Once the tranposition of material and the existence in these reproductions of two interwoven subsets is recognized, the analysis of the responses is routine and shows, except for the transposition of letters for numbers, the same changes and stabilities found in reproductions with untransposed number-letter sets.

59. RECOGNITIONS OF THE SYMBOL PATTERNS

In contrast to the variety of changes brought out in reproductions, the results of the recognition tests are limited to the recognition material. The material consisted of the following nine patterns, presented to the subjects in an array as printed here, but without the labels a to i.

E9D7C5B1A1	E9D3C5B7A1	E9D1C5B7A1
a	b	c
E9D7C5B3A1	E9D5C5B3A1	E9D1C5B5A1
d	e	f
E9D7C5B5A1	E9D3C5B3A1	E9D1C5B3A1
g	h	i

Standard b is the second pattern in the first row, Standard d is the second pattern in the first column. All nine patterns are identical with respect to all letters and all but the second and fourth number. The two standards are the only patterns in which each number occurs only once. The other seven patterns have one repeated number except pattern f, which has two repeated numbers. Patterns a, d, e, and g have no reversals; the other five patterns have two reversals of the trend of numbers.

The recognition choices of the four 6-week groups, shown in Table 16, are representative. Other recognition data are reported in Section 61.

After 6 weeks, 18 of the 27 subjects who had memorized Pattern b with its two reversals chose in recognition the most regular of the unreversed patterns, Pattern d. Conversely, only 1 of 31 subjects who had memorized the more regular Pattern d chose the two-reversal pattern b, 29 subjects chose Pattern d, which they had memorized, and 1 subject chose another unreversed pattern, g. To put it more succinctly, 30 of the 31 subjects who memorized the unreversed Pattern d selected an unreversed pattern 6 weeks later. Of the 27 subjects who memorized Pattern b with two reversals, 18 subjects changed in recognition to an unreversed pattern, 9 selected a pattern with two reversals. The significant dif-

TABLE 16
Recognition of Symbol Pattern b and d
6 Week Interval

	N	No Reversal		Two Reversals		
		d	g	b	c	i
b memorized	27	18	—	**6**	1	2
d memorized	31	**29**	1	1	—	—

Boldface indicates choice of the standard.

ference between the two groups demonstrates that in recognition Pattern d is very stable, whereas the irregular Pattern b changes to a more regular pattern, most often d, the most regular one and the only other pattern in which each number occurred only once.

This recognition experiment, aside from being strong evidence for directed change and for stress theory, is remarkable in another respect. Most choices, regardless of which pattern was memorized, fall on Pattern b or d. Only three choices of the b groups and one choice of the d groups involve a pattern other than b or d. The reason may be that b and d are the only two patterns without duplication of at least one number. Possibly, many subjects, 24 of 27 in the case of Pattern b, narrowed the choice down to d and b because of this structural clue.

60. RELATION BETWEEN VISUAL AND NONVISUAL MEMORY

The reader may have noticed the structural similarity of the nonvisual tasks to two of the visual patterns. Actually, Figs. 63b and d were designed as visual analogues of the symbol patterns. The regularly decreasing bars correspond to the letters EDCBA and the triangular shapes of different sizes to the numbers. The story task was designed to paraphrase some structural features of Fig. 61c and f. The purpose is to show that memory changes depend on structural features, and that the same structural features can be found in different kinds of material.

Until very recently, structure has been assiduously excluded from memory research with the result that the enterprise has become exceedingly artificial. Some, notably Bartlett (1932) and Smirnov (1973), have used richly structured material, but Bartlett at least has failed to analyze it in sufficient depth to know what he was using.

To the extent that the structure of 61c and 61f is analogous to that of the "20" and "22" version of the Story Task, the results of the two experiments, both in

60. RELATION BETWEEN VISUAL AND NONVISUAL MEMORY

recognition and reproduction, agree quite closely. The same agreement obtains between 63*b* and *d* and the Symbol Patterns *b* and *d*.

This agreement confers on the other experiments using visual material increased significance. The results derived from visual material in Chapter 5 and 6 are valid, we claim, for any other material. There are not laws and arrangements in the brain for visual memory and other, totally different arrangements and laws for other modalities, for words, sentences, or "meanings."

However, while vision, hearing, and other modalities are biologically old, language and symbolic mentation are recent, found spontaneously only in man, and largely confined to evolutionary new parts of the brain. The complexities of this new tier of brain functioning are not well-understood. Therefore, we are on safer ground if we build memory theory on the firmer foundation of nonverbal material and extrapolate cautiously from there, as we have done in this chapter.

Another advantage in using visual forms with the right degree of structural complexity but unencumbered by prior experience or familiarity or meaning is this: Such material gives free rein to structural, intrinsic stresses without the possibility of empiristic explanations to confuse the consideration of intrinsic factors.

Research into the *structure* of nonvisual material, nonsensory material to be exact, is gradually coming into its own, after sporadic beginnings with Bartlett's work on stories and Katona's experiments (Katona, 1940/1967) on memory for structured numbers and for problem solutions. More recent work in the same vein is the research by Sachs (1967), Bransford and Franks (1971) and their colleagues, and by Kintsch and his collaborators. Kintsch (1974, 1977) has devoted much effort to the analysis of text in ways relevant to the storage of meaning and gist. A typical result of such analysis (Kintsch & Keenan, 1973) is the finding that: "superordinate propositions were recalled better than propositions which were structurally subordinate [p. 257]." Structurally, subordinate propositions were forgotten more often than superordinate ones, and this difference increased with time (Kintsch, Kozminsky, Streby, McKoon & Keenan, 1975). This result parallels closely Hanawalt's finding of the increasing rate of "forgetting" or loss of the horizontal line of Fig. 71*a,* described in Section 42, and the observations of Kintsch and Van Dijk (1978) on long-term changes of memory for text.

Another investigation fitting into the framework developed here is the experiment by R. C. Anderson (1974) on recall of sentences. In the terminology used here, Anderson found:

1. His subjects learn propositions, not individual words, somewhat as the subjects who learned Fig. 63 *b* and *d* learned a pattern, not individual bars and triangles.
2. Anderson's subjects often used substitute words in recall. "Substitutions were more likely when the language of the original sentence was judged to be infelicitous [p. 535]." This, in our terminology, is an instance of the near-

singular case (b), a change occurring in a sentence with a lower "aptness rating." The change is directed toward a wording intrinsically more consistent with the meaning of the learned sentence.

3. Anderson addresses random fading as applied to change of features: "Suppose that features mutate at random. Then as time passed responses would fan out over a lot of semantic territory. Extralist intrusions not scored as semantically-related would increase in frequency.... These changes did not happen. Extralist intrusions were as rare on the delayed as on the immediate test [p. 538]." This aspect of the results corresponds to the singular case (a). Whereas the *material*, in this instance the words, can change, the *meaning* of the sentence is fixed; no fading or, as Anderson puts it, mutations in case (a).

4. On the other hand, meaning *preserving* substitutions, especially synonyms, are frequent and increase with time from 57% on the immediate test to 68% a day later. This change represents the nonsingular case (c), undirected drift, although with an admixture of case (b) as mentioned in item 2.

The work of Tulving, Craik, and their associates, of Paris (Paris & Carter, 1973; Paris & Lindauer, 1976) and of Brewer (1975) likewise investigates memory for the meaning as distinguished from the memory for words. The concepts of stress theory should be found as applicable to verbal and textual material and be as useful there as they are for visual material.

8
The Dynamics of Change

61. THE TIME COURSE OF CHANGE

The preceding three chapters, 5, 6, and 7, have analyzed the kind and the direction of change. Here, we examine the *time course* of change. The earlier investigators, Wulf (1922), Perkins (1932), Bartlett (1932), and others, proposed that change was *progressive* in time. By that they meant first that change increased with time, and second that change was directed, not random. Bartlett thought the direction is toward culturally prescribed schemata, Perkins investigated intrinsic change toward symmetry, and Wulf and Koffka (1935) proposed "leveling" and "sharpening" as the goal of change. The Progressive Change was thought to be due to either extrinsic schemata (Bartlett) or intrinsic structural characteristics of the trace (Wulf, Koffka, Perkins). The experiments to document these changes used repeated reproductions by the same subject over periods of days, weeks, and longer. An example of this procedure is the experiment by Perkins described in the next section.

The early opponents of this approach (Carmichael et al., 1932; J. J. Gibson, 1929; Hanawalt, 1937; Woodworth, 1938) sought to explain memory change by fading-plus-extrinsic reconstruction. They objected to theories of progressive change on several grounds.

First, there is the possibility that the repeated activations used by Bartlett and by Wulf modify the trace in unknown ways. There might be what is now called destructive read-out. This question is of some interest and could be profitably investigated in the light of the knowledge of the trace structure available today, but actual data are scarce. In any case, this is a hypothetical argument.

Second, the fact that extrinsic influences were shown to change reproductions

230 8. THE DYNAMICS OF CHANGE

led some investigators to the "unitary" and "parsimonious" hypothesis that *all* changes can be explained as extrinsic. This argument is not compelling. It is a manifestation of the empiristic bias so pervasive in psychology. Although it allows for change, the change is assumed to be random, unpredictable in the individual case, predictable at best, statistically. This, too, is in tune with today's shift from causality to probability.

Third, most of the attempts to demonstrate memory changes in *recognition* were unsuccessful. If the trace really changes and if it changes in predictable, lawful ways, then one should be able to demonstrate the change not only in reproductions but also in recognition, by presenting subjects with some of the variants predicted by the theory. In a recognition test, the subjects should then choose a changed stimulus in preference to the memorized original. With a few exceptions (Goldmeier, 1941; Turner & Craig, 1954), this was not accomplished until the present study. Several authors, notably Hebb and Foord (1945), concluded from their failures in this respect that it could not be done. That left only the evidence for change derived from reproductions. Although reproductions certainly are subject to change, they are, as Chapters 6 and 7 amply illustrate, difficult to interpret. Neither Bartlett's nor Wulf's interpretations are convincing, and neither of them was able to derive predictions from his theories, as stress theory does.

The reason for the disagreement and the reason why the differences are irreconcilable is that both sides are partly right, and neither side has the whole truth. Fading-plus-reconstruction assumes for all changes the mechanism of case (c), Section 23, the loss of information through random decay. It does not acknowledge cases (a) and (b). Progressive change fits case (b) only; directed change increasing with time. Progressive change ignores cases (a), stability, and (c), random loss of information. To round out the picture, association theories tend to deal only with No Change, case (a), fixed traces, which are either preserved intact or not. Alternatively, association theory can also handle case (c), as proposed by Estes (1980). Some items become less accurately localized as time goes by. As Estes (1980) put it: "precision of information about an event is slowly lost [p. 65]," which describes our case (c). Estes also agrees with stress theory in ascribing the loss of information to random noise (p. 67). Stress theory alone allows for both intrinsic and extrinsic mechanisms of change, and for all three mechanisms (a), (b), and (c) of Section 23.

To support stress theory against the objections just mentioned, we review Experiment II, which was especially designed for that purpose. The experiment sidesteps the objection against repeated testing of one subject by providing independent groups of subjects for each time interval examined. It neutralizes extrinsic mechanisms of change by investigating two versions of one and the same task. The material is so constructed that both versions would have to be subject to the same extrinsic influences but would differ sharply in intrinsic stress. This affords a comparison of case (a) with either (b) or (c). Finally, this review is

61. THE TIME COURSE OF CHANGE   231

confined to recognitions in order to demonstrate that intrinsic change does occur in recognition, as it should if the trace really does change.

Experiment II was designed to show the time course of change, which differentiates between the three mechanisms of change.

The experiment uses four time intervals: "immediately," 2 weeks, 4 weeks, and 6 weeks after the learning session. Eight of the 16 groups memorized Fig. 68h, the "20" version of the three-brothers story (Section 52), and the irregular version, b (E9D3C5B7A1), of the Symbol Task (Section 54). The other eight groups memorized Fig. 68e (gaps at the cusps), the "22" version of the story, and the more regular version, "d," of the symbol task. Each of the two task triples was given to two separate groups at each of the four time intervals. One of the two groups was tested for recognition first, reproduction second; the other group attempted reproduction first, recognition second. The procedure resulted in two test sequences × two versions of each task × three tasks × four time intervals between learning and testing.

In the tables, the recognitions before and after reproduction are tabulated separately and also combined. However, the separate results do not differ significantly from each other. Therefore, only the combined figures are used in the graphs of Fig. 82. Combining the recognition data leaves two variants of each task × three tasks × four time intervals. Table 17 gives the actual number of subjects on which each report is based. Ideally, the first three numbers and also the second three numbers in each row of Table 17 should be the same, because the three tasks were administered to the same group. Differences occur, however, because some subjects left some answer sheets blank; some answers were disqualified, because the second copy of a task showed a change or because more than one answer was circled. The largest discrepancy, in the second 6-week group (Tasks 68h, 20, b), is due to a procedural mishap explained in Section 51.

Qualitatively, the recognition results were discussed in Chapter 5 and 7. Here, we display the time course of the recognition changes. Figure 82 reports the recognition results for each of the three tasks as percentages of the numbers in Table 17. Because each task has two versions, one regular and one irregular, and four time intervals, the graph for each task has eight data clusters.

Patterns e and h of Fig. 68, Section 35.   Figure 68 pictures the patterns offered for recognition, Fig. 82a, the recognition results. Solid lines connect the data points for Pattern 68e (gaps at cusps); broken lines give the data for Pattern 68h (gaps in center curves). The recognition choices are subdivided into three classes: patterns with gaps in the side curves (68a, b, c, d), those with gaps at the cusps (68e, f and g), and those with gaps in the center curves (68h to l). The graph shows that all subjects who memorized 68e confined their recognitions to one of the three patterns with a gap at the cusps (e, f, g, solid lines) out to the 6-week interval. The trace of this feature is stable, case (a). For those subjects who learned the pattern with two gaps on the center curves, 68h (a contrastruc-

232   8. THE DYNAMICS OF CHANGE

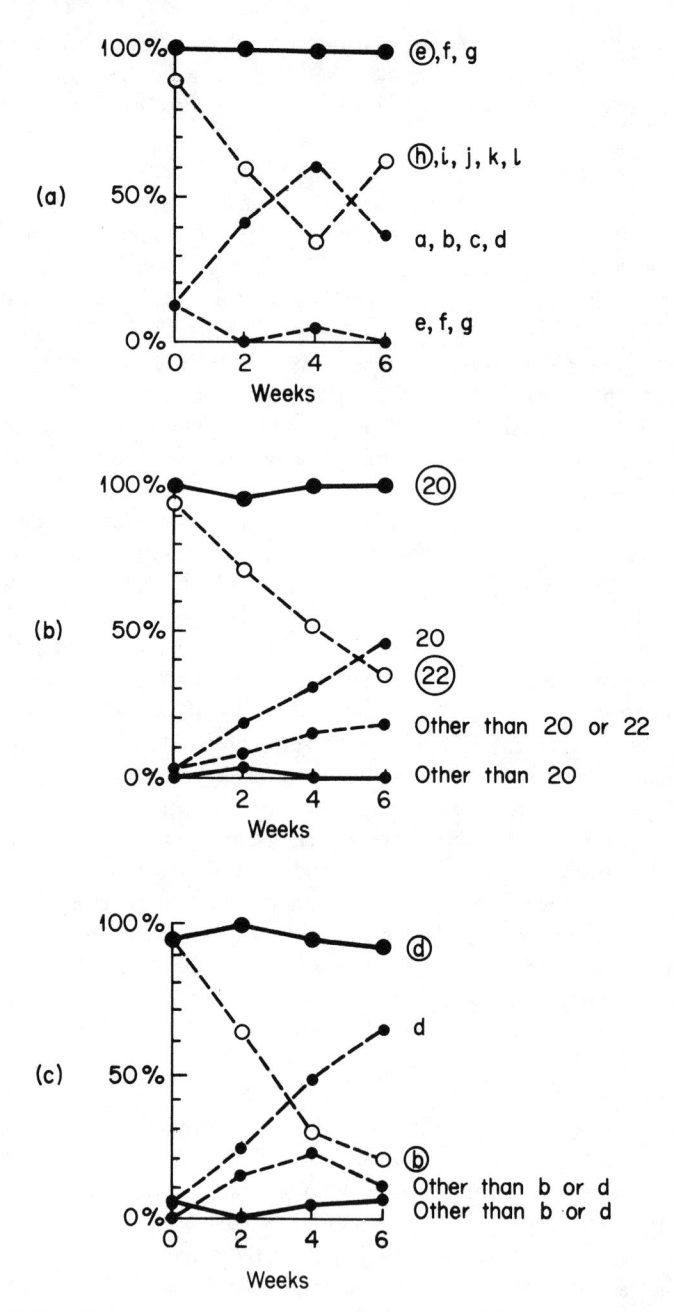

FIG. 82. Time course of the recognitions of patterns *e* and *h* of figure 68 (graph a), of the "20" and the "22" version of the "3 brother" story (graph b), and of the symbol task of section 54 (graph c).

61. THE TIME COURSE OF CHANGE

TABLE 17
Number of Subjects Furnishing Recognitions
in Experiment II for Each Task

	Task					
Time Interval	Fig. 68e	Story "22"	Symbols "d"	Fig. 68h	Story "20"	Symbols "b"
Immed.	39	38	38	27	28	25
2 weeks	31	31	31	22	24	22
4 weeks	29	29	27	31	32	30
6 weeks	31	32	31	17	26	27

tural placement of the gaps), some changes occur immediately, and by 4 weeks a good half of the choices involve patterns with gaps on the side curves. (The 6-week choices should be disregarded because of the procedural errors detailed in Section 51.) The change is progressive with time and represents an example of the spread to other positions as time elapses, typical of case (c). The positions at the cusps are, however, virtually excluded from the spread. The changes are confined to the contrastructural, nonsingular positions. The gap positions on the cusps are singular and represent a different dimension of change. The changes have, however, an admixture of case (b), because the spread, instead of involving randomly all possible positions, is skewed toward the side curves, as discussed in Section 36.

Figure 82b pictures the time course of the "20" and "22" versions of the "3-brother" story (see Section 52), the second one of the three tasks. The regular version, 20, is stable, case (a) of Section 23. It shows no evidence of change even after 4 and 6 weeks. The irregular version (broken lines), which differs only by one number from the regular version, shows marked and progressive change. The learned number 22 is chosen by an ever decreasing percentage of subjects. More and more subjects choose other numbers. The other numbers are not randomly picked. Most of the "wrong" choices go to 20, the one number that gives internal consistency to the story. The increasing trend to 20 makes this outcome an instance of case (b) of Section 23.

Figure 82c reports the recognitions of the Symbol Task, the last task of Experiment II, described in Section 54. The task has a regular version "d" (solid lines) and an irregular version "b" (broken lines). Again, the regular version is essentially stable and does not change progressively, case (a). The recognitions of the irregular version are broken down into three classes: unchanged (choices of "b"), change to the stable pattern d, and all "other" choices. As the graph shows, in the irregular version there are more other choices than in the stable version, but the main change is a progressive decrease of the learned pattern b

234   8. THE DYNAMICS OF CHANGE

and an increase in recognition choices of the regular version, d, which these subjects had never seen.

Figure 82a contrasts the singular case (a) with a fairly pure instance of nonsingularity case (c); Fig. 82b and c illustrate the progressive changes in case (b) by comparison with the stable case (a).

Obviously, the changes cannot be explained by undirected fading. An explanation by fading-plus-reconstruction would have to account for the following findings. In the case of Fig. 68h, the theory would have to predict the loss of information about gap location, whereas in the case of Fig. 68e there is no such loss. Reconstruction would be nearly perfect in 68e, ineffective in 68h, except for excluding the position of the gap at the cusps. In the case of the "story," the 20 version either would not fade or be perfectly reconstructed. The 22 version would fade and increasingly misconstructed to 20 instead of 22. Similarly, in the Symbol Task, either d is fade proof or well-reconstructed, whereas b fades and reconstruction is biased toward d.

In the three tasks, fading-plus-reconstruction can explain the two related outcomes only if reconstruction prevents fading or restores it in our stable case (a) (solid lines in the three graphs), if reconstruction is biased toward singularities in case (b) (22 version of the story, version b in Symbol Task), and is nearly ineffective in case (c), as for instance for Fig. 68h. In other words, fading-plus-reconstruction is explanatory only if it becomes equivalent to stress theory. R. C. Anderson (1974) has made essentially the same argument about reconstruction in the context of sentence memory (p. 537). Within the frame work of stress theory, those changes that are predicted indeed increase with time. The graphs of Fig. 82a, b, c strikingly portray the differences in the fate of singular, nearly singular, and nonsingular features. *Progressive unidirectional change is peculiar to case (b) and cannot be found in material falling under (a) or (c)*. This accounts for the failure of Hanawalt and Hebb and Foord, among others, to demonstrate progressive change.

In a pure instance of the near-singular case (b), sooner or later the little ball of Fig. 58 falls into the well; *change is progressive and directed*. In the nonsingular case (c), the little ball has a good probability to start at or near (Fig. 58) the learned pattern, but, as time goes by, it is likely to be farther and farther away from the learned pattern.

62. GRADUAL VERSUS SUDDEN CHANGE

Experiment II sheds no light on the question whether the progressive changes take place gradually, or abruptly, in discrete steps. It is true that the graphs of Fig. 82 a, b, c show monotonic increase of the changes with time. But such statistics can be read in two ways. They mean either that the traces in all subjects change gradually, or they mean that changes occur abruptly, in jumps, and the

62. GRADUAL VERSUS SUDDEN CHANGE   235

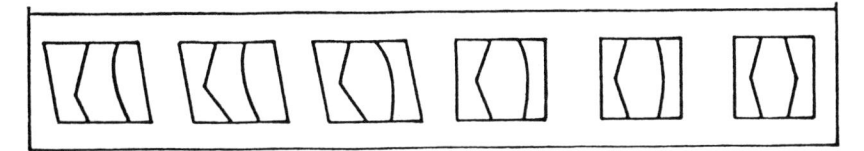

FIG. 83. Reproductions of one of Perkins subjects 2, 3, 9, 16, 30, and 49 days after memorizing the design.

jump takes place after different time intervals in different subjects. Some subjects change immediately, some within 2 weeks, some between 2 and 4 weeks, and by 6 weeks most subjects have changed.

Wulf (1922), Bartlett (1932), and other early investigators assumed that each trace changed continuously over time and assumed further that this change could be monitored by having the same subject recall the items repeatedly. An example of this line of research is shown in Fig. 83, taken from Perkins (1932). The first design is like the standard, which the subject saw for 5 seconds only. The designs of Fig. 83 are reproductions by the same subject 2, 3, 9, 16, 30, and 49 days later. Each succeeding reproduction is somewhat more symmetrical than its predecessor. One can almost see the trace change toward symmetry, progressively and continuously.

But on closer analysis, the seemingly gradual change in Perkin's sequential reproductions dissolves into a series of independent and abrupt changes. Numbering the reproductions from left to right, reproduction 2 shows no change. In number 3, the curvature of the right interior curve has flipped and subsequently remains concave to the left. In number 4, the frame of the pattern changes from slightly oblique to straight, or rectangular, and subsequently remains so. In the last reproduction, the right interior curve becomes an open angle with straight legs, symmetrical to the left interior angle, which has remained unchanged throughout the period of testing. It is thus possible to interpret Perkin's sequence as the result of several sudden changes occurring independently. In terms of stress theory, they can be listed as follows:

1. Stable, unchanged, case (a) are quadrilateral frame, two generally up and down interior curves, the left one a shallow angle, concave toward the midline.

2. Tending toward singularity, case (b) are frame changes to rectangular and equilateral (from nearly so); the right internal curve first turns concave to the midline, like its counterpart, and then turns into a shallow angle, like its counterpart.

3. There are no random changes, case (c).

All changes, separately and together, increase the internal consistency of the pattern. *No change occurs in the opposite direction, away from a more singular value.*

8. THE DYNAMICS OF CHANGE

The evidence is compatible with the assumption that in the near-singular case (b), at least the changes occur in jumps, stepwise, not continuously. These changes would be comparable to the abrupt changes in the perception of ambiguous figures, the inversions of the Necker cube, or the exchange of figure and ground in Rubin's patterns. In the nonsingular case (c), we assume that the trace itself is imprecise. Therefore, change could occur either gradually or in a fairly large number of fairly small steps, a sort of one-dimensional diffusion or random walk. In the singular case (a), there is no change at all, with the exceptions discussed in the following section.

For the trace as a whole, this means that step by step nearly singular aspects of the trace become singular, and nonsingular aspects of the trace are increasingly "smeared out."

63. CHANGE OF SINGULAR TRACES

If a feature has a singular value, then, according to stress theory, this value is precisely coded and is remembered unchanged. We speak of a stable feature, case (a). The graphs of Fig. 82a, b, c contrast this relative stability with the progressive changes in case (b) and the diffuse change in (c). However, the stability in case (a) is not absolute. This section deals with five types of deviations from stability in case (a).

The first kind of deviation consists of the infrequent random errors found for instance in Fig. 82b at the 2-week interval and in Fig. 82c at all except the 2-weeks interval. In both instances, the change is not progressive in time. It represents the unavoidable noise inherent in all information processing and storage systems.

The second deviation is best illustrated by the example of the changes occurring with Fig. 68e as the standard. Table 18 shows that when 68e is learned: (1) recognition choices are confined to the three variants e, f, and g, which have the gap at the cusps. In this respect, the design is stable; (2) even within this limited range, change is uncommon, occurring in only 1.4% of the two shorter time intervals and 15% of the two longer-term storage periods; (3) the incidence of these changes is not like the random fluctuations seen in the regular variants of Task 2 and 3, Fig. 82b and c. Instead, this change is slowly progressive, increasing from 1 in 70 (1.4%) for the shorter terms to 9 in 60 (15%) for the longer intervals; (4) when changes occur, they tend to go from e to g, skipping f. Of 10 changes, only 2 go to f, whereas 8 go to g.

Stress theory accommodates this situation by elaborating the model of Section 22. Case (a) is represented in Fig. 58 as a deep well, so deep that random vibrations are unlikely to lift the ball out of the well. We add to this picture some finer details. Instead of a smooth bottom as in Fig. 58 and in the dotted part of Fig. 84a, we assume the fine structure shown in Fig. 84a by the solid curve. The

TABLE 18
Number (N) of Choices of Fig. 68e, f, or g by Time Interval
Fig. 68e Is the Standard

Time Interval	N	e	f	g
immediately	39	38	—	1
2 weeks	31	31	—	—
Total short intervals	70	69	—	1
4 weeks	29	24	1	4
6 weeks	31	27	1	3
Total long intervals	60	51	2	7

deepest point on the left represents the learned gap location *e*. The shallow middle dip represents variant *f*, and the right deeper hollow represents *g*. With this addition, the ball would still tend to remain within the large well as before, which translates into limitation of recognitions to *e, f,* and *g*. However, it takes much less "vibrational energy" to displace the ball from *e* to *f* or *g*, with *g* much the more likely outcome. This elaboration models all four aspects brought out by examining case (a) in detail. Inside the well, memory assumes some characteristics of the nonsingular case (c), a slow, progressive spread to alternative choices. Outside the well, the trace is stable; memory is confined to *e, f,* or *g*.

A third kind of deviation is typically seen in *reproductions*. In this type, one singular feature is replaced by another one, equally singular and equally prostructural. An example is the inversion of all curves in the 6-weeks reproduction shown in Fig. 80*d*. In this reproduction, the horizontal symmetry of the original is preserved, although all curves are flipped by 180°. Our model represents this change by assuming that one deep well, Fig. 84*b*, stands for horizontal symmetry, but that the well is subdivided by a fairly high barrier into one compartment representing the learned variant and another compartment representing the horizontally symmetrical alternative. The two versions are equivalent as to symmetry, but the learned variant has the advantage of having been experienced in the learning phase: The ball is already there and has a high probability of remaining there. The two compartments in Fig. 84*b* are drawn equally deep to indicate that the two alternatives are assumed to be equally stable.

A similar change is reported by Mandler and Johnson (1977). They used the story of a dog (see also Section 18, Levels of Processing), who crossed a stream on a plank while carrying a piece of meat in his mouth. When he saw his reflection in the water, he tried to snap up the reflected piece of meat as well. But as he opened his mouth, his meat fell into the water "and was never seen again."

238   8. THE DYNAMICS OF CHANGE

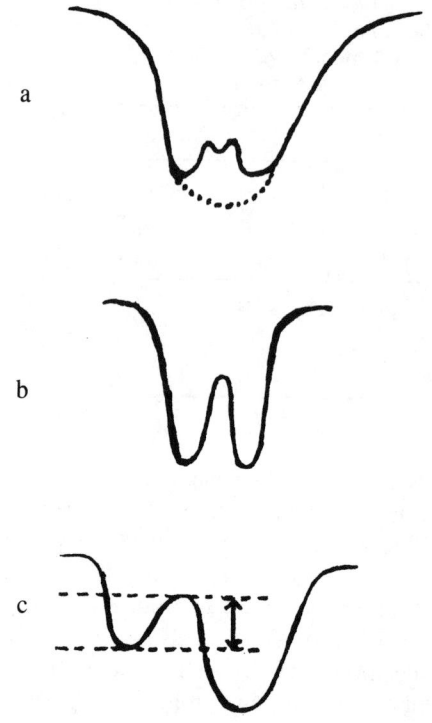

FIG. 84. Deviations from stability within the singular case (a).

This ending is singular, being very consistent with or fitting into the rest of the story. It may be interpreted as Greed Sometimes Causes its Own Punishment. But this particular ending is not the only possible instantiation of the greed–punishment theme. The following reproduction by one of Mandler and Johnson's subjects embodies the theme equally well: "And the dog lost his balance and fell over and that was the end of the dog." Figure 84*b* can represent this example also. The whole well corresponds to the self-consistent greed–punishment theme of the story. The two compartments represent the two endings, and there could be many others sharing the same theme, or the same well.

Another deviation from stability in case (a) was described in Section 23 and 29. It is illustrated by the solid curve of Fig. 62. In this instance, the singularity is represented by a wide, shallow well. The slope of the left wall is steep, the right wall rises more gradually. As a consequence, the singularity is not sharply confined to pattern *c* but extends to pattern *d* and, with small probability, even to pattern *e*. The singularity, in this instance, may be called "weak" or "smeared out."

The last type of deviation from stability to be mentioned here is represented by Fig. 84*c*. The left compartment of the well corresponds to the singularity presented. For the average subject, the feature is stable, the ball remains in the left compartment. It would take a large amount of energy, what in chemistry is called activation energy, to lift the ball from the bottom (lower dotted line) to the top of the barrier (upper dotted line). The "activation energy" is indicated by the double-headed arrow. As long as the "random fluctuations" remain below this level, the feature remains stable. If they exceed this level, the ball may escape the upper well and reach the deeper compartment, to remain there. The diagram would in that case show the transition from a "good" to a "better" or more self-consistent feature.

Many other variants of case (a) are conceivable. Stability can take many forms, and there are many degrees of stability.

64. TRACE SYSTEMS

The notion of an individual trace is no more than a convenient abstraction. It falls short of reality in at least two respects. First traces, once created, do not remain isolated. They quickly form structured aggregates. (That is why lists of disconnected "items" are so unrepresentative as materials for memory research.) Second, as a body of knowledge becomes established in memory, it interacts with new, incoming material. The interaction consists in assimilating new knowledge, but at the same time the new does shape the old. Therefore, as Brown (1979) points out, "an adequate theory must be able to account for major changes in perspective . . . or paradigmatic shifts of theory or world view [p. 232]." In other words, traces interact with each other and with new traces in reciprocal fashion. Much of what we know about this interaction has come from the work of developmental and educational psychologists. (The paper by Brown just cited provides an instructive summary of these fields and a guide to the pertinent literature.) Research will undoubtedly show that the internal structure of entire trace systems follows the same principles of organization and of feature establishment that govern the individual trace, merely at a higher level of the hierarchy. Correspondingly, trace *systems* will be shown to undergo the same changes and exhibit the same stabilities and labilities as those described in Part II for individual traces. The categories and the point of view applied here to individual traces applies equally well to trace systems.

The investigation of trace systems originated with Köhler and von Restorff (von Restorff, 1933). They called these systems trace *fields* in the same sense as physicists speak of gravitational or electromagnetic fields. The stress theory of Chapter 4 is a descendant of this metaphor. These theories are examples of dynamic theorizing that accommodates growth of a conceptual system, rearrangement, new insights, and change of paradigms. It also accommodates the kind of learning that makes a chess master out of a beginner (Chase & Simon, 1973). Learning in that sense is quite different from the feat of learning verbatim the part of Hamlet in Shakespeare's play or being able to recite the English rulers

240   8. THE DYNAMICS OF CHANGE

chronologically with the dates of their birth and death. The latter kind of learning is more suited to topological or static memory models, like Quillian nets (Quillian, 1968) or associative networks (Anderson & Bower, 1973).

However, we don't have to choose between the static and the dynamic models. Biologically, we need both kinds. Much of the time a static memory serves us well. The static memory supplies us with a body of certainty, irreducible facts, with biases, prejudices, stereotypes, clichés, firm convictions, and self-evident truths. On the other hand, when we are young, or new to a job, or in strange surroundings, inexperienced, or confronted with failures or with doubts about our belief systems, then the ability to learn a new terminology, a new classification, a new language, to restructure our trace system, reevaluate our paradigms, "learn from experience," not take things at face value, live with uncertainty, and forget irrelevancies requires a dynamic memory. In short, our memory must provide for both stable storage and flexible restructuring of whole trace systems. The task of devising such a model begins where this account ends.

If traces in general are parts of larger systems, then *extrinsic* effects on a trace, originating within the larger system, are *intrinsic* from a more global point of view. Stress theory as developed here is strictly limited to intrinsic stress. But, if applied to a trace system, a higher level of the hierarchy of traces, the theory should also govern those effects that are *extrinsic* to a trace but *intrinsic* to the relevant trace system. In other words (S. Palmer, personal communication):

> All memory changes are "intrinsic" and can be accounted for by stress theory, but at different levels of organiztion of the "trace". For example, a list of 20 figures (or words) in an experiment is surely a unified memory trace at some larger level of memory structure. To the extent that the entire list is singular at this level (e.g., structured, systematic differences from each figure to the next), then this memory trace should be stable over time. To the extent that the list is nearly singular, it should change toward the singular case, implying certain types of intrusions and not others. And to the extent that it is nonsingular, it should change randomly. In other words, stress theory is as applicable to "extrinsic" cases of memory change as to "intrinsic" ones, except in a more global framework. Given that nearly all memory experiments with "lists of stimuli" are of the nonsingular sort, it is not surprising that stress theory is unnecessary to account for the forgetting (memory change) that occurs. As pointed out many times, in cases of nonsingular structure, stress and fading theory make essentially the same predictions.

These amplifications extend the domain of validity claimed for stress theory to the entire trace system and to intrinsic as well as extrinsic effects on the trace.

65. SYNOPSIS OF MEMORY CHANGE

Intrinsic memory change has long been ignored or declared nonexistent. It was disputed for two reasons. It does not fit into associationistic doctrine, which looks at memory traces as passive deposits and on memory as dead storage. The second reason is that change does not occur with singular and therefore stable traces. The gradual loss of information from *nonsingular* traces seemed explicable by extrinsic mechanisms and by fading, both well-established and easy to demonstrate. Only the knowledge of trace structure, developed in Part I, and stress theory, developed and applied in Part II, make it possible to construct materials, both visual (Chapters 5 and 6) and conceptual (Chapter 7), which reliably and reproducibly exhibit intrinsic change.

The investigation of intrinsic change in Part II serves as a validation of the ideas of Part I about the formation of the trace. These ideas lead to the stress theory of the trace that identifies some traces as exceedingly stable and precise, others as unstable, subject to forgetting, lack of precision, and loss of information. These traces are classified throughout this book as belonging to case (a) and (c), respectively. Another kind of traces, those intermediate between the two others, case (b), progressively change toward singularity and, when they attain singularity, become stable. When these traces have reached a stable state, their information content is decreased. In terms of the traditional *correct-incorrect* memory theories, memory in case (a) is correct, in case (b) incorrect; in case (c), it approaches chance or is forgotten.

This exposition began with biological considerations. It seems fitting to end it by examining the biological utility of the trace structure proposed.

As the trace is formed, all three types of information are acquired and stored. With the passage of time, the singular aspects of the trace tend to survive. Nonsingular information is increasingly lost, and nearly singular information changes to its singular equivalent. The power of an information processor, be it a computer or a brain, depends importantly on the way it utilizes its necessarily finite memory capacity. Singular traces, because of their internal consistency, are most economical to store and later to retrieve. Nonsingular information, being irregular, requires the storage of many independent parameters, as for instance in the case of Fig. 25*b* compared with 25*a* or *c*. Singular information is easily coded; nonsingular information is coded with difficulty. Kintsch and van Dijk have shown that 3 months after a story is learned, recall is very similar to the summaries of the same story obtainable at the time of learning. Both the summary and the 3-months recall are devoid of nonsingular detail, thus freeing up valuable memory capacity.

Change from nearly singular to singular, the change most contested up to now, our case (b), serves to decrease memory load with minimal loss of information. If a businessman, for example, calculates his costs as $597.7964, he will remember something very much like $600. "Rounding off" is a practice of humans as well as computers. The directed change that leads from the almost singular to the nearest singularity eliminates in effect a triviality, costly to store, from an otherwise self-consistent item. As Woodworth (1938) and Bear (1974) have pointed out, the almost singular traces have the structure of schema-plus-correction. The change in memory eliminates the correction, although preserving the pure and simple "schema." It trades a small loss of accuracy for a large gain

242   8. THE DYNAMICS OF CHANGE

in compactness of storage. Bartlett (1932), in his account of long-term recall, notes that in the retelling a story becomes increasingly "more coherent and consequential than in its original form[p. 66];" it becomes "still more concise [p.67]." Bartlett finds for the recall of his "War of the Ghosts" a "strong tendency to rationalize.... Whenever anything appeared incomprehensible, or 'queer' it was either omitted or explained [p. 68]." The omitting and explaining renders the narrative more singular; case (b) changes to case (a). What Bartlett describes in these terms is really not adaptation to a schema or to a social convention as he theorizes. It is a change in the direction of increased self-consistency. Memory change thus gives a maximum of compactness to the trace system.

REFERENCES

Anderson, J. R., & Bower, G. H. *Human associative memory.* New York: Wiley, 1973.
Anderson, R. C. Substance recall of sentences. *Quarterly Journal of Experimental Psychology,* 1974, *20,* 530-541.
Arnheim, R. *Visual thinking.* Berkeley and Los Angeles: University of California Press, 1969.
Asch, S. E. Forming impressions of personality. *Journal of Abnormal and Social Psychology,* 1946, *41*(3). Reprinted in Mary Henle (Ed.), *Documents of gestalt psychology.* Berkeley and Los Angeles: University of California Press, 1961.
Asch, S. E., & Witkin, H. A. Studies in space orientation: I. Perception of the upright with displaced visual fields. *Journal of Experimental Psychology,* 1948, *38,* 325-337. (a)
Asch, S. W., & Witkin, H. A. Studies in space orientation: II. Perception of the upright with displaced visual fields and with body tilted. *Journal of Experimental Psychology,* 1948, *38,* 445-477. (b)
Attneave, F. Dimensions of similarity. *American Journal of Psychology,* 1950, *63,* 516-556.
Attneave, F. Criteria for a tenable theory of form perception. In W. Wathen-Dunn (Ed.), *Models for the perception of speech and visual form.* Cambridge, Mass.: The M.I.T. Press, 1967.
Attneave, F. Multistability in perception. *Scientific American,* 1971, *225*(6), 62-71.
Barclay, J. R. The role of comprehension in remembering sentences. *Cognitive Psychology,* 1973, *4*(2), 229-254.
Barclay, J. R., Bransford, J. D., Franks, J. J., McCarrell, N. S., and Nitsch, K. Comprehension and semantic flexibility. *Journal of Verbal Learning and Verbal Behavior,* 1974, *13,* 471-481.
Bartlett, F. C. *Remembering: An experimental and social study.* Cambridge, Mass.: Cambridge University Press, 1932.
Bates, E., Masling, M., & Kintsch, W. Recognition memory for aspects of dialogue. *Journal of Experimental Psychology: Human Learning and Memory,* 1978, *4*(3), 187-197.
Bear, G. Figural goodness and the predictability of figural elements. *Perception & Psychophysics,* 1973, *13,* 32-40.
Bear, G., Implicit alternatives to a stimulus, difficulty of encoding, and schema-plus-correction representation. *Memory & Cognition,* 1974, *2,* 360-366.
Blesser, B., Shillman, R., Cox, C., Kuklinski, T., Ventura, J., & Eden, M. Character recognition based on phenomenological attributes. *Visible Language,* 1973, *7*(3), 209-223.

REFERENCES

Blum, H. A Transformation for extracting new descriptors of shape. In W. Wathen-Dunn (Ed.), *Models for the perception of speech and visual form*. Cambridge, Mass.: M.I.T. Press, 1967.

Bock, J. K., & Brewer, W. F. Reconstructive recall in sentences with alternative surface structures. *Journal of Experimental Psychology*, 1974, *103*(5), 837–843.

Bower, G. H. Perceptual groups as coding units in immediate memory. *Psychonomic Science*, 1972, 217–219.

Bower, G. H., & Glass, A. Structural units and the redintegrative power of picture fragments. *Journal of Experimental Psychology: Human Learning and Memory*, 1976, *2*, 456–466.

Bower, G. H., & Karlin, M. B. Depth of processing pictures of faces and recognition memory. *Journal of Experimental Psychology*, 1974, *103*, 751–757.

Bower, G. H., Karlin, M. B., & Dueck, A. Comprehension and memory for pictures. *Memory & Cognition*, 1975, *3*(2), 216–220.

Bower, G. H., & Winzenz, D. Group structure, coding and memory for digit series. *Journal of Experimental Psychology*, 1969, *80*, 1–17.

Bransford, J. D., & Franks, J. J. The abstraction of linguistic ideas. *Cognitive Psychology*, 1971, *2*, 331–350.

Bransford, J. D., Franks, J. J., Morris, C. D., & Stein, B. S. Some general constraints on learning and memory research. In L. S. Cermak & F. I. M. Craik (Eds.), *Levels of processing in human memory*. Hillsdale, N.J.: Lawrence Erlbaum Associates, 1979.

Bransford, J. D., & Johnson, M. K. Contextual prerequisites for understanding: Some investigations of comprehension and recall. *Journal of Verbal Learning and Verbal Behavior*, 1972, *11*, 717–726.

Brewer, W. F. Memory for ideas: Synonym substitution. *Memory and Cognition*, 1975, *3*(4), 458–464.

Britton, B. K., Meyer, B. J. F., Simpson, R., Holdredge, T. S., & Curry, C. Effect of the organization of text on memory: Tests of two implications of a selective attention hypothesis. *Journal of Experimental Psychology: Human Learning and Memory*, 1979, *5*, 496–506.

Brown, A. L. Theories of memory and the problems of development. In L.S. Cermak & F. I. M. Craik (Eds.), *Levels of processing in human memory*. Hillsdale, N. J.: Lawrence Erlbaum Associates, 1979.

Bundesen, C., & Larsen, A. Visual transformation of size. *Journal of Experimental Psychology: Human Perception and Performance*, 1975, *1*(3), 214–220.

Carmichael, L., Hogan, H. P., & Walter, A. A. An experimental study of the effect of language on the reproduction of visually perceived forms. *Journal of Experimental Psychology*, 1932, *15*, 73–86.

Cermak, L. S., & Craik, F. I. M. (Eds.). *Levels of processing in human memory*. Hillsdale, N. J.: Lawrence Erlbaum Associates, 1979.

Chase, W. G., & Simon, H. A. The mind's eye in chess. In William G. Chase (Ed.), *Visual information processing*. New York: Academic Press, 1973.

Chomsky, N. *Aspects of the Theory of Syntax*. Cambridge, Mass.: The M.I.T. Press, 1965.

Clement, D. E. Uncertainty and latency of verbal naming responses as correlates of pattern goodness. *Journal of Verbal Learning & Verbal Behavior*, 1964, *3*, 150–157.

Clement, D. E. Paired-associate learning as correlate of pattern goodness. *Journal of Verbal Learning & Verbal Behavior*, 1967, *6*, 112–116.

Cooper, L. A., & Shepard, R. N. Chronometric studies of the rotation of mental images. In William G. Chase (Ed.), *Visual information processing*. New York: Academic Press, 1973.

Corballis, M. C., & Roldan, C. E. Dectection of symmetry as a function of angular orientation. *Journal of Experimental Psychology: Human Perception and Performance*, 1975, *1*(3), 221–230.

Craik, F. I. M., & Lockhart, R. S. Levels of processing: A framework for memory research. *Journal of Verbal Learning and Verbal Behavior*, 1972, *11*, 671–684.

REFERENCES

Craik, F. I. M., & Tulving, E. Depth of processing and the retention of words in episodic memory. *Journal of Experimental Psychology: General,* 1975, *104*(3), 268-294.

Cruse, D., & Clifton, C., Jr. Recoding strategies and the retrieval of information from memory. *Cognitive Psychology,* 1973, *4*(2), 157-193.

Dinnerstein, D., & Wertheimer, M. Some determinants of phenomenal overlapping. *American Journal of Psychology,* 1957, *70,* 21-37.

Duncker, K. Induced motion, 1929. In W. D. Ellis, (Ed. and Trans.), *A source book of gestalt psychology.* New York: Humanities Press, 1950.

Estes, W. K. Is human memory obsolete? *American Scientist,* 1980, *68*(1), 62-69.

Fisher, G. H. Ambiguity of form: Old and new, *Perception & Psychophysics,* 1968, *4*(3), 189-192.

Galli, A., & Zama, A. Untersuchungen über die Wahrnehmung geometrischer Figuren. *Zeitschrift für Psychologie,* 1931, *123.*

Garner, W. R. To perceive is to know. *American Psychologist,* 1966, *21,* 11-19.

Garner, W. R. *The processing of information and structure.* Hillsdale, N. J.: Lawrence Erlbaum Associates, 1974.

Garner, W. R., & Clement, D. E. Goodness of pattern and pattern uncertainty. *Journal of Verbal Learning and Verbal Behavior,* 1963, *2,* 446-452.

Gibson, E. J., & Walk, R. D. The "Visual Cliff." *Scientific American,* April 1960, 2-9.

Gibson, J. J. The reproduction of visually perceived forms. *Journal of Experimental Psychology,* 1929, *12,* 1-39.

Goldmeier, E. Progressive changes in memory traces. *American Journal of Psychology,* 1941, *54*(4), 490-503.

Goldmeier, E. *Similarity in visually perceived forms.* Psychological issues (Monograph 29). New York: International Universities Press, 1972 (originally published in German, in *Psychologische Forschung,* 1936, *21,* 146-208).

Gottschaldt, K. Gestalt factors in repetition. Partial translation in W. D. Ellis, (Ed. and Trans.), *A source book of gestalt psychology.* New York: Humanities Press, 1950 (originally published, 1926 and 1929).

Hanawalt, N. G., Memory trace for figures in recall and recognition. In R. S. Woodworth (Ed.), *Archives of Psychology* (No. 216). New York: Columbia University, 1937.

Hanawalt, N. G., & Demarest, I. H. The effect of verbal suggestion in the recall period upon the reproduction of visually perceived forms. *Journal of Experimental Psychology,* 1939, *25,* 159-174.

Handel, S., & Garner, W. R. The structure of visual pattern associates and pattern goodness. *Perception & Psychophysics,* 1966, *1,* 33-38.

Hebb, D. O., & Foord, E. M. Errors of visual recognition and the nature of the trace. *Journal of Experimental Psychology,* 1945, *35,* 335-348.

Held, R. Plasticity in sensory-motor systems. *Scientific American,* 1965, 231, 84-94.

Held, R. Dissociation of visual functions by deprivation and rearrangement. *Psychologishe Forschung,* 1968, *31,* 338-348.

Honeck, R. P., Riechmann, P., & Hoffman, R. R. Semantic memory for metaphor: The conceptual base hypothesis. *Memory and Cognition,* 1975, *3,* 409-415.

Jenkins, J. J. Four points to remember: A tetrahedral model of memory experiments. In L. S. Cermak & F. I. M. Craik, (Eds.), *Levels of processing in human memory.* Hillsdale, N.J.: Lawrence Erlbaum Associates, 1979.

Julesz, R. *Foundations of Cyclopean perception.* Chicago: University of Chicago Press, 1971.

Kanizsa, R. *Organization in vision.* New York: Praeger, 1979.

Katona, G. *Organizing and memorizing. Studies in the psychology of learning and teaching.* New York & London: Hafner, 1967 (originally published in 1940).

Kintsch, W. *The representation of meaning in memory.* Hillsdale, N.J.: Lawrence Erlbaum Associates, 1974.

REFERENCES

Kintsch, W. Memory for prose. In C. N. Cofer (Ed.), *The Structure of Human Memory.* San Francisco: W. H. Freeman, 1976.

Kintsch, W. *Memory and cognition.* New York: Wiley, 1977.

Kintsch, W., & Bates, E. Recognition memory for statements from a classroom lecture. *Journal of Experimental Psychology: Human Learning and Memory,* 1977, *3*(2), 150-159.

Kintsch, W., & van Dijk, T. A. Toward a model of text comprehension and production. *Psychological Review,* 1978, *85,* 363-394.

Kintsch, W. & Greene, E. The role of culture-specific schemata in the comprehension and recall of stories. *Discourse Processes,* 1978, *1,* 1-13.

Kintsch, W., & Keenan, J. Reading rate and retention as a function of the number of propositions in the base structure of sentences. *Cognitive Psychology,* 1973, *5,* 257-274.

Kintsch, W., Kozminsky, E., Streby, W. J., McKoon, G., & Keenan, J. M. Comprehension and recall of text as a function of content variables. *Journal of Verbal Learning and Verbal Behavior,* 1975, *14,* 196-214.

Kintsch, W., Mandel, T. S., & Kozminsky, E. Summarizing scrambled stories. *Memory and Cognition,* 1977, *5,* 547-552.

Koffka, K. Principles of gestalt psychology. New York: Harcourt, Brace, & World, 1935.

Köhler, W. *Dynamics in psychology.* New York: Liveright, 1940.

Köhler, W. *Gestalt psychology.* New York: Liveright, 1947.

Kolers, P. A. Reading and talking bilingually. *American Journal of Psychology,* 1966, *79,* 357-376.

Kolers, P. A. Some psychological aspects of pattern recognition. In P. A. Kolers & M. Eden (Eds.), *Recognizing patterns.* Cambridge, Mass.: M.I.T. Press, 1968. (a)

Kolers, P. A. Bilingualism and information processing. *Scientific American,* 1968, *218,* 78-86. (b)

Kolers, P. A. A pattern—analyzing basis of recognition. In L. S. Cermak & F. I. M. Craik (Eds.), *Levels of processing in human memory.* Hillsdale, N.J.: Lawrence Erlbaum Associates, 1979.

Kopfermann, H. Psychologische Untersuchungen über die Wirkung Zweidimensionaler Darstellungen Körperlicher Gebilde. *Psychologische Forschung,* 1930, *13,* 293-364.

Kosslyn, S. M. Can imagery be distinguished from other forms of internal representation? Evidence from studies of information retrieval times. *Memory and Cognition,* 1976, *4,* 291-297.

Kozminsky, E. Altering comprehension: The effect of biasing titles on text comprehension. *Memory and Cognition,* 1977, *5*(4), 482-490.

Krolik, W. Über Erfahrungswirkungen beim Bewgungssehen. *Psychologische Forschung,* 1934, *20,* 47-101.

Krumhansl, C. L. Concerning the applicability of geometric models to similarity data: The interrelationship between similarity and spatial density. *Psychological Review,* 1978, *85,* 445-463.

Kruskal, J. B. Multidimensional scaling by optimizing goodness of fit to a nonmetric hypothesis. *Psychometrika,* 1964, *29,* 1-27.

Kuhn, T. S. *The Copernican Revolution.* Cambridge, Mass.: Harvard University Press, 1957.

Kuhn, T. S. *The structure of scientific revolutions.* Chicago: University of Chicago Press. 1970.

Lachman, J. L., & Lachman, R. Comprehension and cognition: A state of the art inquiry. In L. S. Cermak & F. I. M. Craik, (Eds.), *Levels of processing in human memory.* Hillsdale, N.J.: Lawrence Erlbaum Associates, 1979.

Lakoff, G. Hedges: A study in meaning criteria and the logic of fuzzy concepts. *Papers from the eighth regional meeting, Chicago Linguistics Society.* Chicago: University of Chicago Linguistics Department, 1972.

Lockhart, R. S. Remembering events. In L. S. Cermak & F. I. M. Craik (Eds.), *Levels of processing in human memory.* Hillsdale, N.J.: Lawrence Erlbaum Associates, 1979.

Loftus, E. F. The malleability of human memory. *American Scientist,* May-June 1979 *67*: 312-320. (a)

Loftus, E. F. *Eyewitness Testimony.* Cambridge, Mass.: Harvard University Press, 1979. (b)

REFERENCES

Loftus, E. F. Reactions to blatantly contradictory information. *Memory and Cognition,* 1979, *7,* 368-374. (c)

Mandler, J. M., & Johnson, N. S. Some of the thousand words a picture is worth. *Journal of Experimental Psychology: Human Learning and Memory,* 1976, *2,* 529-540.

Mandler, J. M., & Johnson, N. S. Remembrance of things parsed: Story structure and recall. *Cognitive Psychology,* 1977, *9,* 111-150.

Mandler, J. M., & Parker, R. E. Memory for descriptive and spatial information in complex pictures. *Journal of Experimental Psychology: Human Learning and Memory,* 1976, *2,* 38-48.

Markman, E. M., & Seibert, B. Classes and collections: Internal organization and resulting holistic properties. *Cognitive Psychology,* 1976, *8,* 561-577.

Metelli, F. Achromatic color conditions in the perception of transparency. In R. B. Macleod & H. L. Pick (Eds.), *Perception Essays in Honor of James J. Gibson.* Ithaca, N.Y.: Cornell University Press, 1974. (a)

Metelli, F. The perception of transparency. *Scientific American,* 1974, *230,* 90-98. (b)

Metzger, W. Tiefenerscheinungen in optischen Bewegungsfeldern, *Psychologische Forschung,* 1935, *20,* 195-260.

Metzger, W. *Gestze des Sehens.* Frankfurt am Main: Waldemar Kramer, 1975.

Miller, G. A. The magical number seven, plus or minus two. *Psychological Review,* 1956, *63,* 81-97.

Minsky, M. A framework for representing knowledge. In P. H. Winston (Ed.), *The psychology of computer vision.* New York: McGraw-Hill, 1975.

Morris, C. D., Bransford, J. D., & Franks, J. J. Level of processing versus transfer appropriate processing. *Journal of Verbal Learning and Verbal Behavior,* 1977, *16,* 519-533.

Neisser, U. *Cognition and reality.* San Francisco: W. H. Freeman, 1976.

Neisser, U., & Becklen, R. Selective looking: Attending to visually specified events. *Cognitive Psychology,* 1975, *7,* 480-494.

Neisser, U., & Hupcey, J. A. A Sherlockian experiment. *Cognition,* 1975, *3,* 307-311.

Newman, E. H. *Strictly speaking.* Indianapolis: Bobbs-Merrill, 1974.

Nickerson, R. S., & Adams, M. J. Long-term memory for a common object. *Cognitive Psychology,* 1979, *11,* 287-307.

Norman, D. A. *Memory and attention.* New York: Wiley, 1976.

Norman, D. A., & Bobrow, D. G. On the role of active memory processes in perception and cognition. In C. N. Cofer (Ed.), *The structure of human memory,* San Francisco: W. H. Freeman, 1976.

Norman, D. A., & Bobrow, D. G. Descriptions: An intermediate stage in memory retrieval. *Cognitive Psychology,* 1979, *11,* 107-123.

Norman, D. A., & Rumelhart, D. E, *Explorations in Cognition.* San Francisco: W. H. Freeman, 1975.

Oppenheimer, E. Optische Versuche über Ruhe und Bewegung. *Psychologische Forschung,* 1934, *20,* 1-46.

Owens, J., Bower, G. H., & Black, J. B. The "Soap Opera" effect in story recall. *Memory and Cognition,* 1979, *7*(3), 185-191.

Palmer, S. E. Visual perception and world knowledge. In D. A. Norman, D. E. Rumelhart, & LNR Research Group (Eds.), *Exploration in cognition.* San Francisco: W. H. Freeman, 1975. (a)

Palmer, S. E. The effect of contextual scenes on the identification of objects. *Memory and Cognition,* 1975, *3,* 519-526. (b)

Palmer, S. E. Hierarchial structure in perceptual representation. *Cognitive Psychology,* 1977, *9,* 441.

Palmer, S. E. Structural aspects of visual similarity. *Memory and Cognition* 1978, *6*(2), 91-97. (a)

Palmer, S. E. Fundamental aspects of cognitive representation. In E. Rosch & B. Lloyd (Eds.), *Cognition and categorization.* Hillsdale, N.J.: Lawrence Erlbaum Associates, 1978. (b)

REFERENCES

Paris, S. G., & Carter, A. Y. Semantic and constructive aspects of sentence memory in children. *Developmental Psychology,* 1973, *9,* 109-113.

Paris, S. G., & Lindauer, B. K. The role of inference in children's comprehension and memory for sentences. *Cognitive Psychology,* 1976, *8,* 217-227.

Paul, I. H. *Studies in remembering.* New York: International Universities Press, 1959.

Perfetti, C. A. Levels of language and levels of process. In L. S. Cermak & F. I. M. Craik (Eds.), *Levels of processing in human memory.* Hillsdale, N.J.: Lawrence Erlbaum Associates, 1979.

Perkins, F. T. Symmetry in visual recall. *American Journal of Psychology,* 1932, *44,* 473-490.

Peterson, M. J., Meagher, R. B., Jr., Chait, H., & Gillie, S. The abstraction and generalization of dot patterns. *Cognitive Psychology,* 1973, *4,* 378-398.

Posner, M. I., Goldsmith, R., & Welton, K. E., Jr. Perceived distance and the classification of distorted patterns. *Journal of Experimental Psychology,* 1967, *73,* 28-38.

Posner, M.I., & Keele, S.W. On the genesis of abstract ideas. *Journal of Experimental Psychology,* 1968, *77,* Part 1, 353-363.

Postman, L. Learned principles of organization in memory. *Psychological Monographs: General and Applied,* 1954, *68*(3), 1-24.

Quillian, M. R. Semantic memory. In M. L. Minsky (Ed.), *Semantic information processing.* Cambridge, Mass.: M. I. T. Press, 1968.

Reddy, R., & Newell, A. Knowledge and its representation in a speech understanding system. In L. W. Gregg (Ed.), *Knowledge and cognition.* Hillsdale, N.J.: Lawrence Erlbaum Associates, 1974.

Restorff, H., von. Über die Wirkung von Bereichsbildung im Spurenfeld. *Psychologische Forschung,* 1933, *18,* 299-342.

Riley, D. A. Memory for form. In L. Postman (Ed.), *Psychology in the making.* New York: Knopf, 1962.

Rock, I. *Orientation and form.* New York: Academic Press, 1973.

Rock, I. *An Introduction to perception.* New York: MacMillan, 1975.

Rock, I., & Engelstein, P. A study of memory for visual form. *American Journal of Psychology,* 1959, *72,* 221-229.

Rock, I., & Halper, N. R. Form perception without a retinal image. *The American Journal of Psychology,* 1969, *82,* 425-440.

Rock, I., & Leaman, R. An experimental analysis of visual symmetry. *Acta Psychologica,* 1963, *21,* 171-183.

Rosch Heider, E. "Focal" color areas and the development of color names. *Developmental Psychology,* 1971, *4*(3), 447-455.

Rosch Heider, E. Universals in color naming and memory. *Journal of Experimental Psychology,* 1972, *1,* 10-20.

Rosch, E. H. Natural categories. *Cognitive Psychology,* 1973, *4,* 328-350. (a)

Rosch, E. On the internal structure of perceptual and semantic categories. In T. E. Moore (Ed.), *Cognitive development and the acquisition of language.* New York: Academic Press, 1973. (b)

Rosch, E. Cognitive reference points. *Cognitive Psychology,* 1975, *7,* 532-547. (a)

Rosch, E. Cognitive representation of semantic categories. *Journal of Experimental Psychology: General,* 1975, *104,* 192-233. (b)

Rosch, E. Universals and cultural specifics in human categorization. In R. Brislin, S. Bochner, & W. Lonner (Eds.), *Cross-cultural perspectives on learning.* New York: Halsted, 1975. (c)

Rosch, E. Human categorization. In N. Warren (Ed.), *Advances in cross-cultural psychology* (Vol. 1). London: Academic Press, 1977.

Rosch, E. Principles of categorization. In E. Rosch and B. B. Lloyd (Eds.), *Cognition and categorization.* Hillsdale, N.J.: Lawrence Erlbaum Associates, 1978.

Rosch, E., & Mervis, C. B. Family resemblances. *Cognitive Psychology,* 1975, *7,* 575-605.

REFERENCES

Rosch, E., Mervis, C. B., Gray, W., Johnson, D., & Boyes-Braem, P. Basic objects in natural categories. *Cognitive Psychology,* 1976, *8,* 382-439. (a)

Rosch, E., Simpson, C., & Miller, R. S. Structural bases of typicality effects. *Journal of Experimental Psychology: Human Perception and Performance,* 1976, *2*(4), 491-502.(b)

Russell, B. *A history of Western philosophy.* New York: Simon & Schuster, 1945.

Sachs, J. S. Recognition memory for syntactic and semantic aspects of connected discourse. *Perception & Psychophysics,* 1967, *2,* 437-442.

Schulman, A. I. Memory for words recently classified, *Memory and Cognition,* 1974, *2,* 47-52.

Selfridge, O. G., & Neisser, U. Pattern recognition by machine. *Scientific American,* 1960, *203* (Augs.), 60-68.

Shannon, C. E., & Weaver, W. *The mathematical theory of communication.* Urbana: The University of Illinois Press, 1949.

Shepard, R. N. Analysis of proximities as a technique for the study of information processing in man. *Human Factors,* 1963, *5,* 33-48.

Shepard, R. N. Attention and the metric structure of the stimulus space. *Journal of Mathematical Psychology,* 1964, 54-87.

Shepard, R. N. Recognition memory for words, sentences, and pictures. *Journal of Verbal Learning and Verbal Behavior,* 1967, *6,* 156-163.

Shepard, R. N., & Chipman S. Second-order isomorphisms of internal representations; shapes of states. *Cognitive Psychology,* 1970, *1,* 1-17.

Shepard, R. N., & Metzler, J. Mental rotation of three-dimensional objects. *Science,* 1971, *171,* 701-703.

Simon, H. A. Complexity and the representation of patterned sequences of symbols. *Psychological Review,* 1972, *79,* 369-382.

Smirnov, A. A. *Problems of the psychology of memory.* New York: Plenum, 1973.

Ternus, J. The problem of phenomenal identity. Selection 11, p. 149-160. In W. D. Ellis (Ed. and Trans.), *A source book of gestalt psychology.* New York: Humanities Press, 1950 (originally published in 1926).

Treisman, A. The psychological reality of levels of processing. In L. S. Cermak & F. I. M. Craik (Eds.), *Levels of processing in human memory.* Hillsdale, N.J.: Lawrence Erlbaum Associates, 1979.

Tulving, E. Episodic and semantic memory. In E. Tulving & W. Donaldson (Eds.), *Organization of memory.* New York: Academic Press, 1972.

Tulving, E. Cue-dependent forgetting. *American Scientist,* 1974, *62,* 74-82. (a)

Tulving, E. Recall and recognition of semantically encoded words. *Journal of Experimental Psychology,* 1974, *102,* 778-787. (b)

Tulving, E. Relation between encoding specificity and levels of processing. In L. S. Cermak & F. I. M. Craik (Eds.), *Levels of processing in human memory.* Hillsdale, N.J.: Lawrence Erlbaum Associates, 1979.

Tulving, E., & Thomson, D. M. Encoding specificity and retrieval processes in episodic memory. *Psychological Review,* 1973, *80,* 352-373.

Tulving, E., & Watkins, O. C. Recognition failure of words with a single meaning. *Memory and Cognition,* 1977, *5*(5), 513-522.

Turner, M. B., & Craig, E. A. The effect of figural reproduction on recognition. *Journal of Psychology,* 1954, *38,* 265-270.

Tversky, A. Features of similarity. *Psychological Review,* 1977, *84*(4), 327-352.

Tyler, S. W., Hertel, P. T., McCallum, M. C., & Ellis, H. C. Cognitive effort and memory. *Journal of Experimental Psychology: Human Learning and Memory,* 1979, *5,* 607-617.

Wagner, D. A. Memories of Morocco: The influence of age, schooling, and environment on memory. *Cognitive Psychology,* 1978, *10,* 1-28.

REFERENCES

Weber, M. *The methodology of social sciences.* Logos 1917. English translation: The Free Press. New York: Macmillan, 1949.

Weisstein, N., & Harris, C. S. Visual detection of line segements: An object-superiority effect. *Science,* 1974, *186,* 752-755.

Weisstein, N., & Maguire, W. Computing the next step: Psychophysical measures of representation and interpretation. In E. M. Riseman & A. R. Hanson (Eds.), *Computer vision systems.* New York: Academic Press, 1978.

Weisstein, N., Maguire, W., & Berbaum, K. A phantom-motion aftereffect. *Science,* 1977, *198,* 955-958.

Wertheimer, M. Numbers and numerical concepts in primitive peoples. In W. D. Ellis (Ed. and Trans.), *A source book of gestalt psychology.* New York: Humanities Press, 1950 (originally published in 1912).

Wertheimer, M. The syllogism and productive thinking. In W. D. Ellis (Ed. and Trans.), *A source book of gestalt psychology.* New York: Humanities Press, 1950 (originally published in 1920).

Wertheimer, M. Laws of organization in perceptual forms. In W. D. Ellis (Ed. and Trans.), *A source book of gestalt psychology.* New York: Humanities Press, 1950 (originally published in 1923).

Whitman, J. R., & Garner, W. R. Free recall learning of visual figures as a function of form of internal structure. *Journal of Experimental Psychology,* 1962, *64,* 558-564.

Winston, P. H. Learning structural descriptions from examples. In P. H. Winston (Ed.), *The psychology of computer vision.* New York: McGraw-Hill, 1975.

Wiseman, S., & Neisser, U. Perceptual organization as a determinant of visual recognition memory. *American Journal of Psychology,* 1974, *87,* 675-681.

Woodworth, R. S. *Experimental psychology.* New York: Henry Holt, 1938.

Wulf, F. Tendencies in figural variation. In W. D. Ellis (Ed. and Trans.), *A source book of gestalt psychology.* New York: Humanities Press, 1950 (originally published in 1922).

Zangwill, O. L. An investigation of the relationship between the processes of reproducing and recognizing simple figures, with special reference to Koffka's trace theory. *British Journal of Psychology,* 1937, *27,* 250-276.

Author Index

Numbers in *italics* denote pages with complete bibliographic information.

A

Adams, M. J., 16, *247*
Anderson, J. R., x, 3, 90, 105, 106, 240, *243*
Anderson, R. C., 109, 111, 227, 234, *243*
Arnheim, R., 80, *243*
Asch, S. E., 18, 19, 184, *243*
Attneave, F., 1, 20, 22, 23, 26, 66, 75, 153, *243*

B

Barclay, J. R., 70, 90, 91, 120, *243*
Bartlett, F. C., 5, 90, 94, 103, 124, 142, 203, 226, 229, 235, 242, *243*
Bates, E., 87, *243, 246*
Bear, G., 26, 45, 49, 50, 54, 55, 56, 61, 65, 89, 95, 109, 110, 241, *243*
Becklen, R., 71, *247*
Berbaum, K., 84, *250*
Black, J. B., 88, *247*
Blesser, B., 68, 70, 75, 76, 79, *243*
Blum, H. A., 186, *244*
Bobrow, D. G., x, 5, 87, *247*
Bock, J. K., 98, 111, *244*
Bower, G. H., x, 3, 72, 73, 87, 88, 90, 92, 94, 105, 106, 240, *243, 244, 247*
Boyes-Braem, P., 40, 80, 81, 97, 98, 101, *249*

Bransford, J. D., 70, 87, 88, 90, 91, 94, 120, 227, *243, 244, 247*
Brewer, W. F., 98, 111, 228, *244*
Britton, B. K., 91, *244*
Brown, A. L., 96, 239, *244*
Bundesen, C., 23, 24, *244*

C

Carmichael, L., 70, 107, 120, 122, 229, *244*
Carter, A. Y., 92, 228, *248*
Cermak, L. S., x, 4, 92, 94, 134, *244*
Chait, H., 20, 30, 60, 80, 81, *248*
Chase, W. G., 3, 43, 50, 71, 203, 239, *244*
Chipman, S., ix, *249*
Chomsky, N., 87, *244*
Clement, D. E., 44, 45, 46, 47, 75, 80, *244, 245*
Clifton, C., Jr., 87, *245*
Cooper, L. A., 23, *244*
Corballis, M. C., 68, *244*
Cox, C., 68, 70, 75, 76, 79, *243*
Craig, E. A., 135, 230, *249*
Craik, F. I. M., x, 4, 92, 93, 94, 134, *244, 245*
Cruse, D., 87, *245*
Curry, C., 91, *244*

251

D

Demarest, I. H., 106, 107, 122, *245*
Dinnerstein, D., 7, *245*
Dueck, A., 72, 94, *244*
Duncker, K., 184, *245*

E

Eden, M., 68, 70, 75, 76, 79, *243*
Ellis, H. C., 92, *249*
Engelstein, P., 127, 181, *248*
Estes, W. K., 230, *245*

F

Fisher, G. H., 100, *245*
Foord, E. M., 123, 124, 125, 126, 127, 128, 149, 162, 183, 230, *245*
Franks, J. J., 70, 87, 88, 90, 91, 120, 227, *243, 244, 247*

G

Galli, A., 8, 9, 83, *245*
Garner, W. R., 18, 26, 44, 45, 46, 47, 54, 75, 101, 111, 117, *245, 250*
Gibson, E. J., 43, *245*
Gibson, J. J., 107, 120, 229, *245*
Gillie, S., 20, 30, 60, 80, 81, *248*
Glass, A., 73, *244*
Goldmeier, E., 5, 7, 12, 13, 20, 22, 23, 24, 25, 26, 28, 29, 30, 31, 32, 33, 35, 36, 37, 38, 39, 40, 44, 47, 67, 68, 69, 78, 79, 87, 95, 121, 123, 124, 125, 126, 128, 129, 130, 135, 142, 143, 144, 147, 150, 151, 153, 162, 164, 165, 166, 168, 170, 172, 174, 176, 177, 182, 184, 230, *245*
Goldsmith, R., 20, 21, 58, 60, 81, 110, *248*
Gottschaldt, K., 5, 7, 8, 72, 73, 74, 82, *245*
Gray, W., 40, 80, 81, 97, 98, 101 *249*
Greene, E., 95, *246*

H

Halper, N. R., 18, *248*
Hanawalt, N. G., 106, 107, 119, 122, 124, 125, 127, 130, 131, 144, 151, 166, 167, 169, 173, 181, 229, *245*
Handel, S., 44, 54, 111, *245*
Harris, C. S., 84, *250*

Hebb, D. O., 123, 124, 125, 126, 127, 128, 149, 162, 183, 230, *245*
Held, R., 82, *245*
Hertel, P. T., 92, *249*
Hoffmann, R. R., 86, 91, *245*
Hogan, H. P., 70, 107, 120, 122, 229, *244*
Holdredge, T. S., 91, *244*
Honeck, R. P., 86, 91, *245*
Hupcey, J. A., 89, 90, *247*

J

Jenkins, J. J., x, *245*
Johnson, D., 40, 80, 81, 97, 98, 101, *249*
Johnson, M. K., 94, *244*
Johnson, N. S., 11, 95, 97, 237, *247*
Julesz, R., 7, 43, 74, 115, *245*

K

Kanizsa, R., 57, 59, 60, 73, 83, *245*
Karlin, M. B., 72, 92, 94, *244*
Katona, G., 87, 94, 227, *245*
Keele, S. W., 30, 31, 60, 81, 94, *248*
Keenan, J., 88, 227, *246*
Kintsch, W., 3, 87, 88, 91, 94, 95, 96, 106, 109, 111, 112, 227, *243, 245, 246*
Koffka, K., 57, 124, 149, 229, *246*
Köhler, W., 8, 57, *246*
Kolers, P. A., ix, 4, 5, 87, *246*
Kopfermann, H., 5, 7, 43, 84, 95, *246*
Kozminsky, E., 88, 94, 111, 112, 227, *246*
Kosslyn, S. M., 72, *246*
Krolik, W., 11, *246*
Krumhansl, C. L., 47, 138, *246*
Kruskal, J. B., 27, *246*
Kuhn, T. S., 57, *246*
Kuklinski, T., 68, 70, 75, 76, 79, *243*

L

Lachman, J. L., 74, *246*
Lachman, R., 74, *246*
Lakoff, G., 55, *246*
Larsen, A., 23, 24, *244*
Leaman, R., 68, 142, *248*
Lindauer, B. K., 91, 92, 228, *248*
Lockhart, R. S., x, 3, 4, 93, *244, 246*
Loftus, E. F., 107, 203, *246, 247*

AUTHOR INDEX 253

M

Maguire, W., 84, *250*
Mandel, T. S., 94, 111, 112, *246*
Mandler, J. M., 9, 11, 50, 95, 97, 237, *247*
Markman, E. M., 80, 82, *247*
Masling, M., 87, *243*
McCallum, M. C., 92, *249*
McCarrell, N. S., 70, 90, 120, *243*
McKoon, G., 227, *246*
Meagher, R. B., Jr., 20, 30, 60, 80, 81, *248*
Mervis, C. B., 40, 57, 75, 76, 80, 81, 97, 98, 101, *248, 249*
Metelli, F., 59, 83, *247*
Metzger, W., 4, 5, 7, 8, 11, 43, 56, 75, *247*
Metzler, J., 23, *249*
Meyer, B. J. F., 91, *244*
Miller, G. A., 5, *247*
Miller, R. S., 26, 80, 81, 97, *249*
Minsky, M., 94, *247*
Morris, C. D., 87, 88, *244*

N

Neisser, U., 5, 71, 72, 75, 89, 90, 94, 120, *247, 249, 250*
Newell, A., 4, *248*
Newman, E. H., 109, *247*
Nickerson, R. S., 16, *247*
Nitsch, K., 70, 90, 120, *243*
Norman, D. A., x, 3, 5, 16, 87, 94, 102, *247*

O

Oppenheimer, E., 184, *247*
Owens, J., 88, *247*

P

Palmer, S. E., ix, 7, 11, 26, 34, 43, 69, 71, 72, 75, 81, 89, 94, 112, 120, 122, *247*
Paris, S. G., 91, 92, 228, *248*
Parker, R. E., 9, 50, *247*
Paul, I. H., 124, *248*
Perfetti, C. A., 74, *248*
Perkins, F. T., 125, 142, 229, 235, *248*
Peterson, M. J., 20, 30, 60, 80, 81, *248*
Posner, M. I., 20, 21, 30, 31, 58, 60, 81, 94 110, *248*
Postman, L., 81, *248*

Q

Quillian, M. R., 240, *248*

R

Reddy, R., 4, *248*
Restorff, H., von, 239, *248*
Riechmann, P., 86, 91, *245*
Riley, D. A., 107, 122, 124, 130, 164, *248*
Rock, I., 5, 7, 18, 41, 68, 127, 142, 181, *248*
Roldan, C. E., 68, *244*
Rosch, E., 5, 18, 26, 40, 43, 44, 52, 53, 55, 57, 59, 61, 63, 64, 65, 75, 76, 80, 81, 82, 94, 97, 98, 101, 110, 112, 117, 205, *248, 249*
Rumelhart, D. E., x, 16, 94, 102, *247*
Russell, B., 101, *249*

S

Sachs, J. S., 87, 96, 227, *249*
Schulman, A. I., 93, 125, *249*
Seibert, B., 80, 82, *247*
Selfridge, O. G., 75, *249*
Shannon, C. E., 3, 47, *249*
Shepard, R. N., ix, 19, 23, 26, 27, 136, *244, 249*
Shillman, R., 68, 70, 75, 76, 79, *243*
Simon, H. A., 3, 43, 50, 71, 203, 239, *244, 249*
Simpson, C., 26, 80, 81, 97, *249*
Simpson, R., 91, *244*
Smirnov, A. A., 226, *249*
Stein, B. S., 88, *244*
Streby, W. J., 227, *246*

T

Ternus, J., 5, 13, 14, 15, 95, *249*
Thomson, D. M., 99, *249*
Treisman, A., 74, *249*
Tulving, E., x, 4, 88, 90, 92, 99, 100, 120, *245, 249*
Turner, M. B., 135, 230, *249*
Tversky, A., 47, 56, 111, 117, *249*
Tyler, S. W., 92, *249*

V

van Dijick, T. A., 96, 106, 109, 227, *246*
Ventura, J., 68, 70, 75, 76, 79, *243*

W

Wagner, D. A., 71, 101, *249*
Walk, R. D., 43, *245*
Walter, A. A., 70, 107, 120, 122, 229, *244*
Watkins, O. C., 99, 100, 120, *249*
Weaver, W., 3, 47, *249*
Weber, M., 74, 98, *250*
Weisstein, N., 84, *250*
Welton, K. E., Jr., 20, 21, 58, 60, 81, 110, *248*
Wertheimer, Max, 4, 5, 9, 17, 40, 43, 51, 56, 57, 87, 95, 125, 146, 168, *250*
Wertheimer, Michael, 7, *245*
Whitman, J. R., 18, *250*
Winston, P. H., 3, 83, 84, *250*
Winzenz, D., 87, *244*
Wiseman, S., 72, *250*
Witkin, H. A., 184, *243*
Woodworth, R. S., 51, 60, 61, 65, 106, 119, 229, 241, *250*
Wulf, F., 106, 124, 149, 172, 229, 235, *250*

Z

Zama, A., 8, 9, 83, *245*
Zangwill, O. L., 127, 128, *250*

Subject Index

A

Associationism, 11, 43, 72, 97, 105, 106-108, 187, 230, 240
Attention, 11
Autochthonous stress (*see* Intrinsic stress)

C

Case (a) (*see* Singularity)
Case (b) (*see* Near-singularity)
Case (c) (*see* Nonsingularity)
Categories, singularity and, 97-99
Change (*see* Memory change)
Circularity, 124-125
Closure, 196-202
Coding, 108
　as data reduction, 85, 87-88, 100
　of features, 17-19
　of function, 9-16
Coding economy, 43-44, 57-58, 87, 241-242
Coding efficiency (*see* Coding economy)
Coding theory, 102
Context, 67-74, 90-91
Contrastructural features (*see* Prostructural features)

D

Data reduction, 108 (*see also* Coding)
Decay of the trace, 118, 122, 167, 211

Depth of processing (*see* Levels of processing)
Deterioration of traces (*see* Decay, Fragmentary reproductions)
Dimensionality, 26-31
Directed change (*see* Near-singularity)

E

Empirism, 11, 43, 59, 94, 96, 97, 205-207, 214, 230
Empiristic fallacy, 205-207
Encoding specificity, 12, 99-100, 120, 135
Enlargement, 11-13, 23-25
Equivalent set, 44-47, 172
Experience, 52, 70-74, 84, 91-92, 97, 98 (*see also* Empirism, Familiarity)
Extrinsic effects, 67-74, 106-108, 166, 240, 241

F

Fading-plus-reconstruction, 106, 118-123, 167-169, 230, 234 (*see also* Schema-plus-correction)
Fading theory, predictions of, 119-123, 144, 150-152, 155-159, 163, 168-169, 173, 178, 182-183, 185, 187-188, 194-195, 204-205, 208, 212-213, 217, 218, 220, 227-228, 234

255

256 SUBJECT INDEX

Familiarity (*see also* Empirism, Empiristic fallacy) 59, 80-81, 92, 205-206, 217
Feature space, 127-128
Figure assimilation, 130, 166, 194
Forgetting, 167-169, 194
Fragmentary reproductions, 165-166, 191-192
Function of parts, 9-16, 88-90, 95-96, 194

G

Gaps, coding of, 29-30, 76-79, 152-162
Garners five-dot patterns, 44-47, 49, 54-55, 110-111
Goodness, 44-47, 80-82, 239
Grouping, 5-9, 76-78, 86-87

H, I

Hierarchy, 100
Imprinting, 43
Inference, 91-92
Inferred equivalent set (*see* Equivalent set)
Interference, 167, 178
Intrinsic change (*see* Memory change)
Intrinsic stress, 106-112, 113-115, 227-228, 240

L, M

Laocoon statue, 84-86
Levels of processing, 92-94, 101, 108, 121, 134, 220
Material, 10, 12, 23, 213, 220
Memory change, 104, 105-108
  gradual versus sudden, 234-236
  in recognition, 125-129, 130-163
  in reproduction, 125-129, 164-202
  toward self-consistency, 140-142, 144-149, 172-173
  of singular traces, 236-239
  toward singularity, 136-139
  toward symmetry, 142-144, 235
  in trace systems, 239-240
Model of stress, 113-115
Monotonic dependence, 20-31, 33-34

N

Near-singularity, 64-66, 97, 109-112, 113-115, 116-118, 169, 172-173, 234

Nonsingularity, 16, 60-66, 112, 113-115, 116-118, 240, 241
Norm, singularity as, 50-57

O

Object assimilation, 166
Orienting task, 4, 93, 101, 134
Orthogonality axiom, 117, 196

P

Parsimonious hypotheses, 57, 100-101, 102, 122, 230
Parsing (*see* Grouping)
Phenomenally realized parameters, 31-39
Prägnanz (*see* singularity)
Prostructural features, 169-172, 174, 178, 201-202, 231-233
Proverbs, coding of, 86

R

Recognition, intrinsic change in, (*see* Memory change in recognition)
Recognition versus reproduction, 125-129, 180-181
Reconstruction, 166 (*see also* Fading-plus reconstruction)
Regularity, 44-47
Rotation, 13, 23

S

Schema, 72, 74-82, 94-96
Schema-plus-correction, 64-66, 117, 169, 241 (*see also* Near-singularity)
Selective looking, 71-72
Self-consistency, 48-50, 54-55, 91-92, 144-149, 173-181, 186, 206, 207-212, 214, 218, 222
Sensitivity to change, 39-44, 47, 58
Similarity, 29-30, 31-39, 47, 135-136, 140
Singularity, 38-66, 82, 101, 109, 113-115, 116-118, 186
  defining characteristic of, 41, 58-59, 113 (*see also* Sensitivity to change)
  degree of, 63-66 (*see also* Strength of singularity)
  nature of, 57-60

SUBJECT INDEX 257

and schema, 94-96
sources of, 42
Stimulus, 82-86
Strength of gaps, 159-162, 169-172, 200-202
Strength of singularities, 238
Strength of wholes, 6, 9, 49, 76, 107, 117, 168, 174
Stress (*see* Intrinsic stress)
Stress theory, 115-118, 118-123, 230

T

Time, role of, 116-117, 121, 123, 183, 229-234, 241

Trace systems, 107, 239-240
Transposition, 64, 193, 208, 211, 225

U, V

Uniqueness, 44-47
Verbal memory, 86-100
Verbalisation, 166, 176, 179
Visual concepts, 74-82

BF
371
.G64
1982